Qurʾān Quotations Preserved on Papyrus Documents, 7th–10th Centuries

Documenta Coranica

Comité de rédaction

VOLUME 2

The titles published in this series are listed at *brill.com/doco*

Qur'ān Quotations Preserved on Papyrus Documents, 7th–10th Centuries

And the Problem of Carbon Dating Early Qur'āns

Edited by

Andreas Kaplony
Michael Marx

BRILL

LEIDEN | BOSTON

Library of Congress Cataloging-in-Publication Data

Names: Kaplony, Andreas, editor. | Marx, Michael, 1971- editor.
Title: Qur'an quotations preserved on papyrus documents, 7th-10th centuries / edited by Andreas Kaplony, Michael Marx.
Description: Leiden ; Boston : Brill, [2019] | Series: Documenta coranica ; Volume 2 | Includes bibliographical references and index.
Identifiers: LCCN 2018059325 (print) | LCCN 2018060374 (ebook) | ISBN 9789004376977 (E-book) | ISBN 9789004358911 (hardback : alk. paper)
Subjects: LCSH: Quran–Quotations. | Quran as literature. | Manuscripts, Arabic (Papyri)
Classification: LCC BP131.8 (ebook) | LCC BP131.8 .Q775 2019 (print) | DDC 297.1/224–dc23
LC record available at https://lccn.loc.gov/2018059325

Typeface for the Latin, Greek, and Cyrillic scripts: "Brill". See and download: brill.com/brill-typeface.

ISSN 2211-6761
ISBN 978-90-04-35891-1 (hardback)
ISBN 978-90-04-37697-7 (e-book)

This book is printed on acid-free paper and produced in a sustainable manner.

Contents

The Qur'ān's *Sitz im Leben*: Preliminary Remarks on Methodology VII
Andreas Kaplony
Figures XII
Notes on Contributors XV

1 Introduction 1
Michael Josef Marx

2 Qur'ān Quotations in Arabic Papyrus Letters from the 7th to the 10th Centuries 42
Daniel Potthast

3 Qur'an Quotations in Papyrus Legal Documents 86
Leonora Sonego

4 Qur'ānic Quotations in Arabic Papyrus Amulets 112
Ursula Bsees

5 Radiocarbon (^{14}C) Dating of Early Islamic Documents: Background and Prospects 139
Eva Mira Youssef-Grob

6 Radiocarbon (^{14}C) Dating of Qur'ān Manuscripts 188
Michael Josef Marx and Tobias J. Jocham

Quoted Editions 223
Index 232

The Qur'ān's *Sitz im Leben*: Preliminary Remarks On Methodology

Andreas Kaplony

Today, most scholars agree that the texts of the Qur'ān basically (1) were *authored* as part of Muḥammad's mission of about twenty years (up to 632) in Mekka and Medina and, being written in Arabic and with Arabic characters, stressed his mission's distinct Arabness against the background of pre-Islamic Western Arabia, where writing in Arabic with Arabic characters had been marginal; (2) were *compiled into one authoritative text* earlier or later in the pre-Umayyad, Umayyad, and Early ʿAbbāsid *imperial period* (632–800) to display the power of the one Arab-Islamic Empire to Arab Muslims and all others alike; and (3) *strongly influenced* the quite diverse cultures of the *Islamic Ecumene* up to the Fāṭimid period and beyond (800–1000), in which Arabic had become the one *lingua franca* and Arabic writing, so to speak, the one *scriptura franca*. Yet to be honest, we only vaguely know what the Qur'ān's *Sitz im Leben* in these three phases actually was, what exactly the Qur'ān was used for in Muḥammad's own time, how it was placed to display Muslim imperial rule, and how it was later employed by Ismāʿīlīs, Melkites, Sunnites, Zoroasthrians, Karaites, etc. of the Arabic, Coptic, Sabaean, New Persian, Turkish, etc. tongues.

Each of the three phases mentioned has its distinct source profile. (1) For Muḥammad's own time, our best source is probably the text of the *Qur'ān* itself, which stresses that it is not a seer's stammering but a written message and also emphasizes how people should have reacted—and how they actually did react—to Muḥammad and his message, and to earlier messengers and their messages.[1] *North-Arabian inscriptions, statues, and votive offerings* found in the West Arabian towns of Qaryat al-Fāw, Dedān/al-ʿUlā, al-Ḥiǧr/Madā'in Ṣāliḥ, Taymā', etc. similarly refer to themselves and define what writing was meant to be used for.[2] There may also be information in the steadily grow-

1 For the Qur'ān reflecting on itself, see, e.g., Jeffery 1952; Madigan 2001; Jones 2003: 8–15; Boisliveau 2011; 2013; 2014a; 2014b; 2014c; Neuwirth 2015: 13–24.

2 For a survey of archaeological findings on the Arabian Pensinsula, see *Roads of Arabia* 2012. There is a full-text database of South Arabian, Ancient North Arabian, Aramaic, and Nabatean inscriptions on the Arabian Peninsula, the *Digital Archive for the Study of Pre-Islamic Arabian Inscriptions* (DASI) (dasi.cnr.it; last accessed 27 March 2019).

ing but mostly undated *corpus of graffiti* found in West Arabia.[3] The most rewarding, yet almost unexamined treasure is the vast corpus of *Christian and Jewish apocrypha in Syriac, Coptic, Armenian, Ethiopic, Greek*, etc.: these apocrypha—rather than the Bible one step farther back—are both what the Qur'ān directly reacts to and what very much shaped and mirrored the conceptions of religious men and women and their (written) messages in Muḥammad's time.[4] Finally, pre-Islamic *Arabic poetry* occasionally describes how people used writs, and often refers to the role that poets and poetry played; since it was mostly compiled in the eighth century and later but claims to go back to pre-Islamic times, identifying the safely pre-Islamic bits is a challenge of its own.[5]

(2–3) For understanding how the Qur'ān actually was used in the *imperial and lingua franca periods* (632–1000), the sources are much more precise and rich. We might use the *Qur'ān manuscripts* preserved from these same periods examining all traces of compilation left on its text (the order of the Surahs, the use of the Basmala, the Mysterious Letters, etc.) and on the manuscripts (the presentation of Surah titles and verse dividers, verse numbers, the dimensions of the Qur'ān manuscripts, etc.).[6] We need to check how the Qur'ān was quoted and displayed in *inscriptions, coins, papyrus and parchment documents, manuscripts and objects such as potsherds, tiles, etc.* The later we are in this period, the more important become Qur'ānic bits and pieces in the *Ḥadīṯ collections*, in *historiography*, and in *Adab literature*.[7] And there are *full descriptions* of how the Qur'ān was used.

Exactly this is one of the two aims of the present volume: the examination of Qur'ānic quotations in the three most important corpora of papyrus and parchment documents preserved from the *imperial and the lingua franca periods (632–1000)*, i.e., in original letters, agreements, and amulets. The results are quite astonishing. Daniel Potthast in his contribution makes clear that while *original Arabic letters preserved from the imperial period (632–800)* had a clear Muslim-only flavour, *original Arabic letters preserved from the lingua franca period (800–1000)* are generally monotheist and not explicit on their religious

3 For the graffiti from the Arabian Peninsula, see, e.g., Jones 2003: 4; Macdonald 2010; Imbert 2011; 2012; 2013; 2015.

4 For the apocrypha as background to the Qur'ān, see, e.g., Griffith 2008; Kropp 2008; Mourad 2008; Witztum 2011.

5 For pre-Islamic Arabic poetry referring to documents, see Jones 2003: 1–4; Neuwirth 2015: 7–12.

6 For early Qur'ān manuscripts up to 800, see Déroche 2007; 2013; 2014; Puin 2011; Cellard 2015; Chahdi 2015; George 2015; Marx 2015; Small 2015.

7 For Ḥadīṯ collections, historiography, and Adab literature on the Qur'ān, see Motzki 2001; Jones 2003: 5–7; Amir-Moezzi 2013.

affiliation, with only a very few using Qur'ān quotations to stress their Muslim identity. Similarly, Leonora Sonego finds that in *Arabic legal agreements from the lingua franca period* (800–1000)—no earlier ones have been preserved—only divorce and marriage documents quote the Qur'ān; this is probably due to the fact that the Qur'ān has precise legal instructions only on divorce that are quoted in both divorce and marriages documents. Ursula Bsees shows that in *Arabic amulets from the lingua franca period* (800–1000), Qur'ān quotations are displayed in two quite different ways: for those who were illiterate, the dangerous power of amulets was visually represented by the use of archaizing ornamental script and by magical symbols, whereas amulets aimed at the literate population were in a casual script, yet on small strips of low-quality papyrus.

The other aim of this volume is to evaluate how much we might use radiocarbon (^{14}C) for dating early Qur'ān manuscripts. Eva Mira Youssef-Grob, on the one hand, and Michael Josef Marx and Tobias J. Jocham, on the other, convincingly show how radiocarbon dating, if used in a skeptical and well considered way, strongly confirms the paleographical attribution of the early Qur'ān manuscripts to the imperial period (632–800).

This volume is longly overdue, and we wish to thank both all contributors and Brill publishers for their patience. The collections most kindly allowed us to reproduce images, not to mention the fact that some even lent a helping hand for radiocarbon dating.

Bibliography

Amir-Moezzi, Mohammad Ali. 2013. "Le Coran silencieux et le Coran parlant." In *Le Coran: nouvelles approches*, ed. Mehdi Azaiez and Sabrina Mervin. Paris: CNRS, 57–98.

Boisliveau, Anne-Sylvie. 2011. "Canonisation du Coran … par le Coran?" In *Revue des Mondes Musulmans et de la Méditerranée* 129: 154–168.

Boisliveau, Anne-Sylvie. 2013. "Polemics in the Koran: The Koran's Negative Argumentation over Its Own Origin." In *Arabica* 60: 131–145.

Boisliveau, Anne-Sylvie. 2014a. *Le Coran par lui-même: vocabulaire et argumentation du discours coranique autoréférentiel*. Leiden: Brill.

Boisliveau, Anne-Sylvie. 2014b. "'Parole' et 'récitation': aspects du vocabulaire autoréférentiel du Coran." In *Oralité et écriture dans la Bible et le Coran*, ed. Philippe Cassuto / Pierre Larcher. Aix-en-Provence: Presses universitaire de Provence, 71–98.

Cellard, Eléonore. 2015. "La vocalization des manuscrits coraniques dans les premiers siècles de l'Islam." In *Les origines du Coran, le Coran des origines: actes du colloque international ... les 3 et 4 mars 2011*, ed. François Déroche / Christian Julien Robin / Michel Zink. Actes de colloque. Paris: Académie des Inscriptions et Belles-Lettres, 151–176.

Chahdi, Hassan. 2015. "Entre *qirāʾāt* et variantes du *rasm*: l'exemple du fragment Marcel 18." In *Les origines du Coran, le Coran des origines: actes du colloque international ... les 3 et 4 mars 2011*, ed. François Déroche / Christian Julien Robin / Michel Zink. Actes de colloque. Paris: Académie des Inscriptions et Belles-Lettres, 177–189.

Déroche, François. 2007. "Beauté et éfficacité: l'écriture arabe au service de la révélation." In *Results of Contemporary Research on the Qur'ân: The Question of a Historico-critical Text of the Qur'ân*, ed. Manfred S. Kropp. Beiruter Texte und Studien, vol. 100. Beirut: Ergon, 17–31.

Déroche, François. 2013. "Contrôler l'écriture: sur quelques caractéristiques des Corans de la période omeyyade." In *Le Coran: nouvelles approches*, ed. Mehdi Azaiez / Sabrina Mervin. Paris: CNRS, 41–54.

Déroche, François. 2014. *Qur'ans of the Umayyads: A First Overview*. Leiden Studies in Islam and Society, vol. 1. Leiden: Brill.

George, Alain. 2015. "Le palimpseste Lewis-Mingana de Cambridge, témoin ancien de l'histoire du Coran." In *Les origines du Coran, le Coran des origines: actes du colloque international ... les 3 et 4 mars 2011*, ed. François Déroche / Christian Julien Robin / Michel Zink. Actes de colloque. Paris: Académie des Inscriptions et Belles-Lettres, 219–270.

Griffith, Sidney. 2008. "The 'Companions of the Cave' in Sūrat al-Kahf and in Syriac Christian Tradition." In *The Qur'an in Its Historical Context, vol. 1*, ed. Gabriel Said Reynolds. Routledge Studies in the Qur'an. London: Routledge, 109–137.

Imbert, Frédéric. 2011. "L'Islam des pierres: l'expression de la foi dans les graffiti arabes des premiers siècles." In *Revue des Mondes Musulmans et de la Méditerranée* 129: 57–78.

Imbert, Frédéric. 2012. "Réflexions sur les formes de l'écrit à l'aube de l'Islam." In *Proceedings of the Seminar for Arabian Studies* 42 (= *Papers from the Forty-fifth Meeting of the Seminar for Arabian Studies Held at the British Museum, London, 28–30 July 2011*): 119–128.

Imbert, Frédéric. 2013. "Le Coran des pierres: statistiques et premières analyses." In *Le Coran: nouvelles approches*, ed. Mehdi Azaiez / Sabrina Mervin. Paris: CNRS, 99–124.

Imbert, Frédéric. 2015. "Califes, princes et poètes dans les graffiti du début de l'Islam." In *Romano-Arabica* 15 (= *Writing and Street Art in the Arab World*), 59–79.

Jeffery, Arthur. 1952. *Qur'ān as Scripture*, New York: Russell F. Moore.

Jones, Alan 2003. "The Word Made Visible: Arabic Script and the Comitting of the Qur'ān to Writing." In *Texts, Documents and Artefacts: Islamic Studies in Honour of D.S. Richards*, ed. Chase F. Robinson. Islamic History and Civilization: Studies and Texts, vol. 45. Leiden: Brill, 1–16.

Kaplony, Andreas. 2018. "Comparing Qur'ānic Suras with Pre-800 Documents (With an Appendix on Subtypes of Pre-800 Kitāb Documents)." In *Der Islam* 95: 312–366

Kropp, Manfred. 2008. "Beyond Single Words: *mā'ida, Shayṭān, jibt* and *ṭāghūt*. Mechanisms of Transmission into the Ethiopic (Gəʿəz) Bible and the Qur'ānic Text." In *The Qur'an in Its Historical Context, vol. 1*, ed. Gabriel Said Reynolds. Routledge Studies in the Qur'an. London: Routledge, 204–216.

Macdonald, M[ichael] C.A. 2010. "Ancient Arabia and the Written Word." In *The Development of Arabic as a Written Language: Papers from the Special Session of the Seminar for Arabian Studies Held on 24 July, 2009*, ed. M[ichael] C.A. Macdonald. Supplement to the Proceedings of the Seminar for Arabian Studies, vol. 40. Oxford: Archaeopress, 5–28.

Madigan, Daniel A. 2001. *The Qur'ân's Self-image: Writing and Authority in Islam's Scripture*, Princeton: Princeton University Press.

Marx, Michael. 2015. "Le Coran de ʿUthmān dans le traité de Versailles." In *Les origines du Coran, le Coran des origines: actes du colloque international … les 3 et 4 mars 2011*, ed. François Déroche / Christian Julien Robin / Michel Zink. Actes de colloque. Paris: Académie des Inscriptions et Belles-Lettres, 271–295.

Motzki, Harald. 2001. "The Collection of the Qur'ān: A Reconsideration of Western Views in Light of Recent Methodological Developments." In *Der Islam* 78: 1–34.

Mourad, Suleiman, A. 2008. "Mary in the Qur'ān." In *The Qur'ān in Its Historical Context, vol. 1*, ed. Gabriel Said Reynolds. Routledge Studies in the Qur'ān. London: Routledge, 163–174.

Neuwirth, Angelika. 2015. "The 'Discovery of Writing' in the Qur'ān: Tracing and Epistemic Revolution in Arab Late Antiquity." In *Jerusalem Studies in Arabic and Islam* 42: 1–29.

Puin, Gerd-R. 2011. "Vowel Letters and Ortho-epic Writing in the Qur'ān." In *The Qur'an in Its Historical Context, vol. 2: New Perspectives on the Qur'an*, ed. Gabriel Said Reynolds. Routledge Studies in the Qur'an. London: Routledge, 147–190.

Roads of Arabia: Archäologische Schätze aus Saudi-Arabien, ed. Ute Franke / Ali Al-Ghabban / Joachim Gierlichs / Stefan Weber. 2012. [Publikationen des] Museum[s] für Islamische Kunst. Berlin: Wasmuth.

Small, Keith E. 2015. "Textual Transmission and Textual Variants: A Survey of Textual Variants in Early Qur'āns." In *Les origines du Coran, le Coran des origines: actes du colloque international … les 3 et 4 mars 2011*, ed. François Déroche / Christian Julien Robin / Michel Zink. Actes de colloque. Paris: Académie des Inscriptions et Belles-Lettres, 93–109.

Witztum, Joseph. 2011. "Joseph among the Ishmaelites: Q 12 in Light of Syriac sources." In *The Qur'an in Its Historical Context, vol. 2: New Perspectives on the Qur'an*, ed. Gabriel Said Reynolds. Routledge Studies in the Qur'an. London: Routledge, 425–448.

Figures

The bulk of Arabic fragments collected by G. Michaélides (1900–1973) were bought in 1977 by Cambridge University Library. Inv. 32 and Inv. 190 as presented in this volume, however, appear to have never arrived in Cambridge. The images of the two documents are produced from the articles of Adolf Grohmann (1887–1977).

1.1 Fragment of a papyrus with Qur'ānic text (B. Moritz, Arabic Palaeography, Kairo 1905, Panel 43 recto) 15
1.2 Fragment of a papyrus with Qur'ānic text (B. Moritz, Arabic Palaeography, Kairo 1905, Panel 43 verso) 16
1.3 Papyrus with Qur'ānic text (A. Grohmann, The Problem of Dating Early Qur'āns, in: *Der Islam* 33 (1958) pl. 1) 19
1.4 Papyrus with Qur'ānic text (A. Grohmann, The Problem of Dating Early Qur'āns, in: *Der Islam* 33 (1958) pl. 1) 20
1.5 Early fragment of the Qur'ān, recto (P.Mird A 31 a 1) © Jerusalem Papyrus Collection [Image from M.J. Kister, On an Early Fragment of the Qur'ān, in: *Studies in Judaica, Karaitica and Islamica presented to Leon Nemoy on his eightieth birthday*, ed. S.R. Brunswick / J.C. Greenfield. Ramat-Gan: Bar-Ilan University Press 1982, p. 166] 23
1.6 Qur'ān fragment on papyrus (P.Leiden inv. Or. 8264 recto) © Leiden University Library, Papyrus Collection 25
1.7 Qur'ān fragment on papyrus (P.Leiden inv. Or. 8264 verso) © Leiden University Library, Papyrus Collection 26
1.8 Qur'ān fragment on papyrus (P.Stras. inv. Arab. 142 recto) © Bibliothèque nationale et universitaire de Strasbourg 28
1.9 Qur'ān fragment on papyrus (P.Stras. inv. Arab. 142 verso) © Bibliothèque nationale et universitaire de Strasbourg 28
1.10 Qur'ān fragment on papyrus (A. Grohmann, The Problem of Dating Early Qur'āns, in: *Der Islam* 33 (1958) pl. 4) 31
1.11 Qur'ān fragment on papyrus (A. Grohmann, The Problem of Dating Early Qur'āns, in: *Der Islam* 33 (1958) pl. 4) 32
1.12 Qur'ān fragment on papyrus (P.Berl. inv. 24017 recto) © Staatliche Museen zu Berlin, Ägyptisches Museum und Papyrussammlung 35
1.13 Qur'ān fragment on papyrus (P.Berl. inv. 24017 verso) © Staatliche Museen zu Berlin, Ägyptisches Museum und Papyrussammlung 36
1.14 Markup-System for the Arabic text © Tobias J. Jocham 38
2.1 A private letter written in 102/722 that quotes Q 65:2–4 in a different word order

(P.Michael.inv. P. A 560 = P.RagibLettreFamiliale) © Cambridge University Library, Michaelides Papyrus Collection 60
2.2 A business letter from the Fayyūm (9th c.) that contains quotations of Q 9:120–121 (in reversed verse order) and Q 65:12 (P.Louvre inv. E 7057 C = P.Marchands II 26) © Musée du Louvre, Département des Antiquitées Egyptiennes 61
2.3 A business letter from the Fayyūm (9th c.) that quotes Q 41:39 with minor changes influenced by the text of Q 42:9 (P.Louvre inv. E 8258 = P.Marchands, V/1 11) © Musée du Louvre, Département des Antiquitées Egyptiennes 62
2.4 A private letter (9th/10th c.) that quotes Q 14:7 (with a small orthographic variance) (P.Hamb.inv. A.P. 55 = P.Hamb.Arab. II 34) © Staats- und Universitätsbibliothek Hamburg, Papyrus-Sammlung 63
2.5 A business letter (around 800) quoting Q 65:7 (P.Louvre inv. SN 6378 = P.David-WeillLouvre 9) © Musée du Louvre, Département des Antiquitées Egyptiennes 63
3.1 An order to deliver a sheet of papyrus within the administration (dated 196/812). The text on the seal (now lost) had the oldest datable Qurʾān quotation in a legal document. The order is followed by a second, unpublished, text. (P.Vind.inv. A.P. 5557 = P.World p. 145). © Österreichische Nationalbibliothek, Papyrussammlung 91
3.2 A divorce document quoting Q 4:130 (P.Vind.inv. A.P. 832 = P.World p. 199 = Chrest.Khoury I 20) © Österreichische Nationalbibliothek, Papyrussammlung 108
4.1 Magical layout and inscription-style Kufi (P.Vind.inv. A.P. 7719r = PERF 840 = Nilus XXII 46) © Österreichische Nationalbibliothek, Papyrussammlung 121
4.2 Q 36 with some peculiarities (P.Heid.inv. Arab 91 = P.Bad. V 147) 125
5.1 Qurʾān fragment on papyrus (P.Leiden inv. Or. 8264, recto) © Leiden University Library, Papyrus Collection 151
5.2 OxCal plot of the IntCal13 curve, covering the two millenia CE until 1950 ("present") 152
5.3 OxCal single plot of ETH-54173 154
5.4 OxCal curve plot of ETH-54173 156
5.5 OxCal multiple plot of ETH-54173 156
5.6 OxCal plot of extract of IntCal13 curve, covering the centuries between 600 and 1200 CE 157
5.7 Lower part of an official letter on papyrus, dated 710 CE (P.Heid.inv. Arab. 2 = P.Heid.Arab. I 1 lower part) © Universität Heidelberg, Institut für Papyrologie 167
5.8 Lower part of an official letter on papyrus, dated 710 CE (Heid. inv. Arab. 9 = P.Heid.Arab. I 2 lower part) © Universität Heidelberg, Institut für Papyrologie 168

5.9 OxCal curve plot of selected results of measurements on dated papyri 710 CE 170
5.10 Oxcal plot of combined results, three measurements each on two dated papyri 710 CE 171
5.11 Oxcal plot of combined results plus offset as suggested by Dee et al. 2010 172
5.12 Modeled OxCal single plot for papyrus P.Leiden inv. Or. 8264 175
5.13 OxCal single plot for papyrus P.Leiden inv. Or. 8264 175
6.1 Qur'ān in Hiǧāzi Type I (Arabe 328a, fol. 10v) © Bibliotheque national de France 194
6.2 Qur'ān in Hiǧāzi Type II (Arabe 328e, fol. 90v) © Bibliotheque national de France 195
6.3 Qur'ān in Hiǧāzi Type III (Arabe 330a, fol. 1r) © Bibliotheque national de France 196
6.4 Qur'ān in Hiǧāzi Type IV (Arabe 334c, fol. 41r) © Bibliotheque national de France 197
6.5 Basmala of Surah 5 (ms.or.fol. 4313, fol. 2r) © Staatsbibliothek zu Berlin 198
6.6 Basmala of Surah 32 (Is. 1615 I, fol. 7r) © Chester Beatty Library, Dublin 198
6.7 Basmala of Surah 18 (Ma VI 165, fol. 5r) © Universitätsbibliothek Tübingen 199
6.8 Basmala of Surah 18 (We II 1913, fol. 111v) © Staatsbibliothek zu Berlin 199
6.9 OxCal Combined plot and sample image (ms.or.fol. 4313, fol. 2r) © Staatsbibliothek zu Berlin & Tobias J. Jocham 201
6.10 OxCal Combined plot and sample image of the manuscript (Ma VI 165, fol. 23r) © Universitätsbibliothek Tübingen & Tobias J. Jocham 202
6.11 OxCal Combined plot and sample image of the manuscript (Cod.or. 14.545b, fol. 1r) © Leiden University Library & Tobias J. Jocham 203
6.12 OxCal Combined plot and sample image of the manuscript (We II 1913, fol. 104r) © Staatsbibliothek zu Berlin & Tobias J. Jocham 204
6.13 Comparison chart for key words in different Qur'ānic manuscripts © Tobias J. Jocham 208
6.14 Two ways of spelling the word *šay'* in Surah 18 of the Egyptian print of the Qur'ān Cairo (Cairene print 1924) © Michael Marx / Tobias J. Jocham 210

Notes on Contributors

Salome Beridze

has studied Arabic Studies in Tbilisi, Kuwait and Berlin. From 2014–2017 she was working as research assistant in the project *Corpus Coranicum* of the Berlin-Brandenburg Academy of Sciences and Humanities. Currently, she is member of the Graduate School *Manuscript Cultures* of the University of Hamburg where she is preparing a Ph.D. thesis on the palaeography of early Qurʾān manuscripts.

Charlotte Bohm

has studied Jewish, Byzantine and Semitic studies at the FU Berlin. She works as a research assistant in the project *Corpus Coranicum* of the Berlin-Brandenburg Academy of Sciences and Humanities.

Ursula Bsees

Dr.phil. (2015), is a Visiting Research Associate at Wolfson College, University of Cambridge. Funded by an Erwin Schrödinger research fellowship from the Austrian Science Fund, she does research on early hadith scholarship and transmission of texts, based on Arabic papyri. Her research interests lie in Arabic papyri (mostly literary), Medieval Arabic manuscripts, and magic and popular belief in the Arab World. She is currently preparing her doctoral dissertation on the edition and analysis of a Medieval paper scroll from rural Egypt for publication.

Tobias J. Jocham

does research at the Corpus Coranicum at Berlin-Brandenburg Academy of Sciences and Humanities. His main interest and study rests with material analysis of late antique manuscripts and its value as evidence for development of scripts and writing systems. He is preparing his Ph.D. on ink analysis of qurʾānic parchments and papyri.

Andreas Kaplony

Ph.D. (1994), Habilitation (2001), is Chair of Arabic and Islamic Studies at Ludwig-Maximilians-Universität München. He has published widely on Arabic-Islamic history.

Michael Josef Marx

has studied Oriental and Semitic languages and literatures and linguistics in Berlin (FU), Bonn, Tehran and Paris (INALCO and EPHE). Since 2007 he is director of the research department *Corpus Coranicum* of the Berlin-Brandenburg Academy of Sciences, a project founded together with Angelika Neuwirth and Nicolai Sinai in 2005. Together with the TELOTA department of the Academy, Michael has developed the online publication system *Corpus Coranicum* and is currently editor in chief of the online catalogue of ancient Qur'anic manuscripts. Together with François Déroche (Collège de France) and Christian Julien Robin (CNRS) he has been conducting the French-German projects Coranica and Paleocoran, supported by the German Research Council (DFG) and the Agence nationale de la recherche (ANR).

Daniel Potthast

Dr.phil. (2011), teaches and does research at the Chair of Arabic and Islamic Studies at Ludwig-Maximilians-Universität München. His main interest lies in the history of Muslim-Christian contact in the Middle Ages and in Arabic document studies. He has published *Christen und Muslime im Andalus: Andalusische Christen und ihre Literatur nach religionspolemischen Texten des zehnten bis zwölften Jahrhunderts* (2013), several articles on letter exchange in the Western Mediterranean and is preparing a study on diplomatic exchange between Arabic and Latin empires in the fourteenth century.

Leonora Sonego

lic.phil. (2011) is research assistant at the Chair of Arabic and Islamic Studies at Ludwig-Maximilian-Universität München. She has been working for the Arabic Papyrology Database since 2010, keeping newly entered data consistent with the existing corpus. One of her interests is the functioning of legal documents.

Eva Mira Youssef-Grob

Dr.phil. (2009), is a lecturer for Arabic and Arab culture at University of Zurich and ETH Zurich. Her doctoral thesis *Documentary Arabic Private and Business Letters on Papyrus: Form and Function, Content and Context* (2010) emerged in the Zurich/Munich research group of the Arabic Papyrology Database Project in which she was working from 2006 until 2016. Her interests in Arabic Papyrology are broad and cover, besides different aspects of letter writing, especially questions of palaeography and dating.

CHAPTER 1

Introduction

*Michael Josef Marx**

1 Exploring Material Evidence

The present volume is one of the results of *Coranica*, a French-German research project funded by the German *Deutsche Forschungsgemeinschaft* (DFG) and the French *Agence nationale de la recherche* (ANR) between 2012 and 2015. The project's task was to explore material evidence for the early history of the Qurʾān. To date, knowledge of the history of this text relies primarily on the narrative of the Islamic tradition. In order to balance the traditional narrative, material evidence is able to contribute to a new perspective on the Qurʾān and Early Islam. The question about the history of the text and its canonization formed the project's first part, under the title *Manuscripta et Testimonia Coranica*. A second component, *Glossarium Coranicum* focussing on languages in Late Antique Arabia and their impact on the Qurʾānic vocabulary.

The French-German project implements an approach based on material evidence. As part of this empirical approach, it aims to take into account methodological developments, technical innovations, and the latest archaeological discoveries. These include research on the most ancient written witnesses of the text of the Qurʾān, a field of study that lay dormant until the 1980s, when it was revived by manuscript discoveries in Sanaa, St. Petersburg,[1] and Istanbul.[2] With the opening of archaeological excavations on the Arabian Peninsula, a large quantity of another type of material evidence entered the field when important epigraphic and archaeological discoveries were made in Arabia, as illustrated

* In collaboration with Salome Beridze, Charlotte Bohm and Tobias J. Jocham for the edition of seven papyri Qurʾanic fragments.

1 Approximately 130 fragments of early parchment manuscripts, approximatively 1700 *folii*—according to the preliminary catalogue notes of Valery V. Polosin (1939–2014)—are now kept in the National Library of Russia and were acquired by Jean-Joseph Marcel (1776–1856) in Cairo during Bonaparte's expedition to Egypt.

2 A huge collection of early Qurʾānic manuscripts, saved after the 1894 fire in the Umayyad Mosque of Damascus, was brought to Istanbul and awaits study. Images of some manuscripts were published in the catalogue of a 2010 exhibition in the Istanbul Museum of Turkish and Islamic Arts, commemorating the proclamation of the Qurʾān 1400 years ago (measured by the solar calendar); cf. Unustası 2014. In April–May 2016, the special exhibition *Kūfī* in the same museum presented some fragments of the former Damascene collection.

 | DOI:10.1163/9789004376977_002

in the *Roads of Arabia* exhibition at the Louvre (Paris)[3] in 2010, Barcelona in 2011, St. Petersburg in 2011, and the Pergamon Museum (Berlin) in 2012.[4] Some of the texts discovered in Arabia are chronologically and geographically close to the environment of the Qurʾān, and thus give insights into the religious history of pre-Islamic Arabia.

A good example of the relevance of material evidence is the pre-Islamic name of the monotheistic god in Arabia attested to in Ancient South Arabian inscriptions. After the Himyarite kings rejected paganism at the end of the fourth century, the only god mentioned in South Arabian inscriptions, *rḥmn-n* (a Sabaic name, probably pronounced *raḥmān-an*, the syllable -an being the definite article, meaning literally "the Merciful"), is the name of the god worshipped by Arabian Jews and Christians. *Raḥmān-an*, transposed into Arabic as *ar-raḥmān*, is the only name of god attested in Arabian epigraphy after 400, when Christianity and Judaism became the official religions of rulers and aristocracy. In the Qurʾān, the word *ar-raḥmān*, considered by grammarians and theologians as an adjective—in parallel to the adjective *ar-raḥīm*, "merciful," with which it is part of the tripartite formula of the *basmala*—can be seen as an echo of the pre-Islamic period of Arabian monotheism. Looking historically into the issue, the interpretation of *raḥmān* as an adjective corresponds to the analysis of the first Arabic grammarians and lexicographers of the eighth century; however, it ignores the religious development of the peninsula in the pre-Islamic period that this term reflects.

Archeology provides a more accurate picture of the environmental and demographic milieu of Arabia in the second half of the sixth century, including political and economic components; it also illuminates the spread of Christianity and other religions on the peninsula. A good example of the importance of archeological discoveries is the corpus of pre-Islamic inscriptions in Arabic script discovered recently in Biʾr Ḥimā close to the city of Nağrān, in the southwest part of the kingdom of Saudi Arabia. Their texts, memorial inscripitions for Christians, perhaps monks—the later ones apparently commemorating events linked with the massacre of Christians by the Jewish king Yūsuf—are dated in the same calendar that is used in the late Nabataean inscriptions, and also shed light on the genesis of the emergence of Arabic script in the period of Late Antiquity. According to the Biʾr-Ḥimā-Inscriptions,[5] some of which date to the fifth century, the genesis of the Arabic script has to be revised. Traditionally, following descriptions of the origins of the Arabic script such as those men-

3 Detailed *Catalogue Routes d'Arabie* 2010, published in French and English.
4 Catalogue *Roads of Arabia* 2012 of the Berlin Exhibition.
5 Robin 2014.

tioned in Ibn an-Nadīm's *Fihrist* (d. approx. 990) or al-Balāḏurī's (d. 892) *Futūḥ al-buldān*, the history of Arabic script was traced back to the Mesopotamian cities of al-Ḥīra and al-Anbār.

2 Editing the Early Manuscripts of the Qur'ān

Providing a platform for cooperation between scholars in the fields of Ancient Studies and Islamic Studies from Austria, Belgium, England, France, Germany, and Italy, *Coranica* began in 2011, directed by Christian Robin and François Déroche (Académie des Inscriptions et Belles-Lettres, Paris) and Michael Marx and Angelika Neuwirth (Berlin-Brandenburgische Akademie der Wissenschaften, Berlin). The first objective of *Coranica* is to contribute to the history of the Qur'ānic text by producing catalogued inventories and studies of the earliest manuscripts of the Qur'ān. For this task, *Documenta Coranica* was founded in order to publish ancient fragments of Qur'ānic codices, accompanied by a detailed transliteration of the manuscript text. Its first volume, *Codex Amrensis 1*, published in 2018, consists of four dispersed fragments of an eighth-century codex that once belonged to the library of the ʿAmr ibn al-ʿĀṣ Mosque in al-Fusṭāṭ (Old Cairo). Scheduled in the same series are editions of three fragments of Qur'ānic codices from the Great Mosque of Sanaa, of which one is a palimpsest considered to be one of the most ancient extant Qur'ānic fragments.[6]

The task of publishing ancient manuscripts of the Qur'ān had already been undertaken in the 1990s by Sergio Noja Noseda (d. 2008) and François Déroche (in the framework of the *Amari* project). Two facsimile volumes were published, accompanied by a preliminary transliteration using dotted script for the representation of the Arabic text.[7] *Documenta Coranica* is taking up this idea of making the ancient manuscripts of the Qur'ān accessible, in a modified adapted way, by providing a more accurate representation of the included

6 Photographs of these three fragments had been taken by Christian Robin in Sanaa with support of the French ANR in the framework of the *De l'antiquité tardive à l'Islam* (DATI) project in 2008.

7 Déroche/Noseda 1998; Déroche/Noseda 2001. The first volume (1998) contains a manuscript in Ḥiǧāzī script from the Bibliothèque nationale de France (Arabe 328a), consisting of 56 folios. It represents about 25 percent of the text of the Qur'an. The second volume (2001) is an edition of the first half of the oldest Qur'an manuscript conserved by the British Library (Or. 2165), Ḥiǧāzī as well. This manuscript consists of 121 folios representing app. 53 percent of the total text of the Qur'an, of which images of 61 fol. were published in the volume of 2001.

text.[8] Sergio Noja Noseda and François Déroche's first project meanwhile seems to have inspired other scholars in the field: In 2004, Efim A. Rezvan published a Qur'ānic manuscript of which 81 leaves are conserved by the St. Petersburg Institute of Oriental Manuscripts and 16 fol. are conserved in four other places in Uzbekistan.[9] A facsimile-series that has started in Turkey, carried out by the Research Center for Islamic History, Art and Culture (IRCICA), where by 2017 eight large manuscripts had been edited by the Turkish scholar and politician Tayyar Altıkulaç (b. 1943), was perhaps also inspired by the French-Italian project. The first volume of the Turkish series was the 2007 publication of images of an almost complete codex on display in Istanbul's Topkapı Sarayı Museum.[10] This Qur'ān, attributed to Caliph ʿUṯmān ibn ʿAffān, was presented as a gift to the Ottoman Sultan Maḥmud II (1785–1839) by the governor of Egypt Muḥammad ʿAlī (1769–1849). The second volume was the 2011 publication of another codex attributed to ʿUṯmān ibn ʿAffān, once held in the Shrine of Ḥusain in Cairo and now conserved in the Library of Islamic Manuscripts Foundation.[11] These were followed by publications of large codices: one codex kept in the Istanbul Museum of Turkish and Islamic Arts (Türk ve İslam Eserleri Müzesi),[12] a codex attributed to ʿAlī ibn Abī Ṭālib kept in Sanaa,[13] the manuscript Arabe 328a of Paris,[14] and the manuscript Tübingen Ma VI 165.[15] The Turkish series seems to be motivated less by an historical approach to the textual history of the Qur'ān than by the wish to prepare a documentation, the purpose of which remains somewhat difficult to gauge. The volumes have been carefully prepared by Tayyar Altıkulaç; they contain images of the codices and give the Arabic text, albeit fully dotted even if many words do not have dots. Footnotes mention spellings of the preceding edited volumes of the series.

As a methodologically enriched continuation of the *Amari* project, the series *Documenta Coranica* offers a transliteration[16] of each single photo of a manuscript page. This "transliteration," or Arabic text, uses an eight-colour system to

8 See edition of the text of seven papyri containing Qur'ānic text (following this introduction) that are using a colour markup system.

9 Rezvan 2004, facsimile edition of a manuscript (in script style B) attributed to ʿUṯmān of which fragments are preserved in St. Petersburg, Katta-Langar, Bukhara and Tashkent, containing about 40 percent of the Qur'ānic text.

10 Altıkulaç 2007a.

11 Altıkulaç 2011a.

12 Altıkulaç 2007b.

13 Altıkulaç 2011b.

14 Altıkulaç 1436/2015.

15 Altıkulaç 2016.

16 The term "transliteration" is strictly speaking inaccurate here, since the script used in the manuscripts is Arabic and the "transliteration" does not use a different script to represent

indicate (a) degrees of legibility, (b) differences compared with the spelling of the Egyptian print of the Qur'ān (Cairo 1924, the so-called "King Fu'ād Edition"), and (c) modifications (corrections, overwritings, additions, and erasures) of the manuscripts' first layer of ink (see page 38 of this volume).[17] Since the publication of the first volume, *Codex Amrensis 1* (fragments Paris Arabe 326a, St. Petersburg Marcel 9 and fragments today kept in the Museum of Islamic Art in Doḥa (Qatar)) prepared by Eléonore Cellard (Paris), volumes on Tübingen manuscript Ma VI 165 (*Codex Damascensis 1*) and British Library Or. 2165, Paris BNF Arabe 328e and Kuweit LNS 19ab (*Codex Amrensis 2*) DAM 01-27.1 (*Codex Sanaanensis 1*) DAM 01-29.1 and DAM 01-25.1 (*Codex Sanaanensis 2*) are currently under preparation.

3 Carbon Dating Parchment Manuscripts, Wooden Sticks from Yemen, and Papyri

Early Qur'āns of the first four centuries usually have no text indicating the name of the scribe(s), nor where nor when the copy was produced. Exceptions are the so-called "Qur'ān of Amāǧūr" that has an endowment document (*waqfiyya*) dated 262/876, indicating a terminus *ante quo*.[18] Among dated Qur'āns are codices produced around the year 1000, such as "the Nurse's Qur'ān" from Qayrawān (written in 410/1019) and the "Codex of Ibn al-Bawwāb" (Chester Beatty Library Dublin, CBL 1431, dated 391/1000), both dated by colophon. Complete codices include the monumental Qur'ān that is conserved today by the Central Library of Islamic Manuscripts (*al-Maktaba al-markaziyya li-l-maḫṭūṭāt al-islāmiyya*) in Cairo, while other codices datable to the period between 750 and 900 seem to be complete but contain no colophon. We do not know whether or not older codices once had a colophon or other scribal information specifying the date on the first or last page because these pages were especially exposed to damage of all kinds. According to the *Corpus Coranicum* database of Qur'ānic manuscripts,[19] e.g., only two fragments before 750 contain parts of the first Surah: (1) the manuscript DAM 01-25.1, kept in the "House of manuscripts" (*Dār al-maḫṭūṭāt*) in Sanaa and carbon dated to the

---

the text of the manuscript. A more precise term would be simply an "Arabic text" of the manuscripts' contents.

17 The markup-scheme and the colour system have both been developed by Tobias J. Jocham in his Master's thesis "Studien zu den frühen Qur'ān-Handschriften Is. 1615 aus der Chester Beatty Library in Dublin".

18 Déroche 1991–1992: 61.

19 See Manuscripta Coranica, Online Catalogue of Early Qur'ānic Manuscripts, https://corpuscoranicum.de/handschriften/uebersicht.

seventh century, and (2) DAM 20-33.1 from the same collection, with remarkable illuminations dated by art historical comparison of its ornaments to the first decades of the eighth century.

Dating the manuscript evidence plays a central role in understanding the history of the Qurʾān. The problem is intricate because there are different opinions as to the age of what was considered, in the second half of the nineteenth century, the British Library's most ancient Qurʾān. This fragment of a codex (British Library Or. 2165) contains 121 parchment leaves preserved in good condition, covering more than 60 percent of the text. One image of this manuscript was published in a facsimile album by William Wright in 1875.[20] The Austrian scholar Josef von Karabacek (1845–1918) was convinced that this manuscript was written in the seventh century,[21] whereas Bernhard Moritz (1859–1939) in his *Arabic Palaeography* (printed in Cairo 1905) had classified a similar type of script contained in a fragment of the Khedival Library (Cairo) as belonging to the ninth century.[22] From today's perspective, von Karabacek's opinion seems to make sense, whereas Moritz' classification appears odd. Here one should be aware of the fact that since the time of Jakob Georg Christian Adler (1756–1834), who published in 1780 the first study of ancient Qurʾānic manuscripts and the history of the Arabic script in the modern era, scholars have had no reliable framework to classify Qurʾānic fragments chronologically.[23] In the middle of the nineteenth century, Michele Amari (1806–1889), an Italian scholar, who had started to produce the catalogue of the Royal Library in Paris, was convinced that some fragments among this rich Qurʾān collection of Egyptian origin contained a script style described briefly by Ibn an-Nadīm (d. 995) as the writing of Mekka and Medina.[24] One of the founding fathers of Qurʾānic studies in Europe, Theodor Nöldeke (1836–1930), had access to collections in Berlin and Gotha but was not really in a position to understand the age of the documents. Gotthelf Bergsträßer (1886–1933), professor of Islamic studies at the University of Munich, who launched the idea of setting up a photo archive of ancient Qurʾānic manuscripts, remained reluctant to mention dates of the manuscripts studied.[25]

In a small article, Adolf Grohmann (1887–1977) called for the comparison of ancient Qurʾāns with dated Arabic papyri, an idea that offered arguments to

20 Wright 1875–1883: pl. LIX.

21 von Karabacek 1906.

22 Moritz 1905: Table 44. See also Marx/Jocham in this volume for the results of carbon dating of the Berlin fragments of the same codex.

23 Adler 1780.

24 Amari in Derenbourg 1910.

25 Bergsträßer 1930, and Pretzl 1934.

suggest, for instance, a dating for the mentioned London manuscript.[26] However, this promising approach using papyri systematically for the dating of parchment fragments of the Qur'ān before 900 has never been carried out systematically to date. With many more papyrus documents accessible today, one would wish that paleographic evidence coming from script styles of dated Arabic papyri would be given more attention.

Since the 1980s the situation in Qur'ānic paleography has changed substantially, due to the systematic typology of ancient Arabic script styles published by François Déroche on the basis of the fragments in the Bibliothèque Nationale (Paris).[27] This classification of script styles into four categories of Ḥiǧāzī, and a differentiated classification of five Kufic styles, offers today a reference tool for studies of Qur'ānic manuscripts. Concerning the question of dating, Déroche's classification implies somehow a relative chronological order for the development of letter shapes, based on which a vague periodization seems to be plausible. However, crucial issues of dating the manuscripts are still under discussion.

In a discipline of manuscript studies where no early document has a date and paleography mainly indicates a relative chronology, dating based on radiocarbon analysis in a systematic way seems to be attractive. The project's campaign was supported by the collections of Berlin, Dublin, Heidelberg, Leiden, Munich, Oslo, Sanaa, Tbilisi, Tübingen, and a private collection in Stuttgart (for a parchment leaf in Kufic script). All measurements of Arabic, Coptic, Georgian, and Syriac manuscripts, Arabic papyri, and wooden sticks from Yemen with incised text in Ancient South Arabian were carried out in collaboration with the Laboratory of Ion Beam Physics of ETH Zurich (Irka Hajdas)[28]. Since all early manuscripts of the Qur'ān were written on parchment, for comparison a number of dated other parchments with non-Qur'ānic texts from the same region and period in Arabic, Coptic, Georgian, Greek, and Hebrew manuscripts before 1000 CE were consulted. In light of comparative evidence, the actual precision of ^{14}C dates can be better understood for early manuscripts of the Qur'ān as well, as the results of the radiocarbon dating of Georgian and Syriac manuscripts has shown.

26 Grohmann 1958.
27 Déroche 1983.
28 Marx et al. 2014

4 Papyri as Evidence for the History of the Qurʾān

In the text of the Qurʾān, different writing materials are named: lexemes such as *ṣuḥuf* ("sheets"), *raqq* ("parchment"), *ḥibr* ("ink"), *midād* ("ink"), and *qalam* ("pen") reflect the usage of writing in Mekka and Medina.[29] The most frequent word is *kitāb* ("book"), a term that apparently in most instances refers to the heavenly book or "Holy Book" of a religious community, as in *ahl al-kitāb* ("the people of the book"). In Surah 6 the word *qirṭās* appears twice in its plural form *qarāṭīs*, in verses 7 and 91, possibly meaning "papyrus" and in both cases designating the material on which the revelations of former prophets were written down. However, it remains difficult to determine whether *qarāṭīs* means "papyri" here or, instead, the material out of which a book (codex) is produced. Although from a linguistic perspective *qirṭāṣ/qarāṭīs* could be considered a loanword from the Syriac *qarṭīs-ā* (from the Greek *chartēs*), the loaning process would have taken place in the pre-Islamic period, since the term appears in poetry attributed to pre-Islamic authors, e.g., in the *muʿallaqa*-poem of Ṭarafa.[30] Arthur Jeffery lists both "parchment" and "papyrus" as possible meanings, also with reference to Jewish sources (Midrash Leviticus Rabba § 34), where a "document" is referred to as written on material that we cannot identify definitely.[31] One argument for "parchment" could be Ṭarafa's poem, where *qirṭās* is mentioned as "something peculiarly Syrian." In Eleonore Haeuptner's study of the material culture reflected in the Qurʾān, she considers the term *qirṭās* to mean "parchment."[32]

Whether parchment or papyrus, it is striking that among the writing materials mentioned in the Qurʾān, the word *muṣḥaf*—the term for a codex of the Qurʾān—is missing. This word, which is most probably of Ethiopian origin, is today the term for a copy of the Qurʾān. According to the biography of the Prophet Muḥammad (*Sīra*), he employed scribes such as Zaid ibn Ṯābit, yet no official copy of the text of the Qurʾān was apparently produced by Muḥammad. According to Muslim tradition, this step is linked either to the first caliph, Abū Bakr, or to the third, ʿUṯmān, with the latter being seen as the collector and unifier of the text via official copies of the Qurʾān that he is believed to have sent to the most important cities of the Arabic empire—Basra, Damascus, and Kufa—and, according to some sources, also to Bahrain and Yemen. According

---

29 Maraqten 1998.

30 Cf. Tarafa, poem no. 56, line 9, quoted after Arazi/Masalha 1999: 33.

31 Jeffery 1938: 235–236.

32 Haeuptner 1966: 97–110, claiming that Q 52:3 (*fī raqqin manšūrin*) and Q 52:2 (*wa-kitābin masṭūrin*) also point to the meaning "parchment" (rather than "papyrus").

to another scholarly opinion, it was during the Umayyad dynasty (661–750) that the text of the Qur'ān was standardized.[33] In most studies about the textual history of the Qur'ān, material evidence however is neglected.[34]

So far, seven papyri are known that contain (almost) exclusively the text of the Qur'ān: (A) the Moritz fragment, a papyrus at the Egyptian National Library in Cairo, the former Khedival Library, a photo of which is included in Bernhard Moritz's volume *Arabic Palaeography* (Moritz 1905: Table 43); (B) a piece (P.Michael.inv. 32) from the collection of Georges Michaélides (now lost) and (F) a second piece (P.Michael.inv. 190), also inaccessible today;[35] (C) a fragment from the Rockefeller Collection (P.Rockefeller inv. Mird A 31 a 1), discovered at Ḫirbet al-Mird, kept today by the Israel Museum in Jerusalem and described by A. Grohmann and M. Kister; (D) a papyrus kept in Leiden (P.Leiden inv. Or. 8264);[36] (E) a papyrus in Strasbourg (P.Stras.inv. Ar. 142); and (G) a fragment kept by the papyrus collection of the Neues Museum in Berlin (P.Berl.inv. 24017). Documents such as Papyrus No. 274 of Duke University, written in a rather late script style, or Utah Inv. 342, containing a bifolium dated after 800 CE, contain Qur'ānic text. In his article "A Third Koranic Fragment on Papyri" (2003), Sergio Noseda Noja mentions "fragments of a word or two" in papyri of the John Rylands University Library of Manchester[37] that fall instead into the category of Qur'ānic quotations. Many papyri collections, such as the one in Vienna, contain parchment Qur'ānic fragments, e.g., call numbers A Perg. 2 and A Perg 213, that are not considered here. Available information about the seven fragments of Qur'ānic papyri having probably "non-magical" function is limited as it seems to be impossible to reconstruct their context, neither to know their precise date. What can be said is what follows:

(A) Egyptian National Library, Cairo: the Moritz fragment: Little is known about the two small papyri fragments of which Bernhard Moritz's album *Arabic Palaeography* contains an image (Moritz 1905, Table 43). The call number is not given nor do we learn whether the fragments are inscribed on the back side. Moritz seems to have been convinced that the two pieces, on which the script is very similar, are from a codex of the Qur'ān because his caption of the

33 See Casanova 1911.
34 Burton, Crone, Cook, and Wansbrough, all in the 1970s, without material evidence.
35 Papyrus no. 32 of the collection of Georges Michaélides is lost today, while Papyrus no. 190 is at Cambridge University Library, which acquired this collection but cannot provide images for conservational reasons. The two papyri are discussed on the basis of photos included in the articles of Adolf Grohmann.
36 Dated by ^{14}C-analysis to 653–766, $\sigma 2$ (95.4%); see Youssef-Grob 2019.
37 Noja Noseda 2003: 316 n. 11.

image says: "Fragment of a Qur'ān on Papyrus. III cent. Khedivial Library." The word *allaḏīna* (الدس) is written similarly on both fragments, the script being close to Hiǧāzī or Type B of Kufi. The two fragments seem to contain a text from Surah 28: in the image, the fragment on the left (line 1: الحى هم; line 2: اوتى; line 6: ا الدس; line 7: به مما; line 8: اجر يوتون; line 9: ينفقون line 10: اعملا) fits Q 28:48–57, while the text on the fragment on the right is difficult to identify, perhaps Q 28:80–85. The two fragments would then belong originally to one bifolium of a much larger size, in which case the left fragment could be part of the first page of the bifolium, while the right fragment might be a portion of the last part of Q 28. In a review of the Moritz album, Josef von Karabacek recognizes Q 28:48–57, for the fragment on the left but leaves open the identification of the fragment on the right side of the image.[38] Since we have so little information of the two fragments of which we even do not know if they belonged together originally, it would make—strictly speaking—make more sense to consider them as two papyri pieces. For pragmatic reasons, however, we treat them here as one object.

(B) Michaélides Collection (P.Michael.inv. 32): This papyrus (now lost, but illustrated in Grohmann 1958, Plate 1) has some diacritical signs, 14.8 cm × 5.9 cm. Brown, fine papyrus. Recto (left hand side): Q 54:11–38, 20 lines; verso (right): Q 54:45–55; 55:1–32; 18 lines, verse division; end of line 4, the end of verse 50, a verse division mark is visible. Q 54 is divided from 55 by two parallel horizontal lines running over the full width of the page, and filled in with an undulating line with pearls in the compartment.[39] It is possible that this fragment, of which little is known, is from a codex.

(C) Rockefeller Collection, Jerusalem (P.Rockefeller inv. Mird A 31 a 1): Adolf Grohmann (Grohmann 1963: no. 28) erroneously considered this fragment to be from a letter. Against this view, Meir J. Kister published a small article arguing for a Qur'ānic text.[40] Since the text is preceded by non-Qur'ānic text, this papyrus is most probably a fragment of a letter containing a longer quotation from the Qur'ān.

(D) Leiden, University Library (P.Leiden inv. Or. 8264): A quite detailed description of this fragment has been written by Petra Sijpesteijn and was published by Sergio Noja Noseda: "Arabic, papyrus, 1 leaf., set between glass. Qur'an,

38 von Karabacek 1906: 37.
39 Grohmann 1958: 222–228.
40 Kister 1982.

fragment, sura 71:9–19. Recto: 13 lines written in black ink parallel to the papyrus fibres; original cutting lines preserved on right, left, top and bottom; right bottom corner broken off; two small holes in the papyrus. Verso: 7 lines written in black ink at right angles to papyrus fibres; bottom quarter of papyrus blank. On the recto side verses 10–19 of sura 71, on the verso side verses 19–25 of the same sura are written (this was already discovered by C. van Arendonk, the previous owner, as is clear from his comments in the small notebook that is kept with the papyrus (Or. 8264a, below). He indicated that the recto started at verse 9, but it is the fact half way verse 10). The text seems to be a writing exercise dating from the 3rd/9th century. The letters (open ʿayn, bottom of alif bends to the right) and lay-out (words are broken off at the end of a line and continued on the next) are characteristic of papyri from the first two Muslim centuries. It may also be argued that this is probably the result of the fact that the text was written by someone who has not much practice in writing or who was learning how to write. (See also the Leiden papyrus Or. 12.885, below. W. Diem has published a 3rd/9th century letter written by an unpracticed hand, and which looks similar to earlier writings.) The writer made several spelling mistakes (for example: recto 2 *al-samaʾ* is written with *sad* instead of *sin*; verso 2 *lam yaziduhu* is written with an incorrect long *i*; verso 6 *wa-la tuzid* is written with incorrect long *i*). He has left words out (recto 4 one word left out; recto 13 *al-ard* is written above the line; verso 5 second *la* left-out). And he used many orthographical incorrect spellings (recto 2 long *a* not written in first word; recto 5 long *a* corrected and added; verso 1 long *a* not written; verso 3 twice long *a* not written). The text stops in the middle of an *aya*, and at the end of line 5 on the recto side decorations in the form of dots in the shape of a circle are written although there is no end of verse there. Earlier provenance: The papyrus comes apparently from a collection, either private or public, as there is a label pasted on the glass with the mark 'A 1'. The MS was privately acquired by C. van Arendonk (d. 1946) from Erik von Scherling, an antiquarian in Oegstgeest, who may have brought the papyrus from Egypt. Van Arendonk was the learned curator of the Leiden Oriental collections. Added as Or. 8264 bis is the cliché for *Rotulus*. Or. 8264 bis. The cliché used for reproducing Or. 8264 in *Rotulus*. (preserved in the film collection as Or. B 365) Or. 8264 a. Arabic, Dutch, paper, 5 ff., and blanks. Exercise book of C. van Arendonk (d. 1946), containing his notes on Arabic papyri. He may have made these notes when asked for information about the originals, which may have been offered to him by Erik von Scherling, the well-known antiquarian who was based in Oegstgeest (near Leiden), and who published a series of scholarly sales catalogues under the collective title *Rotulus*. This is correct if the assumption that the other fragments mentioned in van Arendonk's exercise book also come from Erik von Scherling. No. 5 (ff. 3a–b) in van Arendonk's notes concerns the fragment which is now known as Leiden Or. 8264. Added are two sets of photographs of Or. 8264, above. (in Ar. 3029)"[41]

(E) Bibliothèque nationale et universitaire, Strasbourg (P.Stras.inv. Ar. 142): This fragment contains a small text from Q 19 that is not known to have any particular magic function.[42] The fragment was published by Naïm Vanthieghem (Vanthieghem 2015), who estimates—since the back side is empty and the text itself is written in a rather unprofessional type of writing—that this fragment is most probably not of a codex of the Qurʾān.[43]

(F) Michaélides Collection (P.Michael.inv. 190): Another damaged, today not accessible papyrus (illustrated in Grohmann 1958, Plate IV), Q 60:5–63:9, written in an early type of a cursive script. Theoretically, this fragment could be a part of a codex, but since we do not know more about it, the evidence remains quite vague.

(G) Neues Museum, Berlin (P.Berl.inv. 24017): This papyrus—a damaged fragment in vertical—contains on its front and back sides text of Q 48, the complete text of Q 49, and the beginning verses of Q 50. It is difficult to exclude the possibility of a magical context for this document because we do not know how the scribe and later owner may have used this document. The included Qurʾānic text is not a passage of reportedly magic function.[44] It is not impossible that this fragment originally belonged to a codex. The same could be said about the Michaélides fragments no. 32 and 190, but the evidence remains weak.

These seven papyrus fragments contain text of the Qurʾān,[45] but they do not offer sufficient evidence for the existence of a Qurʾān codex on papyrus. The two fragments from the Michaélides Collection as well as the Leiden papyrus

41 Noja Noseda 2003: 316–318.

42 In his study "The Qurʾān and Its World", Efim A. Rezvan gives a list of magical functions of Qurʾān verses based on a treatise of the classical period, see Rezvan 1998.

43 Vanthieghem 2015: 421, "Notre fragment ne faisait pas partie d'un codex, puisqu'il n'est écrit que sur une face. On ne peut donc dire avec certitude quelle était la fonction de ce texte. L'écriture étant pour ainsi dire libraire, il paraît difficile d'y voir une amulette, car ce type de document est toujours rédigé dans une écriture hésitante et peu professionelle. La sourate 19 ne paraît par ailleurs pas non plus avoir connu de succès particulier en magie musulmane. Pourrait-il s'agir des vestiges d'une page où un particulier avait fait mettre au propre tout ou une partie de ladite sourate pour l'exercice de sa piété personnelle?"

44 Rezvan 1998: 29, where the magical power of Q 48 is mentioned as preventing illnesses, verses 1–3 to force someone to come to you, and verse 29 against all illnesses.

45 The images and especially the transliterations on the following pages have been prepared and typeset by Tobias J. Jocham.

could possibly stem from larger fragments of the Qurʾān, but it seems impossible to say whether they originally belonged to a complete codex of the Qurʾān or to a collection of Surahs brought together in a portion of a *ǧuzʾ* (1/30) or a *ḥizb* (1/60) of the text. The Qurʾānic text in the Moritz fragment possibly contains a verse separator, but we know too little about this almost illegible fragment to make a precise statement.[46] With regard to the question of papyrus codices, the statement of Joseph von Karabacek concering the Moritz fragment should be mentioned here: "Es ist durchaus zweifelhaft, ob hier Reste eines Korʾāns oder die von Gebeten mit korʾānischen Perikopen und Interpunktationen [...] vorliegen. Bedauerlicherweise vermißt man die Angabe, ob diese Blätter einseitig oder zweiseitig, und in diesem Falle, wie sie beschrieben sind. Ich für meinen Teil muß vorläufig noch an der Existenz von Papyruskorʾānen zweifeln."[47] Naïm Vanthieghem (Paris) recently discovered a fragment of a papyrus codex (with the text of Surah 2) kept in the library of the University of Hamburg and, together with Mathieu Tillier (Paris), is preparing an edition of this so far unique finding. The seven papyri fragments containing Qurʾānic text that introduce this volume do not appear to have functioned as magical documents and stand a bit isolated within the huge corpus of early papyri. They seem to be exceptions to the rule that the material shape of the first Qurʾāns followed the model of codex culture of Late Antiquity, which clearly gave preference to parchment.

Evidence of the early Qurʾān on papyrus will certainly grow in the coming years, as more collections are becoming accessible online and databases are built to facilitate research. The present volume focuses on the use of the Qurʾānic text as reflected in documents other than the codex, and therefore gives some insight into how the text of the Qurʾān was used in society and how Qurʾānic passages were understood. As limited as papyrus evidence for the early history of the Qurʾān may be, these papyri nevertheless present fairly early material, antedating exegetical literature in many cases. They also broaden our understanding of the roles of the Qurʾānic text in early Muslim societies.

---

46 For an overview about late antique codex culture in the Middle East, and parchment taking over against papyri, see Blank 1992: 63 and Schipke 2013: 151.

47 See von Karabacek 1906: 137.

Notes | Text | Line

حاهم الحو مں عىدىا فالوا لولا اوىى مىل ما اوىى موسى اولم ىكفروا ىما
اوتے موسى مں فىل فالوا سحراں ىطهرا وفالوا اىا ىكل كفروں (٤٨) فل فاىوا
ىكٮ مں عىد الله هو اهدى مىهما اىىعه اں كىىم صدفىں (٤٩) فاں لم ىسىحىىوا
لک فاعلم اىما ىىىعوں اهواهم ومں اصل ممں اىىع هوىه ىعىر هدى مں الله
اں الله لا ىهدى الفوم الطلمىں (٥٠) ولفد وصلىا لهم الفول لعلهم ىىدكروں (٥١)
الدىں اىىىهم الكىٮ مں فىله هم ىه ىومىوں (٥٢) وادا ىىلى علىهم فالوا ا
مىا ىه اىه الحو مں رىىا اىا كىا مں فىله مسلمىں (٥٣) اولىک ىو
ىوں اجرهم مرىىں ىما صىروا وىدروں ىالحسىه السىىه ومما ررفىهم
ىىفقوں (٥٤) وادا سمعوا اللعو اعرصوا عىه وفالوا لىا
اعملىا ولكم اعملكم سلم علىكم لا ىىىعى الجهلىں (٥٥) اىک لا ىهدى مں احىىٮ
ولكں الله ىهدى مں ىسا وهو اعلم ىالمهىدىں (٥٦) وفالوا اں ىىىع
الهدى معک ىىحطف مں ارصىا اولم ىمكں لهم حرما امىا ىحىى الىه ىمرٮ

FIGURE 1.1 Fragment of a papyrus with Qur'ānic text: Q 28:48–57 (B. Moritz, Arabic Palaeography, Kairo 1905, Panel 43, left)

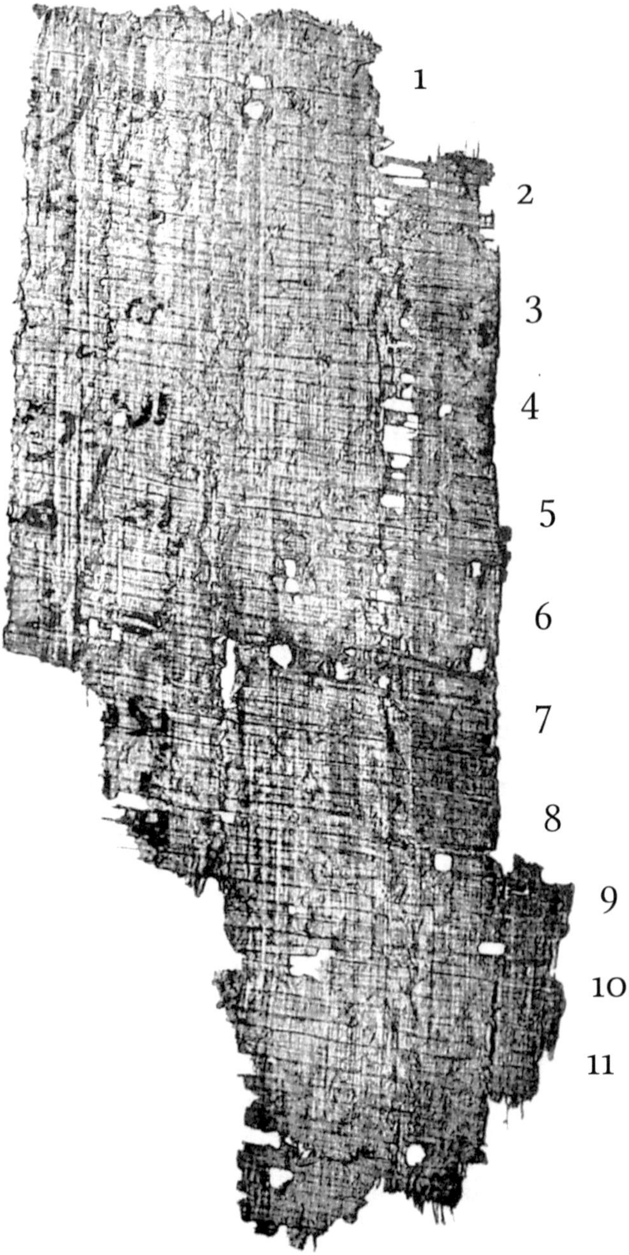

FIGURE 1.2 Fragment of a papyrus with Qurʾānic text: Q 28:61–68 (B. Moritz, Arabic Palaeography, Kairo 1905, Panel 43, right)

Notes | Text | Line

افمں وعدىه وعدا حسىا ڡهو لٯىه كمں
مىعىه مىع الحىوه الدىىا ىم هو ىوم الٯىمه
مں المحصرىں (٦١) وىوم ىىادىهم ڡىٯول اىں سركاى
الدىں كىىم ىرعموں (٦٢) ٯال الدىں حٯ علىهم الٯول
رىىا هولا الدىں اعوىىا اعوىىهم كما عوىىا ىىرانا الىك ما
كاىوا اىاىا ىعىدوں (٦٣) وٯىل ادعوا سركاكم
ڡدعوهم ڡلم ىسىحىىوا لهم وراوا العداں لو اىهم
كاىوا ىهىدوں (٦٤) وىوم ىىادىهم ڡىٯول ماذا احىىم
المرسلىں (٦٥) ڡعمىں علىهم الاىىا ىومىد ڡهم
لا ىىساءلوں (٦٦) ڡاما مں ىاں وامں وعمل صلحا
ڡعسى اں ىكوں مں المڡلحىں (٦٧) ورىك ىحلٯ ما ىسا

Notes	Text
	فصحا ابـــواب الـسـمـا بـما منهمر (١١) وفـحـرىا الارص عـىـوىا فالىقى الما
ألْوَٰحٍ	على امـر قـد قـدر (١٢) وحملىاه على داب الـواح ودسـر (١٣) ىـحرى ىاعىىىا
ءايَةً	حـرا لمں كـان كـفر (١٤) ولـقـد ىركىها ايـٮ فهل مـدكر (١٥) فكىف كان
	عدابى وىـدر (١٦) ولـقـد ىسرىا الـقـران للدكر فهل مں مـدكر (١٧) كدىٮ عاد
	فكىف كـان عـدابـى وىـــدر (١٨) انا ارسـلـىـا علـىهم رىـحا صـرصـرا فى
	ىـوم ىحس مسىمر (١٩) ىـىرع الـىـاس كاىهم اعـجـار ىحل مىقعر (٢٠) فكىف
	كـان عـدابـى وىـدر (٢١) و لـقـد ىسـرىا الـقـران للدكر فـهل مـں مـدكر (٢٢)
	كـدىـٮ ىـمـود ىالـىـدر (٢٣) فـقـالـوا اىـسـرامـىـا وحـــدا ىـىـىعه انا ادا
	لـفى صـلـل وسـعـــر (٢٤) الـقى الـدكر علـىه مـں ىىىىا ىـل هـو كـداب اسـر
	سـىـعـلـمـون غـــدا مـں الـكـداب الاسـر (٢٥) انا مـرسـلـوا الـىـاقـه فىىه
	لـهـم فـارىـقـىـهـم واصـطـبـر (٢٧) وىـىـاهـم ان الـمـا قـسـمـه ىـىـىهم كل
	سـرب محـىـصر (٢٨) فـىـادوا صاحـىهم فـىعاطى فعقر (٢٩) فكىف كان
	عـدابـى وىــدر (٣٠) انا ارسـلـىـا علـىـهم صـىـحه وحـــده فـكـانـوا
	كهـسـىـم المحـىـطر (٣١) ولـقـد ىسـرىا الـقـران للدكر فـهل مـں مـدكر (٣٢)
	كـدىـٮ قـوم لـوط ىالـىـدر (٣٣) انا ارسـلـىـا علـىـهم حاصـىـا الا ال لـوط
	ىحـىـىهم ىسحر (٣٤) ىعمه مـں عـىـدىا كـدلـك ىـحـرى مـں سـكـر (٣٥) ولقد
	ادرهـم ىطـشـىا فـىمـاروا ىالـىـدر (٣٦) ولـقـد راودوه عـں صـىـفه فطمسىا
	اعـىـىهم فـدوقـوا عـدابـى وىـــدر (٣٧) ولـقـد صـىحـهم ىـكـره عـــداب مسىقر

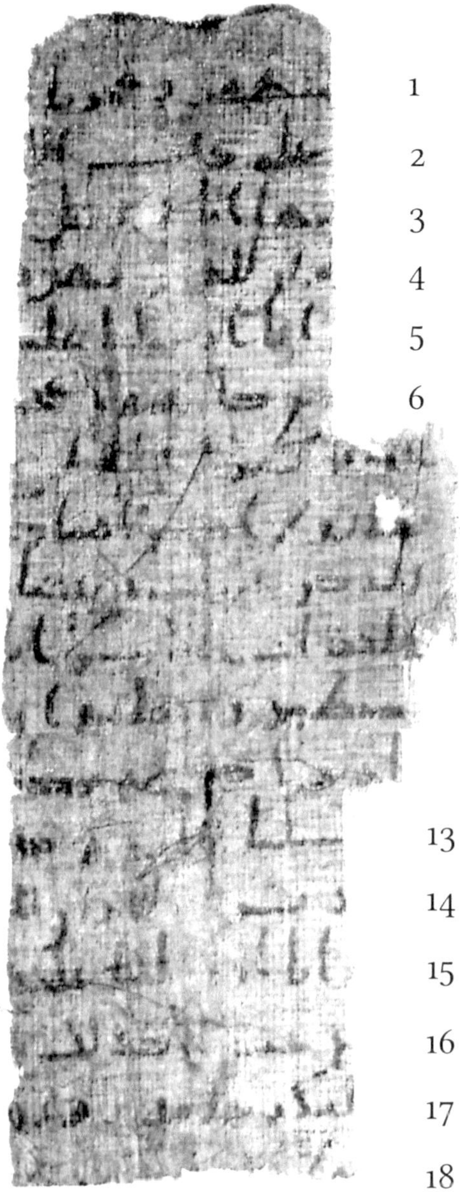

FIGURE 1.3 Papyrus with Qurʾānic text: Q 54:11–38 (A. Grohmann, The Problem of Dating Early Qurʾāns, in: *Der Islam* 33 (1958) pl. 1)

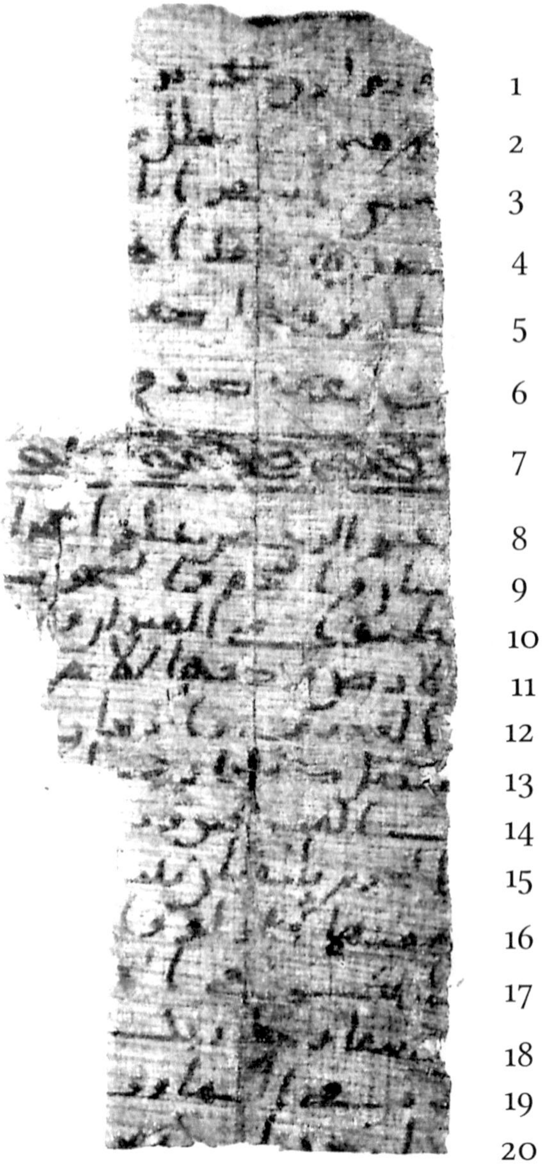

FIGURE 1.4 Papyrus with Qur'ānic text: Q 54:44–55:32 (A. Grohmann, The Problem of Dating Early Qur'āns, in: *Der Islam* 33 (1958) pl. 1)

Notes	Text	Line
	مسصر (٤٤) سهرم الحمع وىولون الدىر (٤٥) ىل الساعه موعدهم والساعه	1
	ادهى وامر (٤٦) ان المحرمىں فى صلل وسعر (٤٧) ىوم ىسحىون فى	2
	الىار على وحوههم دوقوا مس سقر (٤٨) انا كل سى حلقىه ىقدر (٤٩) وما	3
	امرىا الا وحده كلمح ىالىصر (٥٠) ولقد اهلكىا اسىاعكم فهل من مدكر (٥١)	4
	وكل سى فعلوه فى الرىر (٥٢) وكل صعىر وكىر مسىطر (٥٣) ان المىقىں	5
	فى حىىٮ وىهر (٥٤) فى مقعد صدق عىد ملىك مقىدر	6
	Ornament	7
	ىسم الله الرحمں الرحىم (○) الرحمں (١) علم القران (٢) حلق الاىسں (٣) علمه	8
	الىىاں (٤) السمس والقمر ىحسىاں (٥) والىحم والسحر ىسحداں (٦) والسما رفعها	9
	ووصع المىراں (٧) الا ىطعوا فى المىراں (٨) واقىموا الوزں ىالقسط	10
لِلْأَنَامِ	ولا ىحسروا المىراں (٩) و الارص وصعها للاىم (١٠) فىها فكهه والىحل داٮ	11
	الاكمام (١١) والحٮ دو العصف والرىحاں (١٢) فىاى الا رىكما ىكدىاں (١٣)	12
	حلق الاىسں من صلصل كالفحار (١٤) وحلق الحاں من مارح من ىار (١٥) فىاى	13
	الا رىكما ىكدىاں (١٦) رٮ المسرقىں ورٮ المعرىىں (١٧) فىاى الا	14
	رىكما ىكدىاں (١٨) مرح الىحرىں ىلىقىاں (١٩) ىىىهما ىررح لا ىىعىاں (٢٠) فىاى الا	15
	رىكما ىكدىاں (٢١) ىحرح مىهما اللولو والمرحاں (٢٢) فىاى الا رىكما	16
	ىكدىاں (٢٣) وله الحوار المىساٮ فى البحر كالاعلم (٢٤) فىاى الا رىكما	17
وَيَبْقَىٰ	ىكدىاں (٢٥) كل من علىها فاں (٢٦) وىىقا وحه رىك دو الحلل والاكرام (٢٧) فىاى الا	18
ٱلسَّمَٰوَٰتِ	رىكما ىكدىاں (٢٨) ىسله من فى السموٮ والارص كل ىوم هو فى ساں (٢٩)	19
	فىاى الا رىكما ىكدىاں (٣٠) سىفرع لكم اىه الىقلاں (٣١) فىاى	20

Notes	Text	Line
	بسم الله الرحمن الرحيم	1
	من فلان الى سليمن بن حرث	2
	اما بعد فانى احمد اليك الله الذى	3
	لا هو	4
	قال فى كتابه	5
	يايها الذين امنوا	6
	اتقوا الله حق تقاته ولا تموتن	7
	الا وانتم مسلمون ﴿١٠٢﴾ واعتصموا	8
	بحبل الله جميعا ولا تفرقوا	9
نِعْمَتَ	واذكروا نعمه الله	10
		11
		12
	اوحد	a
	حص	b
	الى	c
	السا	d
	ص	e

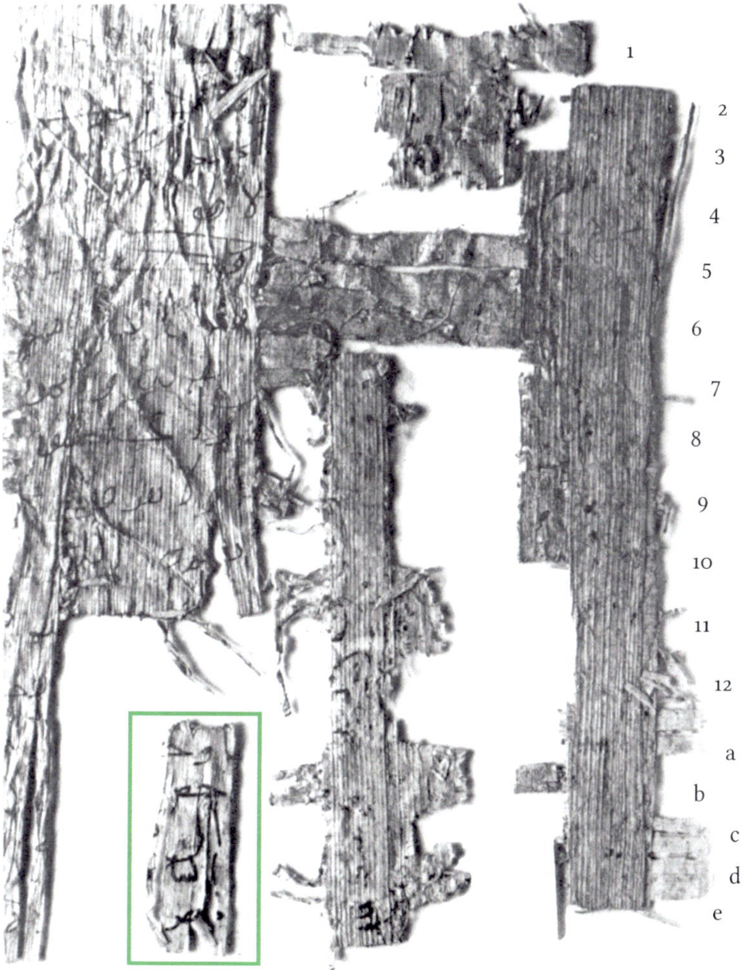

FIGURE 1.5 Early fragment of the Qur'ān, recto: Q 3:102–103 (P.Mird A 31 a 1) © JERUSALEM PAPYRUS COLLECTION [IMAGE FROM M.J. KISTER, ON AN EARLY FRAGMENT OF THE QUR'ĀN, IN: *STUDIES IN JUDAICA, KARAITICA AND ISLAMICA PRESENTED TO LEON NEMOY ON HIS EIGHTIETH BIRTHDAY*, ED. S.R. BRUNSWICK / J.C. GREENFIELD. RAMAT-GAN: BAR-ILAN UNIVERSITY PRESS 1982, P. 166]

Notes	Text
	ركم اىه كان عڡارا ﴿١٠﴾
ٱلسَّمَآ	ىرسل السما علىكم مد
مِّدْرَارًا | يُمْدِدْكُم	رارا ﴿١١﴾ وىمدكم ىا مول وىىں
جَنَّٰتٍ	وىحعل لكم حىاں وىحعل
أَنْهَٰرًا	لكم اىهارا ﴿١٢﴾ ما لكم لا ۞
وَقَارًا	ىرحون لله وڡرا ﴿١٣﴾ وڡد
	حلڡكم اطوارا ﴿١٤﴾ الم ىر
	وا كىڡ حلو الله سىع سموٮ
	طىاڡا ﴿١٥﴾ وحعل العمر ڡىهں ىورا و
	حعل السمس سراحا ﴿١٦﴾ والله ا
يُعِيدُكُمْ	ىىىكم مں الارص ىىىا ﴿١٧﴾ ىم ىعد
إِخْرَاجًا | وَٱللَّهُ	كم ڡىها وىحرحكم احرحا ﴿١٨﴾ ا
بِسَاطًا	لله حعل لكم الارص ىسطا ﴿١٩﴾ لسلكو

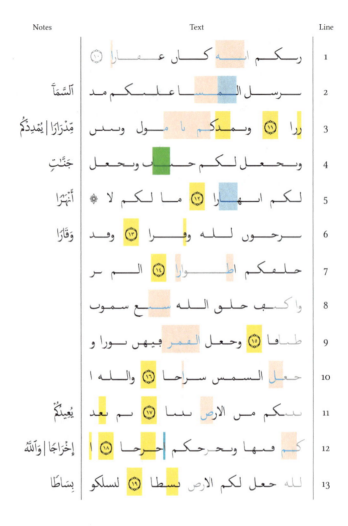

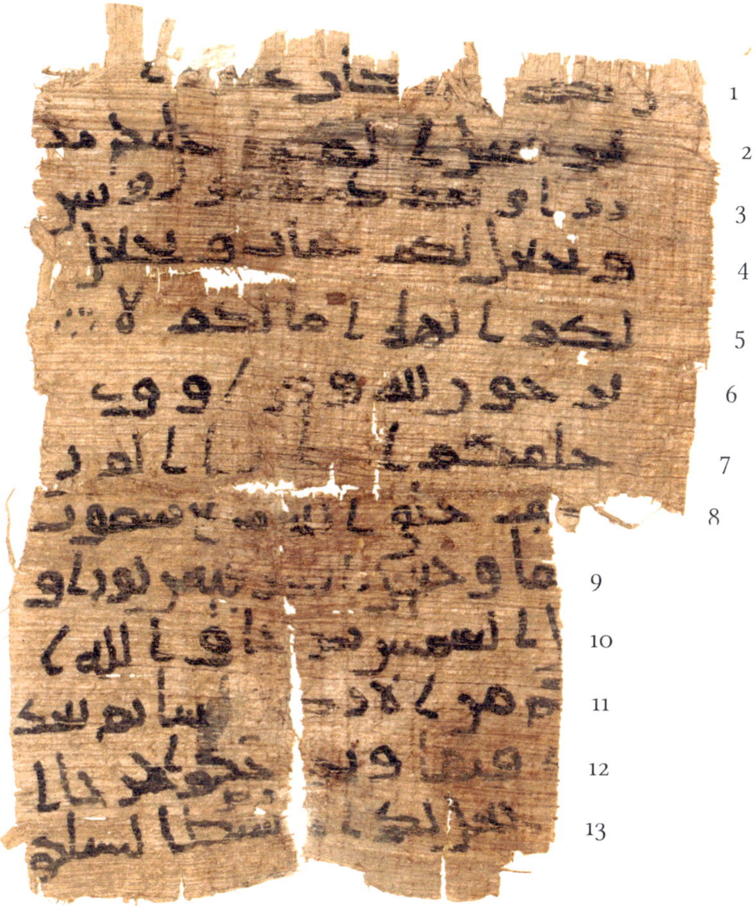

FIGURE 1.6 Qur'ān fragment on papyrus: Q 71:10–20 (P.Leiden inv. Or. 8264, recto) © LEIDEN UNIVERSITY LIBRARY, PAPYRUS COLLECTION

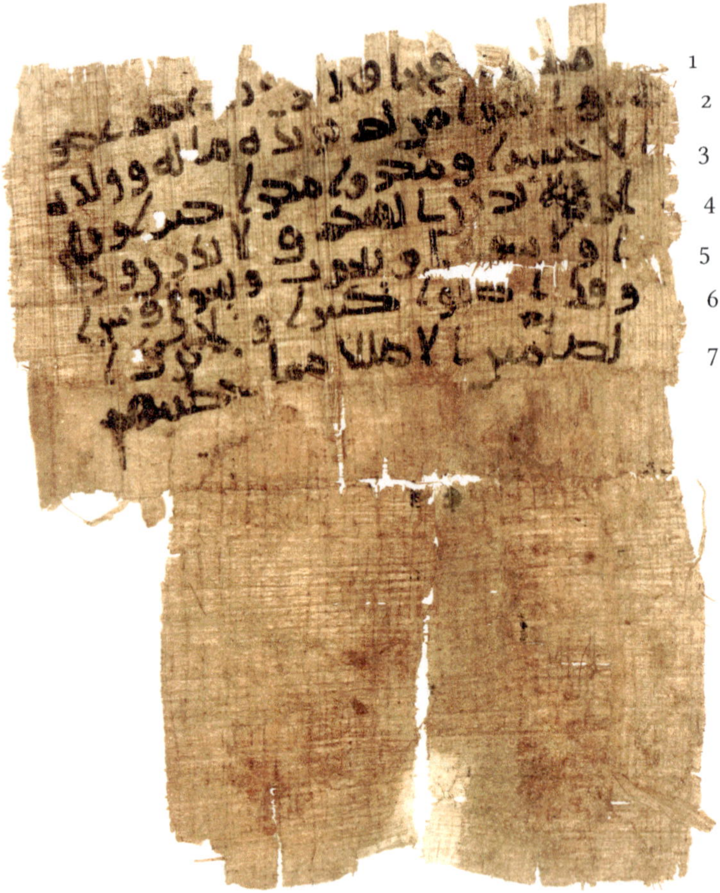

FIGURE 1.7 Qur'ān fragment on papyrus: Q 71:20–25 (P.Leiden inv. Or. 8264, verso)

Notes	Text	Line
فِجَاجًا	ا مںها سںلا فححا ٢٠ فال ںوح رب اهم عصو	1
يَزِدْهُ	ى واںىعوا مں لم ىرده ما له وولده	2
خَسَارًا | كُبَّارًا	الا خسرا ٢١ ومكروا مكرا كىرا ٢٢ وفا	3
	لوا لا ىدرں الهىكم ولا ىدرں ود	4
سُوَاعًا | وَلَا	ا ولا سوعا ويعوب ويعوق وىسرا ٢٣	5
	وفد اصلوا كىىرا ولا ىرد ا	6
ٱلظَّٰلِمِينَ	لصلمىں الا صللا ٢٤ مما حطىىهم	7

FIGURE 1.8 Qurʾān fragment on papyrus: Q 19:43–4[illegible] (P.Stras. inv. Arab. 142, recto)
© BIBLIOTHÈQUE NATIONALE ET UNIVERSITAIRE DE STRASBOURG

FIGURE 1.9 Qurʾān fragment on papyrus (P.Stras. inv. Arab. 142, verso)
© BIBLIOTHÈQUE NATIONALE ET UNIVERSITAIRE DE STRASBOURG

Notes	Text	Line
ٱلشَّيۡطَٰنَ ۖ ٱلشَّيۡطَٰنَ	ىاىک فاىىعىى اهدک صرطا سوىا ٤٣ ىاىت لا ىعىد السىطں اں السىطں كاں	1
لِلشَّيۡطَٰنِ	للرحمں عصىا ٤٤ ىاىت اىى احاف اں ىمسک عذاب مں الرحمں فىكوں للسىطں	2
	ولىا ٤٥ قال اراعب اىت عں الهىى ىاىرهىم لىں لم تنته لارحمنک واهجرنى مليا ٤٦	3
	قال سلم علىک ساسىعفر لک رىى اىه كاں ىى حفىا ٤٧ واعتزلكم وما ىدعوں	4
	مں دوں الله وادعوا رىى عسى الا اكوں ىدعا رىى سقىا ٤٨ فلما اعىرلهم	5

Traces of writing

<table>
<tr><th>Notes</th><th>Text</th><th>Line</th></tr>
<tr><td>ٱللَّهَ</td><td>انک انت العزىر الحكيم (٥) لقد كان لكم فىهم اسوه حسنه لمں كان ىرحوا لله واليوم</td><td>1</td></tr>
<tr><td>يَتَوَلَّ</td><td>الاحر ومں ىىولا فاں الله هو العىى الحمىد (٦) عسى الله اں ىحعل ىىىكم وىں الدىں عادىىم مىهم موده</td><td>2</td></tr>
<tr><td>يَنۡهَىٰكُمُ | يُقَٰتِلُوكُمۡ | دِيَٰرِكُمۡ</td><td>والله قدىر والله عفور رحىم (٧) لا ىىهكم الله عں الدىں لم ىقىلوكم فى الدىں ولم ىحرحوكم مں دىا</td><td>3</td></tr>
<tr><td>تَبَرُّوهُمۡ | يَنۡهَىٰكُمُ | قَٰتَلُوكُمۡ</td><td>ركم اں ىىروهم وىقسطوا الىهم اں الله ىحب المقسطىں (٨) انما ىىهكم الله عں الدىں لم ىقىلوكم فى</td><td>4</td></tr>
<tr><td>دِيَٰرِكُمۡ | وَظَٰهَرُواْ | ٱلظَّٰلِمُونَ</td><td>الدىں واحرحوكم مں دىركم وطهروا على احراحكم اں ىولوهم ومں ىىولهم فاولىک هم الطلموں (٩)</td><td>5</td></tr>
<tr><td>ٱلۡمُؤۡمِنَٰتُ | مُهَٰجِرَٰتٍ | بِإِيمَٰنِهِنَّۖ | فَإِنۡ</td><td>ىاىها الدىں امىوا ادا حاكم المومىٮ مهحرٮ فامىحىوهں الله اعلم ىاىمىهں واں علمىموهں</td><td>6</td></tr>
<tr><td>تَرۡجِعُوهُنَّ | حِلّٞ لَّهُمۡ | يَحِلُّونَ | لَهُنَّۖ | أَنفَقُواْ</td><td>مومىٮ فلا ىرحعوا الى الكفار لا هں حلهم ولا هم ىحلوں لهں واىوهم ما ىفقوا ولا حىاح علىكم اں ىىكحو</td><td>7</td></tr>
<tr><td>تُمۡسِكُواْ | وَسۡـَٔلُواْ</td><td>هں ادا اىىموهں احورهں ولا ىمسكو ىعصم الكوافر وسىلو ما اىفقىم ولىسلوا ما اىفقوا</td><td>8</td></tr>
<tr><td>عَلِيمٌ | أَزۡوَٰجِكُمۡ</td><td>دلكم حكم الله ىحكم ىىىكم والله علم حكىم (١٠) واں فاىكم سى مں اروٰكم الى الكفار فعاقىىم</td><td>9</td></tr>
<tr><td>أَزۡوَٰجُهُم | مُؤۡمِنُونَ</td><td>فاىوا الدىں دهىٮ اروحهم مىل ما اىفقوا واىقوا الله الدى اىىم ىه مومىوں (١١) ىاىها الىىى ادا</td><td>10</td></tr>
<tr><td>Crossed-out text | ٱلۡمُؤۡمِنَٰتُ</td><td>حاک المومىٮ</td><td>11</td></tr>
<tr><td>أَن لَّا | يَزۡنِينَ</td><td>ىىاىعىک على الا ىسركں ىالله سىا ولا ىسرقں ولا ىرىىں ولا ىقىلں او لدهں</td><td>12</td></tr>
<tr><td>بِبُهۡتَٰنٖ | وَٱسۡتَغۡفِرۡ | لَهُنَّ</td><td>ولا ىاىىں ىىهىں ىفىرىىه ىں اىدىهں وارحلهں ولا ىعصىىک فى معروف فىاىعهں وىىىعفر لهں</td><td>13</td></tr>
<tr><td>يَئِسُواْ | غَضِبَ</td><td>الله اں الله عفور رحىم (١٢) ىاىها الدىں امىوا لا ىىولو قوما عصٮ الله علىهم قد ىىسوا مں الاحره</td><td>14</td></tr>
<tr><td></td><td>كما ىىں الكفار مں اصحٮ القىور (١٣) ✡❁❁❁ ىسم الله الرحمں الرحىم ❁❁❁❁</td><td>15</td></tr>
<tr><td>ٱلسَّمَٰوَٰتِ</td><td>اربع ىعسر اىه ىىح لله ما فى السموٮ وما فى الارص وهو العرىر الحكىم (١)</td><td>16</td></tr>
<tr><td></td><td>ىاىها الدىں امىوا لم ىقولوں ما لا ىفعلوں (٢) كىر مقىا عىد الله اں ىقولوا ما لا ىفعلوں (٣) اں الله</td><td>17</td></tr>
<tr><td>بُنۡيَٰنٞ | يَٰقَوۡمِ</td><td>ىحٮ الدىں ىقىلوں ڡے سىىله صفا كاىهم ىىں مرصوص (٤) واد قال موسى لقومه ىقوم لم ىودوىى</td><td>18</td></tr>
<tr><td>أَزَاغَ</td><td>وقد ىعلموں اىى رسول الله الىكم فلما راعوا راعا الله قلوىهم والله لا ىهدى القوم الفسقوں (٥)</td><td>19</td></tr>
<tr><td>يَٰبَنِيٓ | إِسۡرَٰٓءِيلَ | ٱللَّهِ</td><td>واد قال عىسى اىں مرىم ىىى اسرىل اىى رسول الىكم مصدقا لما ىں ىدى مں التورىه ومىسرا</td><td>20</td></tr>
<tr><td></td><td>ىرسول ىاىى مں ىعدى اسمه احمد فلما حاهم ىالىىٮ قالوا هدا سحر مىں (٦) ومں اطلم ممں افىرى</td><td>21</td></tr>
<tr><td>ٱلظَّٰلِمِينَ</td><td>على الله الكدٮ وهو ىدعى الى الاسلم والله لا ىهدى القوم الطلمىں (٧) ىرىدوں لىطفوا ىور الله</td><td>22</td></tr>
</table>

FIGURE 1.10 Qurʾān fragment on papyrus: Q 60:5–61:8 (A. Grohmann, The Problem of Dating Early Qurʾāns, in: *Der Islam* 33 (1958) pl. 4

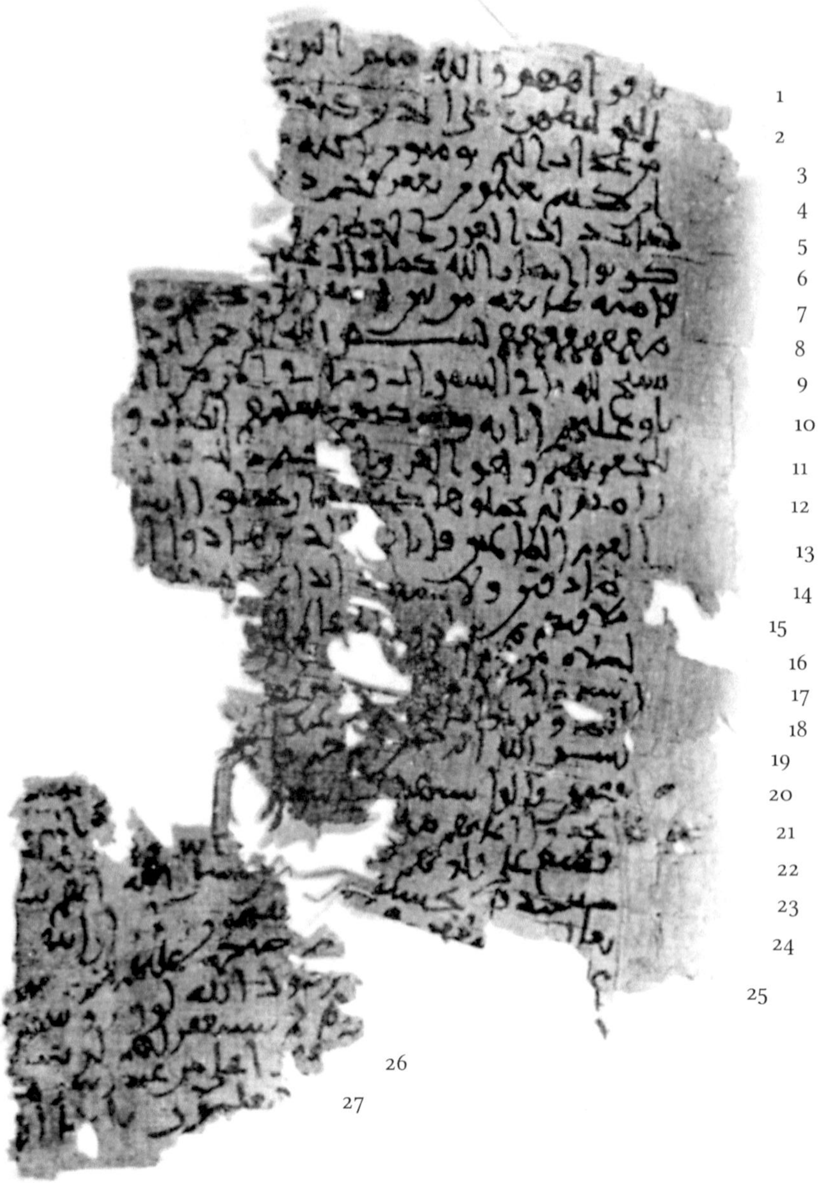

FIGURE 1.11 Qur'ān fragment on papyrus: Q 61:8–63:9 (A. Grohmann, The Problem of Dating Early Qur'āns, in: *Der Islam* 33 (1958) pl. 4)

<table>
<tr><th>Notes</th><th>Text</th></tr>
<tr><td>بِأَفْوَٰهِهِمْ | نُورِهِۦ</td><td>بافـوهـهـم والـلـه مـىم الـىـوره ولـو كـره الـكـفـرون (٨) هـو الـدى ارسـل رسـولـه بالـهـدى ودىـں</td></tr>
<tr><td></td><td>الـحو لىطهره على الـدىں كله ولـو كـره الـمسركون (٩) ىاىـها الـدىں امـىوا هـل ادلكـم على ىحـره ىىحىكم</td></tr>
<tr><td></td><td>مں عـداب الـىم (١٠) ىومىون بالله ورسـولـه وىحـهـدون فـى سـىل الله باموالكـم وانفسكم دلكـم حىر لكم</td></tr>
<tr><td></td><td>ان كىىم ىعلمون (١١) ىعفر لـكـم دىوىكـم ويدحلكـم حىـٮ ىحرى مـں ىحىها الاىـهـر ومسـكں طىىه فى</td></tr>
<tr><td>جَنَّٰتِ | عَدْنٍ</td><td>حىٮ دلك الفور العطىم (١٢) واحـرى ىحىوىها ىصر مں الله وفىح فرىٮ وىسر المومىوں (١٣) ىاىها الدىں امىوا</td></tr>
<tr><td></td><td>كوىـوا اىـصـار الله كما قـال عسى اىں مرىم للحوارىں مـں اىـصـارى الـى الله قـال الـحـوارىـون ىحں اىـصـار الله</td></tr>
<tr><td>فَـَٔامَنَت | إِسْرَٰٓءِيلَ | وَكَفَرَت</td><td>فامىـه طـاىـفـه مـں ىـى اسـراىـل وكـفـره طـاىـفـه فاىدىا الـدىں امـىـوا على عـدوهـم فـاصـبحـوا طـهـرىں (١٤)</td></tr>
<tr><td></td><td>❁❁❁❁ ىسم الله الرحمں الرحىم ( )</td></tr>
<tr><td>ٱلسَّمَٰوَٰتِ</td><td>ىسىح لله ما فى السموٮ وما فى الارض الملك القدوس العرىر الحكىم (١) هو الدى ىعٮ فى الامىں رسولا مىهم</td></tr>
<tr><td>يَتْلُواْ | ءَايَٰتِهِۦ | ٱلْكِتَٰبَ</td><td>ىىلو علىهم اىىه ورىكىهم وىعلمهم الكىٮ والحكمه وان كانوا مں قىل لفى صلل مىىں (٢) واحرىں مىهم لما</td></tr>
<tr><td>يَلْحَقُواْ</td><td>ىلحقو بهم وهو العرىر الحكىم (٣) دلك فصل الله ىوىىه مں ىسا والله دو الفصل العطىم (٤) مىل الدىں حملوا الىو</td></tr>
<tr><td>ٱلتَّوْرَىٰةَ | يَحْمِلُ</td><td>راه ىـم لـم ىحملوها كمىل الـحـمـار ىحملوا اسـفـار ىـىس مـىل الـقـوم الـدىں كـدىـوا ىاىـٮ الله لا ىهدى</td></tr>
<tr><td>ٱلظَّٰلِمِينَ</td><td>الـقوم الطلمىں (٥) قـل ىاىها الـدىں هـادوا ان رعمىم اىكم اولىا لله مـں دوں الـىاس فىمىوا الـموٮ ان كىىم</td></tr>
<tr><td>صَٰدِقِينَ</td><td>صدقىں (٦) ولا ىىمىوىه ابـدا ىما قدمٮ اىدىهم والله علىم بالطلمىں (٧) قل ان الموٮ الـدى ىفرون مىه فاىه</td></tr>
<tr><td>مُلَٰقِيكُمْ ۖ | تُرَدُّونَ | عَٰلِمِ</td><td>ملقىكم ىـم ىـردون الـى عـلـم الغىٮ والـسـهـده فىىىكم ىما كىىم ىعملون (٨) ىاىـهـا الـدىں امـىـوا ادا ىودى</td></tr>
<tr><td>لِلصَّلَوٰةِ</td><td>لصلاه مں ىوم الجمعه فاسعوا الى دكر الله ودروا الىىع دلكم حىر لكم ان كىىم ىعلمون (٩) فـادا قصىٮ الصلوه</td></tr>
<tr><td>فَٱنتَشِرُواْ</td><td>فاىىسروا فى الارض واىىعوا مں فصل الله وادكـروا الله كىىرا لعلكم ىفلحون (١٠) وادا راوا ىحره او لهوا اىفصوا</td></tr>
<tr><td></td><td>الـىـهـا وىـركـوك قـاىـمـا قـل مـا عـىـد الـلـه حـىـر مـں الـلـهـو ومـں الـىـحـره والـلـه حـىـر الـررقـىں (١١)</td></tr>
<tr><td></td><td>ىسم الله الرحمں الرحىم ( ) ادا حاك</td></tr>
<tr><td>ٱلْمُنَٰفِقُونَ</td><td>المىفقون قـالـوا ىسهد اىـك لـرسـول الله والله ىعلم اىـك لـرسـولـه والله ىسهد ان المىفقون لكـدىـون (١)</td></tr>
<tr><td>أَيْمَٰنَهُمْ</td><td>اىـحـدوا اىماىهم حىه فـصـدوا عـں سـىل الله اىـهـم سـا مـا كـاىـوا ىعملون (٢) دلـك ىاىـهـم امـىـوا ىـم كـفـروا</td></tr>
<tr><td></td><td>فطبع على قلوبهم فهم لا ىفقهون (١) وادا راىىهم ىعجىك احسامهم وان ىقولوا ىسمع لقولهم كاىهم حسٮ</td></tr>
<tr><td></td><td>مسـىـده ىحسـىون كـل صىحه علىهم هـم الـعـدو فـاحـدرهـم قىلهم الله اىـى ىوفـكـون (٤) وادا قىل لهم</td></tr>
<tr><td></td><td>ىـعـالـوا ىـسـىـعـفـر لـكـم رسـول الـلـه لـووا روسـهـم وراىـىـهـم ىـصـدون وهـم مـسـىـكـىـرون (٥) سـوا</td></tr>
<tr><td></td><td>علىهم اسـىـعـفـرٮ لـهـم ام لـم ىسىعفر لـهـم لـں ىـعفر الـلـه لـهـم ان الـلـه لا ىـهـدى الـقـوم الـفـسـقىں (٦)</td></tr>
<tr><td></td><td>هم الدىں ىقولون لا ىىفقوا على مں عىد رسول الله حىى ىىفصوا ولله حراىں السموٮ والارض ولكں المىفقىں لا ىفقهون (٧)</td></tr>
<tr><td></td><td>ىقولون لىں رحعىا الى المدىىه لىحرحں الاعر مىها الادل ولله العره ولرسوله وللمومىىں ولكں المىفقىں لا ىعلمون (٨) ىاىها الدىں</td></tr>
</table>

Notes	Text
	لىعىط ىهم الكفار وعد الله الدس امىوا وعملوا الصلحت
	مىهم معفره واحرا عطىما ٢٩
	ىسم الله الرحمں الرحىم ◯ ىاىها الدس امىوا لا ىقدموا ىىں ىدى الله
	ورسوله واىقوا الله ان الله سمىع علىم ١ ىاىها الدس امىوا لا ىرفعوا
أَصْوَٰتَكُمْ	اصوىكم فوق صوت الىىى ولا ىحهروا له ىالقول كحهر ىعصكم
	لىعص ان ىحىط اعملكم واىىم لا ىسعرون ٢ ان الدس ىعصون
	اصوىهم عىد رسول الله اولىك
لِلتَّقْوَىٰ | وَأَجْرٌ | عَظِيمٌ	الدس امىحن الله قلوىهم للىقوا لهم معفره واحرا عطىم ٣ ان الدس ىادوىك من
ٱلْحُجُرَٰتِ | حَتَّىٰ	ورا الححرت اكىرهم لا ىعقلون ٤ ولو اىهم صىروا حىا ىحرح الىهم لكان حىرا
	لهم والله عفور رحىم ٥ ىاىها الدس امىوا ان حاكم فاسق ىىا فىىىوا ان ىصىىوا قوما
بِجَهَٰلَةٍ | نَٰدِمِينَ	ىحهله فىصىحوا على ما فعلىم ىدمىن ٦ واعلموا ان فىكم رسول الله لو ىطىعكم
	فى كىىر من الامر لعىىم ولكن الله حىب الىكم الاىمن ورىىه فى قلوىكم
	وكره الىكم الكفر والفسوق والعصىان اولىك هم الرسدون ٧
	فصلا من الله ونعمه والله علىم حكىم ٨ وان طاىفىان من المومىىن اقىىلوا
إِحْدَىٰهُمَا | ٱلْأُخْرَىٰ | فَقَٰتِلُوا۟	فاصلحوا ىىىهما فان ىعت احداهما على الاحرا فقىلوا الىى ىىعى حىى ىفى الى امر الله فان فات
	فاصلحوا ىىىهما ىالعدل واقسطوا ان الله ىحب المقسطىن ٩ انما المومىون احوه
	فاصلحوا ىىن احوىكم واىقوا الله لعلكم ىرحمون ١٠ ىاىها الدس امىوا لا ىسحر قوم
عَسَىٰٓ | عَسَىٰٓ	من قوم عسا ان ىكوىوا حىرا مىهم ولا ىسا من ىسا عسا ان ىكن حىرا مىهن
بِٱلْأَلْقَٰبِ	ولا ىلمروا انفسكم ولا ىىاىروا ىالالقب ىىس الاسم الفسوق ىعد الاىمن ومن لم ىىب
	فاولىك هم الطلمون ١١ ىاىها الدس امىوا احىىىوا كىىرا من الطن ان ىعص
	الطن اىم ولا ىحسسوا ولا ىعىب ىعصكم ىعصا اىحب احدكم ان
	ىاكل لحم احىه مىىا فكرهىموه واىقوا الله ان الله ىواب رحىم ١٢ ىاىها
خَلَقْنَٰكُم | وَأُنثَىٰ | وَجَعَلْنَٰكُمْ	الىاس انا حلقىكم من دكر واىىى وحعلىكم سعوىا وقىاىل لىعارفوا ان
	اكرمكم عىد الله اىقىكم ان الله علىم حىىر ١٣
	marked line

FIGURE 1.12 Qurʾān fragment on papyrus: Q 48:29–49:13 (P.Berl. inv. 24017, recto)

FIGURE 1.13 Qur'ān fragment on papyrus: Q 49:14–50:29 (P.Berl. inv. 24017, verso)

Notes	Text
ٱلْإِيمَٰنُ	قالت الاعراب امنا قل لم تومنوا ولكن قولوا اسلمنا ولما تدحل الايمان فى قلوبكم وان تطعوا
	الله ورسوله لا تلتكم من اعملكم سا ان الله عفور رحيم (١٤) انما المومنون الدين امنوا
بِأَمْوَٰلِهِمْ	بالله ورسوله ثم لم ترتابوا وجهدوا باموالهم وانفسهم فى سبيل الله
ٱلسَّمَٰوَٰتِ	اولئك هم الصدقون (١٥) قل اتعلمون الله بدينكم والله يعلم ما فى السموت وما فى
إِسْلَٰمَكُم	الارض والله بكل شى عليم (١٦) يمنون عليك ان اسلموا قل لا تمنوا على اسلامكم بل الله
إِسْلَٰمَكُم	يمن عليكم ان هدىكم للايمن ان كنتم صدقين (١٧) ان الله يعلم غيب السموت
	والارض والله بصير بما تعملون (١٨)
	بسم الله الرحمن الرحيم ○ ق والقران المجيد (١) بل عجبوا ان جاهم منذر منهم فقال
	الكفرون هذا شى عجيب (٢) اذا متنا وكنا ترابا ذلك رجع بعيد (٣) قد علمنا ما تنقص
	الارض منهم وعندنا كتب حفيظ (٤) بل كذبوا بالحق لما جاهم فهم فى امر مريج (٥)
بَنَيْنَٰهَا | وَزَيَّنَّٰهَا	افلم ينظروا الى السما فوقهم كيف بنينها وزينها وما لها من فروج (٦) والارض
وَذِكْرَىٰ	مددنها والقينا فيها روسى وانبتنا فيها من كل زوج بهيج (٧) تبصره وذكرا لكل
مُّبَٰرَكًا | جَنَّٰتٍ	عبد منيب (٨) ونزلنا من السما ما مبركا فانبتنا به جنت وحب الحصيد (٩) والنخل با
	سقت لها طلع نضيد (١٠) رزقا للعباد واحيينا به بلده ميتا كذلك
وَأَصْحَٰبُ	الخروج (١١) كذبت قبلهم قوم نوح واصحب الرس وثمود (١٢) وعاد وفرعون
	واخون لوط (١٣) واصحب الايكه وقوم تبع كل كذب الرسل فحق وعيد (١٤)
ٱلْإِنسَٰنَ	افعيينا بالخلق الاول بل هم فى لبس من خلق جديد (١٥) ولقد خلقنا الانسان ونعلم ما توسوس به
يَتَلَقَّى	نفسه ونحن اقرب اليه من حبل الوريد (١٦) اذ يتلقا المتلقيان عن اليمين وعن الشمال قعيد (١٧) ما يلفظ
	[illegible] (١٨) [illegible] (١٩)
وَجَآءَتْ	ونفخ فى الصور ذلك يوم الوعيد (٢٠) فجات كل نفس معها سايق وشهيد (٢١) لقد
	كنت فى غفلة من هذا فكشفنا عنك غطاك فبصرك اليوم حديد (٢٢)
	وقال قرينه هذا ما لدى عتيد (٢٣) القيا فى جهنم كل كفار عنيد (٢٤) مناع للخير
	معتد مريب (٢٥) الذى جعل مع الله الها اخر فالقياه فى العذاب الشديد (٢٦) قال قرينه
ضَلَٰلٍ	ربنا ما اطغيته ولكن كان فى ضلال بعيد (٢٧) قال لا تختصموا لدى وقد قدمت
بِظَلَّٰمٍ	اليكم بالوعيد (٢٨) ما يبدل القول لدى وما انا بظلام للعـــــــــــبيد (٢٩)

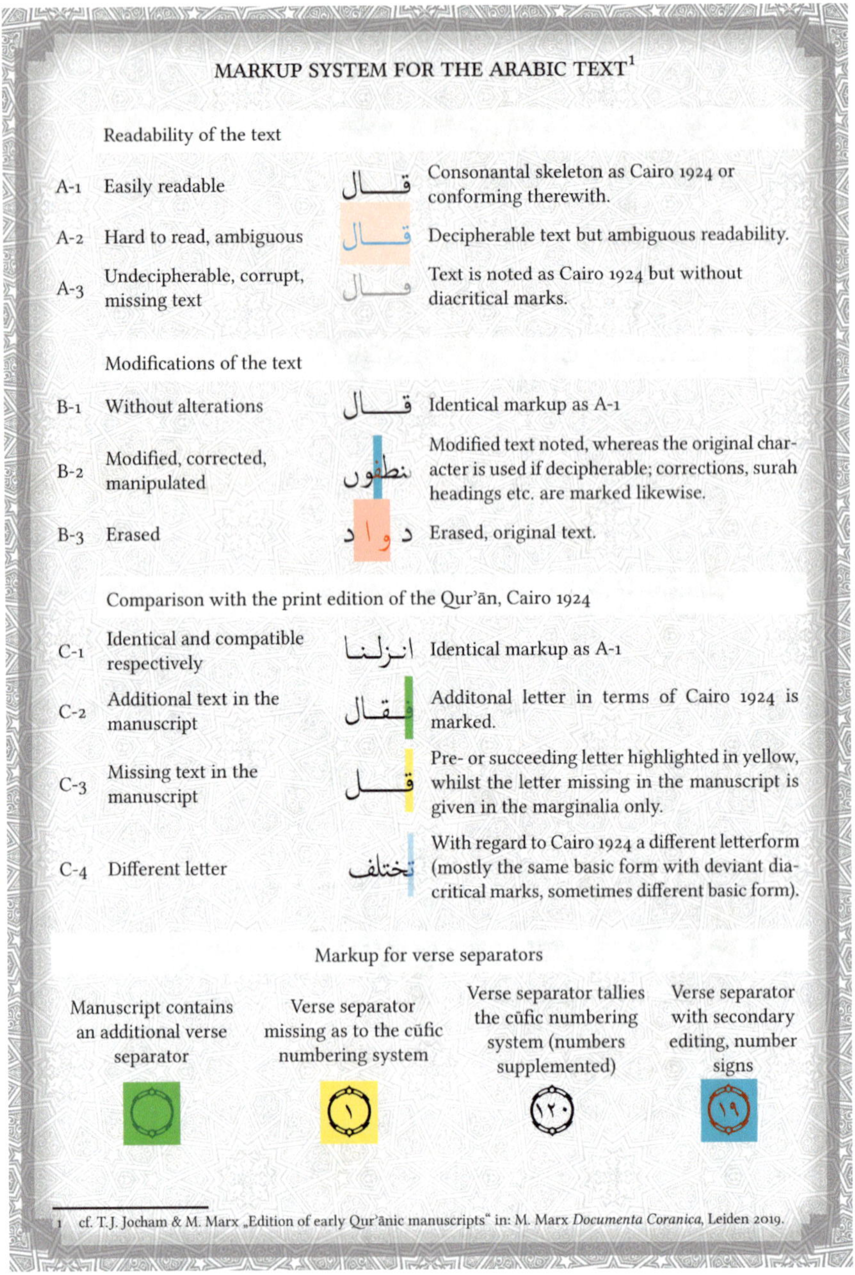
MARKUP SYSTEM FOR THE ARABIC TEXT[1]
Readability of the text
A-1 Easily readable
Consonantal skeleton as Cairo 1924 or conforming therewith.
A-2 Hard to read, ambiguous
Decipherable text but ambiguous readability.
A-3 Undecipherable, corrupt, missing text
Text is noted as Cairo 1924 but without diacritical marks.
Modifications of the text
B-1 Without alterations
Identical markup as A-1
B-2 Modified, corrected, manipulated
Modified text noted, whereas the original character is used if decipherable; corrections, surah headings etc. are marked likewise.
B-3 Erased
Erased, original text.
Comparison with the print edition of the Qurʾān, Cairo 1924
C-1 Identical and compatible respectively
Identical markup as A-1
C-2 Additional text in the manuscript
Additonal letter in terms of Cairo 1924 is marked.
C-3 Missing text in the manuscript
Pre- or succeeding letter highlighted in yellow, whilst the letter missing in the manuscript is given in the marginalia only.
C-4 Different letter
With regard to Cairo 1924 a different letterform (mostly the same basic form with deviant diacritical marks, sometimes different basic form).
Markup for verse separators
Manuscript contains an additional verse separator
Verse separator missing as to the cūfic numbering system
Verse separator tallies the cūfic numbering system (numbers supplemented)
Verse separator with secondary editing, number signs
1 cf. T.J. Jocham & M. Marx „Edition of early Qurʾānic manuscripts" in: M. Marx Documenta Coranica, Leiden 2019.

FIGURE 1.14 Markup-System for the Arabic text
© TOBIAS J. JOCHAM

Bibliography

Adler, Jacob Georg Christian. 1780. *Descriptio codicum quorundam Cuficorum partes Corani exhibentium in Bibliotheca Regia Hafniensi et ex iisdem de scriptura Cufica Arabum observationes novae*. Altona: Eckhard.

Altıkulaç, Tayyar. 2007a. *al-Muṣḥaf al-sharif Attributed to ʿUthmān bin ʿAffān* (*The Copy at the Topkapı Palace Museum*) = *al-Muṣḥaf aš-šarīf al-mansūb ilā ʿUṯmān ibn ʿAffān: nusḫat Topkapı Sarayı*. Silsilat nuṣūṣ muḥaqqaqa, vol. 2. Istanbul: Research Center for Islamic History, Art and Culture.

Altıkulaç, Tayyar. 2007b. *Hz. Osman'a nisbat edilen Mushaf-ı şerîf* (*Türk ve İslâm Eserleri Müzesi Nüshası*) = *al-Muṣḥaf aš-šarīf al-mansūb ilā ʿUṯmān ibn ʿAffān*. 2 volumes. Istanbul: İslâm Araştırmaları Merkezi.

Altıkulaç, Tayyar. 2011a. *Al-Mushaf al-Sharif Attributed to Uthman bin Affan* (*The Copy at al-Mashhad al-Husayni in Cairo*) = *al-Muṣḥaf aš-šarīf al-mansūb ilā ʿUṯmān ibn ʿAffān: nusḫat al Mašhad al-Ḥusaynī bi-l-Qāhira*. Critical Editions Series, vol. 4. Istanbul: İslâm Tarih, Sanat ve Kültür Araştırma Merkezi.

Altıkulaç, Tayyar. 2011b. *al-Mushaf al-Sharīf Attributed to ʿAlī b. Abī Ṭālib* (*the Copy of Sanaa*) = *al-Muṣḥaf aš-šarīf al-mansūb ilā ʿAlī ibn Abī Ṭālib: nusḫat Ṣanʿāʾ*. Critical Editions Series, vol. 6. Istanbul: Research Centre for Islamic History, Art and Culture.

Altıkulaç, Tayyar. 1436/2015. *al-Muṣḥaf aš-Šarīf* (*Bibliothèque Nationale, Paris*) = *Mushaf-ı Şerîf*. İncelemeli metin serisi = Silsilat nuṣūṣ muḥaqqaqa, vol. 8. Istanbul: İslâm Tarih, Sanat ve Kültür Araştırma Merkezi.

Altıkulaç, Tayyar. 2016. *Mushaf-ı Şerîf* (*Tübingen Nüshası*), prepared for publication by Dr. Tayyar Altıkulaç (Text in Arabic and Turkish). Istanbul: IRCICA.

Arazi, Albert and Salma Masalha. 1999. *Six Early Arab Poets: New Edition and Concordance, Based on W. Ahlwardt's The Divans of the Six Ancient Arabic Poets*. The Max Schloessinger Memorial Series. Jerusalem: The Hebrew University of Jerusalem.

Blank, Horst. 1992. *Das Buch in der Antike*. München: C.H. Beck.

Casanova, Paul. 1911. *Mohammed et la fin du monde: étude critique sur l'Islam primitif*, vol. 1. Paris: Geuthner.

Déroche, François. 1983. *Les manuscrits du Coran: aux origines de la calligraphie coranique*. Catalogue des manuscrits arabes, 2ème partie: manuscrits musulmans, tome I, 1. Paris: Bibliothèque Nationale.

Déroche, François. 1990. "The Qurʾān of Amāǧūr." In *Manuscripts of the Middle East* 5, 59–66.

Déroche, François and Sergio Noja Noseda. 1998. *Le manuscrit arabe 328 (a) de la Bibliothèque Nationale de France*. Sources de la transmission du texte coranique, I: Les manuscrits de style ḥijāzī, volume 1. Lesa: Fondazione Ferni Noja Noseda, Studi Arabo Islamici.

Déroche, François and Sergio Noja Noseda. 2001. *Le manuscrit arabe Or. 2165 de la British Library*. Sources de la transmission du texte coranique, I: Les manuscrits de style ḥijāzī, volume 2. Lesa: Fondazione Ferni Noja Noseda, Studi Arabo Islamici.

Graf von Bothmer, Hans-Caspar. 1987. "Architekturbilder im Koran. Eine Prachthandschrift der Umayyadenzeit aus dem Yemen." In *Pantheon: Internationale Jahreszeitschrift für Kunst* 45: 4–20.

Grohmann, Adolf. 1958. "The Problem of Dating Early Qur'āns." In *Der Islam* 33: 213–231.

Grohmann, Adolf. 1963. *Arabic Papyri from Ḫirbet el-Mird*. Bibliothèque du Muséon, vol. 52. Louvain/Leuven: Institut orientaliste.

Haeuptner, Eleonore. 1966. *Koranische Hinweise auf die materielle Kultur der alten Araber*. Tübingen: PhD thesis.

Jeffery, Arthur. 1938. *The Foreign Vocabulary of the Qur'ān*. Gaekwad's Oriental Series, vol. 79. Baroda: Oriental Institute.

Kister, Meir J. 1982. "On an Early Fragment of the Qur'an." In *Studies in Judaica, Karaitica and Islamica Presented to Leon Nemoy on His Eightieth Birthday*, ed. Sheldon R. Brunswick. Ramat-Gan: Bar-Ilan University Press, 163–166.

Maraqten, Mohammed. 1998. "Writing Materials in Pre-Islamic Arabia." In *Journal of Semitic Studies* 43: 287–310.

Marx, Michael (ed.). *Manuscripta Coranica: Online Catalogue of Early Qur'ānic Manuscripts*, https://corpuscoranicum.de/handschriften/uebersicht.

Marx, Michael, Eva Mira Youssef-Grob, Tobias J. Jocham, Irka Hajdas. "The Chronology of Holy Scriptures", ETH Yearbook 2014, www.ams.ethz.ch/publications/annual_reports/2014/037.

Moritz, Bernhard. 1905. *Arabic Palaeography: A Collection of Texts from the First Century of the Hidjra till the Year 1000*. Publications de la Bibliothèque Khédiviale, vol. 16. Cairo and Leipzig: Hiersemann.

Noja Noseda, Sergio. 2004. "A Third Koranic Fragment on Papyrus: An Opportunity for a Revision." In *Rendiconti Classe di lettere e scienze morali e storiche* 137: 313–326.

Rezvan, Efim A. 1998. "The Qur'ān and Its World. VII. Talisman, Shield and Sword." In *Manuscripta Orientalia* 4,3: 13–54.

Rezvan, Efim A. 2004. *Koran 'Usmana: Sankt-Peterburg, Katta-Langar, Bukhara, Tashkent*. St. Petersburg.

Roads of Arabia: Archäologische Schätze aus Saudi-Arabien, ed. Ute Franke et al. 2012. Berlin: Museum für Islamische Kunst.

Robin, Christian. 2014. "Inscriptions antiques récemment découvertes à Najrān (Arabie séoudite méridionale): nouveaux jalons pour l'histoire de l'oasis et celle de l'écriture et de la langue arabes." In *Comptes rendus de l'Académie des Inscriptions et Belles-Lettres*: 1033–1127.

Routes d'Arabie: archéologie et histoire du Royaume d'Arabie Saoudite, ed. Ali Al-Ghabban et al. 2010. Paris: Musée du Louvre.

Schipke, Renate. 2013. *Das Buch in der Spätantike*. Wiesbaden: Reichert Verlag.

Stein, Peter and Tobias J. Jocham and Michael Marx. 2016. "Ancient South Arabian Correspondence on Wooden Sticks: New Radiocarbon Data." In *Proceedings of the Seminar for Arabian Studies* 46: 263–276.

Toral-Niehoff, Isabel. 2014. *Al-Ḥīra: Eine arabische Kulturmetropole im spätantiken Kontext*. Islamic History and Civilization, vol. 104. Leiden: Brill.

Unustası, Müjde (ed.) 2010. 1400. Yılında Kur'an-i Kerim, Istanbul: Antik AŞ, Kültür Yayınları.

Vanthieghem, Naïm. 2015. "Un fragment coranique sur papyrus (Coran 19, 43–49)." In *Chronique d'Égypte* 90: 420–422.

von Karabacek, Josef. 1906. "Arabic Palaeography." In *Wiener Zeitschrift für die Kunde des Morgenlandes* 20: 131–148.

Wright, William. 1875–1883. *Facsimiles of Manuscripts and Inscriptions: 100 Autotype Plates with Letterpress*. The Palaeographical Society Facsimiles of Manuscripts and Inscriptions. Oriental Series, vol. 4. London: Palaeographical Society.

CHAPTER 2

Qur'ān Quotations in Arabic Papyrus Letters from the 7th to the 10th Centuries

Daniel Potthast

1 Corpus of Analyzed Letters

Letters of different kinds form a big part of all published Arabic papyri. Letters usually are further differentiated into private, business, and official letters, but the boundaries between these sub-types are not always clearly defined: For example, the same formulae are used in private and business letters, and with official letters, more specific formulae similar to those used in petitions, orders to subordinates, etc. are used. Since most letters are only preserved in a fragmentary status, it is often difficult to assign the letter to a distinct sub-type, so that in some cases one and the same document has been assigned to different sub-types by different authors. Despite these problems, I differentiate between the sub-types in the hope of showing general trends in the use of Qur'ānic elements. The analyzed letters originated in the Islamic world from the 7th to the 10th centuries CE. Because of the conditions for preservation, almost all documents were found in Egypt, but a few important documents come from Palestine (P.Ness., P.Mird, 76 letters), Syria (P.AbbottMutawakkil, 3 letters), and Khorasan (P.Kratchkovski, 1 letter).

Dating letters is problematic, since *private* and *business* letters almost never carry a date. From the 7th and early 8th centuries, mostly *official* letters have been preserved. The oldest dated letter comes from Naṣṭān in Palestine (P.Ness. 61, written Raǧab 55/1–30 June 675), and a great number of official letters of Qurra b. Šarīk, Governor of Egypt 90–96/709–714, has been preserved (P.BeckerNPAF; P.BeckerPAF; P.Heid.Arab. I; P.GrohmannQorra-Brief; P.Qurra). Following the Arabization of a considerable part of Egypt's population, beginning in the middle of the 8th century, most letters were written for private or economic reasons. Therefore, private and business letters written in a clearly legible, oblique script similar to the script of dated official letters have been dated paleographically to the 8th century. In addition, the different Arabic introductory formulae for letters were consulted for dating letters: for example, letters containing the formula *aḥmadu llāha ilayka* (or: *ilaykum*) *allaḏī lā ilāha illā huwa* were dated to the 8th century. Since this formula is of Qur'ānic origin,

 | DOI:10.1163/9789004376977_003

I discuss the implications of expressing religious identity below.[1] The many letters written in a more cursive, difficult-to-read script are dated to the 9th and partly to the 10th century. When in the 10th century paper replaced papyrus as the writing material, this change was not accompanied by a change in letter-writing formulae. Yet because of the small number of published paper letters attributed to the 10th century, and their minor relevance for the textual history of the Qur'ān, documents on paper have not been analyzed.

The following editions were analyzed for Qur'ān quotations in letters, and since all have been integrated into the Arabic Papyrology Database (www.naher-osten.lmu.de/apd), a thorough search for quotations could be conducted: CPR XVI; P.AbbottMutawakkil; P.AbbottUbaidAllah; P.BeckerNPAF; P.BeckerPAF; P.BeckerPapyrusstudien; P.Berl.Arab. II; P.Cair.Arab.; P.David-WeillEdfou; P.David-WeillLouvre; P.David-WeillMarchand; P.DiemAmtliche-Schreiben; P.DiemAphrodito; P.DiemDienstschreiben; P.DiemFrüheUrkunden; P.DiemGouverneur; P.DiemKontoauszug; P.DiemMauleselin; P.DietrichTopkapi; P.HanafiBusinessLetter; P.HanafiPrivateLetters; P.HanafiTwoArabicDocuments; P.Heid.Arab. I–II; P.HindsNubia; P.Horak 85; P.GrohmannQorra-Brief; P.GrohmannUrkunden; P.GrohmannWirtsch.; P.Jahn; P.Khalili I; P.Kratchkovski; P.Loth; P.Louvre6842; P.Marchands I–III; V/1; P.Ness. III; P.Prag.Arab.; P.Qurra; P.RagibLettres; P.RagibPlusAncienneLettre; P.RagibQurra; P.ReinfandtLeinenhändler; P.ReinfandtWeingutbesitzer; P.SijpesteijnArchivalMind; P.SijpesteijnArmyEconomics; P.World. These editions contain about 500 letters from the first four Islamic centuries, roughly about 200 private, 200 business, and 100 official letters. Additionally, the following editions not accessible in electronic databases were analyzed and searched for longer quotations: P.Hamb.Arab. II; P.Giss.Arab.; P.Mird; P.Philad.Arab.; P.Ryl.Arab. I. These editions contain another 280 letters, mostly dealing with private and business matters.

2 Categorization of Types of Qur'ān Quotations

All editions were read for Qur'ān quotations and allusions. For all identified quotations, all editions were searched using the Arabic Papyrology Database (APD)[2] to determine how regularly they were used. No automated-database-based matching of the text of all editions with the text of the Qur'ān took place.

---

1 For an introduction to the development of Arabic letter writing, and especially formulae, see Grob 2010.

2 Information retrieval was done in autumn 2013.

Therefore is it possible that some quotations are missing in the survey. All references that could be attributed to the Qur'ān have been classified in one of the following three categories:

(1) *Qur'ānic formulae*: Some formulae of Arabic letters are heavily influenced by Qur'ānic verses. While most eulogies have no origin in the Qur'ān, formulae such as the Basmala and the Šahāda, included in almost every letter, have parallels in the Qur'ān. Because of the omnipresence of these formulae in Islamic religious life, we might doubt that scribes understood them as direct quotations. Furthermore, most of them may simply propagate a monotheistic, not necessarily Islamic belief, and as we will see later, almost all of these formulae were also used in Jewish and Christian Arabic letters.

(2) *Short Qur'ānic quotations* (no longer than four words) that do not appear regularly as formulaic references are a gray area. Some of these are rarely used formulae for specific occasions; others are derived from general religious speech, such as God's beautiful names; and some could be very short intended quotations. But there is no unambiguous case in which the scribe refers more to the Qur'ān than to the general religious environment. In any case, there is only a relatively small number of references.

(3) *Full Qur'ānic quotations* are passages (of five words and more). In part, they are explicitly marked as text of the Qur'ān, e.g., by *qāla taʿālà*, "He says (may He be elevated)." One criterion, albeit a weak one, for distinguishing full quotations from short quotations is that a modern Arabic-speaking Muslim would put them in quotation marks. Unlike short quotations (which, for the scribes, may have lost their Qur'ānic nature), and also unlike formulaic allusions (which, for the scribes, had probably even lost their Islamic nature), these full quotations were used in full awareness that they were parts of the Qur'ān. In 780 analyzed letters, only 8 of these most interesting quotations there were found!

3 Qur'ānic Quotations in Papyrus Letters

With full detail, all records with evaluation are specified in the following list:

3.1 *Qur'ānic Formulae*

3.1.1 The Basmala

The Basmala (*bi-smi llāhi r-raḥmāni r-raḥīm, Q* 1:1 and *passim*) is the most used formula, and we might expect it as an introductory invocation in all the letters preserved, even in cases where the beginning of the letter is lost. The Basmala is first attested in letters in 675 CE. No variants are attested (especially no *alifs* in *bi-sm* and *ar-raḥmān*). The Basmala was also used in letters written by Christians, who, however, partially abbreviated or altered it. In Judaeo-Arabic letters, it might be understood as an alternative to the invocation of Hebrew formulae or biblical verses.[3] A pre-Islamic origin of the formulaic use is assumed.[4]

The Basmala is attested:
- in dated private letters: P.Jahn 3 and 4 (both Ǧumādā I 127/8 February–9 March 745); P.RagibLettreFamiliale (24 Ḏū l-qaʿda 102/26 May 721).
- in private letters dated paleographically to the 8th century: CPR XVI 26; 33; P.Berl.Arab. II 25; P.David-WeillLouvre 26; P.Heid.Arab. II 24; P.Jahn 1; 2; 5; 6; 8; 9; P.Louvre6842; P.RagibLettres 4; 9; 11; P.ReinfandtLeinenhändler.
- in private letters dated paleographically to the 9th and 10th centuries: CPR III 1; CPR XVI 23; 24; 25; 28; 29; 30; 34; P.AnawatiPapyrusChrétien, P.Berl.Arab. II 78; 79; P.Cair.Arab. 310; P.David-WeillEdfou A; B; P.David-WeillLouvre 11; P.DietrichTopkapi; P.GrohmannUrkunden 18; P.GrohmannWirtsch. 1; 20; P.Heid.Arab. II 17; 51; 52; 54; 56; 57; 58; 59; 61; 62; 81; P.Horak 85; P.Jahn 10; 12; 13; 15; 16, P.Khalili I 18; 24; 29; 33: 35: 36: P.Marchands II 1; 2; 3; 4; 6; 8; 9; 10; 11; 12; 13; 16; 17; 18; 19; 22; 23; 24; 27; 28; 30; 32; 33; 37; 38; 41; P.Marchands III 29; P.Marchands V/1 11; 17; 22; P.RagibLettres 10; 14; 15; 18; P.Ryl.Arab. I VI 6; 15; 18; P.World p. 182; p. 183.

- in dated business letters: P.GrohmannWirtsch. 9 (23 Epeiph 208/17 July 823).
- in business letters dated paleographically to the late 7th/early 8th century: CPR XVI 18.
- in business letters dated paleographically to the 8th century: P.Berl.Arab. II 50; 51; 52; P.GrohmannWirtsch. 14; P.Heid.Arab. II 26; 27; 42; P.Khalili I 14; 15; 21; P.World p. 162.
- in business letters dated paleographically to the 9th and 10th centuries: CPR XVI 6; 11; 13; 14; 15; 17; 19; 21; 22; 32; P.Cair.Arab. 291; 292; 293; 295; 296; 297; 298; 299; 300; 301; 302; 303; 304; 305; 306; 307; 308; 309; 311; 314; 315; 316, 318; 319; 320; 321; 322; 323; 324; 325; 326; 328; 329; 335; 339; 349; P.Berl.Arab. I 15; P.Berl.Arab. II 29; 38; 39; 40; 41; 42; 43; 55; 57; 59; 60; 61; 62; 63; 64; 66; 67; P.David-WeillLouvre 1; 2; 3; 8; 18; 19; 22; 28; 30; P.DelattreEcrire 1; P.DiemKontoauszug; P.GrohmannUrkunden 19; P.GrohmannWirtsch. 2; 3; 4; 5; 6; 7; 15;

3 Almbladh 2010: 48; 56.

4 Jahn 1937: 159–161.

P.Hamb.Arab. II 1; P.Heid.Arab. II 18; 19; 21; 31; 32; 35; 60; P.Khalili I 17; 19; 23; 25; 26; 30; 31; 34; P.Marchands III 1; 2; 3; 4; 5; 6; 7; 9; 10; 12; 14; 18; 19; 20; 21; 22; 23; 24; 25; 26; 27; 28; 34; 36; 37; 38; 40; 41; 42; 43; 44; P.Marchands V/1 2; 4; 6; 9; 13; 14; 18; P.Prag.Arab. 51; 52; 53; 56; 60; P.RagibLettres 6; 12; 16; 17; P.World p. 139; p. 161; p. 163; p. 173; p. 175.

- in the dated official letters of Qurra b. Šarīk (ruled 708–714, letters mostly from 709–710): P.BeckerNPAF 2; 5; 6; 8; 9; 12; 13; 14; 15; P.BeckerPAF 9; 10; 12; P.BeckerPapyrusstudien; P.GrohmannQorra-Brief; P.Heid.Arab. I 1; 2; 3; 4; 5; 6; 8; 14; 21; 22; a; b; c; d; f; g; h; i; l; P.Qurra 1; 3; P.RagibQurra; P.Ross.-Georg. IV 27 I h; P.World p. 130.
- in other dated official letters from Egypt: P.Cair.Arab. 169 (752); 174 (722); 180 (731–732); P.Clackson 45 (753); P.David-WeillLouvre 16 (713); P.DiemFrüheUrkunden 1 (698); P.HindsNubia (758); P.MargolliouthSelectPapyri 1 (745); 2 (751); 3 (752); P.Ryl.Arab. I IV 1 (751); 5 (759); P.Séoudi 1 (720); P.World p. 132 (793).
- in dated official letters letters not from Egypt: P.AbbottMutawakkil 1; 2 (both 855–856; from Damascus); P.Kratchkovski (717–719; from Zarafšān/Khorasan); P.Ness. 56 (67/28 June–17 July 686; from Naṣṭān/Palestine); P.Ness. 61 (Rağab 55/1–30 June 675; from Naṣṭān/Palestine).
- in official letters dated paleographically to the 7th century: P.Berl.Arab. II 23; P.DiemFrüheUrkunden 2; P.Heid.Arab. I p. 7.
- in official letters dated paleographically to the 8th century: P.Berl.Arab. II 26; 27; 28; 30; P.Heid.Arab. II 5; P.SijpesteijnArchivalMind 1.
- in official letters dated paleographically to the 9th century: CPR XVI 2; 20; P.Cair.Arab. 171; 176; 177; P.David-WeillLouvre 5; P.GrohmannUrkunden 7; 16; P.Heid.Arab. II 9; P.Prag.Arab. 94; 95; P.RémondonEdfou 5; P.SijpesteijnArchivalMind 2.

3.1.2 The Ḥamdala

The Ḥamdala (*al-ḥamdu li-llāhi rabbi l-ʿālamīn*, Q 1:2) is sometimes used in the introduction or, more rarely, as slide-in blessings. A shortened form (sometimes combined with non-Qurʾānic additions such as *kaṯīran, waḥdihi*, etc.) is used more often than the full version of the Ḥamdala. The Ḥamdala is first attested in 721 CE, and is a common feature of formulae since the 9th century. In a shortened version it is also used by Christians.[5] It may have come into regular use later than the Basmala. A verbalized variant of the Ḥamdala is a common ele-

5 Almbladh 2010: 56.

ment of 7th–8th century letter formulae: *aḥmadu llāha ilayka* (or: *ilaykumu*) *llaḏī*, followed by the Šahāda, is first attested in the Qurra letters (709–714); the undated letters CPR XVI 18, P.Berl.Arab. II 23, and RagibPlusAncienneLettre could be still older. It ceased to be used in late 8th century,[6] yet some few letters containing it have been dated by their editors to the 9th century. No variants (such as *al-ʿālamīn* with defective *alif*) have been attested.

(a) The Ḥamdala is quoted, with the addition *rabbi l-ʿālamīn*:
- in private letters dated paleographically to the 9th and 10th centuries: CPR XVI 25; P.David-WeillEdfou A; P.GrohmannUrkunden 18; P.Marchands II 8; 21; 40; P.RagibLettres 15.
- in business letters dated paleographically to the 9th and 10th centuries: P.Berl.Arab. II 53; P.Cair.Arab. 293; 299; 306; 327; 329; 339; P.DiemKontoauszug; P.Heid.Arab. II 39.
- in dated official letters: P.Cair.Arab. 85 (959/960).

(b) The Ḥamdala is quoted, without *rabbi al-ʿālamīn*, but with other additions such as *kaṯīran, waḥdihi* etc.:
- in dated private letters: P.RagibLettreFamiliale (24 Ḏū l-qaʿda 102/26 May 721).
- in private letters dated paleographically to the 8th century: P.Berl.Arab. II 25; P.Jahn 10.
- in private letters dated paleographically to the 9th and 10th centuries: P.AnawatiPapyrusChrétien; P.DelattreEcrire 2; P.Berl.Arab. II 79; P.Heid.Arab. II 61; 82; P.Khalili I 18; 24; P.Marchands II 5; 7; 9; 17; 18; 23; 26; 34; 35; P.RagibLettres 4; 9; P.Ryl.Arab. I VI 15.

- in dated business letters: P.SijpesteijnTravel (10 June 735).
- in business letters dated paleographically to the 9th and 10th centuries: CPR XVI 14; 19; P.Berl.Arab. II 38; 39; 40; 41; 42; 45; 50; 60; 61; P.Cair.Arab. 305; 309; 315; 320; 322; 324; 326; P.DelattreEcrire 1; P.GrohmannWirtsch. 2; P.Heid.Arab. II 10; 29; 32; 34; 36; 39; P.Khalili I 20; 27; 30; P.Marchands III 17; 42; P.Prag.Arab. 56; 57; P.RagibLettres 6; 12; 13.

- in official letters dated paleographically to the 9th and 10th centuries: P.GrohmannUrkunden 7; 16; P.Heid.Arab. II 7; 10.

6 This verbalized Ḥamdala is also attested in later official letters written by Muslim rulers to Christian rulers that are preserved in European archives, so that we might assume that the formula was continuously used in official letters.

(c) The Ḥamdala is quoted, without *rabbi l-ʿālamīn* and with different word order (*wa-li-llāhi/fa-li-llāhi l-ḥamd*):
- in business letters dated paleographically to the 9th and 10th centuries: CPR XVI 12; P.Cair.Arab. 291; 300; 324; P.Hamb.Arab. II 1a; P.Khalili 20.

(d) The verbalized Ḥamdala is quoted, with *aḥmadu llāha ilayka* (or: *ilaykumu*) *llaḏī*, followed by the Šahāda:
- in dated private letters: P.Jahn 3; 4 (both Ǧumādā I 127 AH/8 February–9 March 745); P.RagibLettreFamiliale (24 Ḏū l-qaʿda 102/26 May 722, followed later by a direct quotation).
- in private letters dated paleographically to the 8th century: CPR XVI 33; P.Berl.Arab. II 25; 73; P.Heid.Arab. I p. 7; P.Heid.Arab. II 24; 49; P.Jahn 5; 9; 13; P.Loth 2; P.ReinfandtLeinenhändler.
- in private letters dated paleographically to the 9th century: P.David-WeillLouvre 11; 26; P.Horak 85; P.Jahn 17.

- in business letters dated paleographically to the 7th century: CPR XVI 18 (or early 7th century); P.RagibPlusAncienneLettre (possibly 7th century).
- in business letters dated paleographically to the 8th century: P.Berl.Arab. II 49; P.David-WeillLouvre 30; P.Khalili I 14 (*ʿalayka* instead of *ilayka*); 15.
- In business letters dated paleographically to the 9th century: P.RagibLettres 12.

- in the official letters of Qurra b. Šarīk: P.BeckerNPAF 2; 5; 6; 8; 9; 12; P.BeckerPAF 1; 2; 5; 6; 11; 12; P.GrohmannQorra-Brief; P.Heid.Arab. I 1; 2; 3; 10; 14; P.Qurra 1; 3; P.RagibQurra 1; 2; 3; P.Ross.-Georg. IV 27 I h; P.World p. 132.
- in other dated official letters from Egypt: P.HindsNubia (758).
- in official letters dated paleographically to the 7th century: P.Berl.Arab. II 23.
- in official letters not from Egypt: P.Kratchkovski (717–719; from Zarafšān/Khorasan).

(e) The verbalized Ḥamdala is quoted, with use of *ḥamida* in the imperfect:
- in private letters dated paleographically to the 9th and 10th centuries: P.David-WeillEdfou B (*aḥmadu llāha ʿalayhā*); P.Heid.Arab. II 50 (*naḥmadu llāha ʿalà ḏālika*); 59 (*aḥmadu llāha kaṯīran*); P.Jahn 17 (*fa-naḥmadu llāha ʿalà ḏālika*).

(f) The verbalized Ḥamdala is quoted in private letters, with use of *ḥamida* in the perfect:
- in dated private letters: P.Cair.Arab. 288 (*fa-ḥamidtu llāha ʿalà ḏālika kaṯīran*; 851)
- in private letters dated paleographically to the 9th and 10th centuries: CPR XVI 28 (*fa-ḥamidtu llāha ʿalà ḏālika*); P.Heid.Arab. II 61 (*fa-ḥamidtu llāha ʿalà ḏālika*); P.Marchands II 2 (*fa-ḥamidtu llāha ʿalà ḏālika kaṯīran*); 24 (*fa-ḥamidtu llāha ʿalà ḏālika kaṯīran*); 25 (*fa-ḥamidtu llāha ʿalà ḏālika ḥamdan*); 35 (*fa-ḥamidtu llāha ʿalà ḏālika kaṯīran* and *fa-ḥamidtu llāha ʿalà ḏālika ḥamdan kaṯīran*).

- in business letters dated paleographically to the late 7th/early 8th centuries: CPR XVI 18 (*wa-ḥamidtu llāha ʿalà ʿāfiyatihi*).
- in business letters dated paleographically to the 9th/10th centuries: P.Berl.Arab. II 29 (*fa-ḥamidtu llāha ʿalayhi ḥamdan kaṯīran*); 60 (*wa-ḥamidtu llāha ʿalà ḏālika kaṯīran*); 62 (*fa-ḥamidtu llāha ʿalayhi ḥamdan kaṯīran*); P.DelattreEcrire 1 (*wa-ḥamidtu llāha ʿalà ḏālika*); P.Heid.Arab. II 21 (*fa-ḥamidtu llāha ʿalà ḏālika*); P.Khalili I 17 (*fa-ḥamidtu llāha ʿalayhi ḥamdan kaṯīran*); P.Marchands V/I 18 (*fa-ḥamidtu llāha ʿalayhi ḥamdan kaṯīran*).

(g) *rabbi l-ʿālamīn* without Ḥamdala is only attested:
- in a private letter dated paleographically to the 9th century: P.Marchands II 4.

3.1.3 The First Part of the Šahāda

The first part of the Šahāda (according to the phrase *alladī lā ilāha illā huwa*, Q 59:22; 59:23) emphasizes God's uniqueness. Used almost exclusively as an addition to a verbalized Ḥamdala, it is first attested in the Qurra letters (708–714), unless CPR XVI 18, P.Berl.Arab. II 23, and RagibPlusAncienneLettre are older. The last dated letter that uses this formula is P.World p. 132 (793). A shortened *lā ilāha illā huwa* is attested a few times from the 9th century onward. The shortened form is probably pre-Islamic, influenced by the Samaritan *lit ēlæ iḷḷaʿād*, "There is no god except him."[7]

7 Macuch 1978: 20–26.

(a) The first part of the Šahāda is quoted:
- in dated private letters: P.Jahn 3; 4 (both Ǧumādā I 127/8 February–9 March 745); P.RagibLettreFamiliale (24 Ḏū l-qaʿda 102/26 May 721).
- in private letters dated paleographically to the 8th century: CPR XVI 33 (possibly 7th century); P.Berl.Arab. II 72; 73; P.David-WeillLouvre 26; P.Heid.Arab. I p. 7; P.Heid.Arab. II 24; 25; P.Jahn 5; 9; 12; P.Loth 2; P.RagibLettres 4; 9; P.ReinfandtLeinenhändler.
- in private letters dated paleographically to the 9th/10th centuries: P.David-WeillLouvre 11; P.Horak 85; P.Marchands II 24; 26; P.RagibLettres 10.

- in business letters dated paleographically to the 8th century: CPR XVI 18 (possibly late 7th century); P.Berl.Arab. II 49; P.David-WeillLouvre 30; P.Khalili I 14; 15; P.RagibLettre; P.RagibPlusAncienneLettre (possibly 7th century).

- in the official letters of Qurra b. Šarīk: P.BeckerNPAF 2; 5; 6; 8; 9; 12; P.BeckerPAF 1; 2; 3; 5; 12; P.Heid.Arab. I 1; 2; 3; 10; 14; 16; P.Qurra 1; 2; 3; P.Ross.-Georg. IV 27 I h.
- in another dated official letter: P.World p. 132 (793).
- in official letters dated paleographically to the 7th century: P.Berl.Arab. II 23.
- in official letters not from Egypt: P.Kratchkovski (717–719, from Zarafšān/Khorasan).

(b) Shortened quotations without *allāha llaḏī*, are only attested:
- in private letters dated paleographically to the 9th/10th centuries: P.Berl.Arab. II 81; P.Marchands II 26; 30; 33; 34.

3.1.4 The Second Part of the Šahāda

The second part of the Šahāda (*muḥammadun rasūlu llāh*, Q 48:9), saying that Muḥammad is God's messenger, is not attested in papyrus letters.

3.1.5 The Taṣliya

The Taṣliya (*inna llāha wa-malāʾikatahu yuṣallūna ʿalà n-nabiyyi yā āyyuha llaḏīna āmanū ṣallū ʿalayhi wa-sallimū*, Q 33:56) is sometimes used as eulogy in the introductory formulae, where its basic form is: *ṣallā llāha ʿalà muḥammadin* (or: *ʿalayhi*) *wa-sallama*. Additions preceding *muḥammad*: *sayyidinā*; following *muḥammad*: *an-nabiyyi, wa-ālihi*; additions to *wa-sallama*: *taslīman, kaṯīran*. No addition of *wa-ṣaḥbihi* is attested. Nominalized Taṣliya (*ṣalātun ʿalā* ...) is attested. Apart from P.Cair.Arab. 85 (959/960), no letter is dated, but it seems that the Taṣliya came into use only in the 9th century. According to literary sources, the use of the Taṣliya in official letters was introduced by order of the caliph Hārūn ar-Rašīd.[8]

(a) The Taṣliya is quoted:
- in private letters dated paleographically to the 9th/10th centuries: CPR XVI 25; 31; P.David-WeillLouvre A (addition *ahl baytihi*); B; P.Heid.Arab. II 53; 55; P.Jahn 14; 15; P.Khalili I 18; 36; P.Marchands II 8; 24; 26; 30; 33; 34; P.Prag.Arab. 50.
- in business letters dated paleographically to the 9th/10th centuries: CPR XVI 32; P.Berl.Arab. II 38; 39; 40; 41; 42; 43; P.Cair.Arab. 297; 298; 329; P.DiemKontoauszug; P.Heid.Arab. II 32; P.Khalili I 17; 30; 31; P.Prag.Arab. 56.
- in a dated official letter: P.Cair.Arab. 85 (959/960).

(b) Variants of the Taṣliya, with the Taṣliya as prayer, are only used in business letters:
- in a business letter: CPR XVI 18 (*fa-as'alu llāha an yuṣalliya ʿalā muḥammadin nabiyyinā*, late 7th/early 8th century).

(c) Another variant of the Tasliya, with Taṣliya for ʿAlī:
- in a business letter: P.Cair.Arab. 324 (*ṣallā llāhu ʿalā ʿaliyyin sayyidi l-awwalīna wa-l-āḫarīna wa-ʿalà ālihi ṭ-ṭāhirīna wa-sallama taslīman*, 9th/10th centuries).[9]

3.1.6 The Greeting to Muslims

The greeting to Muslims (*as-salāmu ʿalaykum wa-raḥmatu llāhi wa-barākatuhu*) has two parts. The first part (*salāmun ʿalaykum* Q 6:54; 7:46; 13:24; 16:32; 28:55; 39:73) is an old Semitic greeting, as in the Hebrew and Aramaic *šālōm ləḵā, šəlām lāk/ləkōn, šelāmā ʿalāḵ*. It is found in the Old Testament (Judges

8 Goldziher 1896: 105.

9 Grohmann and Diem, who emended Grohmann's edition (Diem 2012: 57–58), read *ʿalā ʿaliyyin* without further commentary. Since the letter deals with payments, it contains no further hints of a Shiite attitude of the sender and/or the addressee. Muġāwirī 1423/2002: 297 reads … *ʿalā sayyidi l-awwalīna wa-l-āḫarīna* … in his re-publication (P.Alqab 118) of the letter, and understands the second على as an error of the scribe, so that the Taṣliya refers to Muḥammad without mentioning him.

19:20; 2 Sam 18:28, Dan 10:19, 1 Chron 12:19), the Talmud (*šālōm ʿalēkām*), in the Peshitta, Nabatean, and Ṣafaitic inscriptions and pre-Islamic Arabic poetry.[10] In Arabic papyri, mostly the singular is used (*ʿalayka*). According to the literature, in Early Islam often only *salām* was used.

In the second part (*raḥmatu llāhi* wa-*barakātuhu*, Q 11:73, *raḥma* written رحمت, with *tāʾ ṭawīla*), sometimes *wa-barākatuhu* was omitted, and sometimes *allāh* was replaced by *-hi*, so that we cannot decide whether *raḥma* was written in Qurʾānic or modern orthography. The oldest dated letter is P.RagibLettreFamiliale (721); a variant (*muḥammad an-nabī* instead of *-ka* or *-kum*) is found in a letter by Qurra b. Šarīk (709). A few undated letters possibly stem from the 7th century. It seems that the full quotations did not come into use until the 9th century.

According to narrative sources, in Early Islam, the combination of both parts (*tašahhud*) was part of the prayer ritual.

(a) The greeting is quoted, with *tāʾ ṭawīla*:
- in dated private letters: P.RagibLettreFamiliale (24 Ḏū l-qaʿda 102/26 May 721).
- in private letters dated paleographically to the 8th century: P.Berl.Arab. II 73; P.Jahn 5; P.Loth 2.
- in private letters dated paleographically to the 9th century: P.Marchands II 10; 11; 12; 17; 18; 20; 21; 38.

- in business letters dated paleographically to the 7th/8th centuries: CPR XVI 18.
- in business letters dated paleographically to the 9th century: CPR XVI 32; P.GrohmannWirtsch. 2; P.Khalili I 17; 34; P.Marchands V/1 20; P.RagibLettres 12.

- in official letters dated paleographically to the 7th century: P.Berl.Arab. II 23; 24 (or 8th century).

(b) The greeting is quoted, with *tāʾ marbūṭa*:
- in a private letter dated paleographically to the 9th century: P.Marchands II 8.
- in business letters dated paleographically to the 9th/10th centuries: P.Berl.Arab. II 66; P.Cair.Arab. 302; P.Khalili I 32.

---

10 van Arendonk and Gimaret 1995: 915–918.

(c) The greeting is quoted, without *barakātuhu*:
- in dated private letters: P.Jahn 3; 4 (both Ǧumādā I 127/8 February–9 March 745).
- in private letters dated paleographically to the 8th century: P.David-WeillLouvre 26; P.Jahn 1; 8; P.SijpesteijnArmyEconomics; P.RagibLettres 4; 9; P.ReinfandtLeinenhändler.
- in private letters dated paleographically to the 9th century: P.David-WeillLouvre 11; P.Horak 85; P.Marchands II 2; 19; P.Marchands V/1 11.

- in dated business letters: P.SijpesteijnTravel (20 June 735).
- in business letters dated paleographically to the 7th century: P.Hanafi-BusinessLetter; P.RagibPlusAncienneLettre.
- in business letters dated paleographically to the 8th century: P.Berl.Arab. II 49; P.David-WeillLouvre 25; P.DiemMauleselin; P.Khalili I 15; 21.
- in business letters dated paleographically to the 9th century: P.David-WeillLouvre 8; P.GrohmannUrkunden 19; P.GrohmannWirtsch. 3; P.Heid.Arab. II 30 (*wa-barakātuhu* to be assumed); P.RagibLettres 13.

- in dated official letters from Egypt: P.AbbottUbaidAllah (724); P.GrohmannQorra-Brief (*as-salāmu ʿalā muḥammadini n-nabiyyi wa-raḥmatu llāh*, 709).
- in dated official letters from Khorasan: P.Kratchkovski (717–719).

(d) A variant is found:
- possibly in a private letter dated palaeographically to the 9th century: *wa-salāmun ʿalayka wa-ḥasbunā llāhu wa-kafā bihi*: (Q 33:39: *wa-kafà bi-llāhi ḥasīban*): P.Cair.Arab. 295, yet Diem emends: *wa-salāmun alayka wa-raḥmatu llāhi wa-barakātuhu.*[11]

3.1.7 The Greeting to Non-Muslims

The greeting to non-Muslims (*as-salāmu ʿalà man ittabaʿa l-hudà*, Q 20:47) is only attested in the letters by Qurra b. Šarīk and three passports. This special formula was only used in official letters to distinguish between the different religions. In letters about matters of daily life, it was not used. We find this formula later in letters from Muslim to Christian rulers,[12] a further hint of its role

11 Diem 2012: 32.

12 P.Aragon 88; 89; 90; 91; 92 (all written 1323–1330).

in official matters only. Thus the occurrence of the *salām ʿalayka* greeting in private or business letters is no proof that these letters were written from Muslims.

(a) The greeting to non-Muslims is found in official letters only:
- in the dated letters of Qurra b. Šarīk (708–714, mostly 709–710): P.BeckerNPAF 1; 2; 4; 5; 6; 8; 11; 12; P.BeckerNPAF 1; 2; 3; 4; 6; P.Cair.Arab. 157; 158; 159; P.Heid.Arab. I 1; 2; 3; 4; 10; 11; 18; P.Qurra 1; 2; 3; 4; 5; P.RagibQurra 1; 3; P.SijpesteijnQurra.
- in dated passports: P.Cair.Arab. 174 (722); P.RagibSauf-Conduits 2 (722); 3 (734).

(b) Variants:
- P.GrohmannQorra-Brief (*as-salāmu ʿalā muḥammadini n-nabiyyi wa-raḥmatu llāh*, 709); P.HindsNubia (*salāmun ʿalà awliyāʾi llāhi wa-ahli ṭāʿatihi*, 758).

3.1.8 *lā šarīka lahu* (Q 6:163)

While this short statement of God's uniqueness is often attested in protocols (official marks on papyrus scrolls) from the 7th and 8th century, it was not used In letters before the 9th century, where it served to mark the end of the introductory formulae.

lā šarīka lahu is found:
- in private letters dated paleographically to the 9th/10th centuries: P.Berl.Arab. II 79; P.David-WeillEdfou A; P.Marchands II 1; 2; 35; P.Marchands V/1 17.
- in business letters dated paleographically to the 9th/10th centuries: P.Berl.Arab. II 60; 62; P.Cair.Arab. 305; 324; 339; P.David-WeillLouvre 1; P.Heid.Arab. II 32; P.Khalili I 17; 20; P.Marchands III 19; P.Marchands V/1 6; 20.

3.1.9 Istiṯnāʾ (Q 2:70; 6:128)

The formula *in šāʾa llāh* (Q 2:70; 6:128) was added as a statement concerning a coming event to express that the future is subject to God. Its use is similar to the *conditio jacobaea* (following the passage ἐὰν ὁ κύριος θελήσῃ καὶ ζήσομεν / "If it is the Lord's will, we will live," Epistle of James 4:15) in Christian letters.

(a) *in šāʾa llāh* is quoted:
- in private letters dated paleographically to the 7th century: P.SijpesteijnArmyEconomics (possibly 8th century).

- in private letters dated paleographically to the 8th century: P.Berl.Arab. II 72; 73; P.David-WeillLouvre 26; P.Heid.Arab. II 11; 12; 24; P.Jahn 1; 5; 6 (possibly 9th century); 9; P.Loth 2; P.RagibLettres 11; 19 (possibly 9th century).
- in private letters dated paleographically to the 9th/10th centuries: CPR XVI 25; 29; 30; 31; P.Berl.Arab. II 76; 78; 79; 80; 81; P.Cair.Arab. 295; P.David-WeillEdfou A; B; P.David-WeillLouvre 11; P.DelattreEcrire 2; P.HanafiTwoArabicDocuments 2; P.Heid.Arab. II 17; 43; 52; 54; 55; 56; P.Khalili I 18; 33; 35; 36; P.Marchands II 2; 3; 5; 9; 11; 12; 14; 16; 28; 30; 32; 40; P.Marchands V/1 11; P.Prag.Arab. 50; 83; P.RagibLettres 10; 14; P.Ryl.Arab. I VI 1; 6; 15; 18.

- in business letters dated paleographically to the 8th century: P.Diem-Mauleselin; P.World p. 162.
- in business letters dated paleographically to the 9th/10th centuries: CPR XVI 6; 13; 15; 16; 19; 21; 23; 32; P.Berl.Arab. II 29; 38; 39; 40; 41; 42; 43; 51; 55; 56; 57; 60; 61; 62; 64; 66; P.Cair.Arab. 289; 291; 292; 294; 296; 297; 300; 305; 307; 308; 309; 311; 312; 314; 315; 316; 318; 319; 322; 323; 325; 326; 327; 330; 331; 342; P.David-WeillLouvre 8; 22; 28 (possibly older); P.GrohmannUrkunden 19; P.GrohmannWirtsch. 3; 5; 6; 7; 9; P.Hamb.Arab. II 1a; P.Heid.Arab. II 18; 31; 32; 33; P.Khalili I 19; 20; 22; 23; 26; 27; 28; 31; P.Marchands III 4; 6; 13; 22; 37; 40; P.Marchands V/I 4; 6; 12; 16; 20; 23; P.Prag.Arab. 52; 53; 54; 55; 58; 59; 93; P.World p. 161; p. 163; p. 173; p. 175a.

- in official letters of Qurra b. Šarīk (708–714, mostly 709–710): P.BeckerNPAF 1; 2; 4; 6; P.BeckerPAF 5; P.Heid.Arab. I 1; P.Qurra 2; P.RagibQurra 1.
- in other dated official letters: P.AbbottUbaidAllah (724); P.DiemFrühe-Urkunden 3 (779); 5 (775–778); P.Séoudi 1 (720).
- in official letters dated paleographically to the 9th/10th centuries: CPR XVI 2; 20; P.Berl.Arab. II 26; 27; 28; P.Cair.Arab. 176, 177; 178; 179; 290; P.GrohmannUrkunden 7; 16; P.Heid.Arab. II 9; P.Prag.Arab. 95; 96; P.RémondonEdfou 5.

(b) Variants of *in šāʾa llāh*, *in* and *šāʾa* being written together:
- in private letters dated paleographically to the 8th century: P.Ryl.Arab. I I 5 (or later).
- in private letters dated paleographically to the 9th century: P.Marchands II 8; 24.

- in business letters dated paleographically to the 9th century: P.Marchands II 45.

3.1.10 The Ḥasbala

The Ḥasbala (*ḥasbunā llāhu wa-niʿma l-wakīl*, Q 3:173) was used as a formula for closing a letter. It seems that this quotation was used more regularly after the year 1000, and also in official letters for which we have no records on papyrus. It is attested as an introductory formula in Jewish and Christian letters.[13]

The Ḥasbala is quoted:

- in private letters dated paleographically to the 9th/10th century: CPR XVI 29; P.Heid.Arab. II 62; P.Khalili I 36.
- in business letters dated paleographically to the 9th/10th century: P.Cair.Arab. 308; 309; 316; 322; 327; P.Khalili I 22; P.Ryl.Arab. I VI 23.

3.2 *Short Qurʾānic Quotations: Elements Often Used as God's Name, Etc.*

3.2.1 *subḥāna llāh* (Q 10:68; 21:26)

The *subḥāna llāh* formula was usually written with *alif*, but a variant without *alif* is also attested. The formula is also used in Christian letters,[14] although the Qurʾānic verse it is derived from has a peculiar anti-Christian meaning.

subḥāna llāh is found:

- in private letters dated paleographically to the 9th/10th centuries: CPR XVI 23.5; 30r.33; P.AnawatiPapyrusChrétien r.3; P.Marchands II 3.3 (without *alif*); P.Ryl.Arab. I VI 18.3 (possibly older).
- in a business letter dated paleographically to the 9th century: P.Berl.Arab. II 63.4.

3.2.2 *fa-tawakkal ʿalà llāh*, etc.

This encompasses a number of variants (*fa-tawakkal ʿalà llāh*, Q 3:159; 26:217; 27:79; *ʿalà llāh tawakkalnā*, Q 7:89; 10:85; *wa-tawakkal ʿalà llāh*, Q 8:61; 33:3; 33:48; *fa-ʿalà llāhi tawakkaltu*, Q 10:71; *tawakkaltu ʿalà llāh*, Q 11:56). It is attested as an introduction in Jewish letters.[15]

This is only attested:

13 Almbladh 2010: 50; 56.
14 Almbladh 2010: 58.
15 Almbladh 2010: 49.

– in business letters dated paleographically to the 9th century: P.Cair.Arab. 331.9 (*tawakkaltu ʿalā llāh*); P.Marchands III 4r.12 (*yasurruka llāhu wa-qad tawakkaltu ʿalayhi*).

3.2.3 Further Short Quotations

The following short quotations are only attested In single letters and normally had no defined function in the formulary.

(a) *sūʾ al-ʿaḏāb* (Q 2:49; 6:157; 7:141; 7:167; 14:6; 27:5; 39:24; 39:47; 40:45) is found:
- in a private letter dated paleographically to the 7th/8th centuries: P.Mird 63.11 (very fragmentarily preserved; since except for the assumed Qurʾānic quotation *sūʾ al-ʿaḏāb*, no complete words are legible, even Grohmann's identification as a private letter is problematic).

(b) *bi-l-qisṭ* (Q 11:85) is found:
- in a private letter dated paleographically to the 7th/8th centuries: P.Mird. 91.1 (Grohmann identifies this single word as a Qurʾānic quotation, yet since the preceding and following words are lost, I consider this attribution disputable; also the identification as private is problematic, since the fragment consists of only two lines).

(c) *innahu* (Q: *allāha*) *ʿalà kulli šayʾin qadīr* (Q 5:17) is found:
- in private letters dated paleographically to the 9th/10th centuries: P.Hamb.Arab. II 33r.3 (*mā yašāʾu* instead of *kulli šayʾin*); P.HanafiPrivateLetters 2.3–4 (only *kulli šayʾin qadīr* preserved); P.Marchands II 2.3; 2.5.

(d) *innahu* (Q: *innaka*) *samīʿu d-duʿāʾ* (Q 3:38) is found:
- in a private letter dated paleographically to the 9th/10th centuries: P.Marchands II 23.6.
- In a business letter dated paleographically to the 9th/10th centuries: P.Cair.Arab. 301.6.

(e) *fa-innahu* (Q: *innahu*) *raḥīmun samīʿun qarīb* (Q 34:50) is found:
- in a private letter dated paleographically to the 9th/10th centuries: P.Marchands II 26.1.

(f) *fa-rabbuka* (Q: *inna rabbī*) *ʿazīzun raḥīmun "qarībun muǧīb" "lā ilāha illā huwa"* (first quotation: Q 11:61; *ʿazīz* and *raḥīm* are attributes of God, but not used in this combination in the Qurʾān; the Šahāda is based on Q 2:255;

3:2; 3:6; 3:18; 4:87; 6:102; 6:106; 7:158; 9:31; 9:129; 11:14; 13:30; 20:8; 20:98; 23:116; 27:26; 28:70; 40:3; 40:62; 40:65; 44:8; 59:22; 59:13; 64:13) is found:
- in a private letter dated paleographically to the 9th/10th centuries: P.Marchands II 26.26.
- in an official letter dated paleographically to the 9th/10th centuries: P.Prag.Arab. 93.2 (*innahu qarībun muǧīb*; the last *bāʾ* is added by Grohmann).

(g) *innā li-llāhi wa-ilayhi rāǧiʿūn* (Q 2:156) is found:
- in a private letter dated paleographically to the 9th century: P.Jahn 14.15–16 (used as a formula for condolence).
- in private letters dated paleographically to the 9th/10th centuries: P.Marchands III 29r.3; P.Ryl.Arab. I VII 43.1.

(h) *fa-llāhu l-mustaʿān* (Q 12:18) is found:
- in a private or business letter dated paleographically to the 9th century: P.Marchands V/1 11. 18–19.
- in a private letter dated paleographically to the 9th/10th centuries: P.Ryl.Arab. I VI 14.6.
- in business letters dated paleographically to the 9th/10th centuries: P.Berl.Arab. II 41r.10–11 (*wa-llāhu l-masʾūlu l-mustaʿān*); P.Marchands III 8.6 (only *al-mustaʿān*, with *wa-llāh* added by Rāġib).

(i) *allaḏī* (Q: *inna llāha*) *lā yuḫlifu l-mīʿād* (Q 3:9) is found:
- in a private letter dated paleographically to the 9th/10th centuries: P.Ryl.Arab. I VII 43.2 (*miʿād* without *alif*, other than in the Qurʾān).

(j) *allaḏī* (Q: *bi-llaḏī*) *huwa ḫayr* (Q 2:61) is found:
- in a private letter dated paleographically to the 9th/10th centuries: P.Heid.Arab. II 43.5–6.
- in a business letter dated paleographically to the 9th/10th centuries: P.Marchands V/1 6.5–6.

(k) *ǧannāt an-naʿīm* (Q 5:65; 10:9; 22:56; 31:8; 37:43; 56:12; 68:34; *ǧannāt* without *alif*) is found:
- in a private letter dated paleographically to the 9th/10th centuries: P.Hamb.Arab. II 7.11; 45.4 (*ǧannāt* in both papyri with *alif*).
- in an official letter dated paleographically to the 9th/10th centuries: P.Heid.Arab. II 8.2 (*ǧannāt* with *alif*; *an-naʿīm* added by Diem; according to him, instead of *ǧannāt*, rather *ḥasanāt* should be read).

(l) *innahu* (Q: *wa-huwa*) *l-waliyyu l-ḥamīd* (Q 42:28) is found:
- in a private letter dated paleographically to the 9th/10th centuries: P.Hamb.Arab. II 21.4.

(m) *allaḏī ḫalaqa* (Q adds *sabʿa*) *s-samawāti wa-l-arḍ* (Q: *wa-mina l-arḍ*) (Q 65:12) is found:
- in a dated official letter: P.HindsNubia.24–25 (18 Raǧab 141/11 November 758; *samawāt* written in the Qur'ān and on papyrus without *alif*).

(n) *bi-ahli* (Q: *ahl*) *t-taqwà* (Q 74:56) is found:
- in an official letter dated paleographically to the 9th/10th centuries: P.RagibLettres 5.12.

4 Intentional Longer Qur'ān Quotations

Longer Qur'ān quotations are found in only nine letters. In several letters they are explicitly marked by *qāla llāhu* or *qawl allāh*.

(a) P.RagibLettreFamiliale, a dated private letter (written 24 Ḏū l-qāʿda 102/26 May 722):
- l. 10–11: ***"yattaqi llāha"*** *fa-innahu man* (Q: *wa-man*) *"yattaqi llāha yaǧʿalu lahu* ***min amrihi*** *maḫraǧan wa-yarzuquhu min hayṯu* (erroneously with two hooks for the *yā'*) *lā yaḥtasibu"* (Q 65:2–3; bold words inserted from Q 65:4).

(b) P.HindsNubia.7–10; 10–11, a dated official letter from the governor of Egypt Mūsà b. Kaʿb to the king of Nubia Cyriacus (18 Raǧab 141/11 November 758; the script of the letter shows many diacritical dots; yet because the edition by Hinds and Sakkout is based on low-quality pictures, it cannot be determined which dots are written):
- l. 7–10: *wa-llāhu tabāraka wa-taʿālà yaqūlu fī kitābihi awfū* (Q: *wa-awfū*) *"bi-ʿahdi llāhi iḏā ʿahadtum wa-lā tanquḍū l-īmāna baʿda tawkīdihā wa-qad ǧaʿaltumu llāha ʿalaykum kafīlan inna llāha yaʿlamu mā tafʿalūna"* (Q 16:91; *īmān* on papyrus with *alif*, other than in the Qur'ān.)
- l. 10–11: *wa-qāla awfū* (Q: *wa-awfū*) *"bi-ʿahdī ūfi bi-ʿahdikum wa-iyyāya fa-rhabūni"* (Q 2:40; *iyyāya* on papyrus with *alif*, other than in the Cairo print of the Qur'ān, where it is written with alif maqṣūra at the end).

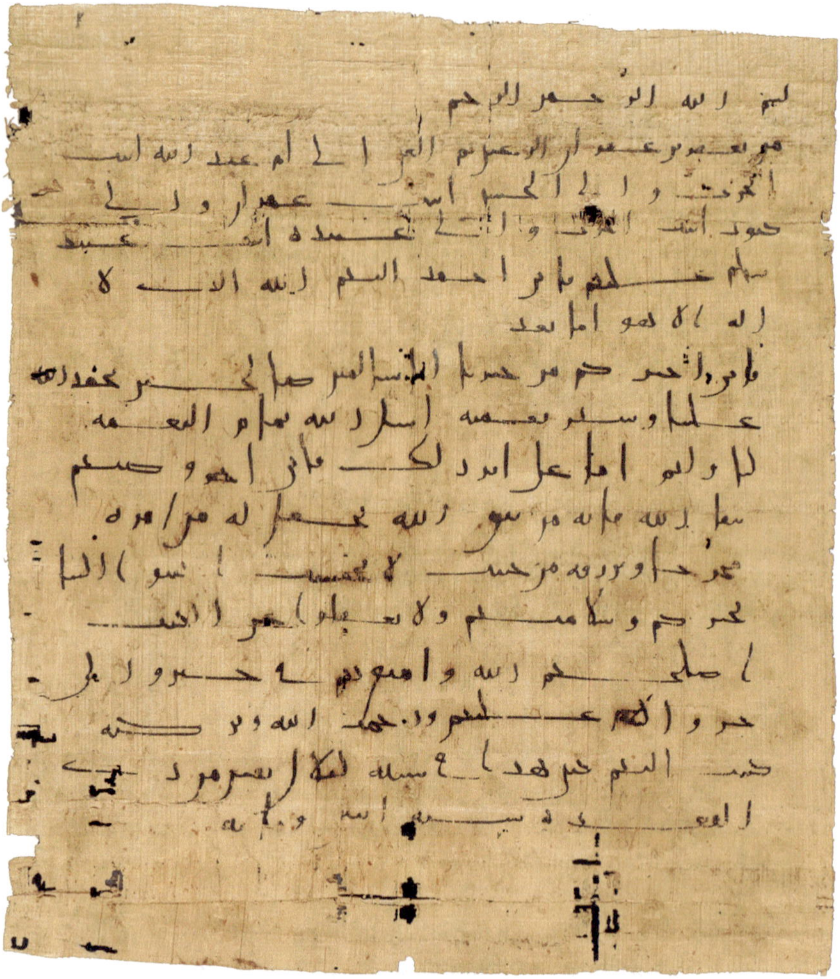
بسم الله الرحمن الرحيم

FIGURE 2.1 A private letter written in 102/722 that quotes Q 65:2–4 in a different word order (P.Michael.inv. P. A 560 = P.RagibLettreFamiliale)

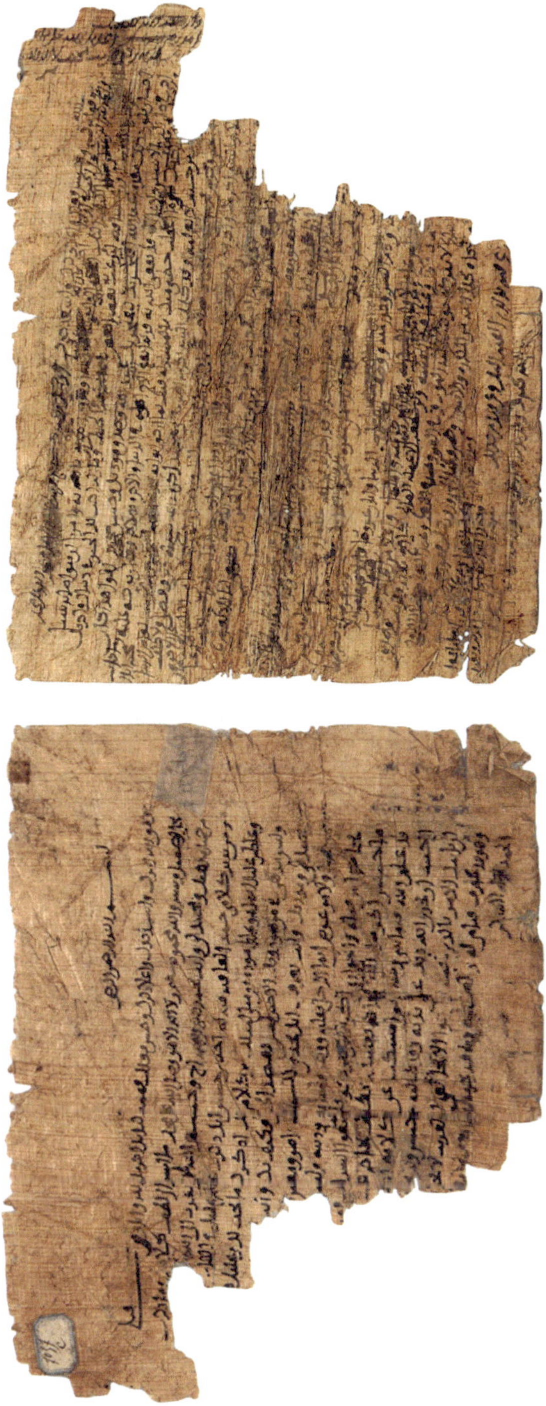

FIGURE 2.2 A business letter from the Fayyūm (9th c.) that contains quotations of Q 9:120–121 (in reversed verse order) and Q 65:12 (P.Louvre inv. E 7057 C = P.Marchands II 26)

FIGURE 2.3 A business letter from the Fayyūm (9th c.) that quotes Q 41:39 with minor changes influenced by the text of Q 42:9 (P.Louvre inv. E 8258 = P.Marchands, V/1 11)

FIGURE 2.4 A private letter (9th/10th c.) that quotes Q 14:7 (with a small orthographic variance) (P.Hamb.inv. A.P. 55 = P.Hamb.Arab. II 34)
© STAATS- UND UNIVERSITÄTSBIBLIOTHEK HAMBURG, PAPYRUS-SAMMLUNG

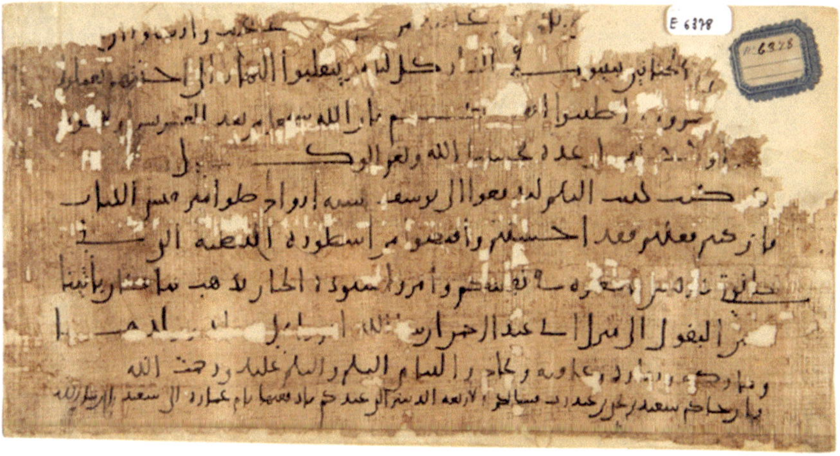

FIGURE 2.5 A a business letter (around 800) with a quotation of Q 65:7 (P.Louvre inv. SN 6378 = P.David-WeillLouvre 9)
© MUSÉE DU LOUVRE, DÉPARTEMENT DES ANTIQUITÉES EGYPTIENNES

(c) P.Mird. 23, an official letter found in Ḫirbat al-Mird/Palestine dated paleographically to the 8th century:
- l. 5: *"wa-qawluhu l-ḥaqq"* (Q 6:73).
- l. 5–6: *"yā ayyuhā llaḏīna ām[inū bi-llāhi wa-]rasūlihi"* (Q 24:62; 49:15; 57:7).
- l. 6: *liya l-amru* (Q: *wa-kāna amran*) *"maqḍiyyan"* (Q 19:21).

(d) P.Mird 28 (= P.KisterQuran), an official letter found in Ḫirbat al-Mird/Palestine dated paleographically to the 8th century:
- l. 5–10: *qāla fī kitābihi* [...] *"yā a[yyuh]ā allaḏī[na] āmanū [ttaqū llāha ḥaqqa] tuqātihi wa-lā tamūtu[nna illā wa-antum muslimūna] wa-ʿtaṣimū [bi-ḥabli llāhi ǧamīʿan] wa-lā tafarraqū [wa-ḏkurū] niʿmata llāhi"* (Q 3:102–103; the quotation is only read by Kister; Grohmann reads only single words).

(e) P.Marchands II 9, a private letter from the Fayyūm/Egypt, dated paleographically to the 9th century:
- l. v5: *qāla llāhu "yaṣilūna mā amara llāhu* (Q adds *bihi*) *an yūṣala"* (Q 13:21).
- l. v5: *qāla "bal ʿibādun mukramūna lā yasbiqūnahu bi-l-qawl"* (Q 21:26–27).
- l. v9–10: *qāla llāhu "fa-man ʿafā wa-aṣ[laḥa fa-ağruhu ʿalà llāhi innahu] lā yuḥibbu ẓ-ẓālimīn"* (Q 42:40; *ẓālimīn* in the Cairo print 1924 and papyrus without *alif*).

(f) P.Marchands II 26, a private letter from the Fayyūm/Egypt, dated paleographically to the 9th century:
- l. v12: *"wa-lā yunfiqūna nafaqatan ṣaǧīratan wa-lā kabīra"* (Q 9:121).
- l. v12: *"wa-lā yaṭaʾūna mawṭiʾan [yaǧī]ẓu l-kuffār"* (Q 9:120; immediately following the preceding quotation; no carrier for the *hamza* in *yaṭaʾūna* neither in the Qurʾān nor in the papyrus).
- l. v14: *"wa-qad aḥāṭa llāhu" bi-ḫalqihi* (Q: *bi-kulli šayʾin*) *"ʿilman" wa-ḫabaran* (Q 65:12).

(g) P.Marchands v/1 11, a private letter from the Fayyūm/Egypt, dated paleographically to the 9th century:
- l. 23–24: *"inna llaḏī" aḥyākum* (Q: *aḥyāhā*) *"la-muḥyī l-mawtà wa-huwa* (thus Q 42:9; yet Q 41:39: *innahu*) *ʿalà kulli šayʾin qadīr"* (Q 41:39).

(h) P.Hamb.Arab. II 34, a private letter dated paleographically to the 9th/10th centuries:
- l. 6: *li-qawli llāhi ʿazza wa-ǧalla "la-in šakartum la-azīdannakum"* (Q 14:7; with *la-in, in* the Qur᾽ān *yā᾽* is used as carrier for the *hamza*, in the papyrus *alif*).

(i) P.David-WeillLouvre 9, a business letter dated paleographically to the late 8th/early 9th century:
- l. 3: *fa-inna llāha "sa-yaǧʿalu* (Q adds *allāh*) *baʿda ʿusrin yusran" wa-yakūnu ḫayran* … (Q 65:7).

5 Evaluation: the Role of the Qur᾽ān in the Daily Life of the Letters' Scribes

Since around 780 letters were analyzed, the lack of Qur᾽ānic quotations in letters is significant. We find long, clearly intentional quotations in only nine letters; this represents only 1% of the corpus. Even when we add all records classified in the second category of short quotations, the Qur᾽ān was used only in around 50 letters, or less than 7% of the corpus. This means that the Qur᾽ān did not play an important role in the matters of daily life with which the letters were concerned.

The content of the nine letters with long Qur᾽ānic quotations does not allow us to determine why their scribes used these quotations. They were probably inserted for personal reasons such as the scribe's above-average interest in religion or wish to demonstrate his education. Despite their low number, intentional quotations present variants to the text of the modern Cairo edition (*riwāyat Ḥafṣ ʿan ʿĀṣim*). These variants range from orthographic changes, especially for the representation of *hamza* and a defective writing of *alif*, as we know this from early Qur᾽ān manuscripts, to a rearrangement of words or even verses. It might even be that these new arrangements are evidence of a variant of Qur᾽ānic text—especially the insertion of text from other verses (e.g., P.RagibLettreFamiliale has two words from Q 65:4 inserted in Q 65:2; and P.Marchands V/1 11 changes the connection of the sentence introduced by *innahu* to *wa-huwa*, as attested for a verse with similar content). Yet the omitting of the grammatically necessary *bihi* (Q 13:21 in P.Marchands II 9) shows that these quotations could originate in a setting where the scribe did not know the Qur᾽ān and the grammar of Qur᾽ānic Arabic perfectly. And I suppose that even the insertions mentioned and the change of verse order in P.Marchands II 26 (Q 9:121 preceding 9:120) could be the result of uncertain remembering, rather than possible evidence of variants common in Early Islamic Egypt.

Qur'ānic quotations were almost never the one main instrument used to mark the religion of the letter's scribe. All the examples quoted are extremely rare in letters on matters of daily life. Since all the letters exhibit an extremely large formulary shaped by religious speech, in the form of eulogies, prayers, and blessings that show a Muslim identity of the scribe, we can suppose that it was these elements rather than Qur'ānic quotations that formed a Muslim identity in the rural communities of Egypt, where the Qur'ān was possibly not known by every Muslim. Apart from some few excerpts used in daily life rituals, especially in prayer, Qur'ānic quotations were not a common element of letters. Obviously, letters do not suffice to claim that in the rural hinterland of Egypt, the Qur'ān was little known, yet the lack of quotations does make one think that probably only a small number of *ḥuffāẓ* lived there.

6 Parallel Epistolary Traditions I: Letters Transmitted in Literary Sources

To be able to estimate to what extent people quoted holy scriptures in letters to construct their religious identity, we will evaluate another three Arabic epistolary traditions: letters transmitted in literary sources, Judaeo-Arabic Letters, and letters written by Christians.

Let us first analyze letters transmitted in literary sources. Since the documentary letters analyzed above show a floating transition from letters in a simple language, influenced by spoken dialect, to artistically constructed letters, we can assume that official letters, especially letters for communication between high-ranking officials, were written in conformity with stylistic ideals of artful prose. It is noteworthy that P.HindsNubia in particular contains long intentional Qur'ānic quotations, since in our corpus this is the letter with the highest-ranking sender (Mūsà b. Kaʿb, governor of Egypt 758–759) and addressee (Cyriacus, king of Nubia c. 747–768). Letters written by educated *kuttāb* and now lost may possibly have more often contained references to the Qur'ān. A reasonably justified judgment must be based on collections of sample letters for the instruction of *kuttāb*.[16] The authenticity of these sample letters cannot be verified; in some cases it is obvious that they are fictious. During the long periods in between the date of the letter and the writing of the

16 Diem 2008: 849–852.

inšā'-works, and the long transmission of *inšā'*-literature by manuscripts, letters were probably adapted to new stylistic ideals. Since these collections were used to improve the style used by the scribes, their authors, to avoid being repetitive, also very often omitted well-known formulae that were already universally employed. Additionally, we must face the fact that until the 11th century—especially for Egypt, the origin of almost our full corpus—no collections of literary letters are preserved. Thus, for purposes of comparison with the documentary letters analyzed here, I consulted mainly the letters ascribed to the Prophet Muḥammad, and to people from his time and the time of the Rightly-Guided Caliphs, and a selection of further early, pre-10th-century letters from Syria and Iraq.

The collection of "original" documents from Early Islam by Hamidullah[17] consists of more than 400 documents. Not all of them are letters, and Hamidullah often refers to letters where no text is transmitted. Yet it is worth mentioning that relatively few of these letters have Qur'ānic quotations. These few quotations are found in letters dealing with politico-religious questions: in invitations to conversion ascribed to Muḥammad (e.g., no. 27 addressed to Emperor Heraclius, Q 4:171 and 9:29; no. 29 addressed to the Patriarch of Constantinople, Q 2:196; no. 49 addressed to a Coptic patriarch, Q 3:64; no. 96–97 addressed to the Christians of Naǧrān, Q 3:64), and in letters attributed to the Rightly-Guided Caliphs concerning the death of the Prophet (e.g., no. 282 attributed to Abū Bakr, Q 3:144; 18:17; 21:34; 33:4; 35:6) or the division of conquered territories and the rule of the caliphs (no. 354–355, ascribed to ʿUmar b. al-Ḫaṭṭāb, containing long parts of Q 59). Even if most of these letters were written to construct a relationship between Muḥammad and the ancestors of politically important people from the first centuries AH, so that the style was of secondary importance, the lack of Qur'ānic quotations in several hundred letters is astonishing. Many of them present a basic formulary that according to Diem's research corresponds to the formulary of papyrus letters.[18] Even if some formulae are not attested in documentary traditions, and even if most blessings and slide-in invocations are lacking in literary tradition, we might suppose that they transmit, or at least mirror, the formulae and style of Early Islamic letters.

This is confirmed by letter collections preserved in *inšā'* literature:[19] since the transmitted letters are much longer than papyrus letters, more quotations

---

17 Ḥamīd Allāh [Hamidullah] 1956.

18 Diem 2008: 857–861.

19 I examined these letters as quoted in al-Qalqašandī's *Subḥ al-aʿšà*, which is based on older collections. Most of his examples are from Fāṭimid and later periods, but he also offers examples from the 7th century onward. See al-Qalqašandī 1913–1919.

are found. But even a letter composed by Abū Isḥāq aṣ-Ṣābiʾ, the leading stylist of ʿAbbāsid epistolography,[20] has next to no direct quotations.[21] Some letters do have quotations, such as a letter ascribed to Muʿāwiya (Q 26:128)[22] and the letters of the ʿAbbāsid caliphs al-Muqtafī (Q 39:36), al-Muʿtaṣim (Q 4:128 and 14:7), and al-Muṭīʿ (Q 8:46 and 3:103).[23] An increase in the use of Qurʾānic quotations can be observed in letters from Ayyūbid and Mamlūk times. Most interestingly, in some Mamlūk letters Qurʾānic quotations are used as invocations, whereby they replace the Basmala.[24] As we will see below, in Judaeo-Arabic letters, verses from the Tanakh also serve as invocations. Obviously, letters transmitted in literary sources have a higher percentage of short and long Qurʾānic quotations than do papyrus letters, so we might conjecture a development from relatively rare quotations in early letters to quite frequent use of quotations in Mamlūk times. But since letters transmitted in literary sources are longer than papyrus letters, the Qurʾānic elements in them are in fact no more common relative to the length of the text than is the case in papyrus letters.

7 Parallel Epistolary Traditions II: Judaeo-Arabic Letters

The second epistolary tradition is a documentary one: by using the Hebrew script while writing Arabic, Arabic-speaking Jews constituted their own identity. Only a small number of these letters were found in circumstances similar to those of the Arabic papyri letters, i.e., by excavation.[25] These letters, probably originating from the 9th century, contain no quotations from the Tanakh; yet, given the very small number preserved, we cannot conclude that the Judaeo-Arabic letter tradition at that time had no quotations from the Tanakh.

Most Judaeo-Arabic letters were preserved in the Cairo Geniza founded in the 11th century. Some documents might be older, or are perhaps copies of older documents, but most letters are younger than the corpus analyzed for Qurʾānic quotations, and they come from a slightly different context: while the Arabic

---

20 aṣ-Ṣābiʾ [1966].

21 See al-Qalqašandī 1913–1919 VI: 562–563; 564–568; VII: 82–84; 104–106; 113–115; VIII: 135–136; 137. Contrary to this image, in another letter written by Abū Isḥāq aṣ-Ṣābiʾ, eight quotations are found (al-Qalqašandī 1913–1919 VI: 483–492).

22 al-Qalqašandī 1913–1919 VI: 388.

23 al-Qalqašandī 1913–1919 VI: 398–413.

24 al-Qalqašandī 1913–1919 VI: 422; 427 (two letters of ʿAbbāsid caliphs in Cairo, the second one quoted by al-Qalqašandī in a chapter entitled “Letters Opening with a Verse from the Qurʾān”); VII: 258 (a letter of the Mamlūk sultan Qalāwūn).

25 P.BlauJudaeoArabicPapyri.

letters originated in the more rural hinterland, the Geniza documents were written in the capital and prove the global entanglement of the Jewish community there. As with the Arabic letters transmitted in literary sources, the length of the Judaeo-Arabic letters stands out. The fact that almost all letters examined seem to be longer than letters in Arabic scripts may be due in part to the conditions of preservation, but regardless of the reason, the probability for scriptural quotations is slightly higher due to their length.[26]

In a larger number of Judaeo-Arabic letters in the Geniza, we find quotations from the Tanakh. They are mostly used as invocations located at the beginning of the letter. Though Judaeo-Arabic letters use the Basmala, either in the standard form or in an abbreviated version, or a Hebrew formula also meaning "In the name of God,"[27] Judaeo-Arabic letters show a higher variance. Besides other formulae also used in Muslim letters but in other places, single verses from the Tanakh, partly combined from different books, initiate letters. According to Almbladh's study, around 1% of her corpus (10 letters out of 935) use quotations as invocations. All these letters mention different verses. The broader introductory formulary also quotes the Tanakh; and more often than in Arabic letters, the Tanakh is quoted in the middle of the text.[28] There are quotations in formulae for special occasions, especially for voyages and condolences.[29] Except for these, all other quotations have been written without defined formulaic reasons. Overall, about every sixth or even every fifth Judaeo-Arabic letter has one or more quotations from the Tanakh.

One reason for this is the one mentioned earlier: the letters from the Geniza are often very long. But this does not explain the proportion of letters quoting or not quoting the respective Holy Scripture. The relatively high numbers of quotations in Judaeo-Arabic letters may be due to the wish to stress religious identity. Although the use of Hebrew script already showed group identity, letter formulary was heavily influenced by the formulary of Arabic letters: as already noted, quotations from the Tanakh sometimes replaced an invocation in Basmala form.

---

26 Since all major editions are in Hebrew, my analysis is based on collections in English translation, where all Hebrew insertions (including quotations from the Tanakh) are marked. I have not been able to check the originals, so the following remarks do not give much more than a general trend.

27 Almbladh 2010: 48.

28 Goitein and Friedman 2008 II: 392–393 no. 35; 435 no. 45a; 548 no. 74; III: 683 no. 29; 754–755 no. 47; 759–761 no. 48; 768 no. 49.

29 For seafaring, see Goitein and Friedman 2008 II: 475 no. 55; 481 nos. 56–57; III: 681 no. 29; 729 no. 41 (all quoting Psalm 107:8); for condolence letters, see Goitein and Friedman 2008 II: 539 no. 71; III: 626 no. 15 (all quoting Isaiah 63:14).

Although the invocation of God is an old Semitic formula, the Basmala proper was introduced by the Arabs. In Hebrew tradition, no invocation was needed to begin a letter, and many Judaeo-Arabic letters have no invocation. The Basmala was possibly perceived as not originally Jewish. This may also have caused the tendency to abbreviate it; to insert it in a Hebrew variant; to substitute for it a quotation from the Tanakh; or, as a fourth option not yet mentioned, to replace it with another Islamic formula, such as the Ḥasbala or formulae based on *tawakkul* references. Although we know these formulae as formulaic quotations from the Qurʾān, they were probably not perceived as of Qurʾānic origin and thereby as clearly connoting Islam. Much later than our letters were written, we find a critical dispute on the usage of Islamic formulae.[30] Since a minority of Judaeo-Arabic letters rejected any possible Islamic connotation to Islam and replaced all formulaic elements with Jewish equivalents, it can be supposed that their scribes tried to ensure their peculiar Jewish identity in a double way—not only by writing Arabic in Hebrew script, but also by eliminating all references to other religions. Thus a major problem of the dearth of pre-10th-century Judaeo-Arabic letters is that we cannot determine whether efforts to affirm a Jewish identity began before Arabic letter formulae were perceived as religiously neutral or only when Jews started to use Arabic as documentary language. I assume that it is more probable that the need for differentiation developed some time after the adoption of Arabic, since the adoption illustrates the Jews' disregard for the necessity of constructing their own identity in daily life writings.

8 Parallel Epistolary Traditions III: Christian-Arabic Letters

The third Arabic epistolary tradition, the Christian-Arabic one, is hardly identifiable, since the Christians of Egypt did not use a different script for their Arabic writings. Christian-Arabic letters have to be identified by their content, yet we have seen that Muslims (and Jews, when not using Hebrew script) did not necessarily integrate signs into their letters to mark the religious identity of their scribes.

Letters probably written by Christians before the year 1000 are: CPR XVI 14; 34; P.AnawatiPapyrusChrétien; P.Heid.Arab. II 2; 34; P.Mird 45; 46; P.Vind.Arab. III 20.[31] They feature the same formulary as all other papyrus letters, so they are

30 Friedman 1980: 92–93.

31 According to to Björnesjö 1996: 97 and 104, P.Jahn 12 also originates from a Christian mi-

listed above if they contain formulae based on Qur'ānic quotations. A Christian origin is only evident by specific Christian formulae—such as a variant Basmala, *bi-smi llāhi l-abi wa-li-bni wa-rūḥi l-qudusi ilāhin wāḥid*—or by the designation of the sender and addressee as Christians, especially if both were monks. In the letters mentioned, substantial parts of formulae correspond to Muslim formulae, even if those are Qur'ānic.[32] To judge whether only these few letters are of Christian origin, we need to know when Christians began to use Arabic as a language for their own communication. Up to the 10th century, we have a parallel Greek and Coptic epistolary tradition; it seems that Coptic letters did not cease to be written until the 11th century.[33] The moment when Christians started to use Arabic to write to other Christians is contested. According to Almbladh, much points to the late 8th century,[34] Richter prefers the 9th/10th centuries for Melkites and the 11th century for Copts.[35]

9 Correlation of Formulaic Changes and of Changing Needs to Express Religious Identity

As mentioned above there was a change in letter formulary. This change mostly concerned the Qur'ānic quotations given under 3.1.3, 3.1.4, and 3.1.6 above. At a certain point in time, the scribes ceased to combine the verbalized Ḥamdala with the first part of the Šahāda. While most formulaic quotations from the Qur'ān were not perceived as Islamic, the Islamic character of a letter was assured by writing this kind of Ḥamdala. Yet in Early Islam, even the use of Arabic language and script was a sign of an affiliation to Islam.

By the process of Arabization, this symbolic character of language and script was lost. Arabized Jews or Christians had to develop their own letter formulary. Since only the part *aḥmadu ilayka llāha llaḏī lā ilāha illā huwa* was understood as Islamic, by omitting this part the complete remaining formulary could be adopted by Christians and Jews. Thus this change may indicate that it was not only Muslims who were writing Arabic letters, but also Christians and Jews.

---

lieu. Though the addressee is a Mēna Pegosh, the use of the formula *fa-innī aḥmadu llāha llaḏī lā ilāha illā huwa* makes this attribution questionable.

32 Almbladh 2010: 58 suggests that the use of the standard Ḥamdala (from the 10th century onward, see above) had been transferred from Christian models into the formulary of Arabic letters.

33 Richter 2008: 743.

34 Almbladh 2010: 56.

35 Richter 2008: 743, who understands P.AnawatiPapyrusChrétien as originating from Melkite tradition.

Unfortunately, because of the lack of dated letters, the period in which this happened cannot be determined. But much points to the end of the 8th century: not only the paleography of the letters but also literary sources indicate that the use of the Taṣliya in letters was introduced under the reign of Hārūn ar-Rašīd (786–809). According to estimations of the percentage of Muslims in Egypt, around the year 900 CE Muslims evolved from a small ruling minority into a visible major group, so that their language became more prominent.[36]

Thus, for Arabic papyrus letters, we need to distinguish between two periods: (1) from the Islamic conquest until the end of the 8th century, and (2) the 9th and the 10th centuries. From the Islamic conquest until the late 8th century, Arabic was the language of the ruling class and was used mainly for official letters, then often accompanied by translations into Greek, and for letters inside the small Muslim communities. An Arabic letter was marked as Islamic (i.e., written by a Muslim) in several ways: (a) by language, since Arabic was not understood by many non-Muslims; (b) by script; and (c) by formulae, namely, (i) with the verbalized Ḥamdala combined with the Šahāda, (ii) sometimes with the greetings *as-salāmu ʿalaykum wa-raḥmatu llāhi wa-barākatuhu* and *salāmun ʿalà man ittabʿa l-hudà*, respectively, with Muslim names, and (iii) very rarely, with Qurʾānic quotations. There was no real need for Qurʾānic quotations because a letter written in Arabic writing and in the Arabic language was already quite strongly defined as Islamic; as already mentioned, the insertion of Qurʾān quotations was prompted by motives such as showing one's own piety or demonstrating the level of one's education. The Christians and Jews maintained their own epistolary traditions, except when in communication with Muslim authorities, especially on tax matters.

Around 800 CE, the language situation in letters became more complicated. Religious affiliation began to be expressed mostly by formulae: while Muslims used the Taṣliya and Christians used trinitarian variants of the Basmala, further means of expression were at the Jews' disposal only by writing in Hebrew script. The Arabic epistolary tradition seemed to break up into three religions. The traditional Christian and Jewish epistolary traditions remained in place during

36 Bulliet 1979, 92–103. Bulliet's study rests upon an analysis of personal names in biographical collections and their differentiation in Muslim and non-Muslim names. Such a differentiation could enlighten documentary sources, but it is debatable whether or not names clearly correlate with religious affiliation. For the Iberian Peninsula, a strong correlation is sometimes denied (see Aguilar 1994: 362), but Latin sources (Alvarus 1973: 314–315) prove that about 150 years after the conquest, Christians began to write in Arabic. We might assume that in most territories of the Islamic conquest, a period of 150 years was necessary for the indigenous population to adopt Arabic.

the period examined here. Nevertheless, and most importantly, not all Arabic letters can be attributed to a specific religion. In fact, letters from the 9th century onward lack signs of religious affiliation: their formulae are monotheistic, and many elements were utilized by followers of all three religions. As a result, the content and formulae of a letter do not suffice to determine the religion of the letter's scribe when all imaginable religious signs beyond monotheism are missing.

Contrary to the assumptions that Jewish and Christian Arabic letters are relatively small groups because their communities had other way to express themselves, and that the majority of Arabic papyrus letters are clearly Islamic, the fourth group—that of monotheistic letters—in fact makes up the great majority. As mentioned earlier, in our corpus of 500 letters examined in detail, of which about 400 are from the 9th and 10th centuries, the Taṣliya is found in 33 letters only; small Qur'ānic quotations are probably used by Muslims only in another 15;[37] and longer quotations in only 4. If we accept that these were the three means by which the scribes of papyrus letters in the 9th and 10th centuries expressed their religious affiliation, then only 52 of around 400 letters are definitely of Muslim origin. If we implement the same method for letters of Christian origin, only 1 is purely Christian (all other Christian letters mentioned were so identified because they were written by monks, contain Coptic, or show their Christian origin in another way). Yet the great majority of letters connote monotheistic belief only. They were not necessarily written between followers of different religions, since it is quite improbable that almost 90 % of these letters are examples of interreligious communication.

Thus we can only conclude that in 9th- and 10th-century Egypt, scribes did not want to expose their religious affiliation. Though every letter is visibly religious, containing religious speech in the form of prayers, eulogies, etc., this marked a shared monotheistic belief and did not serve to delineate between different groups. Only a small number of scribes felt the need to show their religion, and used special signs for it—Muslims, special formulae and Qur'ānic quotations; Christians, special formulae or Coptic; and Jews, Hebrew script.[38]

37 For this, I counted only examples from section 3.2.3 above.

38 Possibly some of the "monotheistic" letters were written by Jews, especially in business matters in between people belonging to different religious groups.

10 Religious Identity in Pre-Islamic Papyrus Letters

In the 7th/8th century, an Arabic letter was clearly Islamic, and Christians and Jews had their own ways of writing letters. The question remains whether the later religious indifference was a new development due to the Arabization of Egypt, or whether the Egyptian letter culture in Egypt had inherited this indifference to showing religious affiliation from earlier times.

In Egypt, letter-writing culture can be traced back far into Antiquity. Especially interesting for comparison are letters from Late Antiquity, as in this period the religious affiliation of most Egyptians changed from paganism/polytheism to Christianity. With respect to languages, we find two epistolary traditions: Greek and Coptic. Greek was used exclusively as a language for writing, although from the 3rd century BCE until the 3rd century CE it was not understood by most Egyptians; up to the 8th century it continued being used in parallel with Coptic, and up to the 11th century, it was sporadically used.[39] According to papyri.info, more than 4,000 Greek letters from all these centuries have been edited.[40] Coptic was used from the 4th century on in parallel with Greek, and from the Islamic conquest in parallel with Arabic, until in the 11th century it was completely replaced by Arabic. According to Richter, about 2,500 Coptic letters have been edited,[41] while a search for the document type "letter" in the *Brussels Coptic Database* (BCD) results in more than 3,700 letters.[42] Coptic letters were often written not on papyrus but on ostraca. According to the *Brussels Coptic Database*, about 2,300 of the 3,700 letters are ostraca. Ostraca was a cheaper writing material for which there existed special formulae excusing the scribe for not honoring the addressee with a papyrus; we might assume that Coptic ostraca originated from a lower social level than Greek and Arabic letters.

When comparing the smaller number of Greek and Coptic with Arabic letters, it is interesting to note that while Greek and Coptic formularies are the same, Arabic letters introduce a completely new kind of formulary. In some Coptic letters we find formulae that are translations from Arabic formulae,[43] but these letters are younger and probably influenced by Arabic letter style. There are "precursors" of the Basmala, such as the Greek *ἐν θεῷ or ἐν κυρίῳ* that sometimes acts as an introducing invocation and the Coptic ϩⲙⲡⲣⲁⲛ ⲙⲡⲛⲟⲩⲧⲉ

39 Richter 2008: 742.
40 papyri.info (last accessed 3 January 2014).
41 Richter 2008: 744.
42 http://dev.ulb.ac.be/philo/bad/copte/ (last accessed 3 January 2014).
43 Richter 2008: 763–768.

(ⲛϣⲟⲣⲡ), "In the name of God (at first)!"; ϲⲩⲛ ⲑⲉⲱ was sometimes used as an invocation in both Greek and Coptic letters. In the concluding formulae of Coptic letters, sometimes a ϩⲙⲡϫⲟⲉⲓⲥ, "in the Lord," is added. In Coptic letters that probably come from pre-Islamic times, sometimes a ϯⲣⲏⲛⲏ ⲛⲁⲕ, "Peace be with you!," is attested. According to Richter, eulogies of the type "God preserves you/prolongs your life/blesses you" are results of the Arabic epistolary style.[44] Compared to Arabic letters with their long formulaic parts, the formulary of Coptic, and even more so of Greek letters, is quite short; it mainly consists of an initial greeting mentioning sender and addressee, a prayer or second greeting, and a farewell. All three parts are built of a few words, and the phrases are only slightly varied. We might deduce that the formulary of Arabic letters was a special development of or derived from a non-Egyptian epistolary tradition.

An examination of Greek and Coptic letters shows that quotations of and allusions to Holy Scriptures appear even more infrequently than do Qur'ānic allusions in Arabic letters. Greek letters from the 3rd/4th centuries have been closely analyzed for biblical quotations, since it was hoped to find early attestations of the Greek New Testament: in a corpus of more than 700 Greek and Coptic letters, only in 14 letters were quotations identified, and in 28 letters allusions found (to the Bible and Tanakh, respectively, and Manichean scriptures).[45] Yet most of these allusions were constructed by modern researchers to allow them to designate letters as of Christian origin(!), since their interest in Jewish and Manichean letters was much lower. Evaluating these passages in a more objective way makes it clear that at most 1% of the corpus contains scriptural reminiscences. For later Coptic letters, there are no studies on biblical quotations; my own reading of BKU I–III, P.Kell.Copt. 1, P.Lond.Copt. 1, P.Ryl.Copt., O.Crum and O.CrumVC (together 986 letters) showed that biblical quotations are as rare as in Greek and older Coptic letters.

Also in this earlier, comparable corpus there is the question how far letters expressed religious affiliation. In Greek papyrology, six criteria have been formulated for identifying a letter as of Christian origin: (1) The use of *θεός* or *κύριος* as a denomination of God in the singular; (2) the use of specific Christian adjectives in the address (such as *ἀγαπητός*); (3) Christian names (mostly biblical) and titles; (4) Bible quotations and reminiscences; (5) the use of *nomina sacra* (names of God abbreviated in the way that only the first and last letter is written); and (6) crosses on letters.[46] According to newer research, most of these

44 Richter 2008: 763–768.
45 Choat 2006: 74–76.
46 Naldini 1968.

criteria are problematic and instead indicate a broader monotheistic, or even pagan, background. In particular, presumably Christian names were assumed by pagans working in temples, presumably Christian formulae were used by non-Christians, pagans wrote their letters in the name of one god and designated him, of course, using the singular, etc.[47]

Therefore, instead of the old classification in which clearly Christian letters replaced pagan ones, modern research acts on the assumption of six categories: (1) pagan/polytheistic; (2) monotheistic; (3) Jewish; (4) Manichean; (5) Christian; and (6) not-attributable. Though many letters can be considered Christian, not-attributable letters are found most often and monotheistic letters also in great numbers. Jewish and Manichean letters (Coptic Manichean letters are only contained in P.Kell.Copt. I) are only known in small numbers; both religions were always minorities.[48]

For the corpus of Coptic letters from the time of the Arabic rule, examination of expressing religious identity in letters is lacking. It seems feasible to postulate the existence of the categories "monotheistic," "Christian," and possibly "not-attributable" and "Jewish." With the change of the Arabic letter formulary that allowed writing in Arabic without denying a Christian identity, the use of Coptic lost its function for displaying a non-Muslim identity.

11 Changing Religious Identities in Egypt according to Papyrus Letters of the First Millennium CE

Therefore, in papyrus letters of Egypt in the first millennium CE, we can discern a number of *distinct* letter-writing cultures that displayed religious identity by language and/or script: an Islamo-Arabic culture in the 7th/8th centuries CE, a Christian-Coptic culture up to the 10th century (and later), and a Judaeo-Arabic culture.

Alongside this, a *common* letter-writing culture existed: in pre-Islamic Egypt, this common culture used first Greek, then Coptic, and starting from the 9th century onward, when it had lost its religious affiliation, Arabic. These multi-religious cultures were based not only on a common language as a medium of communication, but also on a shared monotheistic formulaic language. The main elements of religious speech did not differ. For the time being, we cannot

47 See Luijendijk 2008 for the 3rd century and Choat 2006 for the 4th century.

48 Choat 2006: 152–154 has as a distribution in a corpus of 721 letters: 355 not-attributable, 219 Christian, 73 monotheistic, 40 Manichean, 31 pagan, and 3 Jewish.

say conclusively whether this common letter culture was due to the need for communication across religious borders or instead to an indifference toward religious identity and distinction, for we still need to examine closely all sources on daily life issues.

The parallel existence of letters that are marked as Islamic, Christian, or Jewish hints at an interest in religious distinction, but since only small numbers of letters are clearly assignable to a specific religion, it seems that only a relatively small proportion of the populace was really interested in religion and religious difference. Especially in letters written by Muslims, a need for specific Islamic formulae can be observed. Additionally, the Muslim identity could be expressed by quotations from the Qur'ān. Since formulae such as the Taṣliya sufficed to indicate identity and affiliation, Qur'ānic quotations were more a sign of personal, individual interest in faith, and possibly also a sign to mark elevated education. According to preserved documentary letters, we can assume that in the first Islamic centuries, extensive knowledge of the Qur'ān in the rural hinterlands of Egypt was relatively rare.

Appendix: All Qur'ānic Quotations

On the following pages, I compare all quotations found in papyrus letters with their correspondents in the Qur'ān. Quotations that could be derived from more than one verse are only compared with the first of these verses. In cases of frequent references, only an example quotation, not all records, are shown.

	Text of the papyrus	**Text according to the Cairo Qur'ān (*riwāyat Ḥafṣ ʿan ʿĀṣim*)**
Q 1:1 (P.Ness. 61.1 and many more letters)	سم الله الرحمن الرحم	بِسۡمِ ٱللَّهِ ٱلرَّحۡمَٰنِ ٱلرَّحِيمِ
Q 1:2 (P.RagibLettreFamiliale.7 and many more letters)	حمد الله	ٱلۡحَمۡدُ لِلَّهِ رَبِّ ٱلۡعَٰلَمِينَ

(*cont.*)

	Text of the papyrus	Text according to the Cairo Qur'ān (*riwāyat Ḥafṣ ʿan ʿĀṣim*)
Q 1:2 (CPR XVI 25.13 and many more letters)	الحمد لله رب العلمىں	ٱلْحَمْدُ لِلَّهِ رَبِّ ٱلْعَٰلَمِينَ
Q 1:2 (P.RagibQurra 1.3–4)	فانى احمد الله	ٱلْحَمْدُ لِلَّهِ رَبِّ ٱلْعَٰلَمِينَ
Q 2:40 (P.HindsNubia.10–11)	وفال اوفوا ٮعهدى اوف ٮعهدكم واىاى فارهبون	وَأَوْفُوا بِعَهْدِي أُوفِ بِعَهْدِكُمْ وَإِيَّايَ فَارْهَبُونِ
Q 2:49 et *passim* (P.Mird 63.11)	سو العداب	سُوءَ الْعَذَابِ
Q 2:61 (P.Heid.Arab. II 43.5–6)	الدى هو حىر	بِالَّذِي هُوَ خَيْرٌ
Q 2:61 (P.Marchands V/1 6.5–6)	الدى هو حىر	بِالَّذِي هُوَ خَيْرٌ
Q 2:70; 6:128 (P.SijpesteijnArmyEconomics.4 and other letters)	ان سا الله	إِن شَآءَ ٱللَّهُ
Q 2:104 et *passim* (P.Mird 23.5–6)	ىا اىها الدىں امـ[ـىوا]	يَا أَيُّهَا الَّذِينَ آمَنُوا
Q 2:156 (P.Jahn 14.15–16)	اىا لله والىه راحعوں	إِنَّا لِلَّهِ وَإِنَّا إِلَيْهِ رَاجِعُونَ
Q 2:156 (P.Ryl.Arab. I VII 43.1) Q 2:156 (P.Marchands III 29r.3)	فاىا لله والىه راحعوں	إِنَّا لِلَّهِ وَإِنَّا إِلَيْهِ رَاجِعُونَ

(*cont.*)

	Text of the papyrus	Text according to the Cairo Qur'ān (*riwāyat Ḥafṣ ʿan ʿĀṣim*)
Q 3:9 (P.Ryl.Arab. I VII 43.2)	الدى لا ىحلف المىعد	إِنَّ ٱللَّهَ لَا يُخْلِفُ ٱلْمِيعَادَ
Q 3:38 (P.Marchands II 23.6)	اىه سمىع الدعا	إِنَّكَ سَمِيعُ ٱلدُّعَاءِ
Q 3:38 (P.Cair.Arab. 301.6)	اىه سمىع الدعا	إِنَّكَ سَمِيعُ ٱلدُّعَاءِ
Q 3:173 (CPR XVI 29.9 and other letters)	حسىىا الله وىعم الوكىل	حَسْبُنَا ٱللَّهُ وَنِعْمَ ٱلْوَكِيلُ
Q 5:17 (P.Hamb.Arab. II 33 l. r3)	اىه على ما ىسا ڡدىر	وَٱللَّهُ عَلَىٰ كُلِّ شَيْءٍ قَدِيرٌ
Q 5:17 (HanafiPrivateLetters 2.3–4)	[انه على] كل سى ڡدىر	وَٱللَّهُ عَلَىٰ كُلِّ شَيْءٍ قَدِيرٌ
Q 5:17 (P.Marchands II 2v.2)	اىه على كل سى ڡدىر	وَٱللَّهُ عَلَىٰ كُلِّ شَيْءٍ قَدِيرٌ
Q 5:17 (P.Marchands II 2v.5)	اىه على كل سى ڡدىر	وَٱللَّهُ عَلَىٰ كُلِّ شَيْءٍ قَدِيرٌ
Q 5:65 et *passim* (P.Hamb.Arab. II 7.11)	حىاٮ الىعىم	جَنَّاتِ ٱلنَّعِيمِ
Q 5:65 et *passim* (P.Hamb.Arab. II 45.4)	حىاٮ الىعىم	جَنَّاتِ ٱلنَّعِيمِ
Q 5:65 et *passim* (P.Heid.Arab. II 8.2)	حىاٮ [الىعىم]	جَنَّاتِ ٱلنَّعِيمِ

(*cont.*)

	Text of the papyrus	Text according to the Cairo Qurʾān (*riwāyat Ḥafṣ ʿan ʿĀṣim*)
Q 6:54 et *passim* (P.Jahn 1r.15–16 and many more letters)	والسلم علىک ورحمب الله	فَقُلْ سَلَٰمٌ عَلَيْكُمْ
Q 6:73 (P.Mird. 23.5)	وهوله الحو	قَوْلُهُ ٱلْحَقُّ
Q 6:163 (P.Berl.Arab. II 79r.4 and another 17 letters)	لا سرىک له	لَا شَرِيكَ لَهُۥ
Q 8:29 et *passim* (P.Marchands V/1 6.8)	ىحعل الله لک الـ[ـڡرڡان]	ٱللَّهَ يَجْعَل لَّكُمْ فُرْقَانًا
Q 9:120–121 (P.Marchands II 26v.12)	ولا ىىڡڡون ںڡڡه صعىره ولا كىىر ولا ىطون موطىا [ىعـ]ـط الكڡار	وَلَا يَطَـُٔونَ مَوْطِئًا يَغِيظُ ٱلْكُفَّارَ ... وَلَا يُنفِقُونَ نَفَقَةً صَغِيرَةً وَلَا كَبِيرَةً
Q 10:68 and 21:26 (CPR XVI 23.5)	فسحان الله	قَالُوا۟ ٱتَّخَذَ ٱللَّهُ وَلَدًا سُبْحَٰنَهُۥ
Q 10:68; 21:26 (CPR XVI 30r.3)	سحان الله	قَالُوا۟ ٱتَّخَذَ ٱللَّهُ وَلَدًا سُبْحَٰنَهُۥ
Q 10:68; 21:26 (P.AnawatiPapyrusChrétien r.3)	سحان الله	قَالُوا۟ ٱتَّخَذَ ٱللَّهُ وَلَدًا سُبْحَٰنَهُۥ
Q 10:68; 21:26 (P.Berl.Arab. II 63.4)	سحان الله	قَالُوا۟ ٱتَّخَذَ ٱللَّهُ وَلَدًا سُبْحَٰنَهُۥ
Q 10:68; 21:26 (P.Marchands II 3.3)	سحان الله	قَالُوا۟ ٱتَّخَذَ ٱللَّهُ وَلَدًا سُبْحَٰنَهُۥ

(*cont.*)

	Text of the papyrus	Text according to the Cairo Qur'ān (*riwāyat Ḥafṣ ʿan ʿĀṣim*)
Q 10:68; 21:26 (P.Ryl.Arab. I VI 18.3)	سحاں الله العطم	قَالُوا ٱتَّخَذَ ٱللَّهُ وَلَدًا سُبْحَٰنَهُ
Q 10:68; 11:56; 21:26 (P.Cair.Arab. 331.9)	ٮوكلٮ على الله	إِنِّي تَوَكَّلْتُ عَلَى ٱللَّهِ
Q 11:61 (P.Marchands II 26.26) Q 11:56 (P.Marchands III 3r.12)	ڡرٮک عرٮر رحىم ڡرٮ محٮ لا اله الا هو	إِنَّ رَبِّي قَرِيبٌ مُّجِيبٌ
Q 11:61 (P.Prag.Arab. 93.2)	اںه ڡرٮ محـ[ـٮ]	إِنَّ رَبِّي قَرِيبٌ مُّجِيبٌ
Q 11:73 (P.RagibLettreFamiliale.14 and many more letters)	والسلم علىكم ورحمٮ الله وٮركىه	رَحْمَتُ ٱللَّهِ وَبَرَكَٰتُهُۥ عَلَيْكُمْ
Q 11:85 (P.Mird 91.1)	ٮالڡسط	بِٱلْقِسْطِ
Q 12:18 (P.Berl.Arab. II 41r.10–11)	والله المسول المساں	وَٱللَّهُ ٱلْمُسْتَعَانُ
Q 12:18 (P.Marchands III 8.6)	[والله/ڡالله] المساں	وَٱللَّهُ ٱلْمُسْتَعَانُ
Q 12:18 (P.Marchands V/1 11.18–19)	ڡالله المساں	وَٱللَّهُ ٱلْمُسْتَعَانُ
Q 12:18 (P.Ryl.Arab. I VI 14.6)	ڡالله المساں	وَٱللَّهُ ٱلْمُسْتَعَانُ

(*cont.*)

	Text of the papyrus	Text according to the Cairo Qurʾān (*riwāyat Ḥafṣ ʿan ʿĀṣim*)
Q 13:21 (P.Marchands II 9v.5)	فا[...] الله ىصلون ما امر الله ان ىوصل	وَالَّذِينَ يَصِلُونَ مَا أَمَرَ اللَّهُ بِهِ أَن يُوصَلَ
Q 14:7 (P.Hamb.Arab. II 34.6)	لقول الله عر وحل لان سكرىم لا ربدىكم	لَئِن شَكَرْتُمْ لَأَزِيدَنَّكُمْ
Q 16:91 (P.HindsNubia.7–10)	والله ىارك وىعالى ىقول فى كىابه اوفوا ىعهد الله ادا عهدىم ولا ىىقصوا الاىمان ىعد ىوكىدها وقد حعلىم الله علىكم كفىلا ان الله ىعلم ما ىفعلون	وَأَوْفُوا بِعَهْدِ اللَّهِ إِذَا عَاهَدتُّمْ وَلَا تَنقُضُوا الْأَيْمَانَ بَعْدَ تَوْكِيدِهَا وَقَدْ جَعَلْتُمُ اللَّهَ عَلَيْكُمْ كَفِيلًا إِنَّ اللَّهَ يَعْلَمُ مَا تَفْعَلُونَ
Q 19:21 (P.Mird. 23.6)	لى الامر مقصـ[ـىا]	وَكَانَ أَمْرًا مَّقْضِيًّا
Q 20:47 (P.SijpesteijnQurra.26–27 and many more letters)	والسلم على من اىىع الهدى	وَٱلسَّلَٰمُ عَلَىٰ مَنِ ٱتَّبَعَ ٱلْهُدَىٰٓ
Q 20:47 (P.HindsNubia.67–68)	والسلم على اولىا الله	وَٱلسَّلَٰمُ عَلَىٰ مَنِ ٱتَّبَعَ ٱلْهُدَىٰٓ
Q 20:47 (P. P.GrohmannQorra-Brief.8–9)	والسلم على محمد النى ورحمت الله	وَٱلسَّلَٰمُ عَلَىٰ مَنِ ٱتَّبَعَ ٱلْهُدَىٰٓ
Q 59:22; 59:23 (P.Heid.Arab. I 1.4 and many more letters)	الله الدى لا اله الا هو	هُوَ ٱللَّهُ ٱلَّذِى لَآ إِلَٰهَ إِلَّا هُوَ
Q 21:26–27 (P.Marchands II 9v.5)	قال ىل عىاد مكرمون لا ىسىقوىه ىالقول	بَلْ عِبَادٌ مُّكْرَمُونَ لَا يَسْبِقُونَهُ بِالْقَوْلِ

(*cont.*)

	Text of the papyrus	Text according to the Cairo Qur'ān (*riwāyat Ḥafṣ ʿan ʿĀṣim*)
Q 33:56 (CPR XVI 18r.4)	[ـ]ـل ا[لد]ـه[ىصـ]ـلى على محمد ىسا	إِنَّ ٱللَّهَ وَمَلَٰئِكَتَهُۥ يُصَلُّونَ عَلَى ٱلنَّبِيِّ
Q 33:56 (CPR XVI 25.13–14 and many more letters)	وصلى الله على محمد النى واله وسلم سلىما	إِنَّ ٱللَّهَ وَمَلَٰئِكَتَهُۥ يُصَلُّونَ عَلَى ٱلنَّبِيِّ
Q 33:56 (P.Cair.Arab. 324.3–4)	وصلى الله على على سىد الاولىں والاحرىں وعلى اله الطاهرىں وسلم سلىما	إِنَّ ٱللَّهَ وَمَلَٰئِكَتَهُۥ يُصَلُّونَ عَلَى ٱلنَّبِيِّ
Q 34:50 (P.Marchands II 26.1)	فانه رحىم سمىع ڡرىب	إِنَّهُۥ سَمِيعٌ قَرِيبٌ
Q 41:39 with insertion from Q 42:9 (P.Marchands V/1 11.23–24)	ان الدى احىا كم لمحى الموىا وهو على كل سى ڡدىر	إِنَّ الَّذِي أَحْيَاهَا لَمُحْيِي الْمَوْتَىٰ إِنَّهُ عَلَىٰ كُلِّ شَيْءٍ قَدِيرٌ /فَاللَّهُ هُوَ الْوَلِيُّ وَهُوَ يُحْيِي الْمَوْتَىٰ وَهُوَ عَلَىٰ كُلِّ شَيْءٍ قَدِيرٌ
Q 42:28 (P.Hamb.Arab. II 21.4)	انه الولى الحمىد	وَهُوَ الْوَلِيُّ الْحَمِيدُ
Q 42:40 (P.Marchands II 9v.9–10)	ڡال الله ڡمں عڡا واصـ[ـلح ڡاحره على الله] انه لا ىحب الطالمىں	فَمَنْ عَفَا وَأَصْلَحَ فَأَجْرُهُ عَلَى اللَّهِ إِنَّهُ لَا يُحِبُّ الظَّالِمِينَ
Q 65:2–4 (P.RagibLettreFamiliale.10–11)	[ومن] ىىڡ الله ڡانه مں ىىڡ الله ىحعل مں امره محرحا ويررڡه مں حىٮ لا ىحىسب	وَمَن يَتَّقِ اللَّهَ يَجْعَل لَّهُ مَخْرَجًا وَيَرْزُقْهُ مِنْ حَيْثُ لَا يَحْتَسِبُ ... وَمَن يَتَّقِ اللَّهَ يَجْعَل لَّهُ مِنْ أَمْرِهِ يُسْرًا
Q 65:7 (P.David-WeillLouvre 9.3)	ڡان الله سىحعل ىعد عسر ىسرا	سَيَجْعَلُ اللَّهُ بَعْدَ عُسْرٍ يُسْرًا

(*cont.*)

	Text of the papyrus	Text according to the Cairo Qurʾān (*riwāyat Ḥafṣ ʿan ʿĀṣim*)
Q 65:12 (P.HindsNubia.24–25)	ىالدى حلق السمواب والارص وما سهما	اللّٰهُ الَّذِي خَلَقَ سَبْعَ سَمَاوَاتٍ وَمِنَ الْأَرْضِ مِثْلَهُنَّ
Q 65:12 (P.Marchands ɪɪ 26v.14)	وفد احاط الله ىحلفه علما وحىرا	وَأَنَّ اللّٰهَ قَدْ أَحَاطَ بِكُلِّ شَيْءٍ عِلْمًا
Q 74:56 (P.RagibLettres 5.12)	ىاهل الىموى	هُوَ أَهْلُ التَّقْوٰى وَأَهْلُ الْمَغْفِرَةِ

Bibliography

Aguilar, Victoria. 1994. "Onomástico de origen árabe en el reino de León (siglo x)." In *al-Qanṭara* 15: 351–363.

Almbladh, Karin. 2010. "The 'Basmala' in Medieval Letters in Arabic Written by Jews and Christians." In *Orientalia Suecana* 59: 45–60.

Alvarus. 1973. "Indiculus luminosus." In *Corpvs scriptorm Muzarabicorum, Vol. 2*, ed. Ioannes Gil [Juan Gil]. Madrid: Instituto "Antonio de Nebrija," 270–315.

Björnesjö, Sophie. 1996. "L'arabisation de l'Égypte: le témoignage papyrologique." In *Ègypte/Monde arabe* 27–28: 93–105.

Bulliet, Richard W. 1979. *Conversion to Islam in the Medieval Period: An Essay in Quantitative History*. Cambridge: Harvard University Press.

Choat, Malcolm. 2006. *Belief and Cult in Fourth-Century Papyri*. Studia Antiqua Australiensia, vol. 1. Turnhout: Brepols.

Diem, Werner. 2008. "Arabic Letters in Pre-modern Times: A Survey with Commented Selected Bibliographies." In *Asiatische Studien/Études asiatiques* 62, no. 3 (= *Documentary Letters from the Middle East: The Evidence in Greek, Coptic, South Arabian, Pehlevi, and Arabic (1st–15th c* ce), ed. Eva Mira Grob and Andreas Kaplony. Bern: Lang: 2008): 885–906.

Diem, Werner. 2012. "Philologisches zu arabischen Dokumenten ɪɪ: Dokumente aus der Sammlung der Egyptian Library in Kairo." In *Zeitschrift für arabische Linguistik* 56: 27–78.

Friedman, Akiva Mordechai. 1980. *Jewish Marriage in Palestine: A Cairo Geniza Study, Vol. 1: The Ketubba Traditions of Eretz Israel*. Tel-Aviv: The Jewish Theological Seminary of America.

Ḥamīd Allāh [Hamidullah], Muḥammad. 1956. *Maǧmūʿat al-waṯāʾiq as-siyāsiyya li-l-ʿahd an-nabawī wa-l-ḫilāfa ar-rāšida.* 3rd, revised ed. Beirut: Dār al-Iršād.

Goitein, Shlomo Dov and Mordechai Akiva Friedman. 2008. *India Traders of the Middle Ages: Documents from the Cairo Geniza ("India Book")*. Études sur le Judaïsme Médiéval, vol. 31. Leiden: Brill.

Goldziher, Ignaz. 1896. "Ueber die Eulogien der Muhammedaner." In *Zeitschrift der Deutschen Morgenländischen Gesellschaft* 59: 97–128.

Grob, Eva Mira. 2010. *Documentary Arabic Private and Business Letters on Papyrus: Form and Function, Content and Context.* Archiv für Papyrusforschung und verwandte Gebiete, Beiheft 29. Berlin: de Gruyter.

Jahn, Karl. 1937. "Vom frühislamischen Briefwesen: Studien zur islamischen Epistolographie der ersten drei Jahrhunderte der Hiǧra auf Grund der arabischen Papyri." In *Archiv Orientální* 9: 153–200.

Luijendijk, AnneMarie. 2008. *Greetings in the Lord: Early Christians and the Oxyrhynchus Papyri.* Harvard Theological Studies, vol. 60. Cambridge: Harvard University Press.

Macuch, Rudolf. 1978. "Zur Vorgeschichte der Bekenntnisformel *lā ilāha illā llāhu.*" In *Zeitschrift der Deutschen Morgenländischen Gesellschaft* 128: 20–38.

Muġāwirī Muḥammad, Saʿīd. 1423/2002. *al-Alqāb wa-asmāʾ al-ḥiraf wa-l-waẓāʾif fī ḍawʾ al-bardīyāt al-ʿarabīya, vol. 3.* Cairo: [Manšūrāt] Dār al-kutub wa-l-waṯāʾiq al-qawmīya.

Naldini, Mario. 1968. *Il cristianesimo in Egitto: lettere private nei papiri dei secoli II–IV.* Biblioteca patristica, vol. 32. Fiesole: Nardini.

al-Qalqašandī, Abū l-ʿAbbās Aḥmad. 1913–1919. *Kitāb ṣubḥ al-aʿšà*, ed. Muḥammad ʿAbd ar-Rasūl Ibrāhīm. 14 vols. Cairo: Dār al-kutub as-sulṭāniyya.

Richter, Tonio Sebastian. 2008. "Coptic Letters." In *Asiatische Studien/Études asiatiques* 62, no. 3 (= *Documentary Letters from the Middle East: The Evidence in Greek, Coptic, South Arabian, Pehlevi, and Arabic (1st–15th c CE)*, ed. Eva Mira Grob and Andreas Kaplony. Bern: Lang, 2008), 739–770.

aṣ-Ṣābiʾ, Abu Isḥāq Ibrāhīm b. Hilāl. [1966]. *al-Muḫtār min rasāʾil aṣ-Ṣābiʾ*, ed. Sakīb Arslān. Beirut: Dār an-nahḍa al-ḥadīṯa.

van Arendonk, C[ornelis]. and D[aniel] Gimaret. 1995. "Salām." In *Encyclopaedia of Islam: New Edition* VIII: 915–918.

CHAPTER 3

Qur'ān Quotations in Papyrus Legal Documents

Leonora Sonego

1 Introduction

Egyptian papyri were discovered on the margin of rural areas, in rubbish deposits or in the ruins of deserted settlements, which implies a completely different perspective than the literary sources produced in urban centers, and the information we gather from them on, e.g., financial administration, is quite different from what literary sources tell us.[1] Similarly, one of the hopes of this project is to collect evidence on the presence of the Qur'ān in the first centuries of the Arabic domination over Egypt. Yet not every textual overlap between the Qur'ān and a legal document is a quotation, and a relatively short quote does not prove that the redaction of the Qur'ān had been completed by the time of the document.

Actually, why do we expect to find scriptural quotations in legal documents? Even though lately *Šarīʿa* has been simply translated as "religion" by the *Süddeutsche Zeitung*,[2] does law necessarily refer to religion? Roman Law and Common Law, both used by Christians, were no Christian law, and even Canonical Law does not take the Bible as a main source.[3] In Islamic Law, the Qur'ān may have played a more central central role, yet what about the first centuries when the great reference works, the Ḥadīṯ collections, were about to be written? The legal conceptions of Arabic documents on, e.g., tax administration, leasing land, and selling dwelling houses, had been working long before the Qur'ān was revealed and were independent of it.

Obviously, comparing Islamic Law to Rabbinical Law would be most tempting because both originate roughly speaking in the same area and in the same period; because Jewish and Islamic scholarship have a number of features in

1 Palme 2009: 358.

2 Avenarius 2014 calls the weekly TV program *aš-Šarīʿa wa-l-ḥayāt*, featuring Yūsuf al-Qaraḍāwī, *Die Religion und das Leben*, "Religion and Life."

3 Helmholz 1994 discusses the systematization of canonical law starting from 12th century *Decretum Gratiani*, which essentially relied on existing norms and, when referring to the Bible, only tried to avoid or explain contradictions.

 | DOI:10.1163/9789004376977_004

common, such as the specific relationship between oral vs. written tradition;[4] and because in both cases law was applied before scholarship dealt with it. Yet the Jewish community was in a minority position only, both in the Roman and the Islamic Empire.

In the following, we discuss three types of Qur'ānic quotations: *marginal religious sentences* such as professions of faith added after signatures of witnesses, *short Qur'ānic phrases* integrated into the text, and *Qur'ānic quotations*, i.e., whole sentences, sometimes explicitly introduced as "God's word."

2 Sources and Methodology

In July 2014, the Arabic Papyrology Database (APD) offered, in its public full-text thesaurus the searchable full texts of more than 1,500 published Arabic documents, and in its metadata register, for internal use only, metadata (including category and date) on more than 10,000 published and unpublished documents. Based on this, it was relatively easy to find some 717 published documents dealing with legal matters (see Table 3.1).

Since our main interest was very early documents, all texts from the first three centuries were systematically searched for religious keywords, regardless of whether or not their texts had been entered into the database. (The keywords were essentially "God" and "prophet.") Texts of the 4th century were regularly discussed, yet for them we rely on the APD full-text thesaurus and its automatic search tools. Additionally, we searched the Qur'ān for keywords related to the content of the documents, such as "sale," "lease," and "slavery," and phrases known from the formulary, such as "voluntarily, not coerced." The outcome was surprisingly small except for the topic of divorce, as shown below.

Religious references in these texts are treated in three groups. The first is *Qur'ānic marginal notes*, i.e., confessional statements, free-standing sentences placed somehow on the margins of the texts, be it in the introduction, in the witness clauses, or on seals. The second are *Qur'ānic phrases* integrated completely into the *dispositio*, yet so short that their connection to the Qur'ān must be discussed. The third are indubitable *Qur'ānic quotations* (sometimes variated) that are part and parcel of the legal text.

4 Schoeler 1989: 215.

TABLE 3.1 Published legal documents registered in the Arabic Papryology Database full-text thesaurus and the APD metadata register, as of December 2015

	1st/7th century	2nd/8th century	3rd/9th century	4th/10th century	Undated	Total
Receipt	15	48	124	72	7	266
Written obligation	3	5	57	14	10	89
Lease	0	15	58	11	3	87
Sale	0	4	40	27	9	80
Order for payment or delivery	4	7	37	8	11	67
Signatures	0	2	21	9	2	34
Marriage contract	0	0	16	9	0	25
Divorce documents	0	1	4	2	0	7
Hire of employees	0	0	11	2	0	13
Act of emancipation	0	4	2	2	0	8
Inheritance documents	0	3	2	2	1	8
Certificate of discharge	0	2	2	2	0	6
Deed of gifts	0	0	2	2	0	4
Testimony	0	0	4	0	0	4
[*Waqfiyya*] (pious endowments)	0	0	1	0	0	1
Responsum	0	0	2	0	0	2
Other legal text	0	1	11	1	3	16
Total	22	92	394	163	46	717

The second category, *Qur'ānic phrases*, are found from the year 138/755 onward in acts of emancipation and marriage contracts. The third, explicit *Qur'ānic quotations* and longer religious digressions inside the text of a document, come from marriage contracts, divorce contracts, a draft for a gift, and an act of emancipation, all from the second half of the 3rd/9th century.[5] In both categories, the documents have strong ethical implications. Yet the first category, *Qur'ānic marginal notes*, are instead found on down-to-earth transactions such as orders and receipts for payment and written obligations from the 3rd/9th century onward.

5 A religious digression is found in P.GrohmannBerlin 7, an act of emancipation of 304AH, speaking of *dār al-āḫira* ("the afterlife"), which is to be compared to the younger P.AbbottMarriageContracts 2, a gift between spouses. Such digressions are discussed in section 4 below on Qur'ānic phrases, of which they are an enlargement.

3 Qur'ānic Marginal Notes: Signatures and Seals in Legal Documents

Some pious notes on legal documents are little texts of their own. They are found at the beginning of texts, or between the end of a text and the witness signatures, at the end of individual signatures, in the remarks of judges, after the name of the scribe who drew up an official document, and on seals. This is why we have called them *Qur'ānic marginal notes* to differentiate them from the other two types.

The sentences used appear several times in the Qur'ān. For their use in the documents, these seem to have been variated or combined with other expressions, which makes it quite difficult to distinguish between Qur'ān quotations, Ḥadīṯs, and religious commonplaces. The passages used are taken from the domain of personal devotion, creeds, or monotheist statements. They often mention that (one) God is *sufficient* for His believers, such as Q 3:173 *fa-zādahum īmānan wa-qālū ḥasbunā llāhu wa-niʿma al-wakīlu*, "But it increased them in faith, and they said, 'God is sufficient for us; an excellent Guardian is He'"[6] (quoted P.David-WeillLouvre 9.4, see Table 3.2 below), or Q 9:129 *fa-qul ḥasbiya llāhu lā ilāha illā huwa ʿalayhi tawakkaltu*, "Say: 'God is enough for me. There is no god but He. In Him I have put my trust'" (referred to in P.Khurasan 11.seal, see Table 3.2). The connection with *tawakkul* ("confidence") and *wakīl* ("trustee") also appears in Q 39:38 *qul ḥasbiya llāhu ʿalayhi yatawakkalu l-mutawakkilūna*. "Say: 'God is enough for me; in Him all those put their trust who put their trust.'" This opens up a way to use these quotations in legal documents when speaking about human guardians or trustees, even when only a fragment of the corresponding verse is plainly written.[7]

In one of these mentioned passages, Q 9:129, the "sufficiency" formula is combined with a shortened Šahāda: "There is no god but He." As opposed to this short version, the full Šahāda "There is no god but God" is relatively rare in the Qur'ān; it appears only in Q 37:35 *innahum kānū iḏā qīla lahum la ilāha illā llāhu yastakbirūna*, "For when it was said to them, 'There is no god but God,' they were ever waxing proud," and in Q 47:19 *fa-ʿlam annahu lā ilāha illā llāhu wa-staġfir li-ḏanbika*, "Know thou therefore that there is no god but God, and ask forgiveness for thy sin." The same idea is expressed by *lā šarīka lahu* "He has no associate," as in Q 6:162–163 *qul inna ṣalātī wa-nusukī wa-maḥyāya wa-mamātī li-llāhi rabbi l-ʿālamīna lā sārīka lahu wa-bi-ḏālika umirtu wa-anā*

6 All English translations of the Qur'ān are according to Arberry 1955, unless otherwise indicated. Verse numbers may differ between the quoted text and the translation.

7 *Ḥasbunā llāhu*, "Enough for us is God," is also found in Q 9:59.

TABLE 3.2 The first six Qur'ānic authentication clauses in papyrus legal documents in the APD, which show a large range of the topoi used (the seal of P.Cair Arab. 182 [241/855] is slightly older than P.Prag.Arab. 4, but the formula *"yatiqu bi-llāhi"* is not Qur'ānic; see the following pages.)

Year	Papyrus line	نصّ الوثيقة	نصّ القرآن	Qur'ān
154/771	P.Khurasan 11.seal	حسى [الله] -	فَقُلْ حَسْبِيَ اللَّهُ لَا إِلَٰهَ إِلَّا هُوَ عَلَيْهِ تَوَكَّلْتُ	Q 11:129
196/812	P.World p. 145.seal 3	الحسں ں سعد / ٮومں ٮالله ورسوله	يَا أَيُّهَا الَّذِينَ آمَنُوا آمِنُوا بِاللَّهِ وَرَسُولِهِ	Q 4:136
200/816	P.Terminkauf 1.10	والڡوه لله	وَلَوْ يَرَى الَّذِينَ ظَلَمُوا إِذْ يَرَوْنَ الْعَذَابَ أَنَّ الْقُوَّةَ لِلَّهِ جَمِيعًا وَأَنَّ اللَّهَ شَدِيدُ الْعَذَابِ	Q 2:165
Beginning of 3rd/9th century	P.David-WeillLouvre 9.4	ٮحسٮا الله وٮعم الوكل	فَزَادَهُمْ إِيمَانًا وَقَالُوا حَسْبُنَا اللَّهُ وَنِعْمَ الْوَكِيلُ	Q 3:173
Beginning of 3rd/9th century	CPR XXVI 19.11	[ولا حول] / ولا ڡوه الا ٮالله وكڡا ٮالله سـ[ـهىدا]	وَلَوْلَا إِذْ دَخَلْتَ جَنَّتَكَ قُلْتَ مَا شَاءَ اللَّهُ لَا قُوَّةَ إِلَّا بِاللَّهِ	Q 18:39
246/860	P.Prag.Arab. 4.12	سهد على دلك الله وكڡا ٮالله سهىدا	لَٰكِنِ اللَّهُ يَشْهَدُ بِمَا أَنْزَلَ إِلَيْكَ أَنْزَلَهُ بِعِلْمِهِ وَالْمَلَائِكَةُ يَشْهَدُونَ وَكَفَىٰ بِاللَّهِ شَهِيدًا	Q 4:166

awwalu l-muslimīna, "Say: 'My prayer, my ritual sacrifice, my living, my dying—all belongs to God, the Lord of all Being. No associate has He. Even so I have been commanded, and I am the first of those that surrender.' "[8]

Documents similarly say that all strength (*quwwa*) and success (*tawfīq*) belong to God. Thus documents allude to Q 2:165 *wa-law yarà llaḏīna ẓalamū*

8 *Lā šarīka lahu*, "He has no associate," also appears in the middle of texts after the name of God, for example, in the donation Chrest.Khoury I 89.7 (formulary, camel bone, assigned to the 3rd/9th century) and the marriage contracts P.Cair.Arab. 40.8 (271/885) and 41.12 (279/892), as discussed in section 5 below.

FIGURE 3.1 An order to deliver a sheet of papyrus within the administration (dated 196/812). The text on the seal (now lost) had the oldest datable Qur'ān quotation in a legal document. The order is followed by a second, unpublished, text. (P.Vind.inv. A.P. 5557 = P.World p. 145).
© ÖSTERREICHISCHE NATIONALBIBLIOTHEK, PAPYRUSSAMMLUNG

iḏ yarawna l-ʿaḏāba anna l-quwwata li-llāhi ǧamīʿan, "O if the evildoers might see, when they see the chastisement, that the power altogether belongs to God" (P.Terminkauf 1.10; CPR XXVI 19.11), or to Q 18:39 *wa-law-lā iḏ daḫalta ǧannataka qulta mā šāʾa llāhu lā quwwata illā bi-llāhi*, "Why, when thou wentest into thy garden, didst thou not say, 'As God will; there is no power except in God'?" The only reference to a creed including the Prophet—referring to Q 4:136 *yā ayyuhā allaḏīna āmanū āminū bi-llāhi wa-rasūlihi*, "O believers, believe in God and His Messenger"—is found in P.World p. 145.seal3. The idea that God alone is enough is also expressed by the verb *kafā*, and *kafā bi-llāhi šahīdan*, "God suffices for a witness," appears several times in the Qur'ān (e.g., Q 4:166, see Table 3.2) and in Ḥadīṯs.[9]

Initial and final statements can be considered under three aspects. First, the Ḥamdala quoting, in different variants, Q 1:2 may be functionally considered a simple enlargement of the Basmala.[10] The Ḥamdala-cum-Taṣliya is found as *al-ḥamdu li-l-llāhi rabbi l-ʿālamīna kaṯīran wa-ṣallà llāhu ʿalà muḥammadini n-nabiyyi*, "Many praises belong to God, the Lord of All Being, and God bless Muḥammad, the Prophet" (P.Cair.Arab. 351.10; 262/876); other Ḥamdalas are *al-ḥamdu li-llāhi abadan*, "Praise to God eternally" (P.Cair.Arab. 354.3; 3rd/9th century), and *al-ḥamdu li-llāhi šukran li-llāhi*, "Praise and thanks to God" (P.Cair.Arab. 356.11, 3rd/9th century). There are more than 100 other instances, but the overwhelming majority come from letters (where they are part of the text, not of the heading).

As can be seen from the line numbers, Ḥamdalas are also used instead of or next to signatures (see below): P.GrohmannUrkunden 7.1, 3rd/9th century, official letter, administrative document (order to present somebody to the court); P.World p. 138 b.2, 3rd or 4th/9th or 10th century, other administrative document (notification concerning the level of the Nile); P.Cair.Arab. 354.3 3rd or 4th/9th or 10th century, order for payment or delivery; P.Cair.Arab. 356.recto 11, 3rd/9th century, order for payment or delivery; P.GrohmannUrkunden 16.1, 4th/10th century, order for payment or delivery; P.Heid.Arab. II 34.8 3rd/9th century, business letter, list (note about the sale of cereals, definitely a text with a legal function); P.GrohmannWirtsch. 13.3, 293/906, receipt for payment or delivery; P.GrohmannBerlin 10.18, 295/908, marriage contract; P.Cair.Arab. 73.36, 320/932, contract of sale; P.GrohmannUrkunden 1.5, 326/938 Lease; P.Fay.Monast. 1.28, 335/946, contract of sale; P.Cair.Arab. 85.9, 348/960, official letter, administrative document; P.Steuerquittungen 23.1, 365/976, receipt for payment or delivery; P.FahmiTaaqud 10.1, 369/979, contract of sale; P.Steuerquittungen 27.2, 395/1005, receipt for payment or delivery.

The second function is related to the authentication of documents by the scribe who drew up a document or by the judge who registered it. For authentication, scribes signed in their characteristic handwriting and choice of formulae expressing their personal devotion and/or monotheistic conviction. By such statements, they called on God to hold them responsible for the correctness of

9 *Kafā bi-llāhi wakīlan wa-šahīdan*, "God suffices as trustee and witness."

10 The Basmala is, of course, also a quotation, but it is not specific to legal documents. For an overview of variated and especially abbreviated Basmalas from the Early Islamic period, see Bruning 2015: 360–361.

the content and apologized for possible mistakes. This was probably simply the more polite or modest way to sign a document, and may be related to what we know from Fāṭimid times as *ʿalāma*, attested since the ʿAbbāsid caliph al-Qā'im (422/1031).[11] One group of formulae speaks of entrusting one's concerns to God (forms of *wakkala, fawwaḍa, waṯaqa*). *Wakīl* and *tawakkul* appear in the Qur'ān (see above), while *fawwaḍa ǧābirun amrahu ilā r-raḥmāni r-raḥīmi*, "Ǧābir has entrusted his concerns to the Compassionate and Merciful" (P.RagibSauf-Conduits 6.left seal; P.RagibSauf-Conduits 7.seal; P.RagibSauf-Conduits 8.seal, three permits for persons subject to taxes to leave their district in 133/751), seems to stem from Q 40:44 *wa-ufawwiḍu amrī ilā llāhi*, "and I entrust my concerns to God," and *fawwaḍtu amrī ilayka*, "I have entrusted my concerns to You," appearing in at least six Ḥadīṯ collections in chapters about prayer.[12] *Waṯaqa*, in contrast (see examples in the next paragraph), is not attested in the Qur'ān in that sense. For similar purposes, scribes used monotheistic statements such as *lā ilāha illā llāha*, "There is no god but God"; *ḥasbiya/ḥasbunā llāhu*, "God suffices to me/us"; and *lā quwwata illā bi-llāhi*, "There is no strength but through God."

The practice increases over time. Most documents with Qur'ānic marginal notes are orders for payment or receipt, i.e., documents which require a certain degree of authentication without being contracts, possibly a feature common to documents to be placed in between legal and administrative texts. We do not always know whether they were issued by a public institution, but many of them carry the name of the scribe, obviously a person who was entitled to dispose of the money mentioned in the documents. There is also a sale of a slave girl with no witnesses mentioned, but with a religious formula at the beginning, saying *ḥasbiya llāhu wa-kafā*, "God is enough for me, and He suffices" (P.Vente 6.1). Does the scribe mean "… for a witness"? Some scribes with Christian names used, in writing or in seals, the same formulae as their Muslim colleagues, such as in *nafīsun yaṯiqu bi-llāhi*, "Nafīs trusts in God" (P.Cair.Arab. 182.seal, tax receipt 241/855); *muḥammadu bnu yaḥyā ya[ṯiqu bi-llāhi]* "Muḥammad son of Yaḥyā tr[usts in God]" (P.Cair.Arab. 187.seal, tax receipt 275/888); *wa-kataba yuḥannisu bnu mīnā bi-ḫaṭṭihī / ḥasbiya llāhu*, "Has written John son of Mīnā / my sufficiency is God" (P.Cair.Arab. 192 line 8 and seal, tax receipt 312/924); *kataba yuḥannisu bnu mūnisa bni ṯīyudūra bi-ḫaṭṭihi ḥasbī ṯiqatī bi-llāhi*, "Has written John son of Mūnis son of Theodor, my sufficiency and my confidence is God" (P.GrohmannUrkunden 17.5, receipt

11 Babinger and Bosworth 2000.

12 Wensinck 1936–1969, under the root *f-y-ḍ*.

342/953);[13] *wa-kataba ǧurayǧu bnu qūrīla* [...] *wa-ḥasbunā llāhu waḥdahu*, "Has written George son of Kyrill [...] and our sufficiency is God alone" (P.Cair.Arab. 199.7, tax receipt 346/958). Some purely Coptic documents have Arabic seals, but these have not been registered systematically, e.g., *sabību bnu sahmin ḥasbuhu llāhu*, "Sabīb son of Sahm, his sufficiency is God" (P.Lond.Copt. 1050.seal, entagion, undated). The function of (graphically unimpressive) handwritten phrases seems to be the same as that of seals.

Ḥasb, "sufficiency," also means "calculating," and the formula most often appears in receipts and orders for payment, as well as in business letters. We also expect to find it in accounting. Accounts are beyond the scope of this article, and as far as the texts have been entered into the Arabic Papyrology Database, there is only *wa-ḥasbunā llāhu wa-niʿma l-wakīlu* (P.Cair.Arab. 403r.3 3rd/10th century), an exact rendition of Q 3:173. Two examples are found in deeds, one concerning a donation, the other one a sale (P.Vente 6, 310/923; P.Fay.Monast. 3, 336/947).

As a third group we count formulae referring explicitly to the witnessing of transactions. Modified Q 4:166 *šahida llāhu wa-malāʾikatuhu wa-kafā bi-llāhi šahīdan*, "God and His angels witness to this, and God suffices as a witness" (thus in P.Cair.Arab. 191.8–9, 3rd/9th century) is often abbreviated as *kafā bi-llāhi šahīdan*, "God suffices as a witness," and regularly appears in written obligations drafted by the debtor himself, but with no witnesses,[14] and in unwitnessed documents relating to taxes (e.g., P.Frantz-MurphyContracts 1.3, 261/875), without being limited to these documents.[15] The connection between religion and personal commitment is also shown by a witness stating *ašhadu allā ilāha illā llāhu l-ḥaqqu l-mubīnu wa-ʿalà iqrāri ʿaliyyi bni muḥammadin ...*, "I am witnessing that there is no god but God, the manifest Truth, and to the acknowledgment of ʿAlī b. Muḥammad ..." (P.Marchands I 8.16). This is the only reference to Q 24:25 *yawma-iḏin yūfīhimu llāhu dīnahumu l-ḥaqqa wa-yaʿlimūna anna llāha huwa l-ḥaqqu l-mubīnu*, "Upon that day God will pay them in full their just due, and they shall know that God is the manifest Truth."

Qurʾānic marginal notes are not written in an especially careful or beautiful way and are, unless they are on seals, not distinct from the surrounding text.[16] Sometimes, they are in one stroke, perhaps written more quickly than the rest

13 Quoted according to the emendation by Diem 2011: 114.

14 This phenomenon is described by Thung 2006: 134 in his description of CPR XXVI 26. See also Grohmann 1954: 116.

15 Cf. the document of sale of a slave girl mentioned above, which has no "witnessing" phrase, but a "sufficiency" phrase instead.

16 Sijpesteijn 2014: 56.

of the text, and are smaller, with a thinner line or lighter ink (e.g., CPR XXVI 19.11). Some of them are fully integrated, such as *wa-l-quwwatu li-llāhi* (P.Terminkauf 1.10) quoting Q 2:165, where the scribe dipped his pen three words earlier and then simply continued, whereas other quotations are somehow distinct, such as *lā ilāha illā llāha* (Chrest.Khoury I 17.7) in between two signatures, with the letters being a bit smaller than in the surrounding text, and with thinner lines. Sometimes, they come after a lacuna, such as the Ḥamdala in P.Cair.Arab. 354.3, possibly intended to fill up space in order to prevent later additions. However this cannot have been the case in P.Cair.Arab. 348.4, where the text has been closed up by *kataba l-ḥasanu bi-ḫaṭṭihi*, "al-Ḥasan wrote in his own hand," and the religious formula then fills the empty left hand corner to give the document a more tidy appearance.

4 Qur'ānic Phrases, or: What Is a Qur'ānic Quote inside a Legal Document?

4.1 *Introduction*

The language of legal documents has next to no affinity to the Qur'ān. On the one hand, with the exception of marriage agreements (see section 5.1 below), deeds contain only religious expressions that might, but need not, be Qur'ānic. On the other hand, the Qur'ān provides concrete instructions neither on manumitting slaves nor on inheriting, buying, and selling houses and land, but only a rather general admonition to conduct business in a manner to achieve mutual satisfaction (Q 4:29, see section 4.4 below). Looking for guidance in matters of sale, one is warned not to buy earthly goods at the expense of the afterlife.[17] Houses that are private property are not mentioned; instead, we find houses of God, i.e., places of worship, and dwellings in the world to come.[18] The affairs of this world seem to be left to the believers to a large extent.

The religious expressions listed here (see Table 3.3) may be Qur'ānic quotations or may appear in the Qur'ān in a slightly different form. They are all quite short, consisting of only two or three words, and are more or less pertinent according to whether or not the meaning and function are the same

17 ʿAbd al-Bāqī 1364/[1945]: 381 under the root *š-r-y*. Buying error at the price of right guidance (e.g., Q 2:16) is a frequent topos. The only actual sale is the one of Joseph by his brothers (Q 12:20). Admittedly, the root *b-y-ʿ* leads to more concrete instructions: Q 2:282 recommends writing down sales, yet Q 62:9 makes it clear that praying is more important than trading.

18 Words used for "house" are *bayt allāh*, "the House of God," and *ad-dār al-āḫira*, "the afterlife"; instead of *manzil*, we only find *tanzīl*, "revelation."

TABLE 3.3 The phrases *waǧh allāh, ʿahd allāh, ʿan tarāḍin, ʿuqdat an-nikāḥ, ṭāʾiʿ ġayr mukrah, ṭayyibatan nafsuhu* in their first appearance in papyrus legal documents in the Arabic Papryology Database, compared to the corresponding Qurʾān verses

Year	**Papyrus line**	**نصّ الوثيقة**	**نصّ القرآن**	**Qurʾān**
138/755	P.Khurasan 29.6–7	عمهم لوحه ⟨الله⟩ لىس لاحد علىهم / سىىل	إِنَّمَا نُطْعِمُكُمْ لِوَجْهِ اللَّهِ لَا نُرِيدُ مِنكُمْ جَزَاءً وَلَا شُكُورًا	Q 76:7
146/763	P.Khurasan 31.2–3	وعلى ما / عهد الله ودمه	الَّذِينَ يَنقُضُونَ عَهْدَ اللَّهِ مِن بَعْدِ مِيثَاقِهِ وَيَقْطَعُونَ مَا أَمَرَ اللَّهُ بِهِ أَن يُوصَلَ وَيُفْسِدُونَ فِي الْأَرْضِ أُولَٰئِكَ هُمُ الْخَاسِرُونَ وَيَقْطَعُونَ مَا أَمَرَ اللَّهُ بِهِ أَن يُوصَلَ وَيُفْسِدُونَ فِي الْأَرْضِ أُولَٰئِكَ هُمُ الْخَاسِرُونَ	Q 2:27
239/854	P.Cair.Arab. 56.15	عں راص	يَا أَيُّهَا الَّذِينَ آمَنُوا لَا تَأْكُلُوا أَمْوَالَكُم بَيْنَكُم بِالْبَاطِلِ إِلَّا أَن تَكُونَ تِجَارَةً عَن تَرَاضٍ مِّنكُمْ	Q 4:29
252/866	P.Marchands I 11.4	[ع]ـىد عمده ىكاحه اىاها	وَلَا تَعْزِمُوا عُقْدَةَ النِّكَاحِ حَتَّىٰ يَبْلُغَ الْكِتَابُ أَجَلَهُ	Q 2:235
253/867	P.RémondonEd-fou 1.19	طاىعں عىر مكرهں	أَفَغَيْرَ دِينِ اللَّهِ يَبْغُونَ وَلَهُ أَسْلَمَ مَن فِي السَّمَاوَاتِ وَالْأَرْضِ طَوْعًا وَكَرْهًا وَإِلَيْهِ يُرْجَعُونَ	Q 3:83
339/951	P.FahmiTaaqud 8.13	طىه من انفسهم	وَآتُوا النِّسَاءَ صَدُقَاتِهِنَّ نِحْلَةً فَإِن طِبْنَ لَكُمْ عَن شَيْءٍ مِّنْهُ نَفْسًا فَكُلُوهُ هَنِيئًا مَّرِيئًا	Q 4:4

in the Qurʾān and the contracts. For example, the phrase *ṭayyibatan bi-ḏālika nafsuhu*, "his soul being satisfied with it," has been considered a Qurʾānic quote,[19] yet the Qurʾān talks of divorced wives "being content to give up" the *ṣadāq*, whereas the deeds, which are all sale contracts, talk about "mutually agreeing to a transaction."

19 Frantz-Murphy 1988: 111.

Next, and more importantly, Qur'ānic quotations are necessarily younger than the Qur'ān itself. The texts listed above obviously are younger, but contract formularies evolve slowly, and the formularies used under Islamic law are instead rooted in Late Antique tradition, be it Byzantine, Sasanian, Roman, Hellenistic, Jewish, or Arabic. Thus if any of the overlapping passages are already found in pre-Islamic formularies, they might well be quoted from this earlier formulary and not necessarily from the Qur'ān. Actually, matches between the contracts and the Qur'ān instead show that the Qur'ān was influenced by contemporary, i.e., Late Antique, legal language. A similar case, in a non-Islamic context, has been postulated for the biblical *kōl 'ašer-ḥāpēṣ 'āśāh*, "he does whatever he pleases" (Psalm 95.3), which is also found in a number of contracts of sale from the beginning of the Christian era and probably originates in Aramaic legal language of the second half of the first millennium BCE.[20] Hence we need to take into account contract formularies existing during the time in which the Qur'ān was written and spread in the Near East and North Africa, i.e., before and during the Arab Conquests. One question is what the similarities between legal documents and the Qur'ān are, but the more interesting question is what changes might have been triggered by the nascent Islamic law.

4.2 Li-waǧhi llāh, *"For the Sake of God"*

Some acts of emancipation and donations feature the expression *li-waǧhi llāh*, "for the sake of God," or, in business, "for free," once enlarged into *li-waǧhi llāhi wa-d-dāri l-āḫira*, "for the sake of God and the afterlife." This refers to Q 76:7 *wa-yuṭ'imūna ṭ-ṭa'āma 'alā ḥubbihi miskīnan wa-yatīman wa-asīran/ innamā nuṭ'imukum li-waǧhi llāhi lā nurīdu minkum ǧazā'an wa-lā šukran*, "They give food, for the love of Him, to the needy, the orphan, the captive: 'We feed you only for the Face of God; we desire no recompense from you, no thankfulness.'"

- *'Attaqahum li-waǧhi ⟨llāhi⟩ laysa li-aḥadin 'alayhim sabīlun illā sabīla l-walā'i* "He emancipated them for the sake of God. Nobody has any right over them except the right of patronage." (P.Khurasan 29.6–7, 138/755)[21]
- *A'taqahum li-waǧhi llāhi* "He has emancipated them for the sake of God" (P.Khurasan 30, 160/777, emancipation).
  Ṣadaqatan mā li-waǧhi [llāhi lā urīdu ...] ǧazā'an wa-lā šukūran illā mina llāhi waḥdihi wa-lā šarīka lahu "A gift for the sake of [God. I do not want ...] any recompense nor thankfulness except from God, the one, who has no equal." (Chrest.Khoury I 89.6–7, 3rd/9th century).

20 Hurvitz 1982: 258.

21 English translations by the respective editor, French and German translations by us.

- *Li-waǧhi llāhi wa-d-dāri l-āḫirati lā abtaġī* […] / [*ʿataq*]*nāka li-waǧhi llāhi ʿitqan tāmman* "For the face of God and the afterlife, I do not wish […] / we [set] you [free] for the face of God, a full emancipation" (Chrest.Khoury II 34.2–3, 3rd/9th century, badly preserved blank formulary for an emancipation).
- *Li-waǧhi llāhi wa-d-dāri l-āḫirati* "for the sake of God and the afterlife" (P.GrohmannBerlin 7, 304/916, emancipation)
- *Ṣadaqatan li-waǧhi llāhi ʿazza wa-ǧalla / battatan batlan lā turīdu bi-ḏālika ǧazāʾan wa-lā šukūran illā mina llāhi waḥdihi lā šarīka lahu*, "(This is) an irrevocable charitable grant for the sake of God, to whom be glory and majesty. She desires for this neither reward nor praise except from God alone without any associate" (P.Fay.Monast. 3, 336/947, donation to the monastery of Naqlūn).
- *Ṣadaqatan li-waǧhi llāhi lā yurīdu bi-ḏālika ǧazāʾan wa-lā šukūran*, "He has bestowed this as a charitable endowment for the sake of God, not intending thereby any profit or reward" (P.Cair.Arab. 119, 348/959, donation where both donor and beneficiary have Coptic names).

This is too current an expression to be exclusive to the Qurʾān. But that the expression was felt to be a quote may be shown by Chrest.Khoury I 89.6–7, a template for a man donating a third of his property to his wife, quoting Q 76:8 followed by a statement of Tawḥīd. So, even if the expression was not originally taken from the Qurʾān, it allowed a connection to it. We might call this a quotation by hindsight.

4.3 ʿAhd allāh, *"The Contract of God"*

The expression *ʿahd allāh*, "the promise of God" or "the promise made before God" or "the command of God," appears in Q 2:27 *allaḏīna yanquḍūna ʿahda llāhi min baʿdi mīṯāqihi wa-yaqṭaʿūna mā amara llāhu bihi an yūṣala wa-yufsidūna fī l-arḍi ulāʾika humu l-ḫāsirūn*, "Such as break the covenant of God after its solemn binding, and such as cut what God has commanded should be joined, and such as do corruption in the land—they shall be the losers," and in one emancipation and one marriage contract:

- *Wa-ʿalà qiyā ʿahdu llāhi wa-ḏimmatuhu*, "And Qiyā (the emancipated) is protected by the safeguard of God and his custody" (P.Khurasan 31.2–3, 146/763).
- *Wa-ʿalayhi bi-ḏālika ʿahdu llāhi wa-mīṯāquhu wa-ḏimmatu nabiyyihi muḥammadan* [sic], "And he (the groom) is bound in this regard by the contract of God and his convention and the agreement of His prophet Muḥammad" (P.GrohmannBerlin 10.7, 295/908, marriage contract).

4.4 ʿAn tarāḍin, *"By Mutual Satisfaction"*

The expression *ʿan tarāḍin*, "by mutual satisfaction," quoting Q 4:29 *yā ayyuhā llaḏīna āmanū lā taʾkulū amwālakum baynakum bi-l-bāṭili illā an takūna tiǧāratan ʿan tarāḍin minkum*, "O believers, consume not your goods between you in vanity, except there be trading, by your agreeing together," is also found mainly in contracts of sale. Mutual satisfaction is distinctly Islamic; this was probably due to practical reasons, but the Qurʾān could legitimate it. The expression is also recommended by aṭ-Ṭaḥāwī.[22] Earlier formularies for sales only expressed the satisfaction of the seller, and sales were documented in first-person (subjective style) or third-person (objective style) and formulated from the seller's or the buyer's perspective.[23] In Islamic times, the objective style became the only one used.[24] Of the documents accessible through the Arabic Papyrology Database, four sales each of the 3rd and the 4th century include the expression (P.Cair.Arab. 56.15, 239/854; P.RémondonEdfou 1.16, 253/867; P.FahmiTaaqud 4.15 268/881; P.FahmiTaaqud 5.15, 272/886; P.Fay.Monast. 1.14, 335/946; P.Fahmi-Taaqud 8.12, 339/951; CPR XXVI 8.9, 345/956; P.FahmiTaaqud 10, 369/979). As the number of edited sales decreases in the 4th/10th century (from 40 to 27), this means a slight increase in the use of the formula.

In contrast to *li-waǧhi llāhi* and *ʿahdu llāhi*, the phrase *ʿan tarāḍin* mostly appears in contracts of sale, which have no religious character. It might be interesting to compare the increasing frequency of these formulae to the consolidation of Islamic jurisprudence.

4.5 ʿInda ʿuqdati nikāḥihi, *"At the Conclusion of His Marriage"*

ʿInda ʿuqdati nikāḥihi possibly refers to Q 2:235 *wa-lā taʿzimū ʿuqdata n-nikāḥi ḥattà yabluġa l-kitābu aǧalahu*, "And do not resolve on the knot of marriage until the book has reached its term."

- *ʿInda ʿuqdati nikāḥihi iyyāhā … waliyyu ʿuqdati n-nikāḥi* (P.Marchands I 11.4;8, 252/866).
- P.GrohmannBerlin 11.4 (3rd or 4th/9th or 10th century); CPR XXVI 1.12 (late 3rd/9th century); P.Cair.Arab. 38.15 (259/873); P.Cair.Arab. 39.3 (264/878); P.Cair.Arab. 41.7 (279/892); P.GrohmannBerlin 9.7 (287/900); P.Grohmann Berlin 10.5 (295/908), all marriages up to 400 AH.

Actual knots have been used in marriage ceremonies around the world, but the Qurʾān does not reflect this. Some contracts of sale use *ʿuqda*, too (P.Fay.Monast. 1.13; P.Fay.Monast. 2.13). More research needs to be done on this term.

22 Wakin 1972: Indian pagination 4.
23 Hengstl et al. 2002.
24 Frantz-Murphy 1989: 105.

4.6 Ṭāʾiʿan ġayra mukrahin, *"Voluntarily and Not against His Will"*

The phrase *ṭāʾiʿan ġayra mukrahin* appears in virtually all legal documents, reminiscent of Q 3:83 *a-fa-ġayra dīni llāhi yabġūna wa-lahu aslama man fī s-samawāti wa-l-arḍi ṭawʿan wa-karhan wa-ilayhi yurǧaʿūn*, "What, do they desire another religion than God's, and to Him has surrendered whoso is in the heavens and the earth, willingly or unwillingly, and to Him they shall be returned?" It is generally enlarged by some synonyms at the scribe's discretion, such as:

- *ṭāʾiʿayni ṭālibayni rāġibayni ġayra mukrahayni wa-lā muǧbarayni wa-lā muṭṭahadayni*, "Voluntarily, demanding (and) desiring (it), without compulsion and not against their will, and not under constraint" (P.Cair.Arab. 74.11, 344/955).[25]

We do not count this as Qurʾānic. *Ṭawʿ* and *karh* are probably the most current of the mentioned synonyms for "free will" and "coercion," and the Qurʾān is using current legal speech at this point. The scribes would probably not have spoiled a reference to the Qurʾān, if they had felt it to be one. Counting this as Qurʾānic would also be pointless because it appears in all legal documents as far as their lower half is preserved, at least all documents where one or two parties take up an obligation, with receipts, orders for payment, and leases of state-owned land forming a special group.

4.7 Ṭayyibatan lahu nafsuhu, *"His Soul Being Satisfied with It"*

The volition clause sometimes ends with *ṭayyibatan min anfusihim*, referring to Q 4:4 *wa-ātū n-nisāʾa ṣadaqātihinna niḥlatan fa-in ṭibna lakum ʿan šayʾin minhu nafsan fa-kulūhu hanīʾan marīʾan*, "And give the women their dowries as a gift spontaneous; but if they are pleased to offer you any of it, consume it with wholesome appetite":

- *ṭayyibatan min anfusihim* (P.FahmiTaaqud 8.13, 339/951),
- *ṭayyibatan bi-ḏālika nafsuhu* (P.Cair.Arab. 37.5, 393/1003),
- not attested otherwise before the 5th/11th century: P.Cair.Arab. 60.12, 403/1015; P.HanafiContracts 2.8, 413/1022; P.KölnKauf.16, 414/1024; P.Cair.Arab. 62.14, 429/1037; P.RagibQalamun 2.15, 446/1054,

This is an extremely old expression in contracts, for phrases with "heart" and the root ṭ-y-b already appear in Cuneiform inscriptions and Demotic contracts,[26] as well as in Jewish marriage contracts.[27] Frantz-Murphy nevertheless

25 Enlarging legal phrases with synonyms is no Arabic specialty, cf. Frantz-Murphy 1988: 101; Friedman 1980: 169.

26 Frantz-Murphy 1988: 112.

27 Friedmann 1980: 136.

considers it a Qurʾānic quote, and its late appearance in Arabic deeds is an argument in favor of that. Still, the grammatical construction and the meaning are far distant from the verse alluded to. The formula is not mentioned by aṭ-Ṭaḥāwī.

5 Qurʾānic Quotations in Marriage and Divorce Documents

5.1 *Marriage Contracts*

Clear quotations are found in marriage and divorce documents. Some quotations are explicitly introduced as *qawl allāh*, "the Word of God," while others close up a contract formula. Although of all business matters discussed here, divorce is definitely the one about which we find the most detailed instructions in the Qurʾān, in the 3rd century still only about one-third of the preserved contracts include Qurʾānic quotations.

Marriage contracts are often labeled "contract about the dower" (*iṣdāq*) by the editor, but aṭ-Ṭahāwī suggests that this type of document is to be considered as the actual marriage contract.[28] The texts, if complete and conforming to his layout, say *aṣdaqahā … wa-tazawwaǧahā bihi*, "He gave her … and got married to her by this present [dower]." Some dowers (singular *ṣadāq*) attested in papyri equal the value of rural houses (P.Cair.Arab. 48, 233/847, written obligation for the outstanding portion of a *ṣadāq*, amounting to 10 *dīnar*; P.Cair.Arab. 56, 239/854, where the wife buys a house from her husband for 1 *dīnar*), thereby contributing largely to the financial security of the wife. But we also know of later Mamluk princesses whose *dowry* exceeded their *dower* by multiples, reducing thereby the *ṣadāq* to a symbolic value. At the same time, it becomes the element without which no marriage can be concluded.

Most marriage documents include, at their end and after the establishment of all practical matters, a clause on matrimonial harmony and the correct behavior of the husband. Like any clause in any type of early Islamic contract, this clause might be variated and/or enlarged by the actual scribe. At its core, this clause contains an expression such as *wa-ʿalayhi an yattaqiya llāha fī mraʾatihi*, "He is obliged to fear God in what concerns (sc. his behavior toward) his wife" (or: "to behave with reverence toward his wife"?)[29] and the combina-

---

28 It is this *aṣdaqa* formula which aṭ-Ṭahāwī lists under his *Bāb an-nikāḥ*, "Chapter on Marriage," p. 671. See aṭ-Ṭahāwī, 1974.

29 Q 33:55, in a verse about the Prophet's wives, reminds them that God is witness to everything, i.e., even where nobody else can witness. Perhaps fearing God means following his law even where there is no sanction before death?

tion of *ṣuḥba* and *ʿišra*, both meaning "company." This core is not Qurʾānic,[30] but might be enlarged by Qurʾān quotations or allusions.

The Qurʾānic passages which currently enlarge the traditional marriage clause are three: *wa-lahunna miṯlu llaḏī ʿalayhinna bi-l-maʿrūfi wa-li-r-riǧāli ʿalayhinna daraǧatun*, "Women have such honourable rights as obligations, but their men have a degree above them" (Q 2:228); *aṭ-ṭalāqu marratāni fa-imsākun bi-maʿrūfin aw tasrīḥun bi-iḥsānin*, "Divorce is twice, then honourable retention or setting free kindly" (Q 2:229); and *askinūhunna min ḥayṯu sakantum min wuǧdikum wa-lā tuḍārrūhunna li-tuḍayyiqū ʿalayhinna*, "Lodge them where you are lodging, according to your means, and do not press them, so as to straiten their circumstances" (Q 65:6). Additionally, in some cases, the root *ʿ-š-r* from the traditional core is used in stem III, the *mufāʿala*-form, possibly under the influence of *wa-ʿāširūhunna bi-l-maʿrūfi*, "Consort with them honourably" (Q 4:19). At first sight, *muʿāšara* seems to be younger than *ʿišra*, but this is due to the fact that undated documents attributed to the 3rd century are listed in the end of Table 3.4, whereas they might in fact be older. The data are not sufficient to draw conclusions on a development.

TABLE 3.4 Marital obligations as formulated in marriage contracts from the three first Islamic centuries in the Arabic Papyrology Database, along with one later one, to show what the passage might look like when complete, and aṭ-Ṭaḥāwī's template

Year	Papyrus line	نصّ الوثيقة	Qurʾān passages
Beginning of 3rd/9th century	P.GrohmannBerlin 8.6–9	- [وعلى ...] / ن سعد ان سى الله فى [امراته مريم اس اسمعل ...] / و محس صحتها و[عسرتها ... الامساك] / بالمعروف وسه سه [محمد ...] -	Q 2:229?
259/873	P.Cair.Arab. 38.9–12	وسرط اسمعل مولى / احمد ں مروان لامرته عاسه ىقوى الله العطم محسں الصحته والمعاسره / كما امر الله عر وحل وسه محمد صلى الله علىه وسلم على / الامساك بالمعروف او السرح بالاحسان	(Q 4:19); Q 2:229

30 *Taqwà llāh*, "to fear God," is ubiquitous in the Qurʾān, yet with no specific reference to marriage. The word *ṣuḥba* does not appear.

TABLE 3.4 Marital obligations as formulated in marriage contracts (*cont.*)

Year	Papyrus line	نصّ الوثيقة	Qur'ān passages
264/878	P.Cair.Arab. 39.1–2	وعلىه ان ىىمى الله فىها / [وىحسن صحىتها بالمعروف كما امره الله ىعالى الذى لر]م دكره وحل ىاوه وسنه ىىىا محمد	No quotation
271/885	P.Cair.Arab. 40.8	وعلىه ىىقوا / الله وحده لا سرىك له و[احسان صحىىـ]ـا	No quotation
3rd/9th century	CPR XXVI 1.9–10	[و]ىىـ[ـ]ـرط عىىد لامراىه ىىا / ان ىىمى الله فىهـ[ـا] و[ىحسـ]ـن صحىتها ومعاسرىها	(Q 4:19)
279/892	P.Cair.Arab. 41.11–13	[وعلىه] / [ان ىـ]ـىىو الله وحده لا سرىك له وىحسن صحىتها وعسرىها ولا ىصارىها وىفعل ما امره الـ[ـله] / [وسىه مـ]ـحمد صلى الله علىه وسلم على ما امره الله ىه من الامساك بالمعروف او السرىح باحسـ[ـان]	Q 65:6; Q 2:229
3rd/9th century	P.Cair.Arab. 42.5–7	وعلىه ان ىىمى الله عز وحـ[ـل فىها وىحسن صحىتها ىـ]ـالمعروف كما امره الله ىىارك وىعالى / ىه فى كىابه وسىه محمد رسوله صلى الله علىه وعلى ا[له ... فـ]ـما علىه من دلك ودرحه زائده كقول / الله ىعالى وللرحال علىهن درحه والـلـ[ـه] عزىز حكىم	Q 2:228
287/900	P.GrohmannBerlin 9.5–7	وعلىه ان / [ىىمى الله فىها وىحسن صحىتها] وعسرىها بالرافه والرحمه والاحسا[ن ... «ىحعل» الله ىىار]ك وىعالى وسـ(ـىـ)ـن / [محمد صلى الله علىه وسلم عـ]ـلى ما امر الله ىه من ⟦لا امـ..⟧ الامساك بالمعروف والسرىح باحسان	Q 2:229

TABLE 3.4 Marital obligations as formulated in marriage contracts (*cont.*)

Year	Papyrus line	نصّ الوثيقة	Qurʾān passages
295/908	P.GrohmannBerlin 10.5–7	ان سعى الله فىها وىحسن صحىها / ولا ىصار ىها ويعاسرها بالمعروف [كمـ]ـا اوحب الله عليه من الامساك بالمعروف والسرىح / باحسان وعليه بدلك عهد الله ومىاقه ودمه ىىىه محمدا	Q 65:6; Q 4:19; Q 2:229
336/948	P.AbbottMarriageContracts 1.10, quoted according to Hopkins 1996: 603	بما امر الله به من حسن الصحبه وجمىل العسره	No quotation
337/948	P.MariageSéparation 1.5–6	وعليه ان ىىقى الله / جل وعز فىها ويحسن صحىت[ـها ومعا]شرتها بالمعروف ابدا	(Q 4:19)
Undated papyrus	Chrest.Khoury I 87.5–7	على ان سعى الله عر و{ا}حل فىها وحسن صحىها ومعاسرىها بالمعروف / كما امر الله عر وحل فى كىابه وسىه ىىىه محمد صلى الله عليه وسلم / وله عليها مىل الدى لها عليه من دلك	Q 4:19; Q 2:228
419/1028	P.Cair.Arab. 44.6	[وعليه ان ىىـ]ـى الله الكرىم فىها ويحسن صحىها ومـ[ـعاسرىها] / [ولا ىصارها كما امر الـ]ـله عر وحل به فى كىابه وسىه ىىىا محمد صـ[ـلى الله عليه] وسلم فى الامساك بمعروف او السرىح [باحسان].	Q 4:19 (in lacuna); Q 65:6 (in lacuna); Q 2:229
Died 321/933	aṭ-Ṭaḥāwī 1974: 671 (*Kitāb an-nikāḥ, Bāb an-nikāḥ fī tazwīǧ aṣ-ṣaġīra llatī lam tabluġ min al-raǧul aṣ-ṣaḥīḥ al-ʿāqil al-bāliġ*)	وعليه أن يتّقي الله عزّ وجلّ فيها ويحسن صحبتها ومعاشرتها بالمعروف كما أمره الله عز وجلّ في كتابه وسنّة نبيّه صلّى الله عليه وسلّم وله عليها بعد بلوغها مثل الّذي لها عليه من ذلك ودرجة زائدة عليه	(Q 4:19); Q 2:228

But another feature is rather young, and this is denoting the quotation as such and quoting *verbatim*. While five out of eight marriage documents from the first three centuries claim divine or prophetic authority (even P.Cair.Arab. 39.1–2, where no Qur'ānic text whatsoever is preserved), only one (divorce) document speaks of *qawl allāh*, "the Word of God," and quotes precisely, as do the two Fāṭimid texts. In the older documents, Qur'ānic passages are changed in order to fit the syntactical structure of the contract, whereas in the younger ones, quotations keep their form and therewith become distinct.

For legal reasons, aṭ-Ṭahāwī also variates Qur'ānic formulae. In his *Kitāb an-nikāḥ*, "The Chapter on Marriage," the first formulary concerns the marriage of an adult man with a girl who, as a minor (*ṣaġīra lam tabluġ*), can have no obligations; thus aṭ-Ṭahāwī changes the formula *wa-lahu ʿalayhā miṯlu llaḏī lahā ʿalayhi wa-daraǧatun zāyidatun ʿalayhā*, "and she owes him the same as he owes her, and one degree more at her expense," into *wa-lahu ʿalayhā baʿda bulūghihā miṯlu llaḏī lahā ʿalayhi min ḏalika wa-daraǧatun zāyidatun ʿalayhi* (sic), "and she will owe him, after her majority, the same as he owes her in this respect, and one degree more."

What is the origin of the core clause *wa-ʿalayhi an yuḥsina ṣuḥbatahā wa-ʿišratahā*, "to make her company and association pleasant"?[31] Aṭ-Ṭaḥāwī comments and justifies many of his clauses, but has nothing to say on this one. Yet P.Cair.Arab. 38.9–12, P.GrohmannBerlin 9.5–7, and P.GrohmannBerlin 10.5–7 connect this formula to the one taken from Q 2:229 *imsākun bi-maʿrūfin aw tasrīḥun bi-iḥsānin*, "honourable retention or setting free kindly," and aṭ-Ṭabarī, commenting on Q 2:229, quotes a Ḥadīṯ saying, [...] *an yumsikahā bi-maʿrūfin fa-yuḥsina ṣuḥbatahā aw yusarriḥahā* [...], "that he keeps her, making her company pleasant, or that he sets her free [...]."[32] Yet *aḥsana ṣuḥbatahu* alone was an idiomatic expression at that time with no relation to marriage.[33] *Taqwā llāhi fīhinna* was also used when talking about sisters and daughters.[34] The combination *ṣuḥba wa-ʿišra* occurs in aṭ-Ṭabarī's *Tafsīr*, not in a Ḥadīṯ but in his own summary on Q 2:228,[35] and in al-Buḫārī, again in no Ḥadīṯ but in his introduc-

31 Bauer 2015: 97 has been able to track these matrimonial clauses in exegesis works, aḍ-Ḍaḥḥāk b. Muzāhim al-Hilālī appearing as a main source.

32 aṭ-Ṭabarī [1955] IV: 543.

33 Wensinck 1936–1969 III: 658, second column, lists *aḥsana ṣuḥbatahu* also with male objects. Bauer 2015 found that "*ḥusn aṣ-ṣuḥba* impies caretaking, protection, and solicitous regard."

34 at-Tirmiḏī 2000: 502 (*Kitāb al-birr, Bāb* 13); cf. Also Bauer 2015: 106.

35 aṭ-Ṭabarī [1955] IV: 531.

tion about *ḫulʿ*, "divorce initiated by the wife."[36] The commandment for good relations was thought to be divine and implicit in the Qurʾān, even if the exact phrase is not to be found there.

Contracts with no Qurʾānic quotations show us what the function of quotations actually was. Thus we have a marriage contract between Copts (P.Abbott MarriageContracts 1) that is formuated according to aṭ-Ṭaḥāwī but omits the allusion to the Qurʾān that would otherwise be expected in a 4th-century document. A similar situation has been noticed by Rapoport with respect to P.Cair.Arab. 40, when he identifies another three Arabic marriage contracts concluded by Coptic couples (Chrest.Khoury I 17; P.Cair.Arab. 43; P.Philad.Arab. 38).[37] We should not be too surprised to find Arabic marriage contracts among Copts. Marriages were not celebrated in church before the 6th century. For the Syriac church, a ceremony related to the conclusion of the contract (*mekīrūtā*) is first mentioned at the end of the 8th century. This created a distinction between marriages concluded in and by the church and "civil" marriages, but the latter still existed in the 9th century.[38] Perhaps the recourse to Muslim authorities was the only way to have marriage agreements written down.

5.2 *Two Divorce Documents*

The first example in Table 3.5 is taken from a declaration (*iqrār*) by the husband in which he sets his wife free and gives up any option to turn back to her "until she marries another husband." It shows how the Qurʾānic prescription that a definitely divorced woman (threefold divorce) may not return to her husband

36 al-Buḫārī 2000: 1105 (*Kitāb aṭ-ṭalāq, Bāb* 12).

37 "The documentary evidence includes at least six Arabic documents that bear Coptic names, but these do not seem to differ from contracts concluded by Muslims, except for the omission of religious formulae" (Rapoport 2000: 4). The six documents are Chrest.Khoury I 10 and 15 (= P.AbbottMarriage 1 and 2); 17; P.Cair.Arab. 40; 43; P.Philad.Arab. 38. The two marriage documents do not lack religious formulae: P.Cair.Arab. 40 has a statement of *tawḥīd* (monotheism) in the middle of the marital obligation, and P.Cair.Arab. 43 is not a marriage contract but a fragmentary acknowledgment of a wife, probably that she received or renounced a part of her *ṣadāq*. Rapoport assumes that persons bearing Coptic names are Copts. Only in P.AbbottMarriageContracts 1, the groom is a deacon and the bride the daughter of a priest. Green 1993: 362, in his edition of a 19th-century Arabic marriage contract, gives an overview of Coptic marriage contracts, i.e., marriages in Coptic families in the pre-Islamic and Early Islamic period, be they in Coptic or in Arabic. Like Rapoport after him, he lists the mentioned documents as "Coptic marriages."

38 The synode under the West-Syriac patriarch Dionysios (d. 845) gives the first clear hint that a civil marriage was considered equivalent to fornication (Selb 1992: 4). For the *mekīrūtā*, see Selb 1992: 5; for the wedding celebration (*meštūtā*), Selb 1992: 7.

TABLE 3.5 Two Qur'ānic quotations taken from divorce documents in the Arabic Papyrology Database

Year	Papyrus line	نصّ الوثيقة	نصّ القرآن	Qur'ān
397/909	Chrest.Khoury I 17.3–4	لا رحعه له علها ولا مسوبه حى سكـ[ـح] رو[حا] / عىره	فَإِنْ طَلَّقَهَا فَلَا تَحِلُّ لَهُ مِن بَعْدُ حَتَّى تَنْكِحَ زَوْجًا غَيْرَهُ	Q 2:230
3rd/9th century	P.World p. 199.2–3 = Chrest. Khoury I 20.2–3	وان يتفرقا يغنى / الله كلا من سعته وكان الله واسعا حكيما	وَإِن يَتَفَرَّقَا يُغْنِ اللَّهُ كُلًّا مِّن سَعَتِهِ وَكَانَ اللهُ وَاسِعًا حَكِيمًا	Q 4:130

before having been married to another man was bluntly implemented into the deed by referring to the corresponding passage of the Qur'ān. The couple have Coptic names. The second text is a deed in which former spouses acquit each other of financial claims. It is one of the rare Arabic deeds to have an arenga, including an extended Qur'ānic quotation, which shows a slight deviation from the text, Qur'ānic *yuġni* becoming *yuġnī* in the divorce deed. This fits with none of the current variants by ʿĀṣim or Ibn Kaṯīr, etc.

6 Conclusions

In their transactions, Arabic scribes had not much occasion to quote the Qur'ān. Before the emergence of Islam, legal speech had often been idiomatic, but later became connected to the Qur'ān. This shows that over time, the Qur'ān became better known and more present in daily life. Such a development cannot be observed for mottoes and seal inscriptions. Some of them are exact quotes, others just vary Qur'ānic topoi of piety.

The scarcity of Qur'ānic quotations in legal texts might be due to the scarcity of detailed legal instructions in the Qur'ān. The only exception is divorce, and indeed, the formulary for divorce documents applies Qur'ānic instructions directly. Marriage contracts are a special case, because many cultures emphasize their strong relationship to religion and tradition; Muslim scribes did integrate Qur'ānic quotations into marriage contracts, but had to take them from the passages about divorce.

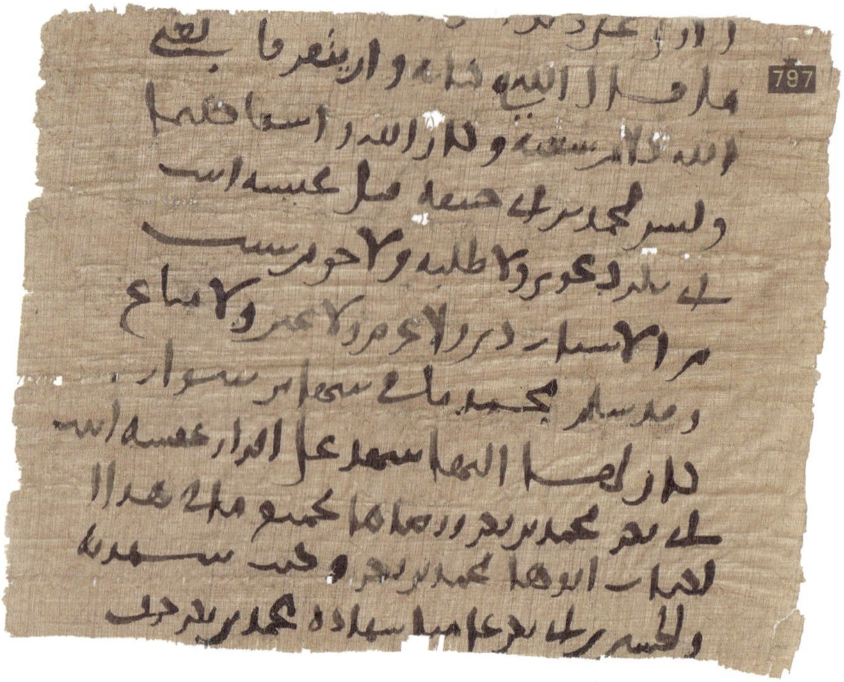

FIGURE 3.2 A divorce document quoting Q 4:130 (P.Vind.inv. A.P. 832 = P.World p. 199 = Chrest.Khoury I 20)
© ÖSTERREICHISCHE NATIONALBIBLIOTHEK, PAPYRUSSAMMLUNG

Bibliography

ʿAbd al-Bāqī, Muḥammad Fu'ād. 1364/[1945]. *al-Muʿǧam al-mufahras li-alfāẓ al-Qurʾān al-karīm*. Cairo: Dār al-Kutub al-Miṣriyya.

Arberry, Arthur John. 1955. *The Koran Interpreted*. London: George Allen and Unwin.

Avenarius, Thomas. 2014. "Tonstörung." In *Süddeutsche Zeitung*, 2.5.2014: 3.

Babinger, Franz, and C. Edmund Bosworth. 2000. "Tawḳīʿ." In *Encyclopedia of Islam. Second Edition, vol. 10*. Leiden: Brill, 392–393.

Balogh, E[lemér], and Paul Eric Kahle. 1953. "Two Coptic Documents Relating to Marriage." In *Aegyptus* 33: 331–340.

Bauer, Karen. 2015. "A Note on the Relationship between Tafsīr and Common Understanding with Reference to Contracts of Marriage." In *Islamic Cultures, Islamic Contexts: Essays in Honor of Professor Patricia Crone*, ed. Behnam Sadeghi et al. Leiden: Brill, 97–111.

Bobzin, Hartmut. 2007. *Der Koran: eine Einführung*. München: Beck.

Bruning, Jelle. 2015. "A Legal Sunna in Dhikr Ḥaqqs from Sufyanid Egypt." In *Islamic Law and Society* 22: 352–374.

al-Buḫārī, Muḥammad ibn Ismāʿīl. 2000. *Ṣaḥīḥ*. Vaduz: Thesaurus Islamicus Foundation.

Cotton, Hannah 1994. "A Cancelled Marriage Contract from the Judaean Desert." In *Journal of Roman Studies* 84: 64–86.

Crone, Patricia. 1987. *Provincial and Islamic Law: The Origins of the Islamic Patronate*. Cambridge: Cambridge University Press.

Crum, Walter Ewing. 1907. "The Coptic Manuscripts." In *Gizeh and Rifeh*, ed. W.M. Flinders Petrie et al. London: School of Archaeology in Egypt, 39–45.

Diem, Werner. 1998. *Fa-waylun li-l-qāsiyati qulūbuhum: Studien zum arabischen adjektivischen Satz*. Wiesbaden: Harrassowitz.

Diem, Werner. 2011. "Philologisches zu arabischen Dokumenten der Österreichischen Nationalbibliothek in Wien." In *Wiener Zeitschrift für die Kunde des Morgenlandes* 101: 75–140.

Frantz-Murphy, Gladys. 1981. "A Comparison of the Arabic and Earlier Egyptian Contract Formularies. Part I: The Arabic Contracts from Egypt (3rd/9th–5th/11th)." In *Journal of Near Eastern Studies* 40: 203–225; 356–357.

Frantz-Murphy, Gladys. 1988. "A Comparison of Arabic and earlier Egyptian Contract Formularies. Part III: The Idiom of Satisfaction." In *Journal of Near Eastern Studies* 47: 105–112.

Frantz-Murphy, Gladys. 1989. "A Comparison of Arabic and Earlier Egyptian Contract Formularies. Part V: Formulaic Evidence." In *Journal of Near Eastern Studies* 48: 97–107.

Frantz-Murphy, Gladys. 2001. *Arabic Agricultural Leases and Tax Receipts from Egypt*. Corpus Papyrorum Raineri, vol. 21. Arabic Papyri, vol. 17. Wien: Hollinek.

Friedmann, Mordechai Akiva. 1980. *Jewish Marriage in Palestine: A Cairo Geniza Study, vol. I: The "Ketubba" Traditions of Eretz Israel*. Tel Aviv; New York: Jewish Theological Seminary of America.

Green, Arnold H. 1993. "A Late 19th Century Coptic Marriage Contract and the Coptic Documentary Tradition." In *Le Muséon* 106: 361–371.

Grob, Eva Mira. 2010. *Documentary Arabic Private and Business Letters on Papyrus: Form and Function, Content and Context*. Archiv für Papyrusforschung und verwandte Gebiete, Beihefte 29. Berlin: de Gruyter.

Grob, Eva Mira. 2013. "A Catalogue of Dating Criteria for Undated Arabic Papyri with 'Cursive' Features." In *Documents et histoire, Islam, VIIe–XVIe s.: Actes des journées d'études Musée du Louvre/EPHE, mai 2008*, ed. Anne Regourd. [Publications de l']École pratique des hautes études, Sciences historiques et philologiques II. Hautes études orientales—Moyen et Proche-Orient, vol. 5/51. Geneva: Droz, 123–143.

Grohmann, Adolf. 1954. *Einführung und Chrestomathie zur arabischen Papyruskunde*. Prag: Státní Pedagogické Nakladalství.

Gronke, Monika. 1984. "La rédaction des actes privés dans le monde musulman médiéval: théorie et pratique." In *Studia Islamica* 59: 159–174.

Helmholz, R.H. 1994. "The Bible in the Service of the Canon Law." In *Chicago-Kent Law Review* 70: 1557–1581.

Hengstl, Joachim, Gottfried Schiemann, and Peter Gröschler. 2002. "Urkunden." In *Der Neue Pauly, Vol. 12,1*, ed. Hubert Cancik and Helmut Schneider. Stuttgart: Metzler.

Hopkins, Simon. 1996. "Arabic Papyri." In *The Elephantine Papyri in English: Three Millennia of Cross Cultural Continuity and Change*, ed. Bezalel Porten et al. Leiden: Brill, 603–607.

Hurvitz, Avi. 1982. "The History of a Legal Formula: *kōl ʾašer-ḥāpēṣ ʿāśāh* (Psalms CXV 3, CXXXV 6)". In *Vetus Testamentum* 32: 257–267.

Imber, Colin. 1997. "Women, Marriage and Property: *Mahr* in the *Behcetü'l-Fetava* of Yenişehirli Abdullah." In *Women in the Ottoman Empire: Middle Eastern Women in the Early Modern Era*, ed. Madeline C. Zilfi. The Ottoman Empire and Its Heritage, vol. 10. Leiden: Brill, 81–104.

Kahle, Paul Eric. 1954. *Bala'izah: Coptic Texts from Deir El-Bala'izah in Upper Egypt*. London: Oxford University Press.

Khan, Geoffrey. 1994. "The Pre-Islamic Background of Muslim Legal Formularies." In *Aram* 6: 193–224.

Khan, Geoffrey. 2008. "Remarks on the Historical Background and Development of Early Arabic Documentary Formulae." In *Asiatische Studien/Études asiatiques* 62,3 (= *Documentary Letters from the Middle East: The Evidence in Greek, Coptic, South Arabian, Pehlevi, and Arabic (1st–15th c CE)*, ed. Eva Mira Grob and Andreas Kaplony. Bern: Lang, 2008), 885–906.

Kraemer, Casper. 1958. *Excavations at Nessana, Vol. 3: Non-Literary Papyri*. Princeton: Princeton University Press.

MacCoull, Leslie. 1979. "A Coptic Marriage Contract in the Pierpont Morgan Library." In *Actes Du XVe Congres International de Papyrologie*, ed. Jean Bingen and Georges Nachtergael. Bruxelles: Fondation Égyptologique Reine Élisabeth, 116–124.

Palme, Bernhard. 2009. "The Range of Documentary Texts: Types and Categories." In *The Oxford Handbook of Papyrology*, ed. Roger S. Bagnall. Oxford: Oxford University Press, 358–394.

Rapoport, Yossef. 2000. "Matrimonial Gifts in Early Islamic Egypt." In *Islamic Law and Society* 7: 1–36.

Schoeler, Gregor. 1989. "Mündliche Thora und Hadith. Überlieferung, Schreibverbot, Redaktion." In *Der Islam* 66: 213–251.

Selb, Walter. 1992. "Zur Christianisierung des Eherechts." In *Eherecht und Familiengut in Antike und Mittelalter*, ed. Dieter Simon. Schriften des Historischen Kollegs: Kolloquien, vol. 22. München: Oldenbourg.

Sijpesteijn, P[etra] M. 2013a. "An Arabic Land Lease from Tutun." In *Papyrological Texts in Honor of Roger S. Bagnall*, ed. Rodney Ast et al. American Studies in Papyrology, vol. 53. Durham: American Society of Papyrologists, 301–306.

Sijpesteijn, Petra M. 2013b. *Shaping a Muslim State: The World of a Mid-Eighth-Century Egyptian Official*. Oxford Studies in Byzantium. Oxford: Oxford University Press.

Sijpesteijn, Petra M. 2014. "Ein Buch und sein Widerhall: zum Gebrauch des Korans im 7.–10. Jahrhundert in Ägypten." In *Kinder Abrahams: die Bibel in Judentum, Christentum und Islam*, ed. Armin Lange and Bernhard Palme. Nilus, vol. 21. Vienna: Phoibos, 47–59; 119–123.

Simonsohn, Uriel I. 2011. *A Common Justice: The Legal Allegiances of Christians and Jews under Early Islam*. Divinations: Rereading Late Ancient Religion. Philadelphia: University of Pennsylvania Press.

Sirat, Colette, Patrice Cauderlier, Michèle Dukan, and Akiva Mordechai Friedman. 1986. *La Ketouba de Cologne: un contrat de mariage juif à Antinoopolis*. Abhandlungen der Rheinisch-Westfälischen Akademie der Wissenschaften, Sonderreihe Papyrologica Coloniensia, vol. 12. Opladen: Westdeutscher Verlag.

aṭ-Ṭabarī, Abū Ǧaʿfar Muḥammad ibn Ǧarīr. [1955]. *Ǧāmiʿ al-bayān ʿan taʾwīl āy al-Qurʾān*. Cairo: Dār al-maʿārif bi-Miṣr.

aṭ-Ṭaḥāwī, Aḥmad. 1974. *Kitāb aš-šurūṭ aṣ-ṣaġīr*, ed. Rūḥī Ūzǧān. Bagdad: Matbaʿat Iʿlānī.

Thung, Michael. 2006. *Arabische juristische Urkunden aus der Papyrussammlung der Österreichischen Nationalbibliothek*. Corpus Papyrorum Raineri, vol. 26. München; Leipzig: Saur.

at-Tirmiḏī, Muḥammad ibn ʿIsā. 2000. *Sunan*. Vaduz: Thesaurus Islamicus Foundation.

Wakin, Jeanette A. 1972. *The Function of Documents in Islamic Law: The Chapters on Sales from Ṭaḥāwīs Kitāb al-šurūṭ al-kabīr*. Albany: State University of New York Press.

Wensinck, Arent J. 1936–1969. *Concordance et indices de la Tradition musulmane*. Leiden: Brill.

CHAPTER 4

Qur'ānic Quotations in Arabic Papyrus Amulets

Ursula Bsees

This article deals with the Qur'ān text as it appears in Arabic papyri that are generally called magical. Additionally, some texts on ostraca, parchment, and cloth have been studied. Due to the restricted time frame for the use of papyrus,[1] texts on paper were not taken into account for the collection of verses found in the texts, but nevertheless served as reference material.

1 The Study of Arabic Amulets

Although the last years have shown a certain increase in the number of editions of Arabic papyri, the percentage of published Arabic papyri is still very small. Consequently, even some of the major editions we work with must be treated with caution, since they are partially outdated and in need of a thorough revision, e.g., Grohmann's *P.Cair.Arab. I–VI* (1938–1962). Yet we have high-quality edition volumes at our disposal, among them those of the Vienna collection in the *Corpus Papyrorum Raineri* (CPR) volumes, such as Diem's *CPR XVI* (1993) and Thung's *CPR XXVI* (2006), as well as papyri from Heidelberg and Berlin in Diem's *P.Heid.Arab. II* (1991) and *P.Berl.Arab. II* (1997) and from the Louvre in David-Weill et al.'s *P.Louvre I–III* (1965–1978). Unfortunately, much material is scattered in articles and chapters of books, now collected and brought together in the Arabic Papyrology Database (www.naher-osten.lmu.de/apd). What we desperately need is a compendium, a handbook on the different domains of Arabic Papyrology, describing the state of the art and gathering the most important insights achieved during the past eighty years.

Arabic papyri amount to roughly 80,000 documents, and the percentage of published papyri is only approximately 3–4%. Of this small quantity, even less work has been devoted to magical papyri—a situation reminiscent of Greek papyrology before Preisendanz's groundbreaking *Papyri Graecae Mag-*

1 Grob 2010: XIV.

 | DOI:10.1163/9789004376977_005

icae (Preisendanz 1928–1941). Before him, there had not been much interest in magical papyri, and some scholars were even outspokenly against studying them in order not to destroy the image of a sophisticated, refined Hellenic culture seemingly incompatible with the often obscure and strange rites and spells found in magical papyri. Betz even says, "How far the dislike of the magical papyri could go is illustrated by a remark made by Ulrich von Wilamowitz-Moellendorff: 'I once heard a well-known scholar complain that these papyri were found because they deprived antiquity of the noble splendor of classicism.'"[2] Ignoring a whole genre of texts because they do not fit the views of some scholars—possibly even the majority—does not really serve the progress of science.

Likewise, the Qur'ān text as represented on papyri, and especially on magical papyri, must be taken into consideration for statements on its early use and history. Otherwise, the gain we have from the study of Qur'ān manuscripts, while definitely not small, lacks an important facet—its use and representation in the daily lives of believers. The degree to which this fact resembles the situation of Greek magical papyri before the efforts of Dietrich and Preisendanz is remarkable—a situation which Betz describes as follows: "Modern views of Greek and Roman religion have long suffered from certain deformities because they were unconsciously shaped by the only remaining sources: the literature of the cultural elite, and the archeological remains of the official cults of the states and cities."[3]

Speaking from today's point of view, it seems that the field of Arabic papyrology is in the same situation. While publications of official documents, legal deeds, and letters of all kinds are extremely valuable and of high quality, literary and magical papyri have mostly been neglected. This study is therefore based on the few editions of magical papyri available to us, which are to be found in Karabacek's *Papyrusfund von El-Faijûm* (1882); Margoliouth's *P.Ryl.Arab. I* (1933); Grohmann's *Zaubertexte* (1934); Dietrich's *P.Hamb.Arab. I* (1937) and *Topkapı* (1958); and Levi Della Vida's *P.Philad.Arab.* (1981). It is symptomatic that the last published edition of magical papyri containing Qur'ān verses was made in 1981.[4] The number of texts that met the criteria applied for this study amounts to 20, some of them small and with only a few lines of text. The reader

2 Betz 1986: XLIIII.

3 Betz 1986: XLI.

4 The Arabic magical texts published later are either on paper, parchment, or other material or do not contain verses from the Qur'ān, such as Diem 1991a, whose texts do not feature Qur'ān verses (nos. 2–3 are re-editions of P.Ryl.Arab. I XIII 6 and XIII 2) or Guo's edition of Arabic documents from al-Quṣayr (Guo 2004), whose texts are written on paper.

must bear in mind that due to the age of the editions used, the images presented therein are all black and white and sometimes of suboptimal quality, at least regarding a thorough examination of the text. P.DietrichTopkapı 4, which is one of the most important papyri discussed by us, is depicted only in some kind of *facsimile* in the handwriting of Albert Dietrich. Moreover, only one edition (Grohmann's *Zaubertexte*) is entirely devoted to magical texts, while the others include only small numbers of magical papyri.

Up to now, nothing has being said about amulets and magical papyri having their own line of transmission of the Qur'ān text, or about their also providing almost unrivaled insight into daily life in Early Islamic Egypt. Unfortunately, statements on these topics must remain mostly assumptions and vague theories, since many aspects of the documents' "setting in life" as well as the archaeological context of our texts are still obscure. Given the small number of published Arabic magical texts, final statements on their background are nearly impossible. This has repercussions for anything that can be said about philological aspects of the papyri. We do not know, for example, whether suggestions about the connection between literacy, script, and writing mistakes might be proven or refuted by future research, given the huge blank areas of the first three centuries of writing in Islam.

2 Arabic Amulets: "Setting in Life" and Preservation

The term "magical" must be regarded as a generic term loosely applied by scholars to a number of categories, such as prayers, imprecations, amulets for positive or negative purposes, and divinatory texts. Tempting as it might be to posit an extensive definition of "magic," an undertaking on this scale would definitely go beyond the focus of this article. That is why we adhere to the different editors' classifications: What they call "magical papyri," "amulets," etc. are treated by us as such.

In the Islamic tradition, such texts very often contain verses from the Qur'ān, which are invested with power that people made use of for manifold purposes.[5] Naturally, some verses offer themselves for curing sickness, while others might be chosen for their protective qualities. The verses chosen either mention these qualities in their text (especially Q 113–114) or have been considered to be powerful with respect to certain purposes in pertinent works of magic, in the Ḥadīṯ collections or in the Tafsīr. They have been collected in groups, e.g., *Āyāt al-ḥifẓ*,

5 On the power of Qur'ānic speech and its miraculous qualities, see Stock 1999: 19–20.

the "Verses of Protection," or *Āyāt aš-šifāʾ*, the "Verses of Healing."[6] The verses were written down on different materials according to the intended purpose. Whereas amulets for protection were worn on the body, e.g., around the neck or on the upper arm, in amulet capsules, texts with healing qualities were oftentimes first written down, then rinsed and the water drunk in order to imbibe the holy text's healing powers.[7] There are even bowls etched with Qur'ān verses and other powerful words, which could be filled with water, into which the words' healing power, the blessing (*baraka*), entered. The water then had to be drunk in order to achieve the transmission of blessing into one's own body. We also find talismanic clothing, most probably for protection in battle.[8]

The most beautiful representations of protective objects are certainly amulets etched in precious stones and metals. They were intended to be worn for protection over a long period of time, unlike amulets for healing purposes or for protection in certain situations, e.g., for relief in childbirth or for curing diseases, whose use was naturally limited to a shorter span.

What might appear as a digression here is actually an essential addition to the mere linguistic examination of magical papyri, since the scarcity of the material forces us to take into consideration other aspects of the texts' background and setting in life. Otherwise, we would gain even less insight into questions such as why a short text was written on a piece of cloth: most probably it had been sewn into a garment. Additional aspects of this kind include archeological evidence such as foldings, creases, or traces of dirt that could shed light on the circumstances of storage a text had been exposed to.

This leads us to the issue of how one disposed of a magical text. Bearing in mind the enormous number of amulets which are being written daily nowadays, it is surprising that magical papyri make up only such a small percentage of the various collections. One possible explanation is the characteristic secrecy with which magical texts must be treated. It is easily understandable that amulets written on behalf of someone, whether for or against certain circumstances, were not meant to be seen by anyone except the wearer, and perhaps not even by him/her, since amulets were often sewn and/or folded into small cloth parcels; opening such a parcel was considered highly dangerous because it could cause the affliction that was to be averted by the amulet to befall the person opening it. We must also consider the possibility of turning

6 Kriss and Kriss-Heinrich 1962: 61. *Āyāt al-ḥifẓ*: end of Q 2:255 *Āyat al-Kursī*; 12:65; 13:12; 15:10; 37:8; 85:21–23. *Āyāt aš-šifāʾ*: Q 9:14; 10:58; 16:70; 17:83; 26:79–81; 41:45.

7 For a papyrus text alluding to such practices, cf. P.Ryl.Arab. I XIII I.1–5.

8 Kriss and Kriss-Heinrich 1962: II 138–139.

an amulet for someone into a harmful spell against the wearer. This could have been the case if it fell into the hands of a person wishing to cause the (former) wearer harm.

Let us keep in mind what has been said above about lack of interest in magical papyri from the scholars' side. It might be that the collections *do* contain large, hitherto undiscovered stocks of amulets and other magical texts, yet we do not know of them due to a lack of interest from the side of the papyrologists who have been working in said collections. Moreover, all magical sciences had operated in a sphere of secrecy ever since Greek magical books had been burnt on a large scale by Augustus, and their authors and those who worked with them had met the same fate. Consequently, magical literature and practice went underground.[9] We might assume that this tradition of secrecy, like many others, was also practiced in the magical sciences in their Islamic form.

It is therefore hard to believe that amulets, even after their use had expired, were discarded carelessly with other rubbish. Without making suggestions that lack proof, we first must ask ourselves why collections *do* contain amulets at all if there was fear of their content's exposure; and second, we must regard them critically since quite a number of them may possibly have been just templates for amulet writers and never used as amulets themselves.[10] A way of testing this is to look at the amulets' folding, but the problem with this approach is that most papyri we are discussing here are accessible only as black-and-white images of sometimes poor quality, so that we must rely on the remarks of the editors who saw the originals.

Consequently, we must say that there is neither proof that all texts in the collections are "real" amulets, nor proof to the contrary, i.e., that they (or at least most of them) are mere templates for texts destroyed after their use. Should it turn out that some of what has been classified as "magical" most probably belongs to another category of text altogether, then such a result could drastically alter not only the conclusions made in this study, but also the direction of future research on the use of the Qur'ān text on papyrus.

Yet we cannot exclude the possibility that some of the so-called amulets preserved in the collections were really used as such. If this is the case, then were there methods of disposal which, under certain circumstances, did not destroy the text?

9 Cf. Betz 1986: XLI.

10 According to Khan 1991–1992: 57, many Qur'ān fragments in the collections were used for private study. If there is no definite evidence, it is best not classify a text as an amulet only because there are some Qur'ān verses on it.

When thinking about the disposal of amulets and other magical papyri, we must bear in mind that due to the sacred character of Qur'ān verses, which represent the Word of God and therefore must be treated with respect, texts made up of or containing Qur'ān verses cannot be discarded like any other kind of text. As Sadan writes, "The literature of Islamic jurisprudence explains the reasons for the concept which requires that worn-out sacred books (usually just Qur'ān volumes), be buried in a special way or treated in any other reverent manner; these reasons are rooted in a zealous religious veneration of the sacred texts."[11]

As in many other matters, Islamic jurisprudence has brought forward suggestions on how to deal with worn-out texts, differentiating between the recommended treatment of Qur'ān exemplars and the treatment of other texts containing citations from the Qur'ān, such as Ḥadīṯ texts or works on grammar. While many jurists recommend burying worn-out Qur'ān exemplars, in an approach analogous to the custom of burying Torah scrolls in Judaism, there is still the fear that the text might be desecrated by dust and earth. Old texts were also re-used for wrapping or binding new books, which was partially permitted depending on the content of both the old and the new text.[12] Another way of recycling old texts was washing or scraping off the ink and using the material again, although this was mostly carried out as the first stage of a longer process of disposal by burial or incineration. Only very few jurists recommend incineration because it is reminiscent of the burning of books that were said to be heretical. Another option was sinking the books in water, although water might also be contaminated with dirt.

As Sadan points out, "One may guess that any local religious leader, hesitating to face the various complications arising in the application of the abovementioned methods in disposing of a worn-out sacred books [*sic*] (since every single method is described, by some of the jurists, as constituting some kind of desecration or defilement) would simply prefer to lock it, at least for a while, somewhere in the library of the local *madrasa*, or in the near-by mosque, or on a shelf in its library."[13] Indeed, Sadan gives evidence for practices akin to the Cairo Genizah in several well-known places, namely the Sīdī 'Uqba Mosque in Kairouan, the Great Mosque of Sanaa, and the Umayyad Mosque in Damascus. Of these three, the latter is of much interest for us, since Ibn Kannān says that there are rumors about small rooms above the pillars of the Umayyad Mosque

11 Sadan 1986: 39.
12 Sadan 1986: 46.
13 Sadan 1986: 53.

"in which written material (viz., *waqf* documents etc.) was kept, together with talismans and incantations against 'snakes, insects, scorpions, beetles, flies, birds, and bats.'"[14]

If we assume that the custom of storing magical texts was known throughout the Islamicate World—and the geographic distance between the mentioned places suggests so—then this would indeed be an explanation for the preservation of magical texts; after all, it is not hard to imagine forgotten storerooms of mosques or *madrasas* as sources of some papyrus finds which have in one way or another entered the papyrus collections.

3 Arabic Amulets: Appearance and Text Layout

The wide range of texts summarized under "magical papyri" is one of the reasons for a similarly wide range of appearances of these texts. Here, we are interested in texts with Qur'ān verses only, but even among these there is no uniform layout that could qualify as standard for an Arabic magical text or an amulet. Many of the amulets are quite small (P.Bad. V 148 measures 2,3 × 3,3 cm), probably a clue to their use in pouches or capsules, but others are not, so small size does not distinguish magical texts from other types of papyri.

One characteristic of magical papyri is magical signs (*charaktēres*), whose origins are unknown, although speculation about them was widespread in Arabic medieval magical writings and still abounds in modern treatises, but without a final explanation on which scholars agree.[15] Apart from magical signs, some of which resemble alphabets, we also find drawings of animals and demons, presumably mostly apotropaic (P.Vind.inv. A.P. 1762v has a big drawing of a scorpion with two other animals and *charaktēres*). Yet drawings appear rarely in Arabic magical papyri, whereas they abound in Greek and Coptic magical papyri and in later Arabic magical paper documents.[16]

14 Ibn Kannān 1998: i 404.

15 For medieval and modern speculation on the origins of magical signs, see Kriss and Kriss-Heinrich 1962: 74–81; Pielow 1995: 156–158. Magical signs are found, e.g., on P.Vind.inv. A.P. 6785v.

16 Examples of such drawings can be found in P.Heid.inv. 1681–1683; P.Heid.inv. 518r; P.Heid. inv. Arab. 500–501; P.Vind.inv. A.Ch. 25618; P.Vind.inv. A.Ch. 16071; P.Vind.inv. A.Ch. 12201.

We might assume that the conquest of Egypt by the Muslim Arabs caused a certain rupture in Egyptian magical tradition, since the Arabs brought with them the concept of the power of the written word and especially of the Qur'ān, the written Word of God. This may have influenced local tradition by offering something more powerful than images of demons, i.e., "images" of Qur'ān verses. The number of elaborate drawings of animals and magical signs in Arabic magical papyri, as compared to Greek and Coptic papyri, is extremely small[17] and their small number might be due to such a shift in the concept of powerful images. The majority of the Egyptian population neither read nor wrote Arabic, but they knew that Arabic was the language of the new elite, the language they saw primarily in manifestations of state power such as inscriptions and coins. Using Arabic meant wielding something of the power of the country's new rulers.[18] This new way of representing power via Arabic script may have replaced the images of demons and the like formerly preferred in amulets. The aspiration to acquire the power of Arabic for oneself does not necessarily demand the use of Qur'ān verses, but in daily life, Arabic was mostly present in inscriptions with Qur'ān verses written in Kūfī script. An imitation of this particular style best transported its power onto papyrus.

In order to extract as much blessing (*baraka*) from the verses as possible, letters were partly written in isolated form, which invokes not only the blessing of the sentence, e.g., the Basmala, but also the blessings of each one of its 19 letters.[19] Arabic isolated letters were also used according to their numerical value, as *abǧad* letters, although they are mostly found in magical squares not yet attested on papyrus.

Furthermore, the sphere of secrecy intrinsic to magical papyri is reflected in deliberately unreadable handwriting and layout. The ways these can be distorted for the purpose of illegibility are as numerous as human imagination allows. P.Vind.inv. A.P. 6175, for example, has tiny, crammed, extremely cursive handwriting and is therefore unreadable.

A unique example of a layout variant in magical papyri can be found in P.Vind.inv. A.P. 10042. The text, which perhaps contains Q 112, is surrounded by a frame reminiscent of the antique *tabula ansata*, or "tablet with handles" style of tablets with Greek and Latin inscriptions. The same style was widely used for Egyptian mummy tablets, especially in the lower classes of the popu-

17 The Vienna collection alone has several fine examples of drawings on Arabic magical papyri (among them P.Vind.inv. A.P. 1762v). Their exact number is still unknown.

18 Kaplony 2019: 5.

19 Pielow 1995: 80.

lation.[20] The *tabula ansata*'s use in the death cult before the Islamic conquest of Egypt could be regarded as its link to a later inclination toward it for magical purposes. Practitioners of magic have always felt an attraction to mysterious, incomprehensible, and strange words and rites. In this respect, the netherworld and some seemingly strange rites connected to it seem predestined to be used by magicians who wanted to evoke the power of a death cult alien to their own cultural and religious background.

Unfortunately, the layout mentioned is unique on papyrus, a specimen without parallels, which makes any definite statement impossible, especially on the question of whether there are any other Arabic magical papyri with a similar layout or whether P.Vind.inv. A.P. 10042 really is one of a kind. However, wooden tablets are a known writing material; they were even used as amulets in pre-Islamic Southern Arabia.[21] Unfortunately, we have no clear evidence for wooden tablets used as amulets in Islamic times. P.Vind.inv. AHT 1 b has Qurʾān verses, but is way too big, as is P.Cair.EgLib.inv. Gen. 39825.[22] P.Cair.IslArt inv. 6003 has the form of a *tabula ansata* and is inscribed with Q 1 and 112, as well as with the beautiful names of God used in the context of healing sickness. Grohmann gives a plate depicting one side of the tablet,[23] but no measurements are added, so size drops out as a criterion for guesses as to its contemporary use. Interestingly, the script is dotted in *maġribī* style, but the *rasm* is written in a low-key, late hand that has added *hamza* even in *as-samāʾ*. Compared to P.Vind.inv. AHT 1 b, which most probably really originates from the Maġrib, the *rasm* looks as though the scribe tried to imitate *maġribī* style with respect to dotting, to the shape of the *dāl*, and to the elongated form of final *yāʾ*. Most wooden tablets were seemingly written too late to fit into our time frame, but at least P.Cair.IslArt inv. 6003 provides us with evidence of the form of *tabula ansata* (although with only one handle) in Arabic wooden tablets. The layout of P.Vind.inv. A.P. 10042 was therefore either chosen for the special qualities attributed to wooden tablets or it was a model for the fabrication of a tablet and never itself used as an amulet.

The next aspect of layout to be considered is the distribution of the texts on recto and verso.[24] Of the 23 papyri dealt with in terms of layout, eleven

20 Herzfeld 1915: 193.

21 Grohmann 1924: 81.

22 Grohmann 1952: 59.

23 Grohmann 1952: pl. VIII.

24 We have also included documents without Qurʾān verses in this list, since it is concerned with matters of layout in general. For the linguistic analysis, naturally, only papyri with Qurʾān verses were consulted.

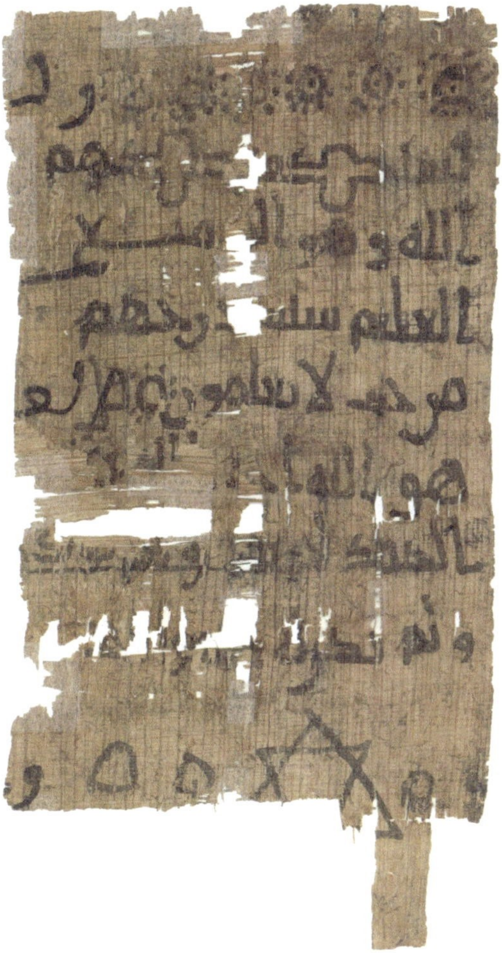

FIGURE 4.1
Magical layout and inscription-style Kufi (P.Vind.inv. A.P. 7719r = PERF 840 = Nilus XXII 46)

documents display a magical text on recto, eight of them with an empty verso. Seven texts are on verso; among them are no papyri with empty recto. Five texts are written on both sides of the papyrus, although it is doubtful whether three of them really are amulets (P.Philad.Arab. 148 and 149;[25] P.Ryl.Arab. I XIII 4). The texts on the other sides of the papyri are all letters, among them two official letters, four private letters, and five letters without classification. P.Vind.inv. A.P. 7719 even displays three texts: an official letter on recto, a pri-

25 P.Philad.Arab. 148 and 149 are most probably Ḥadīṯ texts with decoration. Levi della Vida called them "prayers," thereby neglecting the fact that *duʿāʾ* recommendations are of course part of Ḥadīṯ collections.

vate letter on verso, and an amulet on the margin of recto.[26] This shows the heterogeneity of magical papyri, which were objects of daily use and therefore subject to the circumstances of life they were "born" in. While a professional enchanter, or *šayḫ*, in the city used a new sheet of papyrus for the amulets of his well-to-do clients, in a village writing material was not always at hand and amulets were written on the back of other documents. The same would apply to poorer clients in general, for whom perhaps even a professional enchanter would have written on used papyrus, like his colleague from the village whose "magical" knowledge had been transmitted to him by elders in his family.

4 Qur'ān Verses Quoted in Arabic Papyrus Amulets

There are groups of verses adequate for purposes of healing and protection, but certain verses occur especially frequently in amulets and magical papyri due to the enormous amount of blessing (*baraka*) ascribed to them. The verses represented in the papyri accessed for this study are Q 1 (complete); 2:137; 2:255 *Āyat al-Kursī*; 2:256–257; 2:278; 2:284–286; 7:182; 9:128–129; 18:97–98; 19:1; 20:1; 24:29–30; 30:4; 36:1–12; 42:1–2; 50:39–45; 79:46; 94 (complete); 112 (complete); 113 (complete), 114 (complete). Of these Qur'ān verses, only three are of Medinan origin, the rest are of Meccan origin.

When we encounter words not written according to the text as we know it from the Seven Readings, we must consider two possibilities: either they are writing mistakes due to insufficient or incorrect knowledge of the text or poor writing skills, or they represent variants of the Qur'ān text. In the papyrus texts dealt with for this study, we indeed find examples of unambiguous writing mistakes, but also problematic cases for which it is difficult to decide whether the mistake is a *lapsus calami*, a mistake caused by a misheard recitation, or a variant of the text.

Below we show irregularities in Qur'ān citations as they appear in papyrus amulets, divided into different categories according to the type of mistake they represent. Some examples cannot not be classified unambiguously.

26 Many thanks are due to Eva Youssef-Grob for allowing me to use her previous research on P.Vind.inv. A.P. 7719 as well as on P.Vind.inv. A.P. 1637.

4.1 *Variant Readings*

Papyrus line	Text on document	Standard text	Qur'ān	Variant found in
P.Bad. V 143.3	اهدنا صراط المستقيم	اهدنا الصراط المستقيم	Q 1:5	Ubayy b. Kaʿb; Ibn ʿUmar; Ǧaʿfar aṣ-Ṣādiq
P.DietrichTopkapı 4.3*	اهدن اسراط الم]ست[قيم سراط الذين	اهدنا الصراط المستقيم صراط الذين	Q 1:5	Ibn ʿAbbās (*ṣirāṭ* with *sīn*)

* We give P.DietrichTopkapı 4.3 as dotted in the edition, since Dietrich gives no information on dots.

Concerning *ṣirāṭ al-mustaqīm* as in P.Bad. V 143.3, Hopkins says on papyri in general: "In accordance with a construction very widespread in modern dialects of Arabic, the definite article may be present on an adjectival attribute, but absent from the noun to which the latter refers."[27] The only problem is that his first example is the passage under discussion here, so we want to point out another explanation: Jeffery lists *ihdinā ṣirāṭa l-mustaqīm* as a non-canonic reading of Q 1 *Sūrat al-Fātiḥa*, taken from the Codex of Ubayy b. Kaʿb and likewise found with Ibn ʿUmar and Ǧaʿfar aṣ-Ṣādiq.[28]

Sirāṭ written with *sīn*, as in P.DietrichTopkapı 4.3–4, is both a well-known variant of the word[29] and a known Qur'ān variant found with Ibn ʿAbbās, who reads *sirāṭ* all through the Qur'ān.[30]

4.2 *Grammatical Irregularities and Dialectal Influence*

Papyrus line	Text on document	Standard text	Qur'ān
P.DietrichTopkapı 4.6	لم يلد ولم يلد	لم يلد ولم يولد	Q 112:3
P.Bad. V 143.6	لم يكون له كفوا احد	لم يكن له كفؤا احد	Q 112:4

27 Hopkins 1984: 182.
28 Jeffery 1937: 117; 332.
29 Ibn Manẓūr 1414/1993 VII: 313–314.
30 Jeffery 1937: 195.

Lam yalid wa-lam yulad quoted in P.DietrichTopkapı 4.6: Being conscious of the fact that dialectal influence in Classical Arabic can induce the retention of long vocals in verbs with *infirmae* consonants also in apocopate, the scribe tried to avoid this tendency by creating a hypocorrect form,[31] a form that exists neither in Classical Arabic nor as a dialectal form. Instead of *yūlad*, which he identified with an incorrect realization of the apocopate, he wrote the hypocorrect *yulad*.

The scribe of *lam yakūn* quoted in P.Bad. V 143.6 fell into the exact same trap the first scribe tried to avoid: he constructed an imperfect or subjunctive where apocopate would have been needed. This phenomenon is common in papyri.[32]

4.3 *Misheard or Misunderstood Verses*

Papyrus line	Text on document	Standard text	Qur'ān
P.DietrichTopkapı 4.2	الحمد لله الرب العلامين	الحمد لله رب العلمين	Q 1:1
P.Bad. V 147.4	لسدر قوما ما ادرهم اباهم	لتنذر قوما ما انذر اباؤهم	Q 36:5
P.Bad. V 147.16	فسرهم ٮمعفره	فبشره بمغفرة	Q 36:11
P.Bad. V 147.18	وىكس ما فدهم	ونكتب ما قدموا	Q 36:12

The deviation in Q 1:1 quoted in P.DietrichTopkapı 4.2 could be the result of a misheard recitation. We can assume that almost everyone who knew some Qur'ān verses by heart received this knowledge by listening to recitations. It seems very unlikely that people learned the Qur'ān from written sources, and so the refinement and exactness of their knowledge depended on the clarity of recitations they heard. In *ar-rabb al-ʿalāmīn*, the first article syntactically makes no sense and possibly shows an insufficient grasp of Arabic by the scribe, who heard not only one *rāʾ* as the first letter of *rabb*, but a doubled *rāʾ*.

Li-tunḏira qawman mā anḏarahum quoted in P.Bad. V 147.4 seems at first sight a variant reading of Q 36:5, yet cannot be confirmed as such. The standard text reads *li-tunḏira qawman mā unḏira ābāʾuhum*, so either the scribe added *-hum* of the next word or he misunderstood the passive form of the verb as

31 Versteegh 2005: 4.

32 See CPR XVI 27.5; P.Horak 85.r8; P.Marchands II 1.r10 et al. for the same example with *kāna*.

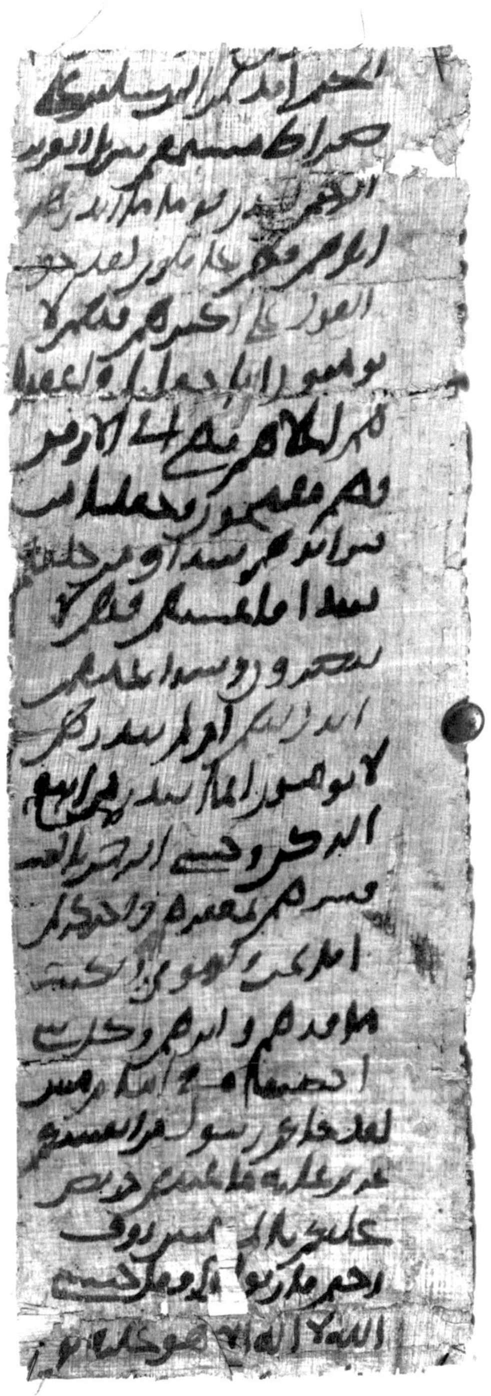

FIGURE 4.2
Q 36 with some peculiarities
(P.Heid.inv. Arab 91 = P.Bad. V 147)

active, added *-hum* as the pronominal suffix for *qawm*, and treated *ābāʾuhum* as the subject of the sentence. Of course we cannot exclude the possibility of a hitherto unknown reading variant, but we have proof for neither assumption.

Fa-bašširhum bi-maġfiratin quoted in P.Bad. V 147.16 confirms that the scribe wrote letter by letter without having a conception of the text as a whole. He mechanically wrote *bašširhum* (instead of *bašširhu*) and added one and the same suffix as well to the next word, which neither makes much sense nor is a known variant. He then corrected the word, which is puzzling with respect to the many mistakes he made (cf. his inability to write *aʿnāqihim*), because it must mean that he did indeed have some concept of what the words were supposed to look like.

It is not clear whether *qaddahum* (instead of *qaddamū*) quoted in P.Bad. V 147.18 is based on a misheard recitation or on interference from the following *wa-āṯārahum*, which might have caused the scribe to add the *-hum* automatically to the previous word as well. Another possible explanation is that he first misheard *qaddahum* and then took it for a noun in a parallel accusative construction, thus reading *wa-naktubu mā qaddahum wa-āṯārahum wa-kulla šayʾin aḥṣaynāhu*.

4.4 *Writing Mistakes*

Papyrus line	Text on Document	Standard text	Qurʾān
P.DietrichTopkapı 4.3–4	اهدن اسراط المـ] ستـ [ـقيم سراط الذين نعم تعلهم غير المغضوب ام/اى	اهدنا الصراط المستقيم صراط الذين انعمت عليهم غير المغضوب عليهم ولا الضالين	Q 1:5–6
P.KarabacekPapyrusfund 5.27	وعف عما	واعف عنا	Q 2:286
P.Bad. V 147.7–8	فى اعمماهم اعلاهم	في اعناقهم اغلالا	Q 36:8
P.Bad. V 147.11 and 19	فاعسىهم ... وكل سى احصىاه	فاغشيناهم ... وكل شيء احصيناه	Q 36:9 and 12
P.Bad. V 147.21	عسم	عنتّم	Q 9:128

(*cont.*)

Papyrus line	Text on Document	Standard text	Qur'ān
P.Bad. V 143.7 and 8	عاسو ... حسد	غاسق ... حاسد	Q 113:3 and 5
P.Bad. V 143.9–10	الوسوس ... الحاس	الوسواس ... الخناس	Q 114:4
P.Bad. V 143a.4	الدى سربوسو ى صـ]د[ور الناس	الذي يوسوس في صدور الناس	Q 114:5

In the first case, the article has been assimilated completely, with no *lām* after *alif*. After *allaḏīna*, where we would expect *ʾnʿmt*, we find *nʿm*. The *tāʾ* is connected to what should be the following word in the standard text, which makes it look like *tʿlhm*, and after *al-maġḍūb* the scribe has written something like *ʿm* or *ʿBy* (without diacritical dots). The scribe had difficulties in giving a correct representation of the end of Q 1, not due to his insufficient knowledge of the text, but to problems in transcribing the text he knew only orally into written form.

Spelling *wa-ʿfu ʿannā* without *alif* in P.KarabacekPapyrusfund 5.27 is, again, nothing but insufficient skill in Arabic orthography. The scribe was not familiar with the correct spelling *ʾʿf* of the imperative of a verb built on the root *ʿ-f-w*. No variant readings are known for this word. Hopkins states that the occurrence of long vowels in imperative and jussive forms in *verba tertiae infirmae* is "extremely common" in the papyri.[33] Did the scribe consciously not manage to write an imperative of the verb, or did he automatically copy a text he had memorized after hearing it? As mentioned above, what he heard or thought he had heard did not necessarily correspond to the rules of Classical grammar. It might not be too bold to suggest that this gives us an insight into literacy at the time: Unlike in our times, reading and writing skills and grammatical knowledge were not as interdependent as we tend to think.

As far as *ʿanittum* written with two *tāʾ* (instead of *tāʾ mašdūda*) in P.Bad. V 147.21 is concerned, there is no more plausible explanation for it than a writing mistake. Hopkins offers no help at this point, since this is the only example on papyrus he presents for repeated consonants instead of *šadda*, well known

33 Hopkins 1984: 85.

from later documents.[34] It is difficult to deduce what the repetition of consonants tells us about the grammar and writing skills of the scribe, since we nowadays consider the realization of *mašdūda* consonants fundamental for the mastering of the Arabic script. This obviously was not the case with the scribe of our papyrus, who was perhaps not familiar with the *šadda* rule or at least had no optical notion of the text. He knew he had to write two consonants, and wrote them consecutively.

ʾʿfmʾhim and *aġlāhum* quoted in P.Bad. v 147.7–8 reveal a definite lack of understanding of the Qurʾān vocabulary. This must be based on a misheard recitation. The scribe could not even approach the correct writing of *aʿnāqihim*, and the word *aġlāl* seems to have evaded his comprehension in a similar way. He tried to write down what he had heard without being told the meaning of the words. This could be a clue to the way the Qurʾān was taught. Obviously, students were taught to memorize the Qurʾān, but the meaning of the verses was not learned at the same time. It seems that the scribe had not attended classes for the latter, so he had probably received only a very basic training in writing, and maybe even less in reading.

Finding a non-*plene alif* in *aġšaynāhum* quoted in P.Bad. v 147.11 is nothing unusual, since non-*plene* writings occur in early documents, as well as in later documents consciously evoking an archaic impression. Interestingly, the scribe has written *aḥṣaynāhu* (l. 19) with *alif*, therefore using *plene* and non-*plene* in the same document and even in the same grammatical construction. While Hopkins states that *plene* and non-*plene* writings both occur frequently in papyri,[35] having them appear both in one document is remarkable. Perhaps the scribe aimed at an archaic style by writing non-*plene*, but occasionally reverted to his habitual style of *alif* plene.

Ḥāsid with non-*plene alif* and the parallel *ġāsiq* with *plene alif* in P.Bad. v 143.8, and non-*plene al-waswās* vs. *plene al-ḫannās* In P.Bad. v 143.9–10, represent further examples of the phenomenon just mentioned above.

The scribe of P.Bad. v 143a (Ostrakon) had problems with writing *yuwaswisu*.

34 Hopkins 1984: 49. A later example is P.MargolriouthMonneret 2.10 on paper.

35 Hopkins 1984: 11.

4.5 *Other Irregularities*

Papyrus line	Text on Document	Standard text	Qur'ān
P.DietrichTopkapı 4.3	وابك نعبد وابك انستعين	اياك نعبد واياك نستعين	Q 1:4
P.KarabacekPapyrus-fund 5.18	لا ٮوده حڡطهما	ولا يئوده حفظهما	Q 2:255
P.Bad. V 147.17	اںا ٮحى الموى	انا نحن نحي الموتى	Q 36:12
P.Vind.inv. A.P. 1637.r7	اںا ٮحں ٮحى الموى	انا نحن نحي ونميت	Q 50:43

The additional *wāw* before *iyyāka* in P.DietrichTopkapı 4.3 is a writing mistake, since it is at the beginning of a new *āya* and is one letter only. This is no known reading variant. The scribe may have wanted to build a parallel to *wa-iyyāka nastaʿīn*, which he achieved by adding a *wāw*. The *alif* before *nastaʿīn* is hard to categorize. It could be a slip of the pen, or the scribe may have had in mind something like *wa-ʾiyyāk ʾa-nastaʿīn* instead of *wa-ʾiyyāka nastaʿīn*.

Wāw missing before *lā yaʾūduhu ḥifẓuhumā* in P.KarabacekPapyrusfund 5.18 can be regarded as a simple writing mistake. This is no attested variant reading.

In *innā* ***naḥnu*** *l-mawtā* (in P.Bad. V 147.17) or *innā* ***nuḥyī*** *l-mawtā* (a reading P.Bad. V pl. 14 suggests) instead of *innā naḥnu nuḥyī l-mawtā*, the scribe probably looked at the *rasm* he had written and, in order to avoid repetition of a word, went on to write *al-mawtā*. Due to his eagerness in avoiding a mistake, he left out one word that looked similar to the one he had just written.

In *nuḥyī l-mawtā* in P.Vind.inv. A.P. 1637r.7, the writer does not quote exactly from Q 50:43, *innā naḥnu nuḥyī wa-numītu*, but rather switches to a passage either from Q 36:12 *innā naḥnu nuḥyī l-mawtā* or Q 42:9 *wa-huwa yuḥyī l-mawtā*.

As the tables above show, mistakes are concentrated on some few of the studied papyri. In reverse, this means that most documents do *not* show mistakes. This could be due to the fact that many verses were well known and much used in amulets. It could also point to the way amulet writers were trained and accustomed to work: the majority had templates from which they copied; the rest relied on oral sources, i.e., on what they were told to write by someone passing his knowledge on to them. Although we might conclude that this shows two different ways of living and working—one with much contact with written material, the other mainly relying on oral sources—it could also mean that the first type of amulet writer was someone who had much contact with the Qur'ān text, such as an Imam or a *muḥaddiṯ*, whereas the person making mistakes in writing the Qur'ān text was a part-time amulet writer not constantly surrounded by written copies of the Qur'ān.

5 Early Ḥadīṯ and Tafsīr Manuals on Qur'ān Verses to Be Used in Amulets

Apart from the inherent blessing that certain Qur'ān verses are said to carry, they have special qualities that are suited to particular purposes, as mentioned in manuals for the practitioner of magic. Thus it would be informative to trace in these manuals of magic all the Qur'ān verses found in magical papyri, in an attempt to draw some preliminary conclusions about the purposes our documents aimed at. The difficulty with this is the inaccessibility of said works of magic for the period of the papyri. No handbook contemporary with our papyri has been preserved—or at least discovered to date—and two comprehensive works, al-Būnī's *Uṣūl al-Ḥikma* and as-Sanūsī's *Kitāb al-Muǧarrabāt*, were composed much later, in the 6th–8th/12th–13th and the 9th/15th centuries, respectively.[36] Something approaching the kind of book we are in need of is at-Tanūḫī's *al-Faraǧ ba'd aš-Šidda* (4th/10th century), even though it does not primarily deal with magic and the composition of amulets as such. Occasionally Qur'ān verses are mentioned, but the book is far from presenting a list of verses together with the corresponding afflictions they can help avert.

As a result, the only way to investigate the particular qualities ascribed to a certain verse is to consult early Ḥadīṯ and Tafsīr manuals such as *Sunan ad-Dārimī*, *Ṣaḥīḥ al-Buḫārī*, *Sunan at-Tirmiḏī*, *Šu'ab al-Īmān* by Bayhaqī, *Tafsīr Muǧāhid* and *Tafsīr 'Abd ar-Razzāq*. They mostly deal with the context in which a given verse was revealed, and with the blessings bestowed on a person reciting it; yet we also find remarks that could lead us to understand why certain verses were chosen for amulets. Not all verses represented in the papyri have a counterpart in Ḥadīṯ and Tafsīr literature. Thus we can only list those verses where the explanation hints at the fact that the verse was to be used in an amulet for healing or protection. For those verses not explicitly said to be applicable for magical purposes, we must content ourselves with short descriptions. For the time being, we cannot determine exactly what made certain verses especially appropriate for use in amulets.

36 Pielow 1995; Dorpmüller 2005.

- On Q 1 *Fātiḥat al-kitāb*, "the Opening of the Book,"[37] al-Bayhaqī cites the Prophet Muḥammad as saying: "The Opening of the Book is a cure for every disease (*fātiḥat al-kitāb šifā' min kull dā'*)."[38] On another occasion, the Prophet describes *al-Fātiḥa* as an ideal incantation (*ruqya*).[39] This advice could explain the high frequency of its appearance in amulets and magical papyri. The *sūra* generally speaks about the omnipotence of God, about believers' relation to Him and their requests for guidance.
- Q 2:137 speaks of God's help for those who truly believe. It contains the words *fa-sayakfiyakahumu llāhu*, whose unusually long appearance makes them interesting for magical use.
- Al-Bayhaqī considers *Āyat al-kursī*, "the Throne Verse" (Q 2:255) to be no less powerful that *al-Fātiḥa*: "He [Abū Ḏārr] said: I said: 'O Messenger of God, which verse that has been sent down to you is the most mighty?' He said: '*Allāhu lā ilāha illā huwa l-ḥayyu l-qayyūm*' until the end of the verse."[40] Although the Throne Verse is quite long, the amount of blessing it is said to contain makes it one of the most popular verses in amulets.[41] Sometimes only the beginning is written due to narrowness of space,[42] but even that is enough to evoke the whole verse's blessings. The Throne Verse mainly describes God's omnipotence and its different manifestations: He does not sleep; He keeps the balance of heaven and earth without tiring from its weight; etc.
- Ad-Dārimī cites the Prophet as saying that the last verses of *Sūrat al-Baqara* (Q 2:285–286) are "from the treasure chests of God's mercy under His throne," and that "four verses from the beginning of *Sūrat al-Baqara*, *Āyat al-Kursī*, then two verses after *Āyat al-Kursī* and three from the end of *Sūrat al-Baqara*, and anyone possessed [by *ǧinn*] will recover."[43]
- Q 7:182 speaks about the humiliation of those who lie about the Qur'ān. This verse could also have been used against slander or adversaries in general.

---

37 On the construction of the expression *Fātiḥat al-kitāb*, see Ullmann 2013: 187.

38 al-Bayhaqī 1423/2003 IV: 42.

39 al-Buḫārī 1422/[2001] VI: 187–188.

40 al Bayhaqī 1423/2003 IV: 55, *qāla qultu yā rasūla llāhi ayyumā āyatin unzilat ʿalayka aʿẓamu? Qāla ʿallāhu lā ilāha illā huwa l-ḥayyu l-qayyūm'.*

41 Pielow 1995: 77.

42 Kriss and Kriss-Heinrich 1962: pl. 71; 72.

43 ad-Dārimī 1421/2000 IV: 2128, *qāla fa-ayyatu āyatin yā nabiyya llāhi tuḥibbu an tuṣībaka wa-ummataka? qāla: suratu l-baqarati, li-annahā min ḫazā'ini raḥmati llāhi min taḥti ʿaršihi*; ad-Dārimī 1421/2000 IV: 2130, *qāla man qara'a arbaʿa ayātin min awwali sūrati al-baqarati, wa-āyata l-kursiyyi wa-āyatayni baʿda āyati l-kursiyyi wa-ṯalāṯan min āḫiri l-baqarati … lā yuqra'na ʿalā maǧnūnin illā afāqa.*

- The last verse from *Sūrat at-Tawba*, Q 9:129 recommends that believers trust wholly in the omnipotence of God.
- Q 18:97–98, which speaks of an enemy's inability to do harm because of God's power and protection, could have been used in an amulet against adversaries.
- Both Q 19:1 and Q 20:1 have been used, probably because they consist of a combination of letters only, without making up comprehensible words. Such inexplicable, enigmatic letters are favored in the composition of amulets. The same can be said of Q 42:1–2.
- With Q 24:39–40, we encounter verses concerned with God's dealing with his enemies, and a thorough description of how unbelievers and God's enemies feel. Their deeds are like a mirage—seemingly good but empty, or like the darkness of a deep ocean in which no light can be found except by God's favor.
- Another verse to be used in an amulet against adversaries is Q 30:4, in which God makes believers prevail over their enemies.
- On Q 36 *Sūrat Yā Sīn*, ad-Dārimī writes: "[…] From Anas, he said: The Prophet—peace be upon him—said: 'Everything has a heart, and the heart of the Qur'ān is *Yā Sīn*. He who recites *Yā Sīn*, God rewards him as if he had recited the [entire] Qur'ān ten times.'"[44] The *sūra* covers a wide range of topics, from the prophets' messages to their peoples to the magnificence of God's creation and His omnipotence, to eschatological matters of reward and punishment and the Day of Judgment.
- In Q 50:39–45, we find directions concerning the times of prayer and how God should be praised, then a part on the Last Judgment and the Qur'ān as a reminder thereof.
- Q 79:46 likewise speaks about Judgment Day and how it will appear to those who have lied about it.
- At-Tanūḫī recommends reciting Q 94 in times of grief and anxiety, especially when they are caused by enemies.[45]
- Perhaps the most popular *sūra* to be found in amulets is Q 112 *Sūrat al-Iḫlāṣ*, "the *Sūra* of the Redemption." On the one hand, it is short and can be fitted even onto small shreds of papyrus or engraved on pendants for necklaces, and on the other hand it carries a great amount of blessings. At-Tirmiḏī cites

44 ad-Dārimī 1421/2000 V: 162, *ʿan anasin qāla: qāla l-nabiyyu ṣallā llāhu ʿalayhi wa-sallama: inna li-kulli šayʾin qalbun, wa-qalbu l-qurʾāni yāsīn, wa-man qaraʾa yāsīn kataba llāhu lahu bi-qirāʾatihā qirāʾata l-qurʾāni ʿašara marrāt.*

45 at-Tanūḫī 1375/1955: 26.

the Prophet himself as saying that whoever recites this *sūra* has recited a third of the Qur'ān.[46] It deals mainly with the omnipotence of God and the description of His attributes, which set Him far apart from humanity.

- The last two *sūras* of the Qur'ān (Q 113–114) are generally mentioned together as *al-Muʿawwiḏatān*, "the Two Exorcist (*Sūras*)."[47] This title already tells us much about their special qualities and the connected uses they can be put to in magical texts. At-Tirmiḏī cites Prophet Muḥammad as calling them "[…] verses the like of which has never been seen."[48] Moreover, their content makes them predestined for amulets, since believers seek refuge from black magic, the evil eye, and demons by reciting them.[49]

The only example for the composition of an amulet found in Tanūḫī's *al-Faraǧ baʿd aš-Šidda* is mentioned in a story about a slave who has been cast out by his master and wants to regain his favor. Tanūḫī composes an amulet containing Q 1, 113–114, 2:255 *Āyat al-Kursī*, 59:21–24, 8:63, 30:21 and 3:103.[50]

6 "Magical Scripts" and General Matters of Representation

There are two main types of magical layouts: the first is a deliberately archaisized angular hand, using magical symbols such as stars, magical letters, and *charaktēres*,[51] striving to convey the special character of the writing into an optical image; the second is written in a casual hand which could as well be used for composing a private letter or even a note. The main functional difference lies in the content to be conveyed to the reader, or, to put it more correctly, the beholder. Accordingly, I distinguish between representative and transmitting script.

In *representative script*, the image itself makes up a substantial part of the message—in our case the message that the script is invested with the power of

46 at-Tirmiḏī 1998 v: 167. At-Tirmiḏī gives a non-standard reading for the second *āya*: *allāhu l-waḥıd aṣ-ṣamad*.

47 ad-Dārimī 1421/2000 IV: 2166; at-Tanūḫī 1375/1955: 55; at-Tirmiḏī 1998 v: 20; al-ʿAsqalāni 1421/2000 VIII: 919

48 at-Tirmiḏī 1998 v: 170.

49 Grohmann 1934: 417 confirms this by saying "[…], gelten doch die beiden letzten Sûren des Qur'âns als besonders zauberkräftig und von Sûra 112 soll der Engel Gabriel bei ihrer Offenbarung gesagt haben, dass jeder gerettet werde, der sie gläubig liest. So wird sie häufig im Augenblick der Gefahr rezitiert und auch als Amulett getragen. Ähnliches gilt auch für die Eröffnungssûre (Fâtiḥa)."

50 at-Tanūḫī 1375/1955: 55.

51 For eyeglass-letters, see Winkler 1930.

the Arabic language and of the Qur'ān verses, as known to the populace from inscriptions. Perhaps these amulets were composed in surroundings with a very high degree of illiteracy, so that adding specific characteristics made them recognizable even to people who had at the most once glanced at a tax demand, at an official letter answering a petition of theirs, or at a contract to which they had been a party. A special layout was the best way to clarify the text's content to someone who distinguished texts mostly by their optical appearance. The importance of the distinction between an amulet and any other text lay in the caution necessary when dealing with religious texts, especially with respect to their safe disposal or (problematic) re-use.[52]

A *transmitting script*, in contrast, is in a cursive, casual style most probably destined for a literate and wealthy audience. It is devoid of magical symbols, its content being more important than its layout. In the case of wealthy clients, even the choice of the writing material—small strips of low-quality papyrus, perhaps already used before—may have qualified as a distinctive feature for recognizing an amulet, since they could afford to write their own documents on big, new, high-quality papyrus sheets. Thus people who were used to amulets in transmitting script recognized them by criteria quite different from those applicable to amulets in representative script. Whereas an amulet in representative script was distinguished from other documents by its archaizing ornamental script alongside magical symbols, amulets in transmitting script stood out among other documents used daily by virtue of their different form and material.

Bibliography

'Abd ar-Razzāq, Abū Bakr b. Hammām b. Nāfi' al-Ḥimyarī al-Yamānī aṣ-Ṣan'ānī 1419/1999. *Tafsīr 'Abd ar-Razzāq*, ed. Maḥmūd Muḥammad 'Abduh. 3 vols. Beirut: Dār al-Kutub al-'Ilmiyya.

al-'Asqalānī, Aḥmad b. 'Alī b. Ḥaǧar. 1421/2000. *Fatḥ al-Bārī: Šarḥ Ṣaḥīḥ al-Buḫārī*, vol. 8, ed. Muḥammad Fu'ād 'Abd al-Bāqī. Riyad: Dār as-Salām.

al-Bayhaqī, Abū Bakr Aḥmad b. al-Ḥusayn. 1423/2003. *al-Ǧāmi' li-šu'ab al-īmān*, ed. 'Abd al-'Alī 'Abd al-Ḥamīd Ḥāmid. 14 vols. Riyad: Maktabat ar-Rušd.

Bergsträsser, Gotthelf. 1993. "Nichtkanonische Koranlesarten im Muḥtasab des Ibn Ginnī." In *Sitzungsberichte der Bayerischen Akademie der Wissenschaften, Philoso-*

52 Khan 1991–1992: 53 takes a similar approach by saying: "The extent to which the standardization of the graphic form was observed also depended on the function which the manuscript played within society."

phisch-historische Abteilung, Jahrgang 1933, Heft 2. Munich: Bayerische Akademie der Wissenschaften.

Betz, Hans-Dieter. 1986. *The Greek Magical Papyri in Translation Including the Demotic Spells, Vol. 1*. Chicago; London: University of Chicago Press.

Blau, Joshua. 1965. *The Emergence and Linguistic Background of Judaeo-Arabic: A Study of the Origins of Middle Arabic*. Oxford: Oxford University Press.

al-Buḫārī, Muḥammad b. Ismāʿīl Abū ʿAbd Allāh. 1422/[2001]. *al-Ǧāmiʿ al-Musnad aṣ-ṣaḥīḥ al-muḫtaṣar min umūr rasūl Allāh ... wa-sunanihi wa-ayyāmihi*, ed. Muḥammad Zuhayr b. Nāṣir an-Nāṣir. 9 vols. Beirut: Dār Ṭawq an-Naǧāt.

Casanova, M. 1921. "Alphabets magiques arabes." In *Journal Asiatique* Series 11, 18: 37–55.

Cohen, Mark. 2006. "Goitein, Magic, and the Geniza." In *Jewish Studies Quarterly* 13: 1–11.

ad-Dārimī, Abū Muḥammad ʿAbd Allāh b. Abd ar-Raḥmān. 1421/2000. *Musnad ad-Dārimī al-maʿrūf bi-sunan ad Dārimī*, ed. Ḥusayn Salīm Asad ad-Dārānī. 4 vols. Riyad: Maktabat al-Muġnī.

David-Weill, Jean et al. 1965; 1971; 1978. "Papyrus arabes du Louvre." In *Journal of Economic and Social History* 8: 277–311; 14: 1–24; 21: 146–164. [P.Louvre I–III].

Diem, Werner. 1991a: "Drei Magische Texte auf Papyrus aus dem 3./9. Jahrhundert." In *Festgabe für Hans-Rudolf Singer zum 65. Geburtstag ...*, ed. Martin Forstner. Frankfurt am Main: Lang, 27–36.

Diem, Werner. 1991b. *Arabische Briefe auf Papyrus und Papier der Heidelberger Papyrus-Sammlung*. [Publications of the] Heidelberger Akademie der Wissenschaften, Philosophisch-historische Klasse, Kommission für Papyrus-Editionen. Wiesbaden: Harrassowitz.

Diem, Werner. 1993. *Arabische Briefe aus dem 7.–10. Jahrhundert*. Corpus Papyrorum Raineri, vol. 16. 2 vols. Vienna: Hollinek.

Diem, Werner. 1997. *Arabische Briefe des 7.–13. Jahrhunderts aus den Staatlichen Museen zu Berlin*. Documenta Arabica Antiqua, vol. 4. 2 vols. Wiesbaden.

Dietrich, Albert. 1937. *Arabische Papyri aus der Hamburger Staats- und Universitätsbibliothek*. Abhandlungen für die Kunde des Morgendlandes, vol. 22,3. Leipzig: Brockhaus.

Dietrich, Albert. 1955. *Arabische Briefe aus der Papyrussammlung der Hamburger Staats- und Universitäts-Bibliothek*. Veröffentlichungen aus der Hamburger Staats- und Universitätsbibliothek, vol. 5. Hamburg: Augustin.

Dietrich, Albert. 1958. "Die arabischen Papyri des Topkapı Sarayı-Museums in Istanbul." In *Der Islam* 33: 37–50.

Dorpmüller, Sabine. 2005. *Religiöse Magie im "Buch der probaten Mittel": Analyse, kritische Edition und Übersetzung des Kitāb al-Muǧarrabāt von Muhammad ibn Yūsuf as-Sanūsī (gest. um 895/1490)*. Arabische Studien, vol. 1. Wiesbaden: Harrassowitz.

Grob, Eva Mira. 2010. *Documentary Arabic Private and Business Letters on Papyrus: Form and Function, Content and Context*. Archiv für Papyrusforschung, Beiheft 29. Berlin: de Gruyter.

Grohmann, Adolf. 1924. *Allgemeine Einführung in die arabischen Papyri*. Corpus Papyrorum Rainer, III: Series Arabica, vol. 1,1. Vienna: Burgverlag.

Grohmann, Adolf. 1934. "Islamische Zaubertexte." In *Griechische, arabische und koptische Texte zur Religion und religiösen Literatur in Ägyptens Spätzeit*, ed. Friedrich Bilabel and Adolf Grohmann. Veröffentlichungen aus den badischen Papyrussammlungen, vol. 5. Heidelberg: Universitätsbibliothek, vol. 1: 415–447; vol. 2: 1–12.

Grohmann, Adolf. 1934–1962. *Arabic Papyri in the Egyptian Library*. 6 vols. Cairo: Egyptian Library Press.

Grohmann, Adolf. 1952. *From the World of Arabic Papyri*. Cairo: Al-Maaref.

Grohmann, Adolf. 1954. *Einführung und Chrestomathie zur arabischen Papyruskunde*. Monografie Archivu Orientálního, vol. 13. Prague: Státní Pedagogické Nakladatelství.

Grohmann, Adolf. 1958. "The Problem of Dating Early Qurʾāns." In *Der Islam* 33: 213–231.

Guo, Li. 2004. *Commerce, Culture and Community in a Red Sea Port in the Thirteenth Century: The Arabic Documents from Quseir*. Islamic History and Civilization: Studies and Texts, vol. 52. Leiden: Brill.

Hamdan, Omar. 2006. *Studien zur Kanonisierung des Korantextes: Al-Ḥasan al-Baṣrīs Beiträge zur Geschichte des Korans*. Diskurse der Arabistik, vol. 10. Wiesbaden: Harrassowitz.

Hentschel, Kornelius. 1997. *Geister, Magier und Muslime: Dämonenwelt und Geisteraustreibung im Islam*. Diederichs Gelbe Reihe, vol. 134. Munich: Diederichs.

Herzfeld, Ernst E. 1915. "Die Tabula ansata in der islamischen Epigraphik und Ornamentik." In *Der Islam* 6: 189–199.

Hopkins, Simon. 1984. *Studies in the Grammar of Early Arabic Based upon Papyri Datable to Before 300 A.H./912 A.D.* London Oriental Series, vol. 37. Oxford: Oxford University Press.

Ibn Kannān, Muḥammad b. ʿĪsā. 1998. *al-Mawākib al-islāmiyya*, ed. Ḥikmat Ismāʿīl, vol. 1. Dammām: Maktabat al-Mutanabbī.

Ibn Manẓūr, Abū l-Faḍl Muḥammad b. Mukarram. 1414/1993. *Lisān al-ʿArab*, 3rd edition. 15 vols. Beirut: Dār Ṣādir.

Jeffery, Arthur. 1937. *Materials for the History of the Text of the Qurʾān, vol. 1*. Leiden: Brill.

Jeffery, Arthur. 1952/1980. *The Qurʾān as Scripture*. New York: Moore; Reprint New York: Arno.

Kaplony, Andreas. 2019. "Scribal Traditions in Documentary Arabic: From the One Imperial Standard Language to the One (Jewish) Language for Transnational Communication (7th–12th Centuries)." In *Jewish History 31* (= *Documentary Genizah Research in the 21st Century*, ed. Jessica Goldberg).

Karabacek, Josef. 1882. *Der Papyrusfund von El-Faijûm*. Denkschrift der Philosophisch-historischen Classe der Kaiserlichen Akademie der Wissenschaften, vol. 33. Vienna: Kaiserliche Akademie der Wissenschaften.

Khan, Geoffrey. 1991–1992. "Standardisation and Variation in the Orthography of Hebrew Bible and Arabic Qur'ān Manuscripts." In *Manuscripts of the Middle East* 5 (= *The Role of the Book in the Civilisations of the Near East*, ed. John Barlett; David Wasserstein; David James): 53–58.

Khoury, Adel Theodor. 1990–2001. *Der Koran Arabisch-Deutsch: Übersetzung und wissenschaftlicher Kommentar*. 12 vols. Gütersloh: Mohn.

Kriss, Rudolf and Hubert Kriss-Heinrich. 1962. *Volksglaube im Bereich des Islam, Vol. 2: Amulette, Zauberformeln und Beschwörungen*. Wiesbaden: Harrassowitz.

Levi Della Vida, Giorgio. 1881. *Arabic Papyri in the University Museum in Philadelphia (Pennsylvania)*. Atti della Accademia Nazionale dei Lincei, serie 8/25, fasc. 1. Rome: Accademia Nazionale dei Lincei.

Loth, Otto. 1880. "Zwei arabische Papyrus." In *Zeitschrift der Deutschen Morgenländischen Gesellschaft* 34: 685–691.

Margoliouth, D[avid] S. 1933. *Catalogue of Arabic Papyri in the John Rylands Library Manchester*. Manchester: Manchester University Press.

Margoliouth, David S. and E.J. Holmyard. 1930. "Arabic Documents from the Monneret Collection." In *Islamica* 4: 249–271.

Muǧāhid, Abū l-Ḥaǧǧāǧ b. Ǧabr al-Maḫzūmī. n.d. *Tafsīr Muǧāhid*, ed. ʿAbd ar-Raḥmān aṭ-Ṭāhir b. Muḥammad as-Suwartī. 2 vols. Beirut: al-Manšūrāt al-ʿIlmīya.

Pielow, Dorothee Anna Maria. 1995. *Die Quellen der Weisheit: die arabische Magie im Spiegel des Uṣūl al-Ḥikma von Aḥmad Ibn ʿAlī al-Būnī*. Arabistische Texte und Studien, vol. 8. Hildesheim: Olms.

Preisendanz, Karl. 1928–1941. *Papyri Graecae Magicae: die griechischen Zauberpapyri*. 3 vols. Berlin: Teubner.

Rāġib, Yūsuf. 1982–1996. *Marchands d'étoffes du Fayyoum au IIIe/IXe siècle d'après leurs archives (actes et lettres), vol. 1–3; 5,1*. Suppléments aux Annales Islamologiques, cahiers 2; 5; 14; 16. Publications de l'Institut Français d'Archéologie Orientale, vol. 586; 631; 727; 768. Cairo: Institut Français d'Archéologie Orientale.

Sadan, Joseph. 1986. "Genizah and Genizah-Like Practices in Islamic and Jewish Traditions." In *Bibliotheca Orientalis* 43: 36–58.

Sadan, Joseph. 2007. "Purity, Impurity and the Disposal of Defiled Books in Islam, in Comparison with Judaism." In *Jerusalem Studies in Arabic and Islam* 33: 193–218.

Schaefer, Karl R. 2006. *Enigmatic Charms: Medieval Arabic Block Printed Amulets in American and European Libraries and Museums*. Handbook of Oriental Studies, vol. 82. Leiden: Brill.

Sijpesteijn, Petra M. 2004. "Request to Buy Coloured Silk." In *Gedenkschrift Ulrike Horak*, ed. Hermann Harrauer and Rosario Pintaudi. Papyrologica Florentina, vol. 34. Florence: Gonnelli, 255–272; pl. 50.

Stock, Kristina. 1999. *Sprache als ein Instrument der Macht. Strategien der arabischen politischen Rhetorik im 20. Jahrhundert.* Wiesbaden: Reichert.

at-Tanūḫī, Abū ʿAlī al-Muḥassin b. Abī l-Qāsim. 1375/1955. *al-Farağ baʿd aš-šidda: al-aṣl maʾḫūḏ min nusḫa ḫaṭṭiyya maḥfūẓa bi-Dār al-kutub al-miṣriyya.* Cairo: Maktabat al-Ḫānǧī.

Thung, Michael. 2006. *Arabische juristische Urkunden aus der Papyrussammlung der Österreichischen Nationalbibliothek.* Corpus Papyrorum Raineri, vol. 26. Munich; Leipzig: Saur.

at-Tirmiḏī, Abū ʿĪsā Muḥammad b. ʿĪsā. 1998. *al-Ǧāmiʿ al-kabīr: sunan at-Tirmiḏī, Vol. 5*, ed. Baššār ʿAwwād Maʿrūf. Beirut: Dār al-Ġarb al-Islāmī.

Ullmann, Manfred. 2013. *Beiträge zur arabischen Grammatik.* Wiesbaden: Harrassowitz.

Versteegh, Kees. 2005. "Breaking the Rules without Wanting to: Hypercorrections in Middle Arabic Texts." In *Investigating Arabic: Current Parameters in Analysis and Learning*, ed. Alaa Elgibali. Leiden: Brill, 3–18.

Winkler, Hans A. 1930. *Siegel und Charaktere in der muhammedanischen Zauberei.* Studien zur Geschichte und Kultur des islamischen Orients, vol. 7. Berlin: de Gruyter.

CHAPTER 5

Radiocarbon (^{14}C) Dating of Early Islamic Documents: Background and Prospects

Eva Mira Youssef-Grob

1 Introduction

Even though the first few centuries of Islam are crucial to our understanding and perception of later Islamic history and faith, they provide us only few sources, compared to later centuries. Early original sources, such as Qurʾān manuscripts, administrative papyri, and inscriptions, are therefore of great historical importance, and their chronological classification is a major question in itself. Moreover, most of these sources do not bear any date and need to be assigned to a period of time on the basis of paleographic, linguistic, textual, or other evidence. In this context, the alternative of a more technical approach seems promising. Radiocarbon dating (^{14}C dating) has been used in archaeology for many decades already, but has only in the last few years been expanded more broadly to manuscripts and small artifacts of more recent times. For the study of Early Islamic history, resorting to radiocarbon dating is still viewed with reluctance. Many scholars see it as too technical, bearing results whose significance is hard to evaluate.

Does radiocarbon dating provide useful results for studying Early Islamic history? This chapter has been written in the context of a series of ^{14}C tests on early Qurʾān manuscripts and other Early Islamic and Christian sources, initiated by the Coranica project. In the field of Qurʾānic studies, this was the first time ^{14}C testing had been done on a large scale. Here, however, I concentrate less on the results than on the issue of ^{14}C dating itself. In what follows, I show which factors play the crucial roles for radiocarbon dating and what one can expect from the results.

The purpose of this chapter is to serve as an orientation for anyone considering using radiocarbon for dating the material she or he is working on, and also to assist in approaching and working with collections whose curators may not be enthusiastic about allowing the destruction of even a small strip of a unique early source. Besides parchment, I mainly concentrate on papyrus and show the challenges and advantages of testing the two materials. In addition to presenting general considerations and compilations of data in order to assess the

 | DOI:10.1163/9789004376977_006

exactness and significance of radiocarbon dating between ca. 600 to 1000 CE, I illustrate my arguments with the first test results from the ongoing Coranica project.[1]

2 A Short History of Radiocarbon Dating on Oriental Manuscripts

Since its discovery in 1949 by Libby, radiocarbon dating has had a profound influence on and widespread application to dating in archaeology. Only recently, however, due to the much smaller sample size needed in Accelerator Mass Spectrometry (AMS) technology, has radiocarbon dating begun to be applied to parchment and papyrus documents. Before AMS, the only technique available was detecting the radioactive decay of individual carbon atoms, which required eradicating much original material evidence.[2] This is less a problem in archaeology, but obviously posed a large obstacle to a wider application of the method in manuscript studies: who wanted (or was allowed) to destroy a big part of the manuscript she or he was working on? Thus the application of AMS technology for radiocarbon dating, in the late 70s, was pivotal in opening the door to a wider application of the method. Suddenly, only a very small fraction of the material evidence was needed for testing. However, precision was not higher with AMS dating; rather, what had changed was that much smaller samples were datable, allowing testing that had been beyond reach before (see section 4 below for more technical aspects). Higher accuracy of the results was based not on the method itself but on a deeper understanding and longer application of the technique, combined with refinements in the areas of calibration and pre-treatments of samples.

2.1 *Using Radiocarbon Dating on the Dead Sea Scrolls (the Qumran Documents)*

The most prominent and pioneering tests were surely those done on the Dead Sea Scrolls (Qumran Documents). Their results have yielded to much discussion and can serve as a model of many aspects of the evolution of AMS radiocarbon dating, such as improvements in calibration, new awareness about the importance of adequate pre-treatment, and the interpreting of results.

---

1 For the Coranica project, see www.coranica.de (last accessed 15 January 2016); for its radiocarbon subproject, see www.coranica.de/computatio-radiocarbonica-en (last accessed 15 January 2016).

2 For textiles, see the photographs in van Strydonck 2014: 2, showing what was destroyed for a radiocarbon analysis back in the 1960s.

After Libby's pioneering test in 1949, in which he tested, *inter alia*, a linen cloth found at Qumran,[3] the first series of AMS tests was conducted by Bonani et al. 1991 and 1992, with later tests by Jull et al. 1995. The results were initially interpreted in a way that supported the thesis that some of the documents (the so-called "sectarian works") were related to Christian origins. But later this became a very controversial issue, discussed, questioned, and reinterpreted many times. One of the basic problems was, and still is, not only the accuracy of the dating itself but how to reconcile the AMS results with other information: especially what is to be considered "good agreement" between AMS results and estimates—on paleographic and textual grounds—or even between the AMS results and dated documents.

The initial studies by Bonani et al. 1992 offered quite optimistic results.[4] However, the data and graphics given were not as concise as expected, and the results were reinterpreted by Rodley 1993, who introduced a systematic offset in calibration.[5] The questions of the storage conditions and physical treatment of the Scrolls (both in Antiquity and after their discovery in modern times) were raised by Caldararo 1995. Caldararo insisted on the importance of further investigations, for these considerations have a crucial impact on the dating of the documents with respect to the radiocarbon method. Had the level of radiocarbon measured in the samples been skewed by the addition of chemicals that themselves contained radiocarbon? Later, this was especially discussed within the frame of a probable contamination by castor oil, proposed by Doudna 1998[6] and further developed by Rasmussen et al. 2001 and 2009.[7] The question of

3 Libby 1951. At that time, the raw datum 1917 ^{14}C-years was measured with a standard deviation (1σ) of ± 200 years.

4 Bonani sounded positive with caution, referring to a generally "good agreement" between radiocarbon dating and paleographic estimates. He concluded (Bonani 1992: 847): "The true ages of the four date-bearing manuscripts (Samples 1, 12, 13 and 14) lie within or close to the respective $1\ \sigma$ ranges. This indicates no significant methodological offset, either in the ^{14}C method or in the calibration curve based on measurements on American bristlecone pine and Irish oak trees. Good agreement between radiocarbon and paleographic dates is also observed in 9 of the remaining 10 samples."

5 In favor of the validity and significance of radiocarbon dating, Rodley 1993 postulated a reanalysis of the data. He suggested that the raw data had been imprecisely calibrated, and presented newly calculated ages including a systematic offset. On this base, the newly calculated ages were presented as "more significant than initially indicated" (Rodley 1993: 336), suggesting "that a general accuracy of about ± 25 yr has been achieved, making the method especially useful for documents whose ages are otherwise in doubt" (Rodley 1993: 337). In retrospect, these statements sound rather naïve.

6 Doudna 1998: 441, and elaborated on pp. 448–452.

7 For the subsequent discussion of castor oil contamination, see Rasmussen et al. 2001; Carmi

adequate pre-treatment became a major issue, alongside the question of calibration itself, including possible regional offsets or offsets between labs.[8]

The first measurements by Bonani 1992 were supplemented by a new set of measurements on Dead Sea Scrolls in 1995 by Jull et al. This set had dealt with documents written on parchment, papyrus, and linen, some of which bore a date in the text. The results were presented as being in "good" or "reasonable" agreement with the estimated or known age of the documents.[9] However, a closer look at the data was rather disillusioning.[10] For a historian working on texts and looking for an instrument for *removing* uncertainty in dating, and especially for an answer as to whether some of the documents had been written BCE or CE, the tests gave no final answer. Actually, the radiocarbon results gave only a very general picture of a time frame of a few hundred years spanning the period from BCE to CE—useful at most in rejecting the hypothesis of a medieval origin of the documents.

Nevertheless, the studies by Bonani and Jull were used both to support and also to challenge the argument that some scrolls were connected to Christian-

2002; Rasmussen et al. 2003; Rasmussen et al. 2009. Rasmussen 2001 argued for a corruption of some results of the two tests based on the observation that castor oil had been widely applied to some of the manuscripts both in Antiquity and in the process of restoration. Castor oil is a source of radiocarbon itself, and insufficient removal of traces leads to skewed results in radiocarbon analysis. In an experimental setting, Rasmussen showed that the pre-treatments of the two sets of test by Bonani and Jull were insufficient to remove all potential remains of castor oil. The validity of the study and its implications were, however, completely rejected by Carmi 2002. In their reply, Rasmussen et al. 2003 refused all objections by Carmi 2002, pointing again to the shortcomings of conventional acid-base-acid (ABA) pre-treatment. Rasmussen et al. 2009 provides studies on different pre-treatment methods meant to remove remains of castor oil, and suggests that for some important documents, a completely new dating with appropriate pre-treatment should be conducted.

8 The contribution of Doudna 1998 is especially worth reading: it gives a good insight into the variety of problems and uncertainties connected, to radiocarbon dating at that time.

9 "^{14}C ages of 14 parchment and 4 papyrus samples found in caves in the Judaean Desert have been measured by AMS. Measurements on samples of known ages are in good agreement with those known ages. Ages determined from ^{14}C measurements on the remainder of the Dead Sea Scroll samples are in reasonable agreement with paleographic estimates of such ages, in the cases where those estimates are available" (Jull et al. 1995: 17).

10 In the case of three dated papyrus documents, "good" was perceived as the date written in the text falling into the 1σ range (calculated 68.2% probability) (Jull et al. 1995: 17). Note that the 1σ range of the two papyrus comprised 191 and 108 calendar years, respectively. The date of the third papyrus failed the 2σ range (calculated 95.4%) by 10 years. However, Jull stresses that a different calibrating curve would have positioned the third papyrus within 2σ (Jull et al. 1995: 15).

ity. Doudna 1998 most prominently rejected this connection, *inter alia* because of the results of the radiocarbon tests (and their reanalysis).[11]

Doudna's study gave rise to discussion by defenders of the radiocarbon method: Rodley and Thiering 1999 addressed the issue of calibration once more.[12] In the same article, Rodley and Thiering discussed possible contamination in order to explain some of the radiocarbon results that do not match the overall picture at all. As mentioned above, pre-treatment methods came into focus and were reconsidered. Beside these more technical aspects, Rodley and Thiering acknowledged the paramount importance of assessing text-internal and external features (such as paleography) to develop arguments of dating further, even though, in the details, they did not agree with Doudna 1998.

In any case, the different studies and the evolution of the arguments clearly show how important it is for dating not just to look at test results, but to incorporate in a holistic way all available information, including from related documents, and to be cautious about projecting investigators' own expectations into "flexible" results. This "flexibility" was addressed by Atwill and Braunheim 2004, pointing to several shortcomings of the two tests done by Bonani and Jull. They concentrated on statistics, developing the argument that the means of interpreting the results were not accurate. Atwill and Braunheim argued that radiocarbon testing is in itself too imprecise to provide conclusive evidence for assigning the documents to a timespan as short as needed to settle the question of when the controversial scrolls were written.[13] Pinning the problem down they stated: "The average amount of error between the radiocarbon and the paleographic medians for the samples is virtually the same length of time or longer as the parameters of the debate of when the scrolls were written. Generally speaking, a measuring instrument that has an average degree of error as large as the phenomenon it is designed to measure is largely without use."[14] They also addressed the problem of single samples and their uncertainties.[15]

---

11 See Doudna 1998: 461–464, proposing "a single-generation hypothesis" on the basis of a new understanding of the present radiocarbon information in the first century BCE.

12 Rodley and Thiering 1999 referred to the then newly released calibration-curve of Stuiver et al. 1998 and applied it to the raw data. Since that time, a few additional updates of calibration-curves have been launched (IntCal04, IntCal09, IntCal13). However, if we compare these results with the newest IntCal13curve, the results would shift only by about 10 years at most, which shows that calibration has made major progress in the last two decades.

13 Atwill and Braunheim 2004: 145.

14 Atwill and Braunheim 2004: 148.

15 Atwill and Braunheim 2004: 152: "when using only a single sample any variation that would exist between different samples that came from the same host is lost and the imprecision

Thus the Dead Sea Scrolls teach us how radiocarbon dating should (not) be approached, for it rarely provides us with hard facts. However, there is no need to be to pessimistic, either, for if applied properly and with caution, it can be a powerful tool.

In this context, a new vigilance emerged as to how to interpret the results of radiocarbon dating. In the eyes of many, the extensive discussion about the dating of the Dead Sea Scrolls discredited the method, and it definitely quenched the primary enthusiasm for it to a large degree. Yet it is important to be aware of the progress that radiocarbon dating has made in the last two decades—its potential as well as its limits—in order to decide whether or not testing a given document (or series of documents) could be useful.

2.2 *Recent Test Series and the Study of the Chronology of Egypt*

In recent years, ever-increasing numbers of manuscripts have been tested by ^{14}C dating, and it seems to have become more and more common praxis to use radiocarbon dating with intriguing documents of doubted age. At the same time, the claims associated with radiocarbon results are generally made with more caution than in the past.[16] Large-scale studies on the applicability of radiocarbon dating shed even more light on this approach.

One milestone was the project "Radiocarbon and the Chronologies of Ancient Egypt." More than 200 objects from Egypt were dated and, even more importantly, the results were discussed and analyzed by leading scholars in Egyptology and radiocarbon dating. The most important findings and data were published in 2010.[17] The 2013 publication of an edited volume provides true insights into the study and the discussion associated with interpreting the results.[18]

As the introduction to the 2013 edited volume stated, the main object of the project was "a check of whether radiocarbon dating 'worked' in Ancient Egypt, and discovering if not, why not."[19] The contributors to the volume did

of the measurement technique becomes the predominant contributor to the reported variance."

16 See, for example, Fedi et al. 2010 for the famous Artemidorus papyrus. In total, five samples were sent to two different labs for radiocarbon dating, and for the ink, ion beam analysis was used. Eventually, the antique provenance of the papyrus was established, and the highly probable antiquity also of the writing, so that the hypothesis of a medieval or modern forgery could be ruled out. However, the study gives no exact date of the origin.

17 Bronk Ramsey et al. 2010 with supporting online material (list with annotated test results); Dee et al. 2010.

18 Shortland and Bronk Ramsey 2013.

19 Shortland and Bronk Ramsey 2013: v.

not confine themselves to addressing technical issues but approached dating in a much more comprehensive way. They included considerations such as how to select suitable samples, the protocoling of the sampling, and the role and application of pre-treatments—as well as the further stages of inference when considering the nature of each sample itself, its context, and its relationship to events for which the radiocarbon dates need to be modeled, both in site-based models and in models of political or cultural change.[20] Thus this study is significant not only in its large dimensions but much more in being a model of how historical and scientific dating and considerations should intertwine. Furthermore, radiocarbon dates were visualized and modeled in different ways using Bayesian analysis, which proved to be a powerful tool for dealing with questions of chronology.

Tests were all done on plant-based materials, of which papyrus formed about one-sixth, besides wood, textile, seeds, and other short-lived plants.[21] While calibrating results, a test series on pre-industrial plant samples of known ages was used to check on the general reliability of radiocarbon results and in order to postulate a small regional offset for Egypt (see section 3.3 below). Eventually, the question of the applicability of radiocarbon dating for Egyptian chronology was clearly and positively answered: "The successful radiocarbon dating of Egyptian history therefore has major ramifications for the chronologies and cultural syntheses of the wider east Mediterranean and ancient Near East in the prehistoric period. [...] A proper synchronization of the civilizations of the east Mediterranean in the second millennium BC may now be possible."[22]

2.3 *Radiocarbon Dating of Early Islamic Manuscripts*

As for Early Islamic manuscripts, radiocarbon dating has been done only on a handful of objects and the results have been met with much reluctance. The reasons are manifold. The technique is still expensive, and there is a moral reservation about destroying unique evidence (even if only about 1 square centimeter). Primarily, however, radiocarbon testing has simply had a very bad start. On the one hand, the first test mentioned in the literature was commissioned by the auction house Christie's, on a parchment fragment of a famous Qur'ān attributed to ʿUṯmān of which several folios were sold in

20 For the latter points, see Bronk Ramsey 2013: 33–34.
21 Brock and Dee 2013: 44 and appendices.
22 Manning et al. 2013: 141.

1992 and 1993.[23] What the actual measurement was can only be guessed at now. No raw data were given—just calibrated timespans of 260 and 125 years, respectively.[24] The main part of this manuscript is held today in Tashkent.[25] Another codex attributed to caliph ʿUṯmān, of which 81 fol. are kept in St. Petersburg and four other fragments in Uzbekistan, has been tested by Efim A. Rezvan. It has yielded a time slot between 775 and 995 CE, i.e., 200 years for the 95.4% confidence range.[26] On the other hand, at about the same time a fragment of one of the famous Sanaa Qurʾān manuscripts was tested.[27] The result was referred to as "assigning the period of genesis between 657 and 690 AD," thus only 33 years.[28] Of course, it was the 68.2% confidence range that was referred to in this case—but with no raw data, calibration curve, or explanations given, the result was rather misleading and surely did not help to build trust.

Subsequent publications approached the dating with more caution and insight. Blair 2006, having her own experience with radiocarbon testing on textiles,[29] referred to earlier tests, gave explanations on the technique, and encouraged further testing "with a coherent and standard protocol."[30] Indeed, the last ten years have witnessed further publications of radiocarbon tests on Early Islamic manuscripts that have approached the technique with more understanding and have also provided raw data and full results. Dutton 2007 published the test result of an early Qurʾānic fragment that was analyzed in 2001 yielding the result 1363 BP ± 33 ^{14}C years. Calibrated back then by

23 Lots 225–225a, sold on 20 October 1992; Lots 29–30, sold on 19 October 1993 (Rezvan 2000: 22 footnote 4).

24 Rezvan 2000: 19: "According to the results of this analysis, the fragment is dated to between 595 and 855 A.D. with a likelihood of 95%. Paleographic dating also indicates the turn to the eighth-ninth centuries." As for the 68.2% confidence range, one finds both the range 640–705 CE (Sam Fogg 2003: 12) and 640–765 CE (Déroche 2003: 261). However, the statement in the Sam Fogg catalogue must be a typographical error, as stated by the website "Islamic Awareness" (www.islamic-awareness.org/Quran/Text/Mss/radio.html, last accessed 16 January 2016). In every case, 765 CE makes more sense if we consider the calibration curve.

25 Blair 2006: 138–139 footnote 93; Déroche 2003.

26 Rezvan 2000: 22 with graphs on pp. 20 and 21; raw data on p. 22; no further explanations and comments are given.

27 See von Bothmer et al. 1999: 45; see also Blair 2006: 139 footnote 95.

28 "Eine später, und ohne Kenntnis meiner Datierung durchgeführte naturwissenschaftliche Untersuchung nach der ^{14}C-Methode hat nach dem noch unveröffentlichten Untersuchungsbericht, als kalibriertes Ergebnis einen Entstehungszeitraum 'zwischen 657 und 690', bestimmt" (von Bothmer et al. 1999: 45).

29 Blair et al. 1992.

30 Blair 2006: 125.

the IntCal98 calibration curve,[31] Dutton calibrated anew with IntCal04.[32] The results[33] matched the paleographic and textual estimate very well and, due to a steep calibration curve, featured narrow timespans (see section 3 below). He concluded: "Furthermore, despite what may be said about this method of dating, these results provide important additional, and corroborating, evidence to that provided by the more traditional methods used by paleographers and art historians."[34] Shorty later, Sadeghi and Bergmann 2010 presented a test on the Standford 07 fragment of the famous Sanaa 1 palimpsest. The raw data (1407 BP ± 36 ^{14}C years) was calibrated to 614–656 CE for the 68.2% confidence range, and 578–669 CE for the 95.4% confidence range.[35] They optimistically infer a high probability "that the Ṣanaʿāʾ 1 manuscript was produced no more than 15 years after the death of the Prophet Muḥammad."[36]

However, it must be objected in both cases that only one measurement on a single target was made, which reduces its explanatory power considerably. Such a claim can easily be contested (see section 5 below). This is probably why Déroche 2014 concludes that "although recent publications seem overconfident in their reliance on the ^{14}C method, the last word should stay with the philologist, the historian or the palaeographer." Déroche mentions two further tests on the same manuscript by Sadeghi and Bergmann, yielding (too) early results "which simply cannot be accepted," i.e., if we assume that the parchment written upon is not much older than the writing itself.[37] He refers also to yet another two tests on two well studied and dated Qurʾān manuscripts (early 11th and early 10th centuries, respectively) for both of which the assumed date of production lies outside the calibrated 95.4% confidence range.[38] However, in the same publication, Déroche gives an account of a test series he had set up to test the accuracy of radiocarbon analysis: two labs were each provided with a set of three pieces stemming from three controversial copies of the Qurʾān. The test results were congruent and lead Déroche to conclude that the attri-

31 Stuiver et al. 1998.

32 Reimer et al. 2004.

33 68.2% confidence range: 644–675; 95.4% confidence range: 609–694 CE + 702–706 CE + 748–765 CE (Dutton 2007: 63–64).

34 Dutton 2007: 64.

35 Sadeghi and Bergmann 2010: 348; 353.

36 Sadeghi and Bergmann 2010: 353.

37 Déroche 2014: 13. Only calibrated confidence ranges are given in these cases (obviously citing the 95.4% confidence range), but no raw data: first folio: 543–599 CE; second folio: 433–599 CE.

38 For test results including raw data and sample code, see Déroche 2014: 12–13.

bution to the early 11th century CE based on the *waqfiyya* associated with the three pieces stands on firm ground, and that an attribution to the 9th century can be ruled out.[39]

Over the last twenty years, our view of radiocarbon dating has changed considerably, from naïve and unskillful acceptance to skeptical and active challenging of the technique. The time had definitely come for a large-scale comparative study such as the Coranica Project. Interestingly, awareness of the potential and the limits of radiocarbon dating developed earlier with respect to Early Islamic textiles than with respect to manuscripts. This is due to textiles' proximity to archaeology (especially within Egyptology/Coptic studies).[40] And it is archaeology that has a long history with radiocarbon dating, having decisively shaped its evolution.

2.4 *The Coranica Project: Context for the Text*

This project approaches the material history of the Qur'ān from a number of angles. A subproject, led by Tobias J. Jocham, Michael Marx, and Eva M. Youssef-Grob, began in 2014[41] with the purpose of conducting large-scale radiocarbon tests on samples from different Qur'ān manuscripts, focusing on very early pieces that are thought to stem from the 1st and 2nd century Hijra, alongside other manuscripts on parchment and papyrus serving comparative purposes.

The project started with an interlaboratory comparison. A sample of the controversial Sanaa 1 manuscript, dated by a preceding test as being peculiarly early, was cut into three pieces and sent to different labs. Finally, the Laboratory of Ion Beam Physics at ETH Zurich was chosen for the subsequent test series.

Then, in a first test battery, manuscripts from the Leiden University collection were tested, and subsequently samples provided by the Tübingen and Heidelberg collections. The results caused a sensation.[42] Radiocarbon tests were clearly in favor of an early date for the Qur'ān manuscripts in Ḥiǧāzī script.

---

39 See Déroche 2014: 13, who unfortunately gives only calibrated ranges of probability but no raw data.

40 See Blair et al. 1992; de Moor et al. 2006; van Strydonck and Boudin 2007; van Strydonck 2014.

41 For the radiocarbon subproject, see www.coranica.de/computatio-radiocarbonica-en (last accessed 15 January 2015).

42 Tests in Leiden led to interviews with the press and a conference on "the Qur'ān as book" in December 2014; see www.library.leiden.edu/special-collections/special/ancient-quran-fragments.html (last accessed 14 November 2015). Tests in Tübingen even made it to the main news bulletin of ARD television; see www.ardmediathek.de/tv/Tagesschau/tagesschau-20-00-Uhr/Das-Erste/Video?documentId=24643718&bcastId=4326&mpage=page.download (last accessed 14 November 2015).

The favorable calibration curve for the sector until ca. 680 CE and a test setup featuring analysis of multiple targets of the same manuscript, supported the argument much more strongly than ever before. Outside the Early Islamic time range, there was an associated project on the development of the Southern Arabian minuscule, under the direction of Peter Stein in Jena, applying radiocarbon testing on a highly relevant sample series of wooden sticks, featuring simple and multiple tests on the material.

In further test series, samples from more collections were and are going to be sent to the ETH lab. Results and derived models and insights will be the subject of forthcoming publications, of which this paper is a first general introduction and gives only some illustrative examples—leaving us with the prospect of new insights into the history of Early Islam.

3 Results of Radiocarbon Tests and Their Calibration

In the last decades, the technique of radiocarbon dating in general and the interpretation of results in particular have witnessed a number of smaller and bigger revolutions. I will keep the technical section short and generally understandable, yet understanding how the analysis works is crucial to understanding the main factors that influence the accuracy of the results.[43]

Radiocarbon (^{14}C) is the unstable radioactive isotope of carbon (C). It is produced by a number of reactions, the most important of which takes place in the upper atmosphere. What matters for the technique of dating is the ratio between radiocarbon (^{14}C) and stable carbon (^{12}C) in the atmosphere, which is fairly constant, apart from changes due to the cosmic-ray flux incidence on the solar system and to variations in the Earth's magnetic field.[44] Once radiocarbon is produced in the upper atmosphere, its atoms oxidize to carbon dioxide $^{14}CO_2$, then mix into the lower atmosphere and disperse.[45]

Radiocarbon (as well as carbon) is incorporated into plants by photosynthesis of carbon dioxide. Thus a living plant holds a record of the ratio between radiocarbon (^{14}C) and stable carbon (^{12}C) in the atmosphere. Starting from the death of the organism, the exchange with the atmosphere stops and the incor-

43 For more technical details, see Bronk Ramsey 2008, in itself a great introduction.

44 Bronk Ramsey 2008: 250–251. For our considerations here, the effects of 20th-century nuclear bomb tests are of no immediate relevance.

45 The level, diffusion, and incorporation of radiocarbon into oceans, lakes, and rivers is not our topic here, nor is the incorporation of radiocarbon into algae and corals or in peat. Yet for an overview, see Bronk Ramsey 2008: 252–253.

porated radiocarbon gradually decays, with a half-life of just over 5,500 years.[46] In other words, in the dead organism, the ratio between radiocarbon (^{14}C) and the stable carbon (^{12}C) is continuously falling. Detecting the actual ratio between radiocarbon (^{14}C) and stable carbon (^{12}C), and concluding the time when the organism died, is what radiocarbon dating is ultimately all about.

3.1 *"Radiocarbon Years" and Calibration to Calendar Years*

In AMS radiocarbon testing, the ratio between ^{14}C and the stable ^{12}C of a sample is measured, as is between stable ^{13}C and stable ^{12}C ($\delta^{13}C$) to account for isotopic fractionation.[47] Corrected for isotopic fractionation, the ratio of ^{14}C compared to ^{12}C is calculated based on the half-life of the ^{14}C isotope, and the age of a sample is given in radiocarbon (^{14}C) years "before present" (BP). "Present" was fixed as 1950, when radiocarbon dating was launched and before nuclear bomb tests considerably changed the level of ^{14}C in the atmosphere.

In addition to the radiocarbon year BP, the standard deviation 1σ, i.e., the precision of the measurement, is given as a ± range of a certain number of radiocarbon years. Roughly speaking, 1σ comprises the calculated range into which about two of three results will fall if the measurement is repeated with exactly the same facility and settings.[48] The result is given as a normal curve of distribution: from the outset, radiocarbon testing is all about probabilities! In the case of multiple targets taken from the same host, the lab states the combined result with error-weighted mean and sample variance, exhibiting a smaller 1σ than the two distributions on their own.

In a nutshell, the sample-code—a number of ^{14}C years BP ± 1σ (in ^{14}C years)—is the "raw data" of a test that should in every case be provided by the lab, even though it is not the kind of data that one can immediately work with.

> **Example 1:** ETH-54173, a sample of the Leiden Qurʾān fragment on papyrus (UB Leiden inv. Or. 8264) tested by ETH Zurich (Fig. 5.1). The result is given as "1324 ± 24," meaning: "1324 calculated ^{14}C years (not calendar years) before 1950, with a precision of ± 24 ^{14}C years."

46 The half-life of radiocarbon is nowadays stated as 5730 ± 40 years (so-called Cambridge half-life). However, for radiocarbon dating, the Libby half-life of 5568 ± 30 is used, i.e., the half-life of radiocarbon as it was believed to be at the time of the development of the radiocarbon dating method in order to have comparable results. The results are therefore also known as giving the "conventional ^{14}C age."

47 On the importance and technique of isotopic fractionation correction, see Bronk Ramsey et al. 2004: 19–20.

48 For a more detailed account on different stages of measurement and associated uncertainties, see section 4 below.

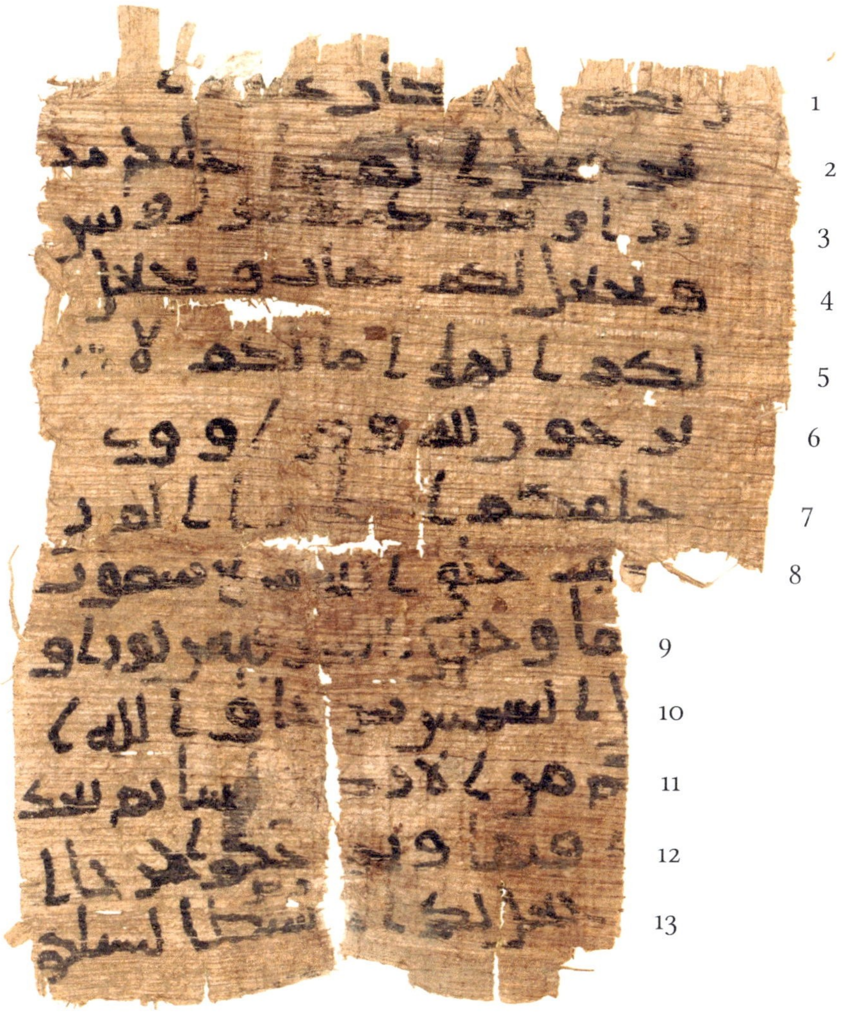

FIGURE 5.1 Qur'ān fragment on papyrus (P.Leiden inv. Or. 8264)
© LEIDEN UNIVERSITY LIBRARY, PAPYRUS COLLECTION

Radiocarbon years do not correspond to calendar years because over the years, the concentration of radiocarbon in the atmosphere has not been stable but has fluctuated on a small scale. In order to receive calendar years from the measured ^{14}C level of a sample, one needs to compare the measured ^{14}C level to ^{14}C levels of samples of known age, in a process of calibration. In the evolution of radiocarbon dating, not only has measurement technique itself has made huge progress but, besides more deeper understanding of the cycle and

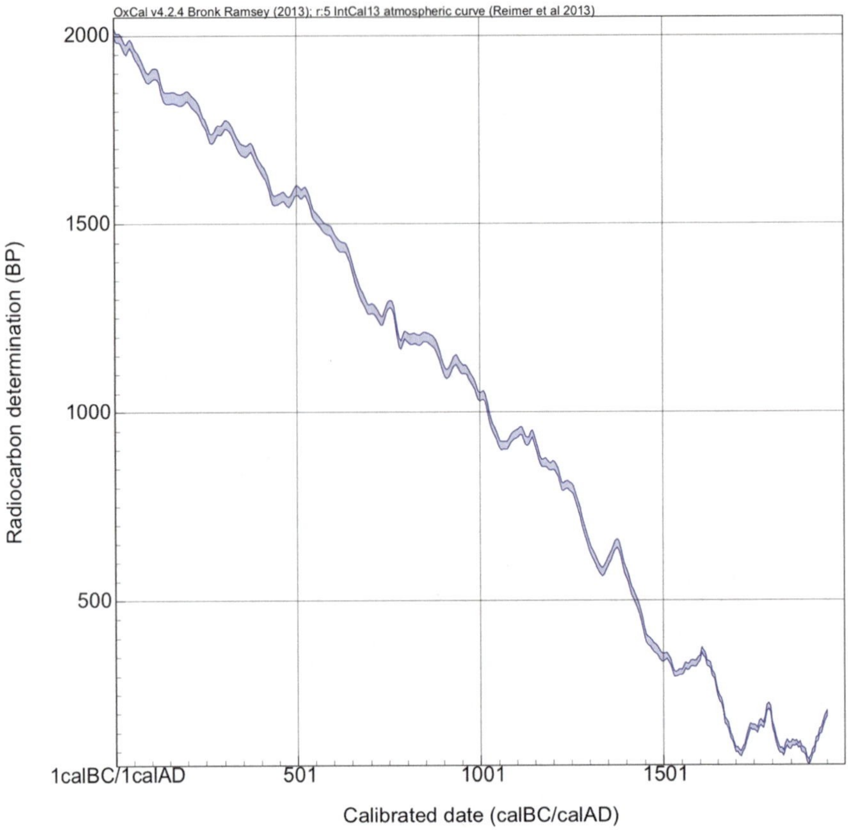

FIGURE 5.2 OxCal plot of the IntCal13 curve, covering the two millenia CE until 1950 ("present")

incorporation of radiocarbon in nature, continuous progress in calibrating has added immensely to accuracy. The internationally standardized and approved calibration curves show the measured level of ^{14}C of material of known age.[49] Figure 5.2 gives a detail of the recently released IntCal13 calibration curve of 2013,[50] namely, the two millennia CE where, later on, the section from 600 to

49 Data for the radiocarbon calibration curves is collected by the IntCal Working Group (IWG). Updates and extensions to the terrestrial and marine calibration curves are subsequently presented and ratified at International Radiocarbon conferences (Reimer et al. 2013b: 1924). The IWG also works on defining and developing standards for the procedures connected to radiocarbon dating, such as sample pre-treatments, blanks, secondary standards for measurements, and interlaboratory comparisons (Reimer et al. 2013b: 1930).

50 Reimer et al. 2013a.

1000 CE is of special interest (see section 3.2 below). The vertical axis refers to radiocarbon years, and the horizontal axis to calendar years. Radiocarbon years do not exactly correspond to calendar years because the concentration of ^{14}C as measured in samples of known age has been unsteady. Peaks and plateaus in this curve ("wiggles") show the difficulty in assigning radiocarbon years to calendar years and how ambiguous the interpretation of results in radiocarbon years can be. In many cases, one and the same concentration of ^{14}C has been measured in samples where real age differs much more than 100 calendar years!

How has this calibration curve been computed? For pre-modern times, we have no direct access to ^{14}C concentration by measuring in the atmosphere, yet at least for the two millennia mentioned, data stem from dendrochonology, namely, from measuring radiocarbon incorporated into tree-rings. These chronologies can be used to calibrate radiocarbon dating in continuous records back to 12,000 BCE.[51]

As longer-living plants, trees incorporate radiocarbon by photosynthesis over a greater period, and tree-rings show different levels of ^{14}C according to their age. However, measurements and models of concentration derived from tree-rings average across the decade and not the single years.[52] This is one of the obstacles for high-precision dating. The standard procedure in dating samples for archaeology has long been a precision of ± 50 radiocarbon years. With AMS dating and with demands for higher precision, labs now offer high-precision dating of ± 20 radiocarbon years. Combining the results of measurements of multiple targets can yield to even smaller standard deviations (discussed below in section 4.2). However, it must always be born in mind that the data set under-

51 Chronologies reach back until 13.900 cal BP. Before that, macrofossil data are used until the end of the range of the dating record at ca. 50,000 BCE (Reimer et al. 2013a: 1870). For different chronologies (Irish oak, German oak, trees from the West Coast of North America, Swiss and German pines etc.) incorporated into the newest IntCal13 calibration data set, see Reimer et al. 2013b: 1933–1934. Some chronologies are floating, i.e., they are fitted into the calibration curve by "wiggle matching," a technique of testing the tree-rings of a wooden sample at such short intervals that the produced pattern can be matched onto the patterns ("wiggles") of the calibration curve.

52 See also the update of IntCal13 (with respect to the previous calibration curve IntCal09) in Reimer et al. 2013a: 1872, where samples of Irish oaks are added to the timespans important for our purposes. However, measurements all average over the decade, while for some studies calibration dates have been produced for single years, with amazing possibilities, especially for wiggle-matching of other datasets based on measurement of short intervals (e.g., Wacker et al. 2014). Generally on wiggle-matching, see Bronk Ramsey et al. 2001; Bronk Ramsey 2008: 264.

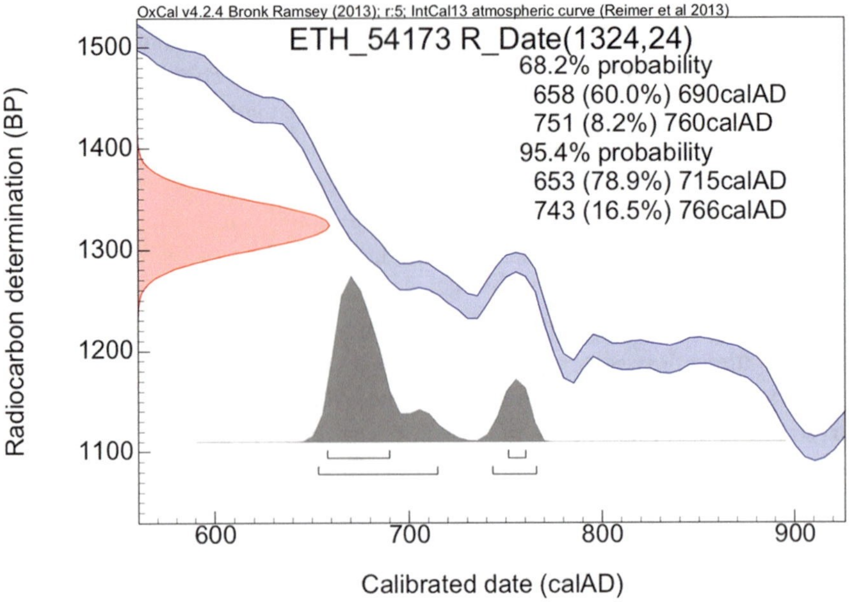

FIGURE 5.3 OxCal single plot of ETH-54173

lying calibration puts its own limits on the precision of the calibrated age![53] Actually, this is the bottleneck in the chain of reasoning.[54]

To return to Example 1 above, the Leiden papyrus Qurʾān fragment (Fig. 5.1) and its raw data ETH-54173: 1324 ± 24: in Figure 5.3 above, these raw data are represented by the red normal curve of distribution on the horizontal axis, now to be calibrated with help of the calibration curve—the wiggly blue line—in order to gain calendar years.[55] For this, two methods are at our disposal. The straightforward interception method at one or two standard deviations visually examines the overlap between the measurement made and the reference curve, while the standard method is used to calculate a probability density function for the age of the sample with the help of a calibration program.[56] The

53 See, for example, Bronk Ramsey 2008: 262: "Although moving from a precision of ± 60 to ± 30 does make a significance difference, further improvements in precision only give a marginal improvement in calendar resolution for most true ages."

54 Bronk Ramsey 2008: 268.

55 The calibration curve is not only represented by a line but as a line plus added confidence range 1σ. Depending on the distribution of the underlying data, the width of the confidence range is wider or smaller.

56 For an overview, see www.radiocarbon.org/Info/ (last recall 15 January 2015). All internationally accepted calibration programs use the IntCal curve(s) for calibration. Yet algorithms implemented and features for inpuy and output might be different. The most

range of probable values can be calculated using the highest probability density (HPD) range, typically at the 95.4% (2σ) level (the grey function in Fig. 5.3). On the basis of this HPD range, the program will provide the probable timespans again by stating 1σ and 2σ: thus probabilities of 68.2% and 95.4% imply that actual results, based on the probabilities given by the measurement, lie within this timespan. In case of plateaus and peaks, some of these timespans will be divided into two or even more single spans, as seen in both the 68.2% and the 95.4% probability span in Figure 5.3 above.

Note that the calculated timespans are not distributed following a normal curve of distribution. It is not 710 CE, the mean of 653 CE and 766 CE (representing the extreme boundaries of the given 95.4% ranges) that represents the most probable result, but rather a date between 653 and 715 CE. However, one should avoid building an argument on a single measurement (see sections 4.2 and 5 below).

Beside the common representation just shown, the density cloud can also be mapped directly on the calibration curve (Fig. 5.4) or—leaving the calibration curve aside—with respect to the axis of calendar years (Fig. 5.5). This last version is preferred in the representation of multiple test results.

3.2 *Peculiarities of Calibration for Early Islamic Times*

As has been shown with Example 1, leveling of the calibration curve determines the precision achievable by calibration to a large degree. Peaks and plateaus in the calibration curve result in long timespans, even if the measured results have a small standard deviation, and allow for "precise results."

Figure 5.6 below shows the ^{14}C concentration curve for the six centuries between 600 and 1200 CE that are of particular interest for research on Early Islamic sources. This section of the curve shows five important timespans until 1000 CE, as marked in the graph. Precision in calibration varies considerably. Until 680 CE, the calibration curve is steep, with no plateaus or peaks. The expected calendar years by calibration will give narrow timespans lying within a few decades, and thus "precise results." Later, the curve is marked by three plateaus or peaks, and thus yields "imprecise results," i.e., in most cases the assignation of about a century, even for the 1σ confidence range. Around

widely used methods for our time range and material are OxCal by Bronk Ramsey of the Oxford Radiocarbon Accelerator Unit (ORAU), on https://c14.arch.ox.ac.uk/embed.php?File=oxcal.html (Bronk Ramsey and Lee 2013), and CALIB by Stuiver, Reimer and Reimer of the Quaternary Isotope Lab, University of Washington, and the Queens University of Belfast, on http://calib.qub.ac.uk/calib/ (Stuiver and Reimer 1993).

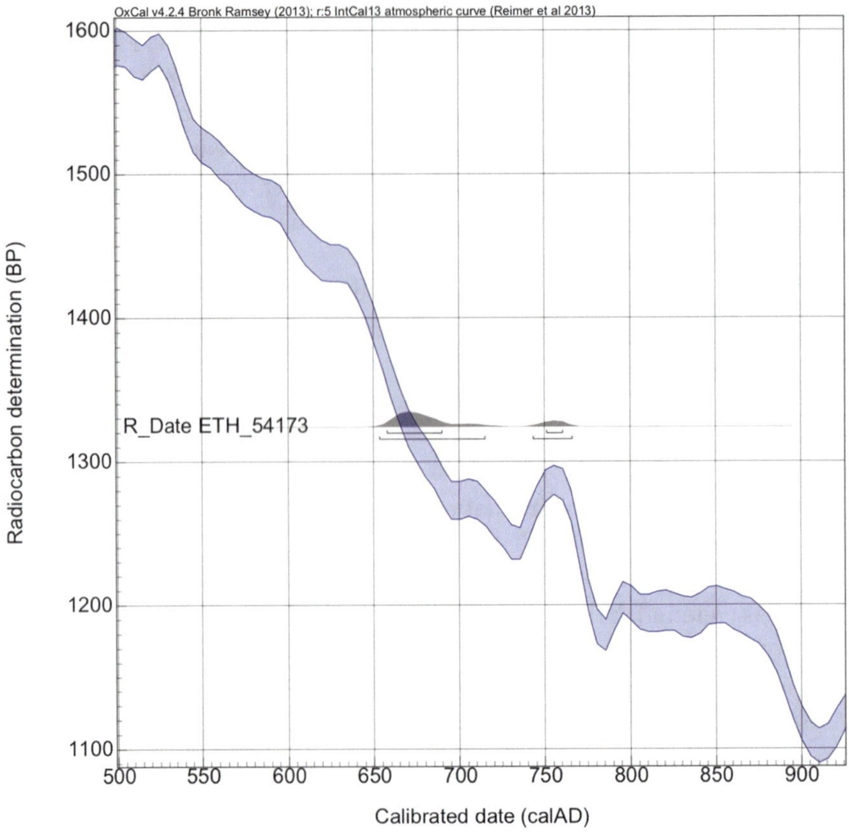

FIGURE 5.4 OxCal curve plot of ETH-54173

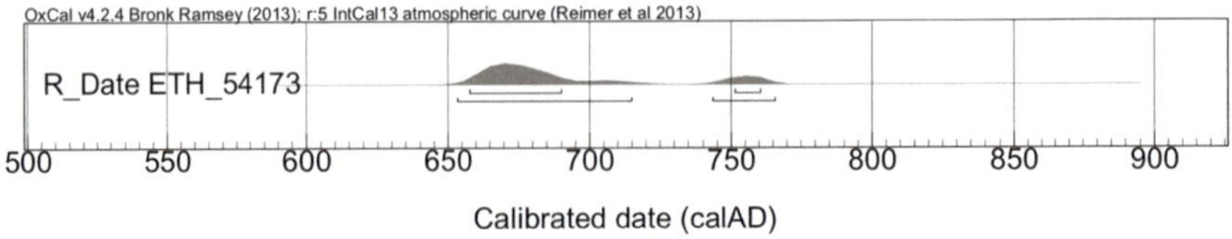

FIGURE 5.5 OxCal multiple plot of ETH-54173

1000 CE, the curve has again a short steep phase and expected calibrated ages again lie within a few decades.

Therefore, not every phase of Early Islamic time yields the same precision for ^{14}C testing. Suppose the expected result of a test falls in one of the "imprecise" phases: will it nevertheless be a result worth going for? It might be, of course, if additional internal or external hints can further narrow the timespan, or if the assignation to the span of about a century is already what one is looking for.

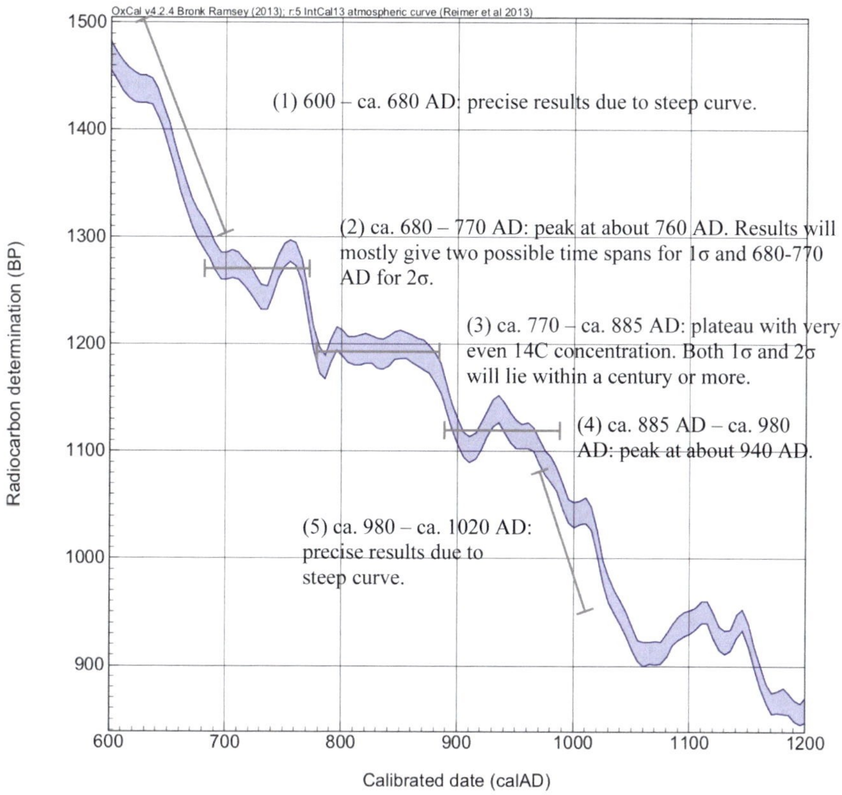

FIGURE 5.6 OxCal plot of extract of IntCal13 curve, covering the centuries between 600 and 1200 CE

3.3 *Offsets in Calibration*

Within a given hemisphere, no great regional variation in the concentration of radiocarbon has been traced, because winds even out differences rather quickly. Also the oceans, being radiocarbon reservoirs of their own, are a balancing force. However, small-scale effects have been detected, most likely attributable to different growing seasons or to reservoir effects.[57]

As for Egypt, Dee et al. 2010 have shown a slight 0.25% difference in radiocarbon concentration from the Northern Hemisphere consensus values, based on a test series of 66 preindustrial short-lived plants whose exact date was known. The difference might look small, yet it results in an average offset of 19 ± 5 radiocarbon years, i.e., most plants prove to be slightly younger than ^{14}C dating with

57 Bronk Ramsey 2008: 251. For a compilation of different studies of regional ^{14}C offsets, see also Manning et al. 2014: 401.

conventional calibration suggested. Dee et al. 2010 explain this with growing seasons as follows: "atmospheric ^{14}C concentrations range from a minimum in late winter/early spring to a peak in late summer due to variations in the timing and location of the injection of $^{14}CO_2$ from the stratosphere into the troposphere."[58] In pre-modern Egypt, the main growing season was in spring, after the Nile flood in winter. But for Europe and its trees, which form the basic data set for the calibration curve, the main growing season lags somewhat behind and is more concentrated in summer and autumn. Therefore, a slightly lower level of radiocarbon can be expected for plants growing in Egypt as compared to Europe.

This offset of 19 ± 5 radiocarbon years was added to all the results from the test series on the "chronology of Egypt" (see section 2.2 above) and successfully applied to data from Amarna by Manning et al. 2013.[59] However, in the frame of the Coranica project, very precise results have been achieved on two dated papyri from Egypt (in triple testing) without applying the offset (see 4.2 below, Example 2).

4 The Accelerator Mass Spectrometry (AMS) Measurement Process and Its Precision

In section 3, questions of calibration were the focus. Although they substantially add to uncertainties connected to radiocarbon dating, they are crucial to our understanding. Yet up to now, not much has been said about Accelerator Mass Spectrometry (AMS) measurement and measurement precision. With AMS, radiocarbon atoms are detected directly (in contrast to the standard decay counting). Thus precision depends on detection efficiency, instrument stability, and sample purity.[60] In the end, the real challenge remains how to deal with results that are not hard and fast facts (see also section 5 below, on the interpretation of results).

The level of ^{14}C decreases over time; the older the sample, the fewer ^{14}C atoms are to be detected—which also sets limits on sample size. In a high-precision measurement with a precision/standard deviation of ± 25 years, for a modern sample one needs the presence of at least 2 μg C. Much older samples, such as a sample 12,000 years old, require the considerably higher amount

58 Dee et al. 2010: 690.

59 "The success of the correlation with the standard Egyptian historical chronology partly depends on the use of the 19 ± 5 years seasonal offset" (Manning et al. 2013: 138).

60 See Bronk Ramsey 2008: 258.

of about 10 µg C. In the measurement itself, the typical total AMS detection efficiency is about 1%, at best about 5%. Therefore, for a modern sample, the threshold for an actual carbon sample size is about 40–200 µg C, not the 2 µg C as stated above.[61] However, the typical sample size for an AMS measurement is standardized by the labs on a milligram of carbon/graphite. As for parchment and papyrus, for one sample, this typically corresponds to about 1 cm^2 of material in total.

The different stages of a measurement include:[62]

- Pre-treatment of the sample. Depending on the material, a pre-treatment is applied in order to clean the sample of all kinds of contamination that could skew the results.
- The sample is loaded into a capsule and combusted to CO_2.[63]
- An aliquot of standardized weight (0.9–2 mg C) is reduced to graphite (existing almost exclusively out of carbon atoms) and pressed into a target for measurement.
- Loading of targets into the measurement cassette. The measurement cassette typically includes oxalic acid II "standards" of standard ^{13}C and ^{14}C levels; so-called "blanks" or "backgrounds," e.g., anthracite technically void of ^{14}C; known-age samples (mostly tree-rings) ("secondary standards"); possibly further quality assurance and background samples; and the targets to test. Each lab has its own standard procedure of how to assemble the measurement cassettes, which is modified according to precision aimed at and the nature of samples to test.[64]
- Cassettes are inserted into the Accelerator Mass Spectrometer and measured in different runs, depending on the precision to achieve.[65]

61 Bronk Ramsey 2008: 258.

62 For detailed accounts of the procedure in the Oxford lab, see Bronk Ramsey et al. 2004; for the procedure in the ETH Zurich lab, see Wacker et al. 2010; Christl et al. 2013. For a general overview, see Reimer et al. 2013b: 1930–1931.

63 At combustion, an analysis of the CO_2 in a gas chromatograph is carried out, giving hints of contaminants that could not be removed. For very small samples, radiocarbon measurement directly of CO_2 is offered.

64 At Oxford, there are up to 56 targets on one cassette, of which about 10 targets are standards and blanks (Bronk Ramsey et al. 2004: 19). At Zurich, there are up to 20 targets on one cassette, including 3 standards and 2 blanks, for high-precision dating 4 to 6 standards and at least 3 blanks (Wacker et al. 2010: 253).

65 As for Zurich: "All samples of a cassette are measured at least 5–6 times. A single measurement is subdivided into 10 cycles of 45 s each. For high-precision measurements, we used 4–6 standards and at least 3 blanks and the measurement time of 30–60 min per sample

TABLE 5.1 Proportion of measurements on different target types lying within 1, 2, and 3 σ of expected values (reproduction of Bronk Ramsey et al. 2004: 21)

Range offset from true value as a factor of uncertainty (σ)	Proportion of 203 HOXII measurements lying within range	Proportion of 96 tree-ring measurements lying within range	Proportion of 66 duplicate AMS measurements on 30 samples lying within range	Proportion of 55 duplicate measurements (including pre-treatment) on 27 samples lying within range
−3 to 3	100.0%	100.0%	100.0%	100.0%
−2 to 2	97.5%	95.8%	95.5%	94.6%
−1 to 1	75.9%	75.0%	69.7%	65.5%

- The final result is calculated based on the measurements of the different target types, taking into account additional uncertainty reflecting the reproducibility of results.[66]

With the AMS instruments introduced about two decades ago, instrument stability no longer puts significant limits on precision of measurement. High precision is achieved by a multitude of measurement runs on the same targets, longer measurement time, and more standards in the same cassette. Numbers of runs are not always stated in the results given by the AMS labs but specified on demand and stated in the standard protocols. Stated standard deviations for radiocarbon measurement results 1σ are calculated based on results of different measurements and on long-term observation. As an illustration, see the Table 5.1, given by Bronk Bronk Ramsey et al. 2004: 21, on performance of the AMS system in Oxford on standards (columns 2 and 3) and known-age material (columns 4 and 5):

was increased to 2–3 hr by extending the cycle time to 60 s and by measuring each sample 10–15 times" (Wacker et al. 2010: 253).

66 The results of "standards" assure the internal consistency of the measurement; they contribute to determine the precision achieved and serve in determining the ^{13}C-^{14}C ratio. Blanks—technically void of any ^{14}C are graphitized in the same way as the test samples—account for AMS background noise and would indicate radiocarbon being added through the process of graphitization (Bronk Ramsey et al. 2004: 19; Wacker et al. 2010: 254; Reimer et al. 2013b: 1930–1931).

"These measurements essentially show the repeatability of the combustion, graphitization, target pressing, and AMS measurement."[67] Table 5.1 shows in the second column that oxalic acid standards yield the most precise results, followed by tree-ring measurements. In case of duplicate samples (two targets), pre-treatment clearly adds uncertainty: whereas 69.7% of the duplicate samples (splitting after pre-treatment) were lying within 1σ, this was reduced to only 65.5% in case of duplicate samples with separate pre-treatment.[68] In principle, the precision of a given radiocarbon measurement can be trusted. Except for the smallest samples, combusting and graphitization are nowadays no longer critical in effecting precision, whereas pre-treatment still is.[69]

4.1 *Sample Purity and Differences between Papyrus and Parchment*

^{14}C levels in simple and long-living plants that had incorporated CO_2 from the atmosphere over photosynthesis are at the core of radiocarbon dating technique and its calibration—leaving maritime and mixed environments aside. As compared with other material, papyrus as a short-lived plant (even in its form as a writing supply) is unproblematic in radiocarbon testing.

As for animals, their carbon also goes back to plants, either directly (in the case of herbivores) or indirectly (in the case of carnivores and omnivores). In all these cases, however, the animal's diet stems from the last few years before death and not from a distant past. Whereas plants deposit radiocarbon in large molecules of the polymer cellulose, animals lay down radiocarbon into polymers such as keratin (horn, nails, feather, and hair) and other proteins. Some other structures (such as bones) also contain mineral components. Thus the interpretation of radiocarbon analysis of animals' remains is more complex than the interpretation of the remains of short-lived plants. Moreover, not all deposits within an animal cease to exchange carbon with the rest of the organism.[70]

67 Bronk Ramsey et al. 2004: 21.

68 Systematic offsets by the AMS system itself are not accounted for in this setup but need to be ruled out by interlaboratory comparisons. For interlaboratory comparisons, see the special issue of the journal *Radiocarbon* 45/3 (2003), devoted to International Radiocarbon Intercomparison.

69 For AMS uncertainties, see Reimer et al. 2013b: 1932–1933. On different kinds of contamination affecting measured radiocarbon age, see Bronk Ramsey 2008: 256.

70 Bronk Ramsey 2008: 253–254.

TABLE 5.2 Main stable molecular forms of carbon used in ^{14}C dating, from Bronk Ramsey 2008: 255

Molecular form	Material
Cellulose (polysaccharide)	Wood and plant remains
Chitin (polysaccharide)	Arthropod exoskeletons
Collagen (protein)	Bone and teeth
Keratin (protein)	Hair, horn, nails, claws and beaks
Lipids (glycerides)	Animal fats and vegetable oils
Aragonite (calcium carbonate)	Mollusk shells, corals, and speleothems
Amorphous carbon (elemental carbon)	Charcoal or charred plant remains

The main stable molecular forms of carbon used in ^{14}C dating are compiled in Table 5.2 above.[71]

Interestingly, if we have a look at the proportions of the materials tested in AMS labs, samples on the base of cellulose are in fact the minority. On top are collagen-containing, charcoal, and charred material.[72]

In the case of parchment, radiocarbon is stored in its collagen (the main structural protein of the skin that amounts to about 90–95% of a parchment's weight).[73] Stemming from cattle, a diet of green plants can be supposed, which eases assessing the organism's position in the environment.[74]

Whereas manufacturing of papyrus is quite simple and does not include application of chemicals,[75] manufacturing of parchment is much more complex, involving many steps and the use of different chemical substances. Over time, different methods in manufacturing have evolved, for many of which we

71 Bronk Ramsey 2008: 255.

72 As for the Oxford Radiocarbon Acceleration Unit: collagen-containing material (i.e., bone, tooth, antler, ivory) 43%; charcoal and charred material (e.g., wood and seeds), 23%; cellulose-containing material (wood, seeds, plant remains, textiles, paper), 16%; shells, other carbonates, and cremated bones, 5%; other material (e.g., hair, sediments, carbonized pottery residues), 14% (Brock et al. 2010: 103). For the Zurich AMS lab, see the diagram in Hajdas 2009: 80.

73 Brock 2013: 353; 357.

74 Radiocarbon stored in the collagen of an organism may also come from a mixed diet, including—over the food-chain or directly—drawing on the CO_2 reservoir of the ocean. On the set of problems associated especially with human bones, see Bronk Ramsey 2008: 260–261.

75 On papyrus manufacturing, see Grohmann 1952: 30–31; Bülow-Jacobsen 2009: 4–10.

have no written sources describing them exactly.[76] In any case, "parchment is a complex, inhomogeneous material, and its chemistry and state of preservation can be affected by a range of external factors such as environmental pollution, harsh cleaning, improper conservation and restoration."[77] Parchments from the Middle East from Early Islamic times have been produced by the same or similar procedures as somewhat later parchments in Europe, for which there are more studies or written sources available about production.[78]

From a technical point of view, testing of Early Islamic papyrus promises fewer complications than testing of parchment for a variety of reasons:

(a) *Short-lived plant vs. complex animal product*: Papyrus is a short-lived *plant*, providing a kind of snapshot of one year. We can easily test the radiocarbon level of its cellulose fiber. Overall, this is the material best suited for radiocarbon testing[79] (second only to wood with tree-rings, on which the calibration curve is based and on which also the technique of wiggle-matching can be applied).[80]

Parchment is a much more complex animal product in which, as far as we know, mostly skins of very young animals were used and radiocarbon exchange can be almost neglected: radiocarbon level is mostly herbal, with an animal "storage" of a few years.

(b) *Provenance*: Most papyrus documents stem from Egypt, which was the main producer of papyrus. This gives us the chance to apply the regional calibration-offset as described by Dee et al. 2010.

For parchment manuscripts, the situation is in most cases very difficult because we cannot say for sure where they were produced. The writing, a possible colophon, declarations of ownership or annotations can give a hint, but can hardly determine the origin with security. But even if we knew the origin, to my knowledge there are no studies on regional variation of radiocarbon concentration for the Middle East that could be of assistance in this respect.[81]

---

76 Brock 2013: 353. For a comprehensive account of parchment and leather manufacturing from ancient to medieval times, see Reed 1972. See also Caldararo 1995: 25 for a concise visual overview of the stages included in producing parchments.

77 Brock 2013: 353.

78 Reed 1972. For the historical context of parchment and leather production and technology transfer from the Middle East to Europe, mainly via Spain, by the Arabs, see Chapter 4.

79 See Dee et al. 2012: 879; 881.

80 See Bronk Ramsey et al. 2001. Wiggle-matching refers to the technique of testing the tree-rings of a wooden sample in such intervals that the produced pattern can be matched onto the patterns ("wiggles") of the calibration curve. This is especially helpful in cases of plateaus in the calibration curve.

81 For a compilation of different studies to regional ^{14}C offsets, see Manning et al. 2014: 401.

(c) *Chemicals and pre-treatment*: Producing papyrus as a writing material involves no chemical treatment that could distort the primary radiocarbon-level, nor do current preservation techniques in papyrus collections. In most cases, before testing, a fairly simple pre-treatment is sufficient—acid-base-acid (ABA) wash, also called acid-alkali-acid (AAA) sequential wash—and serves as the standard procedure for organic sources before testing.[82] However, to adjust pre-treatment accordingly, one has to look out for any kind of conspicuous coat (remnants of glue or conservatives?) and consult restoration diaries.[83] In case of treatment with conservatives, a Soxhlet-type extraction could precede the ABA wash to remove some of the conventionally applied conservatives—even if, ultimately, not all of them are soluble.[84]

The pre-treatment of a parchment sample is sometimes much more complex, even with clean-looking and well-preserved samples. Yet for dated parchment samples, Brock 2013 has shown that a conventional (not too weak) acid-base-acid (ABA) sequential wash is the most favorable pre-treatment, yielding good results with samples of 2–4 mg and bigger. Collagen extraction is also possible, although the additional work does not result in higher accuracy of results.[85] However, in some cases, parchment samples are decomposing in the standard pre-treatments, which yields to reducing the strength of the acid and base solutions in order to preserve enough material for the radiocarbon dating. Sometimes samples even get lost.[86] With parchments from the Dead Sea Scrolls, the use of castor oil (a source of radiocarbon itself) and its skewing impact on test results have been discussed—with suggestions of how remnants can be removed most effectively.[87]

An additional handicap consists of limitations in taking samples from precious parchment manuscripts: manuscript collections normally agree only to giving up a small piece of a margin with no script on it. However, the margins

82 "For organic samples, these methods are usually variants of the acid–base–acid (ABA) methods in which an initial acid treatment removes carbonate precipitated onto the samples from groundwater, the base (or alkali) stage removes humic acid contaminants from the sediment and a final acid stage removes any carbonate dissolved from the air during the pre-treatment" (Bronk Ramsey 2008: 256). For actual procedures and standards at the Oxford lab, see e.g., Brock et al. 2010: 103–104; for those at the Zurich lab, see Hajdas et al. 2004: 268–269.

83 On a papyrus of the Berlin collection (P.Berl.inv. 10038 b+c) with adhesive contamination, see Dee et al. 2012: 879.

84 See Bruhn et al. 2001.

85 Brock 2013: 361.

86 On some samples of the Dead Sea Scrolls, see Doudna 1998: 442.

87 See Rasmussen et al. 2009.

are often much more contaminated than the rest of the piece. In any case, an exact description and close inspection of the parchment sample are indispensable (with recourse to journals of restoration if available).

(d) *Time between production and use*: The literature mentions the high cost of high-quality papyrus such as that used for official letters.[88] We can assume that institutions did not have large papyrus stocks, for this would have been a waste of money—especially in Egypt, the flourishing main producer of papyrus, where no shortage was to be expected.[89] Therefore, we may suppose that the time between production and use was conventionally just a few months to a few years.[90]

We can also assume that a piece of parchment was ready for use as writing material no more than a few months after the death of the animal of whose skin it was made. Parchment to be used for codices was probably produced on demand, and thus very close in time to the writing itself. However, in the case of parchment, opistography was a constant possibility, i.e., that a text formed the upper layer, concealing an older layer of text that had been washed off or erased.

Many papyrus sheets were also reused. Although sometimes the script was washed off,[91] in the vast majority of cases the old text was not canceled out. Instead, the younger text was simply written in a blank space, i.e., on the margins or on verso.[92] This reveals differences between the two writing materials on a deeper level: parchment was surely a very expensive material, perceived as suitable for a holy text such as the Qur'ān, whereas papyrus (speaking of Egypt now) was used for a huge variety of purposes—from wrapping material to chancery writing—and was obviously available in many different qualities and price classes.

88 Karabacek 1894: XVI; Grohmann 1924: 33; Grohmann 1952: 44; Khan 1993: 18.

89 However, we know from Early ʿAbbāsid Iraq that unreliable supply from Egypt accounted for stocks of papyrus in the state Dīwān; see Grohmann 1924: 28–29.

90 It might be interesting to make tests on protocol sheets (cover sheets of papyrus rolls). These are in many instances datable to a year or to a period of time due to historiography (by reference to rulers or officials in charge of the papyrus production) or the fomulary. Writing on protocol sheets most probably was carried out right after the production of a papyrus roll.

91 For a short overview on ink on Arabic papyri, see Grohmann 1952: 67–68. On the solubility of different kind of inks, see Frösén 2009: 82. On inks used, up to the 5th/11th century, in Early Islamic papyrus, paper, and parchment manuscripts, see the comprehensive work of Schopen 2006.

92 On opistography in Arabic documents, see the survey in Diem 1995: 448–453; Grob 2010: 182–183.

4.2 *Multiple Samples/Targets*

In order to enhance the precision of radiocarbon dating, the measurement process itself needs to be adjusted: more standards in the cassettes, longer runs, and more runs. Nevertheless, there are limits given by instrument stability, for AMS instruments themselves put a limit on how long a single target can be measured with high stability. For high precision, the literature strongly recommends measuring several targets from the same host.[93] The results of the different targets are then combined.[94]

> **Example 2:** The enhancement of precision as illustrated by test results on two dated Arabic papyri from Heidelberg[95] undertaken by the Coranica project at ETH Zurich.[96]

Figures 5.7 and 5.8 show parts of two famous Qurra letters (Heid.inv. Arab. 2; Heid.inv. Arab. 9).[97] Both belong to an archive dated by a multitude of documents to 709–710 CE, and both letters carry the explicit date Rabīʿ I 91/7 January–5 February 710.

From both letters, a sample measuring ca. 1×3 cm has been cut off (marked by dotted rectangles in Figs. 5.7–5.8 below). Both samples underwent pre-treatment and were thereafter cut into three pieces each, to be measured separately (i.e., three targets each). Assuming that with both documents, the papyrus was produced only a few months or years at most before it was written upon, all six measurement should yield about the same result, or at least lie very close together. See Table 5.3 for a compilation of raw data:

93 See, for example, Bronk Ramsey 2008: 258; Doudna 1998: 443.

94 It is quite important to distinguish between the number of runs on a single sample/target and the number of samples/targets taken from the same host. In the latter case, we must also distinguish between whether the different samples underwent pre-treatment together or independently.

95 I want to express my gratitude to the Heidelberg papyrus collection for providing us with material for the radiocarbon tests, especially with the dated material whose radiocarbon results is of no immediate interest to the collection but important for interpreting results in a general way.

96 For references to the AMS facilities at ETH Zurich, see Wacker et al. 2010; Christl et al. 2013.

97 P.Heid.inv. Arab. 2 forms, together with P.Heid.inv. Arab. 1, an official letter written by the chancery of Qurra ibn Šarīk. Both fragments together have been edited as P.Heid.Arab. I 1 by Becker 1906. Likewise, P.Heid.inv. Arab. 9 has been joined to P.Heid.inv. Arab. 8 and edited as P.Heid.Arab. I 2.

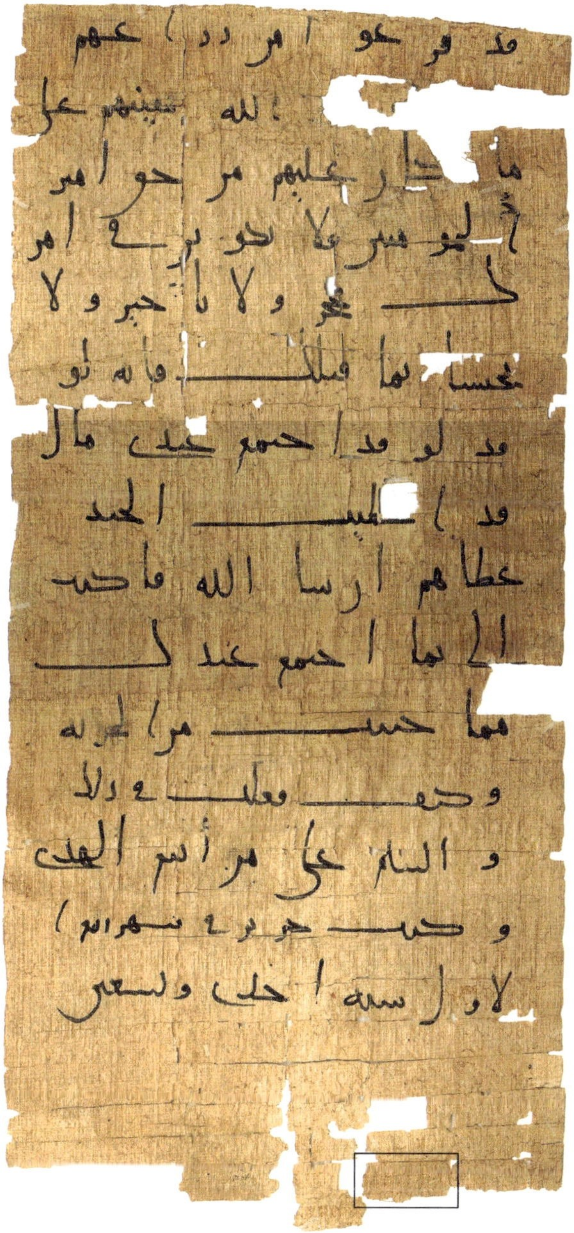

FIGURE 5.7 Lower part of an official letter on papyrus, dated 710 CE (P.Heid.inv. Arab. 2 = P.Heid.Arab. I 1 lower part)

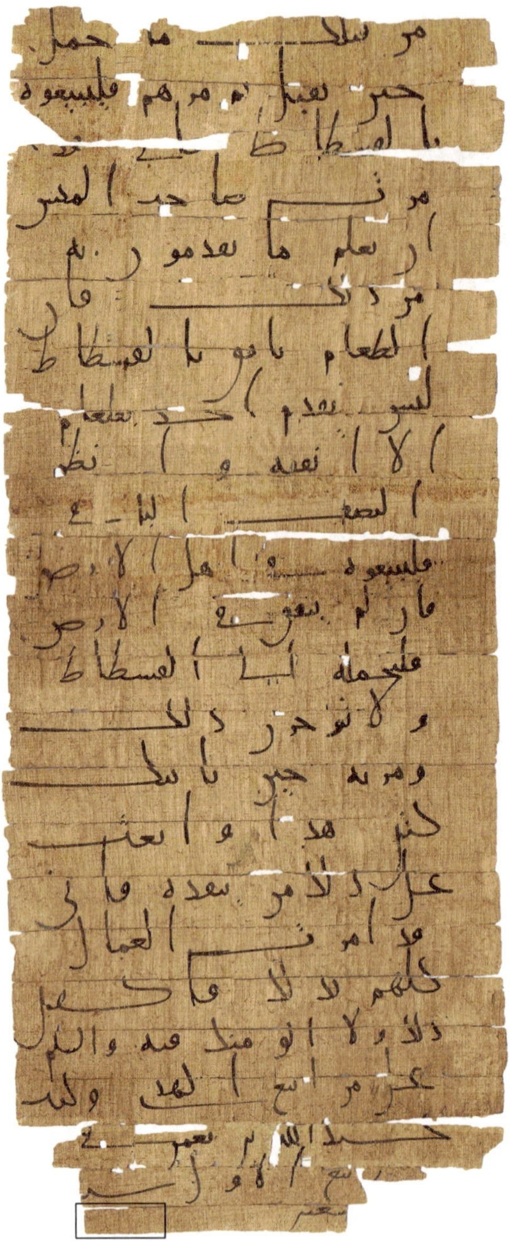

FIGURE 5.8 Lower part of an official letter on papyrus, dated 710 CE (Heid. inv. Arab. 9 = P.Heid.Arab. I 2 lower part)
© UNIVERSITÄT HEIDELBERG, INSTITUT FÜR PAPYROLOGIE

TABLE 5.3 Radiocarbon results of papyri Heid.inv. Arab. 2 and Heid.inv. Arab. 9

		^{14}C years BP	1σ
Heid.inv. Arab. 2	ETH-55666 (target 1)	1262	± 28
Heid.inv. Arab. 2	ETH-55666 (target 2)	1290	± 28
Heid.inv. Arab. 2	ETH-55666 (target 3)	1243	± 28
Heid.inv. Arab. 9	ETH-55667 (target 1)	1267	± 28
Heid.inv. Arab. 9	ETH-55667 (target 2)	1269	± 28
Heid.inv. Arab. 9	ETH-55667 (target 3)	1277	± 28

TABLE 5.4 Calibration of two radiocarbon measurements of papyrus Heid.inv. Arab. 2

		^{14}C years BP	1σ	Calibrated range for 1σ (68.2% confidence)	Calibrated range for 2σ (95.4% confidence)
Heid.inv. Arab. 2	ETH-55666 (target 2)	1290	± 28	675–714 AD (42.8%); 744–765 AD (25.4%)	665–770 AD (95.4%)
Heid.inv. Arab. 2	ETH-55666 (target 3)	1243	± 28	688–777 AD (64.8%); 793–801 AD (3.4%)	681–780 AD (67.3%); 788–875 AD (28.1%)

In fact, all six results are scattered between 1243 BP and 1290 BP, thus within less than 50 ^{14}C years, exhibiting in their distribution statistically expected variation.[98] Furthermore, the real age of the sample (assuming that the papyrus was manufactured in the few years before 710 CE) lies within the 68.2% confidence range of all results, which is considered an excellent result. Yet for a historian, these six results differ considerably, given that exactly the same procedure has been applied to all targets and the same instruments were used for measuring.

Now, let us compare the calibrated results at the margins, 1243 ± 28 and 1290 ± 28, keeping in mind that both could have been the only results if it were the case that only a single sample had been measured. Calibrated confidence range for 1σ and 2σ is as follows (see Table 5.4 above).

98 The six results pass chi-square "goodness-of-fit test" well.

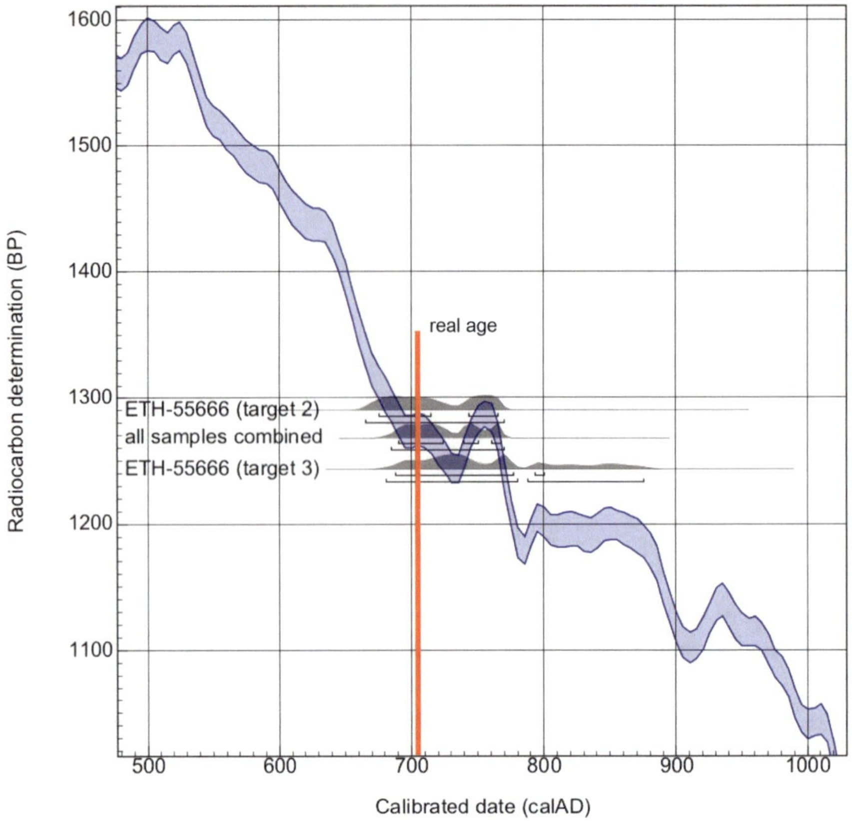

FIGURE 5.9 OxCal curve plot of selected results of measurements on dated papyri 710 CE

In case of a single measurement, the 2σ confidence range is the most secure to work with. In the case of target 2, this lies within about a century. However, for target 3, the 2σ confidence range spans about over 200 calendar years! And both measurements were made with the same high precision and are totally acceptable with respect to the real age and the statistically expected variance of a radiocarbon measurement. So why are calibrated ranges so different? The difference is due to the leveling of the calibration curve. This is visualized in Figure 5.9 by plotting the highest probability density (HPD) range of the two results on the calibration curve plus the combined results of all targets (see explanation below). The small brackets below the HDP ranges indicate the 1σ and 2σ ranges, respectively.

Fortunately, in our case, each of the two papyri was tested with three targets. Therefore, the results can be combined for each papyrus separately, and can also be combined all together, since it is highly probable that both documents were written on papyrus cut in the same year or within some very few

TABLE 5.5 Combined results of radiocarbon measurement on papyri Heid.inv. Arab. 2 and Heid.inv. Arab. 9

	^{14}C years BP	1σ
ETH-55666 (three targets combined)	1265	± 16
ETH-55667 (three targets combined)	1271	± 16
ETH-55666+55667 (all combined)	1268	± 12

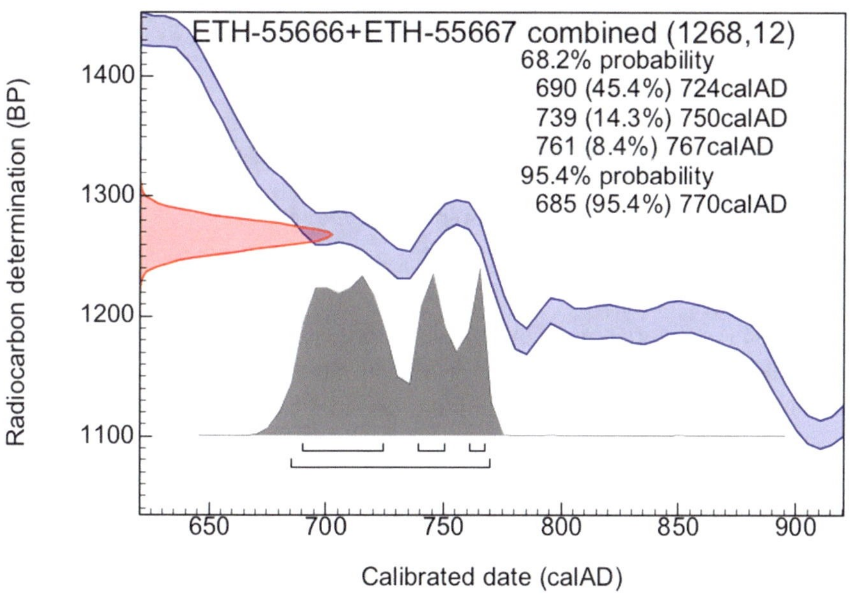

FIGURE 5.10 Oxcal plot of combined results, three measurements each on two dated papyri 710 CE

years.[99] Note that the combined results displayed in Table 5.5 above show a significantly reduced 1σ. They are much more precise than single measurements and yield shorter confidence ranges for 1σ and 2σ in calibration (compare the "three targets combined" ranges in Table 5.5 to the ranges of the two measurements selected in Table 5.4 above).

The combination of all measurements proves to be the most accurate of all (see Table 5.5). For the model of all combined results, see Figure 5.10. However, note that in this small test series, the offset of 19 ± 5 ^{14}C years postulated by Dee

99 On the preconditions to combine results, see Bronk Ramsey 2008: 263–264.

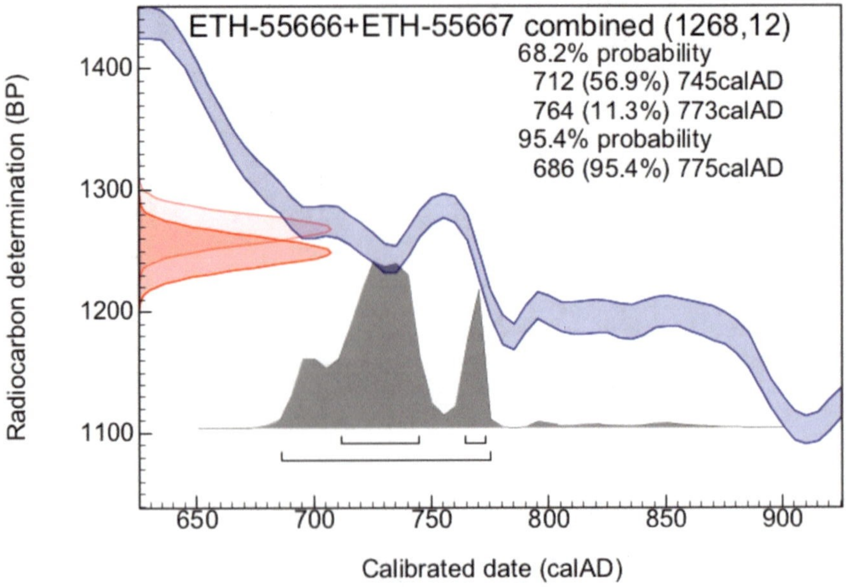

FIGURE 5.11 Oxcal plot of combined results plus offset as suggested by Dee et al. 2010

et al. 2010 for material from Egypt (see section 3.3 above) is not confirmed. Figure 5.11 visualizes the offset and gives the calibrated ranges. If the offset is taken account of, real age moves outside the 1σ confidence range.

4.3 *Modeling Results*

In the frame of the Coranica Project, the majority of the tested documents have been tested with multiple targets, mostly with two, because precision of combined radiocarbon dating is considerably higher than with just one measurement. To enhance explanatory power further, we need to look at specific results against the wider background of results on related groups. Instead of dating one document only, considerations of its age should be made in relation to other datings. However, this kind of relating to different data cannot be done in an impressionistic way but needs proper modeling.

For Early Islamic manuscripts, up to now the limiting factor has been the scarcity of published radiocarbon results. The Coranica Project will therefore open up new possibilities. The more datasets of interrelated documents we have at our disposal, the more powerful our analysis will be, and the more likely it is to lead to much more accurate absolute dating, or to very precious relative dating of the type "probably older than ... by ... to ... years."

In archaeology, models of phases and sequences are widely used when modeling radiocarbon dates, and online programs provide solutions for many different situations.[100] This is illustrated by incorporating the test results of the Leiden Qurʾān papyrus fragment (Example 1, Fig. 5.1) into a set of results from other manuscripts exhibiting Ḥiǧāzī type of script, yet leaving aside, for the moment, the famous Sanaa palimpsest.[101] The model was computed by the online program OxCal 4.2.

> **Example 3**: As described in section 3.1 above, the Qurʾān papyrus fragment UB Leiden inv. Or. 8264 has been tested within the Coranica test series with a single sample/target: ETH-54173, 1324 ± 24. This single measurement has only limited significance for establishing the age of the manuscript, even if aligned carefully with further evidence.

Yet, taken together with other testings of Ḥiǧāzī manuscripts, in the frame of the Coranica Project, and the measurement by Dutton 2007, it forms a whole set of test results (see Table 5.6 below).

For modeling, first results of samples from the same manuscript (even if stemming from different folios) have been combined. In Table 5.6, the five results in grey were entered into a phase model template provided by OxCal.[102] With these data, the model yields an overall index of agreement of 153.3%, which is very high. Figure 5.12 shows the modeled probability distribution of ETH-54173; seeing it thus in the context of other manuscripts in Ḥiǧāzī script. Compare this to a reproduction in Figure 5.13 showing unmodeled data.

Modeled data not only provide narrower confidence ranges but in this case also exclude multiple ranges. However, let us keep in mind that some limits are given to precision, especially by the nature of the calibration curve in the 8th-century CE range.

5 Evaluating Radiocarbon Results

As has been repeatedly stated above and widely illustrated, ^{14}C testing is all about probability. A number of factors might help increase probability, but even with the instruments of measurement and the precision of calibration

100 Bronk Ramsey 2008: 265 for references.

101 Folios from the famous Sanaa 1 palimpsest have been measured by different projects and different labs, yet most results are still unpublished. Many results are intriguingly early, dating the parchment actually into pre-Islamic times.

102 Raw code: Plot(){Sequence(){Boundary("Start 1"); Phase("Hijazi") {R_Date("ETH-54173", 1324, 24); R_Date("OxA-10860", 1363, 33); R_Date("UB Leiden Or. 14.545a (comb.)", 1329, 17); R_Date("UB Leiden Or. 14.545b,c (comb.)", 1329, 17); R_Date("UB Tübingen MA VI 165 (comb.)", 1355, 14);};Boundary("End 1");};};

TABLE 5.6 Compilation of radiocarbon measurements on manuscripts exhibiting Ḥiǧāzī script

			^{14}C years BP	1σ
1	UB Leiden inv. Or. 8264	ETH-54173	1324	± 24
	UB Leiden inv. Or. 14.545a, fol. 4	ETH-54174	1335	± 24
	UB Leiden inv. Or. 14.545a, fol. 2–3	ETH-54175	1322	± 24
2	UB Leiden inv. Or. 14.545a (combined)	ETH-54174 and ETH-54175	1329	± 17
	UB Leiden inv. Or. 14.545b, fol. 1	ETH-54176	1327	± 24
	UB Leiden inv. Or. 14.545c, fol. 1	ETH-54177	1331	± 24
3	UB Leiden inv. Or. 14.545b/c (combined)	ETH-54176 and ETH-54177	1329	± 17
	UB Tübingen MA VI 165, fol. 23	ETH-54180	1357	± 24
	UB Tübingen MA VI 165, fol. 28	ETH-54181	1388	± 24
	UB Tübingen MA VI 165, fol. 37	ETH-54182	1319	± 24
4	UB Tübingen MA VI 165 (combined)	ETH-54180 and ETH-54181 and ETH-54182	1355	± 14
5	Dutton 2007	OxA-10860	1363	± 33

at our disposal nowadays, we will never manage to narrow our results down to one year or even to a single decade.[103]

Furthermore, results do not give the time when the manuscript was written, but only the time of death of the vegetable or animal organism serving as the writing support. In addition, results are severely skewed in case of opistography or of long storage of a writing support before actual use. To cut a long story short: the interpretation and evaluation of a radiocarbon date are shaped by a long chain of assumptions, models, and probabilities.

Fortunately, manuscripts are in many respects quite unproblematic for ^{14}C testing compared to excavated material, where archaeological context and stratification play a major role. Nevertheless, calibrated radiocarbon dates must always be carefully aligned with further evidence, such as that of paleographic,

103 This restriction of precision refers to radiocarbon dating of parchments and papyri. For wood, in some favorable settings assignment to a year has been possible (Wacker et al. 2014).

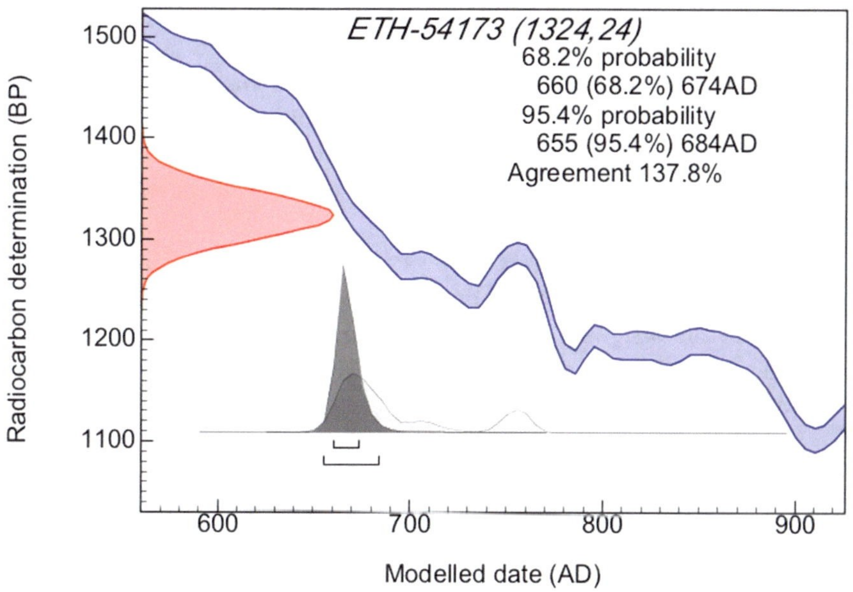

FIGURE 5.12 Modeled OxCal single plot for papyrus P.Leiden inv. Or. 8264

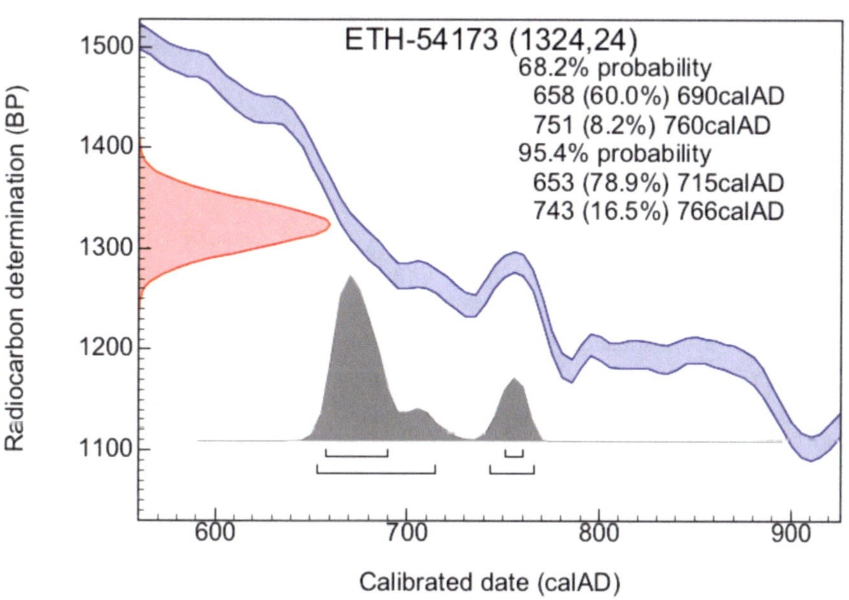

FIGURE 5.13 OxCal single plot for papyrus P.Leiden inv. Or. 8264

stylistic, or internal textual nature. Radiocarbon dates add only one further aspect to the broad picture that might assign a document a probable age. As Bronk Ramsey 2008 states: "Although the measurements themselves have become markedly more precise (and hopefully not less accurate), this means that we need to be even more careful now about the chain of reasoning that allows us to go from a radiocarbon measurement to an understanding of chronology."[104]

The following section focuses on how to interpret results and highlight common errors in interpreting the results. Keep in mind that precision refers to the size of the scale with which a target is measured, while accuracy refers to the actual age of a sample. A given result may be highly precise but not at all accurate. What we long for, of course, is high precision and accuracy.

5.1 *Mind the Traps*

5.1.1 Trap 1: Reading Precision of Measurement as Precision in Calendar Years

A high-precision measurement with a standard deviation of ± 25 ^{14}C years cannot be read as being accurate on ± 25 calendar years, because calibration plays a major role. This might be shown in the samples of Example 2 (see section 4.2 above). ETH-55666 (target 2) was measured as 1290 ± 28 ^{14}C years BP (see Table 5.7 below, line 1). Due to a peak in the calibration curve, the 68.2% confidence range contains two time-windows of 60 years, spanning over 90 years. Thus, after calibration, the intuitive precision of the measurement yields ± 45 calendar years and not ± 28 years. The true *terminus ante quem* age of 710 CE does not lie in the middle of the 68.2% confidence range (675–765 CE), nor exactly in the middle of the first range given for it (675–714 CE).

In the specification of confidence ranges, the precision of one year obscures the fact that the calibration curve itself is computed not for single years but averages over decades. Taking this into consideration, some labs state the confidence ranges rounded to decades (see Table 5.7, line 2). In our example, intuitive precision rises now to ± 50 calendar years.

5.1.2 Trap 2: Building an Argument on a Single Measurement

A single ^{14}C test has only very limited significance, and its results need to be interpreted with caution. Because of error ranges associated with the measurement process and their amplifying impact on calibrated calendar years, only the 95.4% range should be considered. Again: the 1σ range of ± a certain num-

104 Bronk Ramsey 2008: 266.

TABLE 5.7 Calibration of ETH-55666 (target 2)

		^{14}C years BP	1σ	**Calibrated range for 1σ (68.2% confidence)**	**Calibrated range for 2σ (95.4% confidence)**
Heid.inv. Arab. 2	ETH-55666 (target 2)	1290	± 28	675–714 AD (42.8%); 744–765 AD (25.4%)	665–770 AD (95.4%)
Heid.inv. Arab. 2	ETH-55666 (target 2)	1290	± 28	rounded on decades: 670–720 AD (42.8%) 740–770 AD (25.4%)	rounded on decades: 660–770 AD (95.4%)

ber of ^{14}C years implies that if the measurement were repeated several times with identical parameters, *about two of three measurements would fall into that range*. Two valid measurements belonging to exactly the same host can yield a result with a difference of several decades. Depending on the leveling of the calibration curve, the calibration may produce very uneven long confidence ranges. Only multiple samples/targets from the same host and the integration of results in a set of measurements will enhance accuracy and informative value considerably. A single measurement on a fragment of an Early Islamic manuscript can give, at best, a good hint for the assigning of a century, and that only if the testing process and the calibration are combined with further evidence.

5.1.3 Trap 3: Taking the Mean Confidence Range as the Most Probable Date

Working with confidence ranges only obscures the fact that the function behind the calibration for calendar years is *not* a normal curve of distribution. One needs to have a look at the calibration curve in order to grasp what the impact of its leveling on the confidence ranges is (see Fig. 5.2 above). Never take from the outset the mean of the ranges given to be a handy date to work with. It is more adequate to focus attention on the limits of the 1σ and the 2σ ranges.[105]

105 Doudna 1998: 438.

5.2 *Checklist for Evaluating a Given Radiocarbon Dating*

5.2.1 What Is the Test Result and How Is It Presented?

Beside confidence ranges, a radiocarbon test result should always present raw data as ^{14}C years before present (BP) and standard variation 1σ (precision of measurement). If not stated, the author is either deliberately hiding information or, possibly due to lack of familiarity with radiocarbon dating, is not aware of their overall importance. In either case, one must be cautious about the conclusions the author is drawing from the test results.

If raw data are given, the first thing to check is precision (standard variation 1σ) of testing. Nowadays, AMS high-precision dating is measured with a precision of about ± 25 ^{14}C years, whereas in the past, measurements had a precision of ± 50 ^{14}C years. Considering the progress of radiocarbon dating and calibration during the last fifteen years, results with a precision of ± 50 ^{14}C years today should be viewed with reserve, yet access to the raw data enables the calibration of older results anew. A new calibration by the IntCal13 calibration curve is especially advisable for tests done with IntCal98, not to mention tests done earlier. For this, several online program are at our disposal and easy to operate.[106]

If only confidence ranges are given, the calibration curve has to be checked. Confidence ranges tend to give the impression that the distribution of possible dates features a normal curve of distribution, which is definitely not the case!

5.2.2 Isolated Result or Part of a Test Series?

An isolated result must always be viewed with caution. We would be wise only to consider the 95.4% confidence range of the calibration, and that also with caution (see section 5.1 above, Traps 2 and 3).

In case of a series of tests, the informative value is much higher, especially if set in relation with and modeled to dated objects to allow statements such as "later than," "younger than," or "contemporaneous with." But also in these cases, we need to understand whether test results were simply compared in an impressionistic way, or whether there is well-based statistic behind them.

In every case, has the radiocarbon test been carefully aligned with other evidence? It should be just one factor among many.

106 See for an overview www.radiocarbon.org/Info/ (last recall 17 February 2016). All internationally accepted calibration programs use the IntCal curve(s) for calibration. However, the algorithms implemented and several features for in- and output are different. The most widely used for our time range and materials are OxCal by Bronk Ramsey of the Oxford Radiocarbon Accelerator Unit (ORAU): https://c14.arch.ox.ac.uk/embed.php?File=oxcal.html (Bronk Ramsey and Lee 2013) and Calib by Stuiver, Reimer and Reimer of the Quaternary Isotope Lab, University of Washington, and the Queens University of Belfast on http://calib.qub.ac.uk/calib/ (Stuiver and Reimer 1993).

6 Checklist for Scholars Considering Doing Radiocarbon Dating on a Document

6.1 *Will the Test Make Sense?*

Before testing a document, one should be aware of one's own expectations and the possible outcome of a radiocarbon dating. This is important in communicating with collections in order to prepare a sampling. The following checklist aims at helping scholars decide whether ^{14}C dating will meet one's expectations, and if so, under which conditions.

6.1.1 What to Expect from ^{14}C Dating?

As shown above, ^{14}C dating alone, with no further evidence available, hardly yields meaningful and hard results. A single test result may prove that a document, i.e., the material it is written upon, is medieval and no modern forgery. Under good conditions and with a careful experimental setup (with multiple samples, a favorable calibration curve, and using modeling), we might reach a highly probable 50-year window for dating, but day-to-day business is rather the assignment of a century. In any case, ^{14}C results have to be interpreted from different angles and with the help of further internal and external evidence (paleographic, stylistic, contextual, etc.) which must be carefully aligned with it.

6.1.2 Restrictions by Calibration Curve?

Into which time frame does one's document probably fall? Checking the calibration curve (see section 2.3 above) will show the limitations set by plateaus or peaks in the calibration curve. A plateau in the calibration curve easily destroys ambitions for a narrow timespan (i.e., 50 years), even if multiple samples are tested.

In case one's document falls into a plateau, will this be a result worth going for? Even a long timespan may be very helpful if combined with further textual and contextual evidence narrowing it down, e.g., at the end or the beginning of this particular time span. In any case, it is highly recommended that scholars become acquainted with an online calibration program before doing any testing and enter expected results.

6.1.3 How Many Samples Can Be Taken?

The more (or bigger) samples one can have, providing several targets for measuring, the better. In case collections or budget allow for only a single sample to be tested, scholars must be aware of the limited significance of the result (see section 4.2 above). For tests with multiple targets, the AMS lab might give you a price reduction, since pre-treatment usually is applied only once and the sample then divided into two or more pieces for testing thereafter.

6.1.4 Comparative Material

Having access to the ^{14}C results of related documents will allow for comparative, relative dating. In a first and easy step, "most probably earlier than" or "most probably later than" is often more meaningful than probabilities in calendar years. Interpretation of results against a group of samples is from the outset more promising, and the more shared parameters there are—material, provenance, etc.—the better (see sections 4.2 and 4.3 above). To enhance comparability, scholars should work with raw data and calibrate time ranges anew. For the centuries in our focus, differences between the last three calibration curves (IntCal 14, IntCal 09, and IntCal 04) are very small, and IntCal 98 is not far away: results differ within a range of up to 10 years only. However, a given result often does not allow us to see whether computed ranges were rounded by 5 or 10 years or not at all. Thus, calibrating anew is safer and just two mouse clicks away.

Comparative data sets will allow for modeling data, e.g., with Bayesian statistics, a strong tool that helps beyond "this looks like ..." and gives probabilities for coincidence, sequence of groups, etc.[107] In archaeology, Bayesian analysis is being applied with radiocarbon measurements on a regular basis and has proved to be very useful.[108]

6.2 *Testing*[109]

6.2.1 Contacting an AMS Lab

Many different labs offer AMS radiocarbon dating.[110] In comparing different labs, price (and whether taxes will be added or not!), how fast results can be expected, and customer friendliness are most important. One might prefer a lab that has tested samples that could serve as comparative material. Procedures in different labs are much the same and regular quality controls guarantee comparable results, yet one might feel more comfortable in comparing one's result(s) to former results in the knowledge that exactly the same pretreatments and machines were used. Each AMS lab will provide the protocol scheme of how samples must be delivered.

---

107 Free calibration programs like OxCal provide many ready-made models and options. Even for the non-expert in statistics, access to Bayesian analysis is possible.

108 In archaeology, mainly two situations are dealt with with Bayesian statistics: single sites where radiocarbon measurements come (as groups) from different stratigraphic layers, and studies on the chronology of whole regions or cultures that imply many different processes and overlappings (Bronk Ramsey 2008: 265–269).

109 On sample selection for radiocarbon dating, see also Brock and Dee 2013.

110 A list of all radiocarbon labs (conventional and AMS) with their codes can be found on www.radiocarbon.org/Info/Labs.pdf (last accessed 17 February 2016).

6.2.2 Sample Size

With parchment and papyrus, 1 cm^2 is a good standard size that is sure to provide enough material for one sample to be tested by an AMS lab. However, there is no need to cut the sample from the document in square format: small slices taken from the margins are almost invisible.[111] When communicating with the curators of manuscript collections, one may wish to send a picture of the document indicating where one intends to cut the tiny sample(s) of material. The collection may be relieved to see from the beginning that the document will not be badly deformed.

6.2.3 Protocol of Sampling

Sampling needs to be protocoled carefully in order to trace where exactly the sample is cut off. This includes taking pictures before and after and looking out for contamination (traces of glue, etc.). If collections provide restoration protocols, one should have a look at them and mark possible contaminants on the sheet to be sent with the sample to the AMS lab.

6.2.4 Sample Extraction

Most collections prefer sample extraction to be done by their own conservator, preferably in your presence. Extracts should be put in a small transparent plastic bag with a zip lock top, with details written on it, and sent with the standardized sample protocol sheet to the AMS lab.

6.3 *Interpreting and Presenting Results*

6.3.1 Interpreting Results

Radiocarbon dating itself normally takes between one and six months, depending on the policy and capacity of the lab. As soon as labs have provided the set of raw data and the calibrated output, the main work of interpreting and possibly modeling starts. This is quite easy if the radiocarbon dating confirms what one has hypothesized from textual evidence. However, what if it does not? Since radiocarbon dating is in the end all about probabilities, the weighing of the significance of the test must be done properly (see section 4 above). Trying to compare results and setting them in relation to as many other tests as possible will raise their explanatory power. In doing this, one should think of relative, *terminus post quem* and *ante quem* chronology and be aware that it is the writing material that is being dated, not the text of the document.

111 But be aware of contamination at the margins due to their exposure to wear and tear and contamination.

In case the calibrated age is much older than expected, one might be dealing with a case of opistography; especially with papyrus, the material might have been cut out of an older piece of papyrus or have been washed off and reused. If the calibrated age is much younger than expected, the document might be a copy or imitation of an older document. In general, what further hints are there to the document's material history? The possibility of contamination should also be taken into consideration (see section 4.1 above). In all these cases, tests with multiple targets are strongly suggested.

If one has access to sets of comparable data, one should model data with Bayesian analysis. In using "group events," sets of data can be put into different kinds of chronological relation, i.e., in phases joining each other without break or discontinuity between them, in phases following each other (continuously or not), or in phases that may be "overlapping" if part of the two phases were contemporary. The particular model(s) for certain data sets will be chosen according to general historical evidence and the probability of exactly these assumptions will also be analyzed by Bayesian analysis itself.[112]

If the radiocarbon date seems to be an outlier that makes no sense at all, there may be a measurement problem due to contamination, etc. However, more often, and especially in archaeology, the sample context may have been misinterpreted.[113]

6.3.2 Presenting Results

To provide transparency, when referring to results raw data should always be given with confidence ranges. Mentioning the lab and the code of the sample given by the lab will ease finding and quoting results. With multiple targets, it is best to state how many targets were tested. It is also best to speak of probabilities, not of hard and fast facts, and to mention which of the two conventional confidence ranges you are referring to.

Readers unfamiliar with radiocarbon dating appreciate explanations of exactly what short and long confidence ranges are. To make results transparent and comprehensible, a plot of the output featuring the calibration curve might be helpful, within the text or at least in an appendix. The graphic display will also show that the mean of the given confidence ranges is not the most probable date of origin.

112 In this respect, the calibration program OxCal features many easily accessible models and is user-friendly also for non-expert in statistics.

113 Bronk Ramsey 2008: 263.

If you model your data with a program such as OxCal, you might also provide the raw code in an appendix to ensure reproducibility.[114]

Bibliography

Atwill, Joseph and Steve Braunheim. 2004. "Redating the Radiocarbon Dating of the Dead Sea Scrolls." In *Dead Sea Discoveries* 11, no. 2: 143–157.

Becker, Carl Heinrich 1906. *Papyri Schott-Reinhardt, Vol. 1.* Veröffentlichungen aus der Heidelberger Papyrussammlung [VHP], vol. 3. Heidelberg: Winter. [P.Heid. Arab. 1].

Blair, Sheila S. 2006. *Islamic Calligraphy.* Edinburgh: Edinburgh University Press.

Blair, Sheila S., Jonathan M. Bloom, and Anne E. Wardwell. 1992. "Reevaluating the Date of the 'Buyid' Silks by Epigraphic and Radiocarbon Analysis." In *Ars Orientalis* 22: 1–41.

Bonani, Georges, Magen Broshi, Israel Carmi, Susan Ivy, John Strugnell, and Willy Wölfli. 1991. "Radiocarbon Dating of the Dead Sea Scrolls." In *Atiqot* 20: 27–32.

Bonani, Georges, Suan Ivy, Willy Wölfli, Magen Broshi, Israel Carmi, and John Strugnell. 1992, "Radiocarbon Dating of Fourteen Dead Sea Scrolls." In *Radiocarbon* 34, no. 3: 843–849.

Brock, Fiona. 2013. "Radiocarbon Dating of Historical Parchments." In *Radiocarbon* 55, nos. 2–3: 353–363.

Brock, Fiona and Michael W. Dee. 2013. "Sample Selection for Radiocarbon Dating." In *Radiocarbon and the Chronologies of Ancient Egypt*, ed. Andrew J. Shortland and Christopher Bronk Ramsey. Oxford: Oxbow Books, 40–47.

Brock, Fiona, Thomas Higham, Peter Ditchfield, and Christopher Bronk Ramsey. 2010. "Current Pretreatment Methods for AMS Radiocarbon Dating at the Oxford Radiocarbon Accelerator Unit (ORAU)." In *Radiocarbon* 52, no. 1: 103–112.

Bronk Ramsey, Christopher. 2008. "Radiocarbon Dating: Revolutions in Understanding." In *Archaeometry* 50, no. 2: 249–275.

Bronk Ramsey, Christopher. 2013. "Using Radiocarbon Evidence in Egyptian Chronological Research." In *Radiocarbon and the Chronologies of Ancient Egypt*, ed. Andrew J. Shortland and Christopher Bronk Ramsey. Oxford: Oxbow Books, 29–39.

Bronk Ramsey, Christopher, Johannes van der Plicht, and Bernhard Weninger. 2001. "'Wiggle Matching' Radiocarbon Dates." In *Radiocarbon* 43, no. 2A: 381–389.

Bronk Ramsey, Christopher, Thomas Higham, and Philip Leach. 2004. "Towards High-Precision AMS: Progress and Limitations." In *Radiocarbon* 46, no. 1: 17–24.

114 See studies like Shortland and Bronk Ramsey 2013: 277–284; Manning et al. 2013: 142.

Bronk Ramsey, Christopher, Michael W. Dee, Joanne M. Rowland, Thomas F. Higham, Stephen A. Harris, Fiona Brock, Anita Quiles, Eva M. Wild, Ezra S. Marcus, and Andrew J. Shortland. 2010. "Radiocarbon-Based Chronology for Dynastic Egypt." In *Science* 328: 1554–1557.

Bronk Ramsey, Christopher and Sharen Lee. 2013. "Recent and Planned Developments of the Program OxCal." In *Radiocarbon* 55, nos. 2–3: 720–730.

Bruhn, Frank, Alexander Duhr, Pieter M. Grootes, Annette Minitrop, and Marie-Josée Nadeau. 2001. "Chemical Removal of Conservation Substances by 'Soxhlet'-Type Extraction." In *Radiocarbon* 43, no. 2A: 229–237.

Bülow-Jacobsen, Adam. 2009. "Writing Materials in the Ancient World." In *The Oxford Handbook of Papyrology*, ed. Roger S. Bagnall. Oxford: Oxford University Press, 3–29.

Caldararo, Niccolo 1995. "Storage Conditions and Physical Treatments Relating to the Dating of the Dead Sea Scrolls." In *Radiocarbon* 37, no. 1: 21–31.

Carmi, Israel 2002. "Are the ^{14}C Dates of the Dead Sea Scrolls Affected by Castor Oil Contamination?" In *Radiocarbon* 44, no. 1: 213–216.

Christl, M., C. Vockenhuber, P.W. Kubik, L. Wacker, J. Lachner, V. Alfimov, and H.-A. Synal. 2013. "The ETH Zurich AMS Facilities: Performance Parameters and Reference Materials." In *Nuclear Instruments and Methods in Physics Research, Section B* 294: 29–38.

de Moor, Antoine, Chris Verkechen-Lammens, and Mark van Strydonck. 2006. "Relevance and Irrelevance of Radiocarbon Dating of Inscribed Textiles." In *Textile Messages: Inscribed Fabrics from Roman to Abbasid Egypt*, ed. Cäcilia Fluck and Gisela Helmecke. Studies in Textile and Costume History, vol. 4. Leiden: Brill, 223–232.

Dee, Michael W., Fiona Brock, Stephen A. Harris, Christopher Bronk Ramsey, Andrew J. Shortland, Thomas F.G. Higham, and Jo M. Rowland. 2010. "Investigating the Likelihood of a Reservoir Effect in the Radiocarbon Record for Ancient Egypt." In *Journal of Archaeological Science* 37: 687–693.

Dee, Michael W., Joanne M. Rowland, Thomas F.G. Higham, Andrew J. Shortland, Fiona Brock, Stephen A. Harris, and Christopher Bronk Ramsey. 2012. "Synchronising Radiocarbon Dating and the Egyptian Historical Chronology by Improved Sample Selection." In *Antiquity* 86: 868–883.

Déroche, François. 2003. "Manuscripts of the Qurʾān." In: *Encyclopaedia of the Qurʾăn*, ed. Jane D. McAuliffe, vol. 3. Leiden: Brill, 254–274.

Déroche, François. 2014. *Qurʾans of the Umayyads: A First Overview*. Leiden Studies in Islam and Society, vol. 1. Leiden: Brill.

Diem, Werner. 1995. *Arabische Geschäfsbriefe des 10. bis 14. Jahrhunderts aus der Österreichischen Nationalbibliothek in Wien*. Documenta Arabica Antiqua, vol. 1. Wiesbaden: Harrassowitz.

Doudna, Gregory 1998. "Dating the Scrolls on the Basis of Radiocarbon Analysis." In *The Dead Sea Scrolls After Fifty Years: A Comprehensive Assessment, Vol. 1*, ed. Peter W. Flint. Leiden: Brill, 430–471.

Dutton, Yasin. 2007. "An Umayyad Fragment of the Qur'ān and Its Dating." In *Journal of Qur'anic Studies* 9: 58–87.

Fedi, M.E., L. Carraresi, N. Grassi, A. Migliori, F. Taccetti, F. Terrasi, P.A. Mando. 2010. "The Artemidorus Papyrus: Solving an Ancient Puzzle with Radiocarbon and Ion Beam Analysis Measurements." In *Radiocarbon* 52, nos. 2–3: 356–363.

Frösén, Jaakko. 2009. "Conservation of Ancient Papyrus Materials." In *The Oxford Handbook of Papyrology*, ed. Roger S. Bagnall. Oxford: Oxford University Press, 79–100.

Grob, Eva Mira. 2010. *Documentary Arabic Private and Business Letters on Papyrus: Form and Function, Content and Context*. Archiv für Paprusforschung und verwandte Gebiete, Beiheft 29. Berlin; New-York: De Gruyter.

Grohmann, Adolf. 1924. *Allgemeine Einführung in die arabischen Papyri*. Corpus Papyrorum Raineri. Series arabica vol. 1,1. Wien: Burgverlag.

Grohmann, Adolf. 1952. *From the World of Arabic Papyri*. Cairo: Al-Maaref Press.

Hajdas, Irka 2009. "Application of Radiocarbon Dating Method." In *Radiocarbon* 51, no. 1: 79–90.

Hajdas, Irka, Georges Bonani, Jürg Thut, Gianni Leone, Rudolf Pfenninger, and Colin Maden. 2004. "A Report on Sample Preparation at the ETH/PSI AMS Facility in Zurich." In *Nuclear Instruments and Methods in Physics Research, Section B* 223–224: 267–271.

Jull, A.J. Timothy, J. Donahue Douglas, Magen Broshi, and Emanuel Tov. 1995. "Radiocarbon Dating of Scrolls and Linen Fragments from the Judean Desert." In *Radiocarbon* 37, no. 1: 11–19.

Karabacek, Joseph. 1894. *Papyrus Erzherzog Rainer: Führer durch die Ausstellung*. Wien: Selbstverlag der Sammlung.

Khan, Geoffrey. 1993. *Bills, Letters and Deeds: Arabic Papyri of the 7th to 11th Centuries*. [Publications of] The Nasser D. Khalili Collection of Islamic Art, vol. 6. London; New York: Azimuth; Oxford University Press.

Libby, Willard F. 1951. "Radiocarbon Dates II." In *Science* 114: 291–296.

Manning, Sturt W., Bernd Kromer, Michael W. Dee, Michael Friedrich, and Thomas F.G. Higham. 2013. "Radiocarbon Calibration in the Mid to Later 14th Century BC and Radiocarbon Dating Tell El-Amarna, Egypt." In *Radiocarbon and the Chronologies of Ancient Egypt*, ed. Andrew J. Shortland and Christopher Bronk Ramsey. Oxford: Oxbow Books, 121–145.

Manning, Sturt W., Michael W. Dee, Eva M. Wild, Christopher Bronk Ramsey, Kathryn Brandy, Pearce Paul Creasman, Carol B. Griggs, Charlotte L. Pearson, Andrew J. Shortland, and Peter Steier. 2014. "High-Precision Dendro-^{14}C Dating of Two Cedar Wood

Sequences From First Intermediate Period and Middle Kingdom Egypt and a Small Regional Climate-Related ^{14}C Divergence." In *Journal of Archaeological Science* 46: 401–415.

Rasmussen, Kaare L., Johannes van der Plicht, Frederick H. Cryer, Gregory Doudna, Frank M. Cross, and John Strugnell. 2001. "The Effects of Possible Contamination on the Radiocarbon Dating of the Dead Sea Scrolls I: Castor Oil." In *Radiocarbon* 43, no. 1: 127–132.

Rasmussen, Kaare L., Johannes van der Plicht, Gregory Doudna, Frank M. Cross, John Strugnell. 2003. "Reply to Israel Carmi (2002): 'Are the ^{14}C Dates of the Dead Sea Scrolls Affected by Castor Oil Contamination?'" In *Radiocarbon* 45, no. 3: 497–499.

Rasmussen, Kaare L., Johannes van der Plicht, Gregory Doudna, Frederik Nielsen, Peter Hojrup, Erling Halfdan Stenby, and Carl Th. Pedersen. 2009. "The Effects of Possible Contamination on the Radiocarbon Dating of the Dead Sea Scrolls II: Empirical Methods to Remove Castor Oil and Suggestings for Redating." In *Radiocarbon* 51, no. 3: 1005–1022.

Reed, R. 1972. *Ancient Skins, Parchments and Leather*. Studies in Archaeological Science. New York: Seminar Press.

Reimer, Paula J. et al. 2004. "IntCal04 Terrestrial Radiocarbon Age Calibration, 0–26 CAL KYR BP." In *Radiocarbon* 46, no. 3: 1029–1058.

Reimer, Paula J. et al. 2013a. "IntCal13 and Marine13 Radiocarbon Age Calibration Curves 0–50,000 years CAL BP." In *Radiocarbon* 55, no. 4: 1869–1887.

Reimer, Paula J. et al. 2013b. "Selection and Treatment of Data for Radiocarbon Calibration: An Update to the International Calibration (IntCal) Criteria." In *Radiocarbon* 55, no. 4: 1923–1945.

Rezvan, Efim A. 2000. "On the Dating of an 'Uthmanic Qur'an from Saint Petersburg." In *Manuscripta Orientalia* 6, no. 3: 19–22.

Rodley, G.A. 1993. "An Assessment of the Radiocarbon Dating of the Dead Sea Scrolls." In *Radiocarbon* 35, no. 2: 335–338.

Rodley, G.A. and B.E. Thiering. 1999. "Use of Radiocarbon Dating in Assessing Christian Connections to the Dead Sea Scrolls." In *Radiocarbon* 41, no. 2: 169–182.

Sadeghi, Behnam and Uwe Bergmann. 2010. "The Codex of a Companion of the Prophet and the Qur'an of the Prophet." In *Arabica* 57: 348–353.

Sam Fogg. 2003. *Islamic Calligraphy*. Catalogue 27. London: Sam Fogg Rare Books and Manuscripts.

Schopen, Armin. 2006. *Tinten und Tuschen des arabisch-islamischen Mittelalters. Dokumentation, Analyse, Rekonstruktion: ein Beitrag zur materiellen Kultur des Vorderen Orients*. Abhandlungen der Akademie der Wissenschaften zu Göttingen, Philologisch-historische Klasse, 3. Folge, vol. 269. Göttingen: Vandenhoeck & Ruprecht.

Shortland, Andrew J. and Christopher Bronk Ramsey, eds. 2013. *Radiocarbon and the Chronologies of Ancient Egypt*. Oxford: Oxbow Books.

Stuiver, Minze and Paula J. Reimer. 1993. "Extended ^{14}C Database and Revised CALIB Radiocarbon Calibration Program." In *Radiocarbon* 35: 215–230.

Stuiver, Minze, Paula J. Reimer, Edouard Bard, J. Warren Beck, G.S. Burr, Konrad A. Hughen, Bernd Kromer, Gerry McCormac, Johannes van der Plicht, and Marco Spurk. 1998. "INTCAL98 Radiocarbon Age Calibration, 24,000–0 cal BP." In *Radiocarbon* 40, no. 3: 1041–1083.

van Strydonck, Mark 2014. "Four Coptic Textiles from the Louvre Collection ^{14}C Redated after 55 Years." In *Radiocarbon* 56, no. 1: 1–5.

van Strydonck, Mark and Mathieu Boudin. 2007. "Possibilities and Limitations of Radiocarbon as a Tool for Dating Coptic Textiles." In *Actes du huitième congrès international d'études coptes, Paris, 28 juin–3 juillet 2004*, ed. Nathalie Bosson and Anne Boud'hors. Orientalia Lovaniensia Analecta, vol. 163. Leuven: Peeters, 381–390.

von Bothmer, Graf Hans-Caspar, Karl-Heinz Ohlig, and Gerd-Rüdiger Puin. 1999. "Neue Wege in der Koranforschung." In *Magazin Forschung* 1: 33–46.

Wacker, Lukas, Georges Bonani, M. Friedrich, Irka Hajdas, B. Kromer, M. Nemec, M. Ruff, Martin Suter, Hans-Arno Synal, and Christof Vockernuber. 2010. "MICADAS: Routine and High-Precision Radiocarbon Dating." In *Radiocarbon* 52, no. 2: 252–262.

Wacker, Lukas, D. Güttler, J. Goll, J.P. Hurni, Hans-Arno Synal, and N. Walti. 2014. "Radiocarbon Dating to a Single Year by Means of Rapid Atmospheric ^{14}C Changes." In *Radiocarbon* 56, no. 2: 573–579.

CHAPTER 6

Radiocarbon (^{14}C) Dating of Qur'ān Manuscripts

Michael Josef Marx and Tobias J. Jocham

According to ^{14}C measurements, the four Qur'ān fragments University Library Tübingen Ma VI 165, Berlin State Library We. II 1913 and ms. or. fol. 4313, and University Library Leiden Cod. or. 14.545b/c are older than had been presumed due to their paleographical characteristics. Within the framework of the joint German-French project *Coranica*, Qur'ān manuscripts and other texts of Late Antiquity (Syriac Bible manuscripts, Georgian manuscripts, dated Arabic papyri, etc.) have been dated for comparison and turn out to be reliable according to dating by ^{14}C measurement. This article emphasizes the importance of combining ^{14}C measurements with paleographical characteristics and orthography when dating Qur'ān fragments. The archaic spelling that appears within the four fragments (e.g., of the words *Dāwūd*, *ḏū*, or *šay'*) demonstrates that Arabic orthography in the text of the Qur'ān was still developing during the 7th and 8th centuries. The fact that the long vowel /ā/ was—in the early manuscripts—spelled using *wāw* or *yā'* in the middle of a word, rarely using *alif* whose original phonetic value is the glottal stop (*hamza*), led to spellings that are now obsolete. Alongside orthographic and paleographical questions, the large number of fragments in Ḥiǧāzī spelling urges us to reconsider the role that written transmission plays within the textual history of the Qur'ān.

1 Introduction

In the last years, several manuscripts of the Qur'ān and other texts of Late Antiquity have been dated by ^{14}C measurement within the framework of the joint German-French project *Coranica*.[1] The measuring results of the manu-

1 *Coranica* was a joint German-French project conducted from 2011 until 2014 by the project Corpus Coranicum of the Berlin-Brandenburgische Akademie der Wissenschaften (BBAW), Berlin/Potsdam, by UMR 8167 "Orient et Méditerranée—Mondes sémitiques" of the Centre National de la Recherche Scientifique (CNRS), Paris, and the Académie des Inscriptions et Belles Lettres (Paris), and was headed by François Déroche, Michael Marx, Angelika Neuwirth, and Christian Julien Robin; see www.coranica.de/computatio-radiocarbonica-de (last accessed 16 September 2016). We would like to thank the Deutsche Forschungsgemeinschaft (DFG) and the Agence Nationale de la Recherche (ANR) for their generous funding.

scripts University Library Tübingen Ma VI 165,[2] University Library Leiden Cod. or. 14.545b/c,[3] and Berlin State Library ms. or. fol. 4313[4] have sparked a big media response. A press release by the University Library Leiden[5] on the dating of three Qur'ān fragments and a Qur'ān papyrus was picked up by Dutch media[6] and triggered a debate about the authenticity of the Qur'ān during which the University of Leiden organized a study day on short notice on 12 December 2014[7] to clarify the situation. The press release of the University of Tübingen[8] on the dating of manuscript Ma VI 165 also garnered wide attention and reached the news program *Tagesschau* (ARD) on 11 November 2014[9] via *Südwestfunk* (*SWR*) regional news (Henning 2014), from where it reached other media. Arabic,[10] Persian,[11] Russian,[12] and Turkish[13] media reports showed the worldwide interest, and within social media networks there was speculation about possi-

2 We would like to express our gratitude to the director of the University Library Dr. Marianne Dörr, the head of the Oriental department Kerstin Strotmann, and former director Dr. Walter Werkmeister for their kind permission and cooperation to carry out the sample taking.

3 Special thanks to the director of the University Library Dr. Arnoud Vrolijk, who helped to speed up the start-up phase of the dating project immensely due to his quick consent to sample taking, as well as to the restorer Dr. Karin Scheper, who facilitated a successful cooperation in the sample taking process.

4 Our thanks to Christoph Rauch, the head of the Oriental department of the Staatsbibliothek zu Berlin, for his commitment concerning the rather time-consuming sample taking of the manuscripts of Berlin State Library, which e.g. required removing the glass of ms. or. fol. 4313.

5 Anon. "Oldest Quran Fragments in Leiden," n.d. For full details on internet media reports, see the Bibliography.

6 E.g., Vlasbom 2014.

7 Measurement results obtained by the laboratory of ETH Zurich were presented by Tobias J. Jocham and discussed with Hans van der Plicht, Center for Isotope Research, University Groningen in a workshop organized by the University of Leiden; see hum.leidenuniv.nl/lucis/past-events/quran-study-day.html (last accessed 30 April 2015).

8 See https://www.uni-tuebingen.de/aktuelles/pressemitteilungen/newsfullview-pressemitteilungen/article/raritaet-entdeckt-koranhandschrift-stammt-aus-der-fruehzeit-des-islam.html (last accessed 12 November 2018).

9 ARD *Tagesschau* of 10 November 2014, 8:00 pm, accessed under tagesschau.de/multimedia/sendung/ts-5347.html (last accessed 12 November 2018); the report runs from minutes 11:42 to 12:10.

10 Salāma, Khālid. "Aqdam maḫṭūṭa li-ağzā' min al-Qur'ān tastaqṭib al-aḍwā' fī Barlīn," 18 April 2015. www.dw.de/p/1F9zU (last accessed 12 November 2018).

11 www.mashreghnews.ir/fa/mobile/365829 and bbc.co.uk/persian/world/2014/12/141209_sam_koran (both last accessed 12 September 2016).

12 tass.ru/obschestvo/1563280 (last accessed 12 November 2018).

13 haberciniz.biz/almanyada-14-asirlik-kuran-i-kerim-sayfalari-korunuyor-3382078h.htm (last accessed 12 November 2018).

ble scribes or owners of the manuscript, e.g., ʿAlī b. Abī Ṭālib (Husain 2014). The University of Birmingham Library had been asked by our project in 2013 to give permission for carbon dating of an ancient fragment of the Qurʾān (M 1572). The university took samples of that fragment to send them to the laboratory of Oxford University. The obtained measurement dated the carbon of M 1572a (a fragment containing 2 fol.) to be from the interval between 568 and 645 CE. In what appeared to be a kind of competition, Birmingham turned out to hold the most ancient Qurʾānic manuscript although precise rankings are impossible to give. The university had launched the press release in a professional way, so that the discovery of the "Birmingham Qurʾān" was echoed in media around the globe.

Why the manuscripts had been dated and what problems might result from the dating were not part of the news coverage; the mere existence of old Qurʾān text fragments apparently was enough to make the story newsworthy. At a conference of the Frankfurt Institute for Islamic Theology[14] held in September 2014, Michael Marx and Tobias J. Jocham presented a paper on the importance of using material evidence for the textual history of the Qurʾān. Of special importance to the discussion was the fact that alternative and counter-arguments about the emergence of the Qurʾān, such as the one by John Wansbrough (1928–2002; see Wansbrough 1977), were definitely refuted. Enthusiasm, emotion, and fascination must not mislead one into thinking that the conducted dating has ended the debates on Qurʾān textual history, even though they make the hypothesis of Islam emerging in the 8th century highly unlikely. Much more significant is probably the fact that the dating will contribute new findings to the research of textual history, although the limits of dating by ^{14}C measurement have also to be kept in mind.[15]

In order to be able to analyze the history of the Qurʾān text systematically, an online database ("Manuscripta Coranica")[16] was set up for the project Corpus Coranicum of the Berlin-Brandenburg Academy of Sciences, founded in 2007, offering an overview of the oldest available textual witnesses. For its work on the textual history of the Qurʾān, the Potsdam-based project sees its research work as a continuation of the "Apparatus Criticus" project on the text of the Qurʾān that the Commission of Semitic Philology of the Bavarian Academy of

14 Conference "Horizonte der Islamischen Theologie"; see www.uni-frankfurt.de/48320986/kongress?legacy_request=1 (last accessed 12 November 2018).

15 See the objection by François Déroche: "the contribution of C14 [sic] dating to the overall history of the handwritten transmission of the Qurʾān in Umayyad times should not be neglected, but the results of such analysis need (…) to be taken cautiously" (Déroche 2014: 11).

16 See corpuscoranicum.de/handschriften (last accessed 12 November 2018).

Sciences and Humanities established in 1930. That project was initiated and led first by Gotthelf Bergsträßer (1886–1933), professor of Arabic studies at the University of Munich, and after his death was continued by Otto Pretzl (1893–1941)[17] until World War II. The photo archives of the Munich project, containing some 450 Agfa film rolls with some 11,000 images of Qur'ānic manuscripts from collections in Egypt, France, Morocco, Spain, and Turkey that had survived the war, were the starting point of the online database. Bergsträßer saw his research as being complementary to the project to produce a huge documentation on variant readings on the Qur'ān registered in the Muslim scholarly tradition run by the Australian researcher Arthur Jeffery (1892–1959). The Munich project had ceased to exist before the first pages of its scheduled critical apparatus on the text of the Qur'ān were ever published; what was scheduled, according to Bergsträßer's description (Plan eines Apparatus Criticus),[18] was a kind of catalogue of variant spellings that could be referred to for what Bergsträßer considered an almost perfect text edition of the Qur'ān in the Egyptian print (Cairo 1924) that was produced on the orders of the Egyptian king Fu'ād (1868–1936). Research on Qur'ānic manuscripts at that time was still a new discipline in which a reliable paleographical system was lacking, as were comparative studies that would compare Qur'ānic fragments with dated materials like papyri, such as the studies that Adolf Grohmann (1887–1977) would produce thirty years later.[19] Bergsträßer's appraisal of the Egyptian print is based on his observation that this new print, quite distinct in orthography from Qur'ānic codices of the Ottoman empire, to which Egypt had belonged since the 16th century, would strictly follow sources of reference works of Muslim scholarship for orthography and verse separation system.[20]

Bergsträßer had to admit that manuscripts of the Qur'ān were unfortunately not used for the spelling of the Cairene print which is in fact, as he states, a kind of "*Um*schreibung des Textes der beiden älteren offiziellen ägyptischen Ausgaben in die othmanische Orthographie mit Hilfe jüngerer Schriften über diese" (p. 391), i.e., a kind of transposition of the text of two older official Egyptian editions into 'uṯmānic orthography, a style of spelling attributed to the caliph 'Uṯmān, who is considered in a large number of Muslim narratives to be the political leader who established a unified text of the Qur'ān by sending reference copies to the important cities of the Arab empire.

17 See Bergsträßer 1930; Pretzl 1934. On the conception and the realization of the academic project in Potsdam that has been carried out so far, see Marx 2015a: 253–278.

18 Bergsträßer 1930: 395–396.

19 Grohmann 1958.

20 Bergsträßer 1930: 391.

Concerning the chronological classification of manuscripts, our project is based on the paleographic system deployed by François Déroche on the classification of the Qur'ānic fragments kept by the French National Library.[21] The so-called Ḥiǧāzī style of writing of the earliest Qur'ān manuscripts strikes us as a rather uncalligraphic style that can also be recognized in dated papyri of the 7th century.[22] Some letters resemble the late Nabatean ones from which the Arabic alphabet evolved.[23] The rightward-leaning ascender of *alif*, the occasionally widely drawn-back final bow of *yā'*, and the *qāf* that reminds one of the letter *ṣād*—all these are typical of the Ḥiǧāzī style of writing. The term "Ḥiǧāzī" itself (i.e., "in a style of writing of the Ḥiǧāz") goes back to the Italian scholar Michele Amari (1806–1889), who drew upon the research on the origin and formation of the Arabic script by Antoine-Isaac Silvestre de Sacy (1758–1838).[24] Silvestre de Sacy had consulted a short paragraph from Ibn an-Nadīms *Fihrist* (d. 995 or 998) on the oldest style in Arabic,[25] a description of a script style that Amari had identified in the writing of the Paris manuscript Arabe 328 (Bibliothèque nationale de France) as "the script of Mecca and Medina,"[26] followed by Josef Karabacek,[27] Gotthelf Bergsträßer ("ḥiǧāzenisch"),[28] and Nabia Abbott.[29]

Study of the written transmission of the Qur'ān in the West goes back to the theologian Jakob Georg Christian Adler (1756–1834), the first scholar to pursue the idea of studying Arabic paleography and the history of Arabic

21 Déroche 1983, vol. I: 19–22.

22 Grohmann 1958: 213–231; 1959: 272–273.

23 On the emergence of the Arabic scripture from the late Nabatean scripture, see Nehmé 2010: 47–88. Nehmé speaks about "écriture tardo-nabatéenne," i.e., late-Nabatean scripture as precursor of the Arabic script. Letter shapes in the pre-Islamic Arabic inscriptions (without diacritical signs, without vowel signs, and without *alif* in a middle position for the long vowel /ā/) are easily found in the evidence given by her. The hypothesis (e.g., Starcky 1964) that the Arabic script originates from the Syriac one seems less plausible, despite the fact that Arabic and Syriac script share similar aesthetics, such as the unitary baseline. On the development of Arabic script, see the fundamental article by Robin 2006.

24 Silvestre de Sacy 1808: 247–440; 253–254.

25 *Qāla Muḥammad b. Isḥāq fa-awwalu l-ḫuṭūṭi l-ʿarabīyati l-makkī wa-baʿdahu l-madanī ṯumma l-baṣrī ṯumma l-kūfī fa-ammā l-makkī wa-l-madanī fa-fī alifātihī taʿwīǧun ilā yumnati l-yadi wa-aʿlā l-aṣābiʿi wa-fī šaklihī nḍiǧāʿun yasīrun …*; Ibn an-Nadīm 2006: 6. The English translation reads: "Thus saith Muḥammad ibn Isḥāq [an-Nadīm]: the first of the Arab scripts was the script of Makkah, the next of al-Madīnah, then of al-Baṣrah, and then of al-Kūfah. For the alifs of the scripts of Makkah and al-Madīnah there is a turning of the hand to the right and lengthening of the strokes, one form having a slight slant." Dodge 1970, 10.

26 On Amari's "script of Mecca and Medina," see Amari/Derenbourg 1908.

27 Von Karabacek 1891: 323.

28 Bergsträßer 1938: 251–256.

29 Abbott 1939.

script by means of Qur'ān manuscripts. At the time he had only consulted Qur'ān manuscripts of the Royal Library of Copenhagen which are all written in Kufic.[30] His small study on the history of the Arabic script prompted a discussion (Adler 1780) among scholars, and Adler's presentation of the history of Arabic script was adopted by Silvestre de Sacy and substantially enhanced by Amari, who was in charge of cataloguing the Bibliothèque royale's extensive collection of Qur'ānic manuscripts acquired in Cairo.[31] The first groundbreaking, systematic paleography of Qur'ānic manuscripts was presented almost 150 years later, in 1983, by François Déroche with his catalogue of Qur'ān scriptures of the Bibliothèque nationale de France (Paris). It specifies the following four types of the Ḥiǧāzī style (Déroche 1983, vol. I), classified as the most ancient script style.

Déroche's typology is based on the largest accessible collection of ancient Qur'ānic manuscripts, and probably the classification of the 263 Parisian Qur'ān fragments (classified in 26 paleographic groups, four Ḥiǧāzī, 22 Kūfī) will not suffice to classify fragments to be discovered in the future. The scripts of some manuscripts, like Arabe 330g (19 fol.),[32] have no place ("non-classé")[33] in the typology, and manuscripts like Ma VI 165 (Tübingen) and We. II 1913 (Berlin)[34]—despite their age—are to be classified as a script of the style known as Kufic B. Seven sheets of Berlin State Library ms. or. fol. 4313 are considered Ḥiǧāzī, although it is not clear if they are to be classified as type I or type II. Due to the fact that a much larger number of Qur'ān manuscripts is accessible by now, the paleographical types as they were described broadly by Déroche in his catalogue need to be in some respects adjusted, extended, and perhaps slightly modified. Figs. 6.1–6.4 give four exemples of script styles still difficult-to-classify in the existing typology, illustrated with the text of the Basmala introduction formula of Surahs, which are written in the early manuscripts always in the same ink as the Qur'ān text itself.

Because paleographical identification and the chronological classification of these four manuscripts showing features of an ancient script style remain unclear, ^{14}C measurements are of particular interest. So far, ^{14}C has only occasionally been used for dating Oriental manuscripts. In the field of Qur'ānic philology, results were published in three cases i.e., by Yassin Dutton, by Beh-

30 See ms. Cod. Arabe. 36–42 of the Danish National Library in Copenhagen.

31 On the discussion of the oldest Qur'ān fragments, see Déroche 1999: 563–576.

32 There are four pages of the fragment's manuscript Is. 1615 II belonging to the Chester Beatty Library in Dublin.

33 Déroche 1985, vol. I: 143–150.

34 Apparently the six folios of Arabe 6087 (Paris) belong to the same codex.

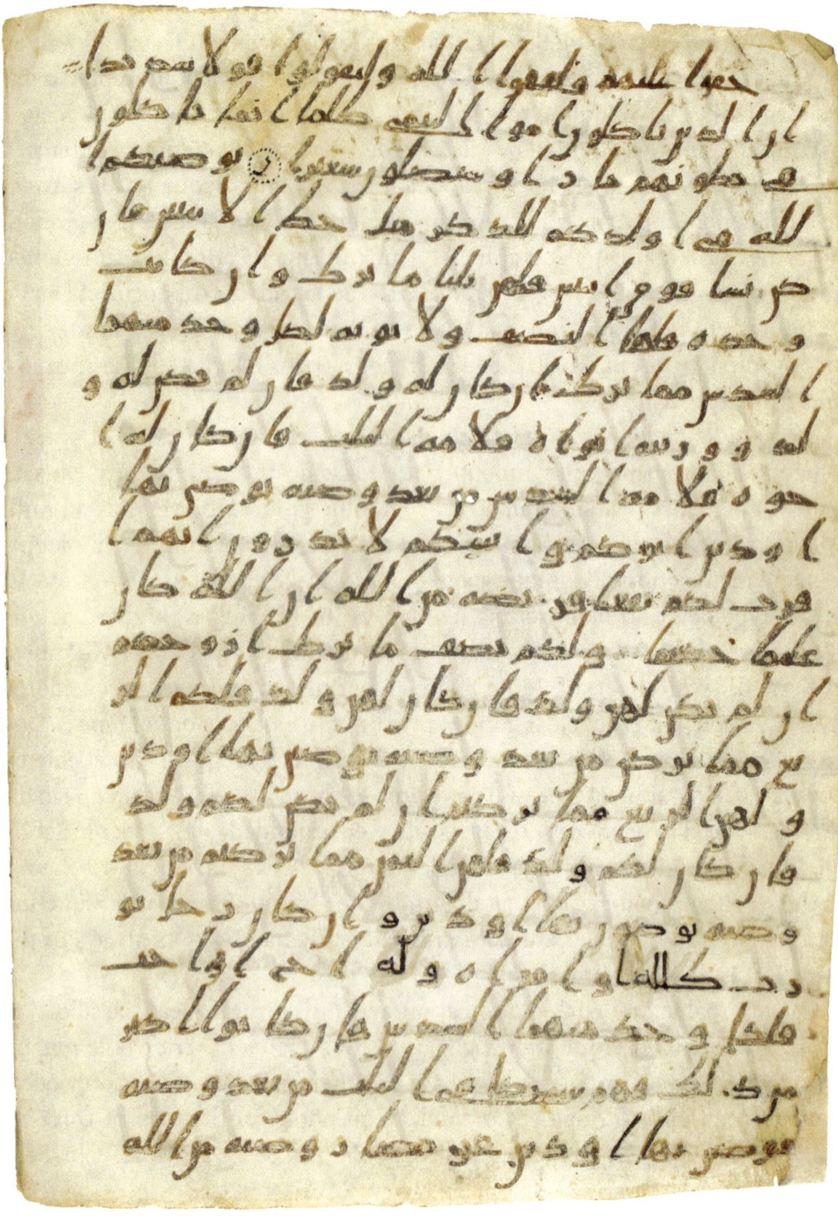

FIGURE 6.1 Qurʾān in Hiǧāzi Type I (Arabe 328a, fol. 10v)

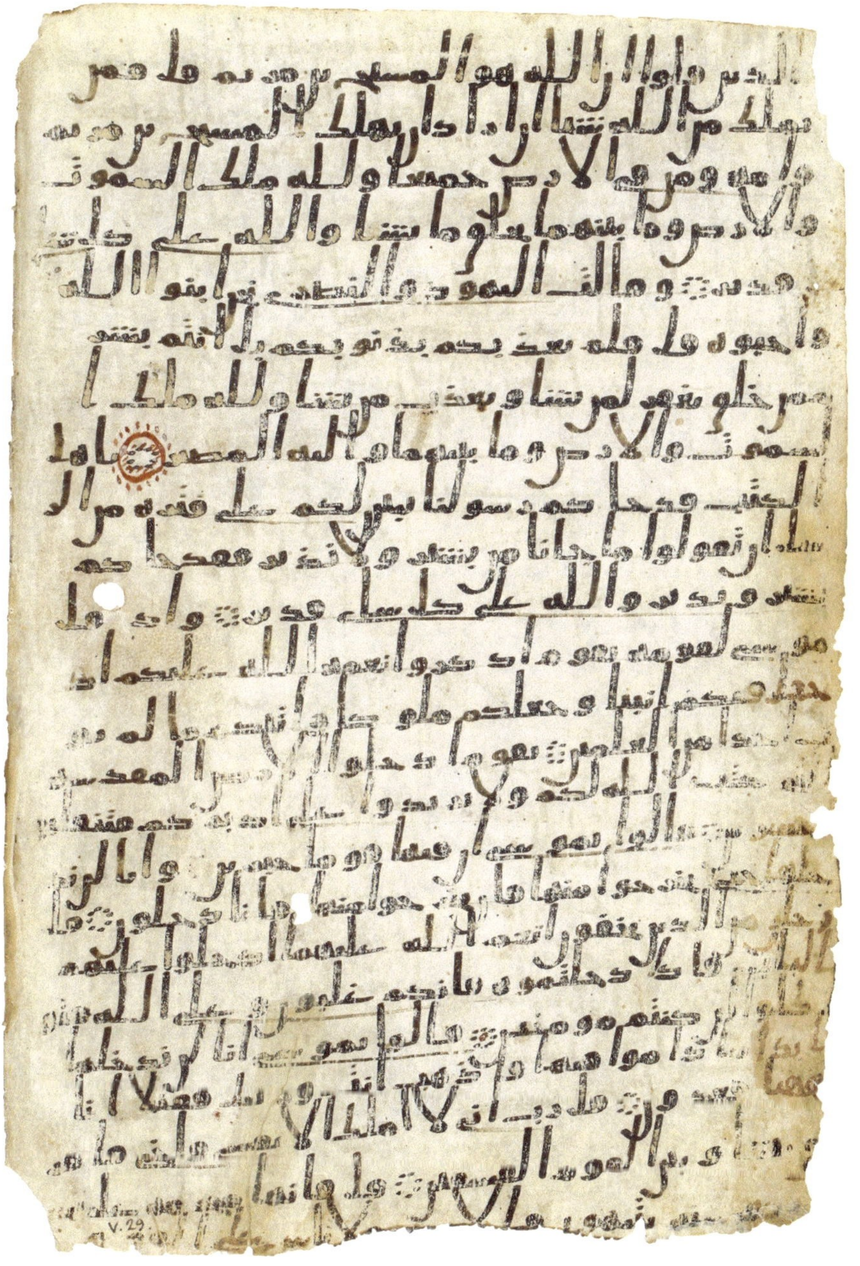

FIGURE 6.2 Qur'ān in Hiǧāzi Type II (Arabe 328e, fol. 90v)
© BIBLIOTHEQUE NATIONAL DE FRANCE

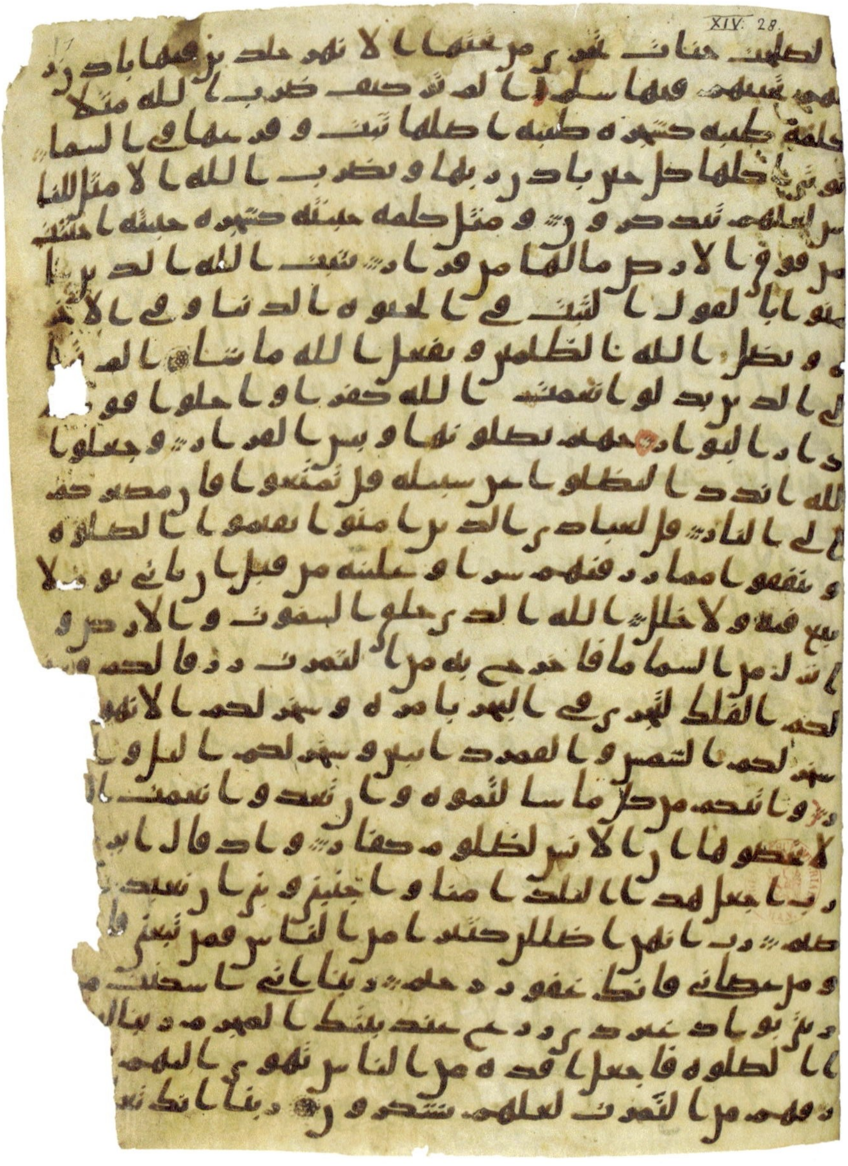

FIGURE 6.3 Qur'ān in Hiǧāzi Type III (Arabe 330a, fol. 1r)
© BIBLIOTHEQUE NATIONAL DE FRANCE

FIGURE 6.4 Qur'ān in Hiğāzi Type IV (Arabe 334c, fol. 41r)
© BIBLIOTHEQUE NATIONAL DE FRANCE

nam Sadeghi, and by Efim A. Rezvan;[35] the time span of the result, but not the exact measurement, was stated in another two instances, in von Bothmer's article on a Sanaa Qur'ān and in the catalogue of the auction house Christie's (Lot 225).[36] François Déroche arranged for the dating of two Qur'ān fragments from Kairouan, through a lab in Lyon: the so-called *muṣḥaf al-ḥāḍina* ("codex of the nurse", with colophon, according to which the manuscript was copied in 1020 CE), and another manuscript with a note of a foundation (*waqfīya*) from 907 CE. The results (1130 BP ±30 for the "*muṣḥaf al-ḥāḍina*" and 1205 BP ±30 for the other ms.) still require a thorough evaluation, though.[37] Contamination of

35 Dutton 2007: 57–87, especially 63ff.; Sadeghi/Bergmann 2010: 343–436, especially 348–354; Rezvan 2000: 19–22.

36 von Bothmer/Ohlig/Puin 1999: 45; Christie's 1992: 88. ^{14}C datings should at least include the absolute measurement value in radiocarbon years and its measurement's accuracy, information about the laboratory entrusted with the measurements, the number of measurements, and possibly further data such as the isotope fractionation.

37 Déroche 2013: 11–13.

FIGURE 6.5 Basmala of Surah 5 (ms.or.fol. 4313, fol. 2r)

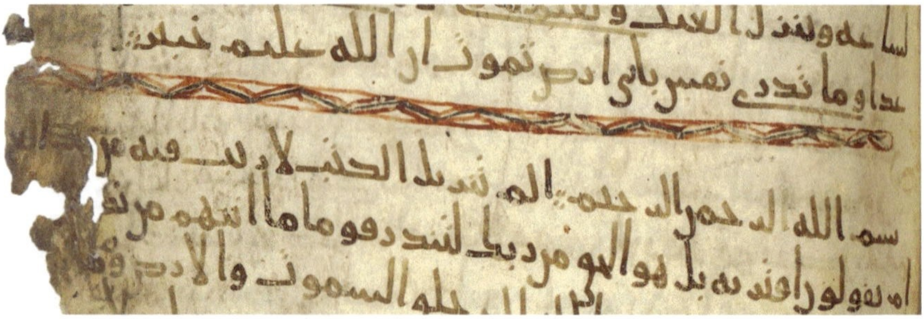

FIGURE 6.6 Basmala of Surah 32 (Is. 1615 I, fol. 7r)
Note: See the facsimile edition of the manuscript by Tobias J. Jocham in the series "Documenta Coranica," *Is. 1615 I (Chester Beatty Library) + fragments (Museum of Islamic Art* et al.). In preparation.

the material may be the reason for these "odd results," but also technical failures of the machines could be a reason.

Within the framework of *Coranica*, carbon dating[38] was applied to more than 50 documents, among others, the four manuscripts Ma VI 165, ms. or. fol. 4313, We. II 1913, and Cod. or. 14.545b/c. Since this procedure entails the removal of testing material, this is not entirely unobjectionable from the point of view of conservation. As compared to the first measurements at the discovery of the method,[39] the required sample amount has been reduced to 1–2 mg pure carbon and still offers great precision in measurement, thanks to technical development and the usage of *Accelerated Mass Spectrometry* (AMS). In order to obtain this amount of pure carbon the removal of about 20 mg is suf-

38 After a first comparison between different laboratories, we decided on the laboratory of the ETH Zurich where all *Coranica* datings were carried out; for the ETH Zurich lab, see www.ams.ethz.ch (last accessed 12 November 2018).

39 Arnold/Libby 1949: 678–680.

FIGURE 6.7 Basmala of Surah 18 (Ma VI 165, fol. 5r)
© UNIVERSITÄTSBIBLIOTHEK TÜBINGEN

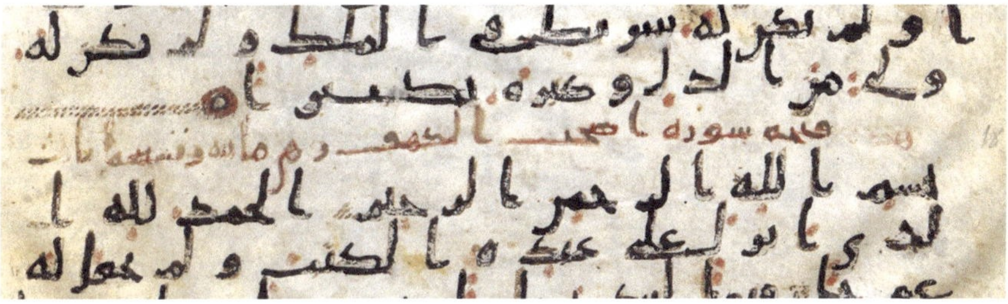

FIGURE 6.8 Basmala of Surah 18 (We II 1913, fol. 111v)
© STAATSBIBLIOTHEK ZU BERLIN

ficient, depending on the initial substance, which in the case of parchment and papyrus corresponds to a surface of approximately 1 cm^2. This sample has to undergo an extensive, multi-level chemical cleaning process before it is transformed into graphite by burning. This material is fixed to a metal core together with other samples (including blank samples to control the accuracy of measurement). By means of AMS the percentage of the radioactive carbon isotope ^{14}C can then be determined in the sample.

Dating organic material is based on the Nobel-Prize-winning research (1960) conducted by Williard F. Libby (1908–1980), which shows that living organisms absorb through their metabolism not only the non-radioactive carbon isotope ^{12}C but also the aforementioned ^{14}C, which evolves due to cosmic radiation in the atmosphere and forms only to an astonishingly small degree (1–10 %) part of the air's carbon content. Because of the radioactive decay[40] of ^{14}C, its percentage in the carbon content of organic material decreases continually, so that

40 The originally calculated radioactive half-life by Libby of 5,568 years for ^{14}C was later corrected to 5,715.

in tenfold radioactive half-life (= ten times the period of time of about 5,600 years) the remaining ^{14}C-percentage falls underneath the detection limit: dating organic material therefore is only possible until approximately 55,000 BCE. All in all, the ^{14}C method has assisted research considerably in pre- and protohistory and is considered a reliable dating technique, applied by numerous specialized laboratories worldwide (see Arnold/Libby 1949: 77–123). This method is rarely used to date written sources, however, most likely due to already existing and well-established forms of dating through paleography and glossary techniques, such as have been used with texts of the European Middle Ages. With the help of a mass spectrometer the percentage proportion of the particular parts of ^{12}C and ^{14}C are elaborated, and the result is then converted into the so-called radioactive carbon age before it can be stated together with the precision of measurements in terms of standard deviation. This radioactive carbon age is expressed in "years BP (= before present)", "present" having been fixed as being the year 1950.[41] The following diagrams reflect these data in the captions within brackets, e.g., the Tübingen manuscript has a radioactive carbon age of 1,357 years BP with a measurement precision of ±14 years BP. Therefore it is necessary to convert the measurement result into the dates of the Gregorian calendar. This in turn limits the precision of the measurements, because the nonlinearity of the ^{14}C concentration in the atmosphere has to be considered, which is expressed in the so-called calibration curve. This is depicted by a light-blue band spanning from the top left to the bottom right within the diagrams (see below) and is based upon dendrochronological data.[42] The y-axis shows the abovementioned radioactive carbon age as a red sine curve which is exposed through folding above the calibration curve on the x-axis as dates in the Christian calendar. Here, a grey curve depicts the probability of the distribution of these dates, whereas the written part of the diagrams indicates the span of possible data from the $\sigma 2$-confidence interval (95.4% probability).[43]

41 The unit "radioactive carbon age" could also be expressed as a percentage of the still extant ratio of ^{14}C in the sample, but this rather unclear term was historically determined and kept until now.

42 Here the comparative data were found by the ^{14}C method in continuous annual ring calendars which reach back to the year 12,000 BCE via overlapping comparisons of slices of trees. These comparative data were solid for the project's time scale and do not exhibit any variations. Only concerning the pre-Christian time period the data situation has not yet been settled; see Creasman 2014: 85–92.

43 Partly occurring "voids" in the time periods (see the datings of We. II and Cod. or. 14.545b/c) are due to the re-rise of ^{14}C content within the atmosphere between 735 and 760 CE.

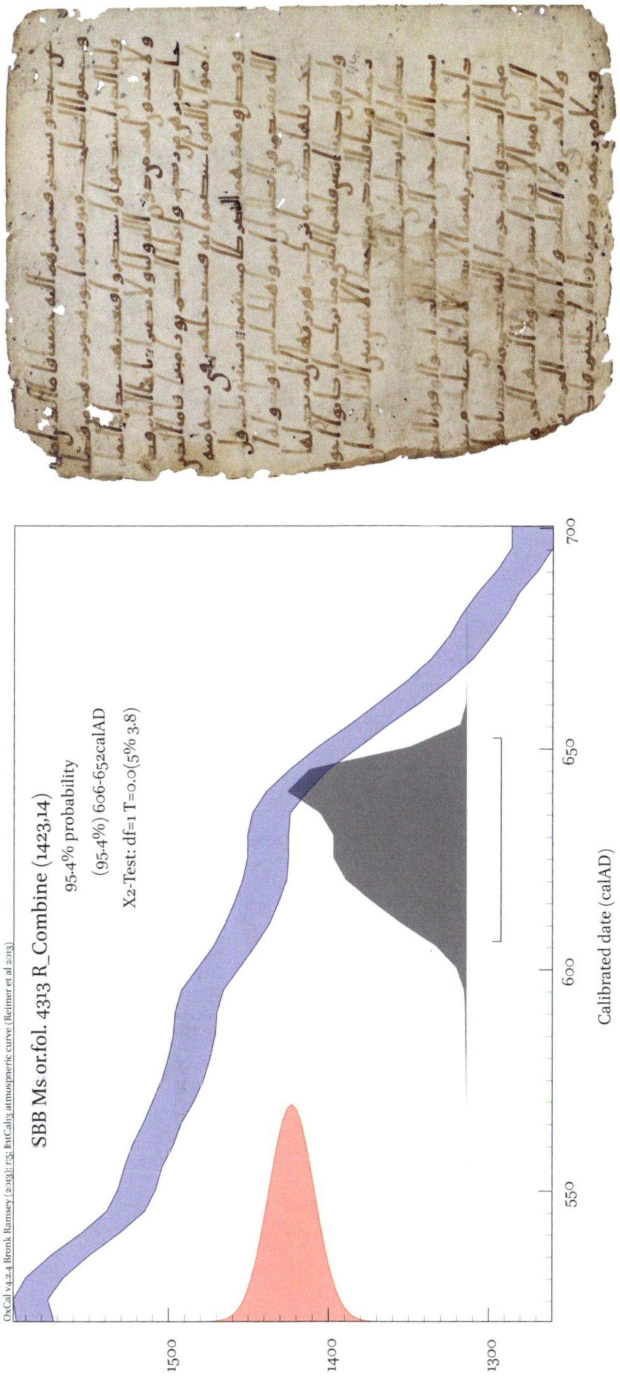

FIGURE 6.9 OxCal Combined plot and sample image (ms.or.fol. 4313, fol. 2r)
© STAATSBIBLIOTHEK ZU BERLIN & TOBIAS J. JOCHAM

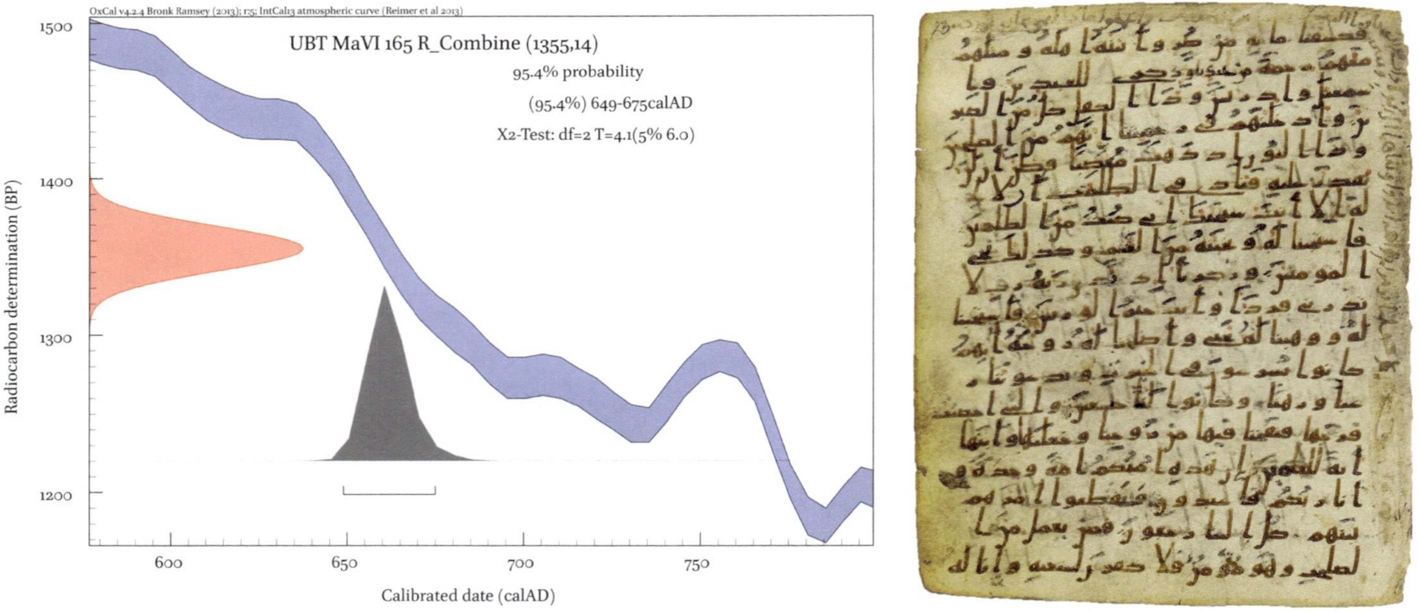

FIGURE 6.10 OxCal Combined plot and sample image of the manuscript (Ma VI 165, fol. 23r)

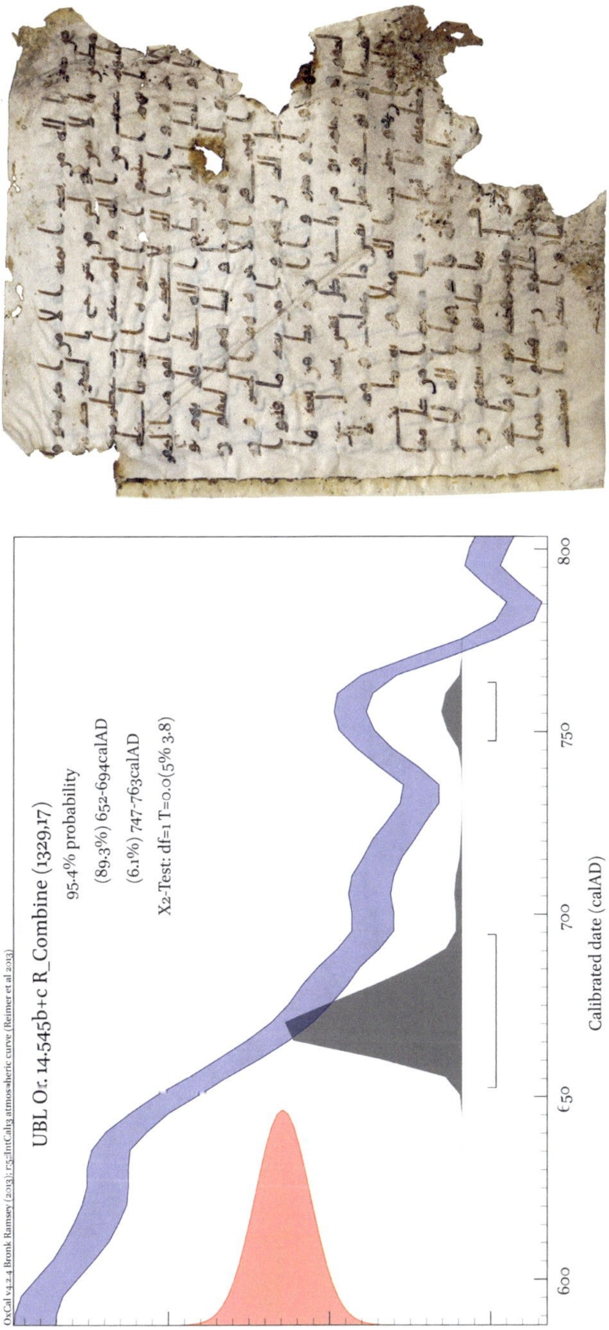

FIGURE 6.11 OxCal Combined plot and sample image of the manuscript (Cod.or. 14.545b, fol. 1v)
© LEIDEN UNIVERSITY LIBRARY & TOBIAS J. JOCHAM

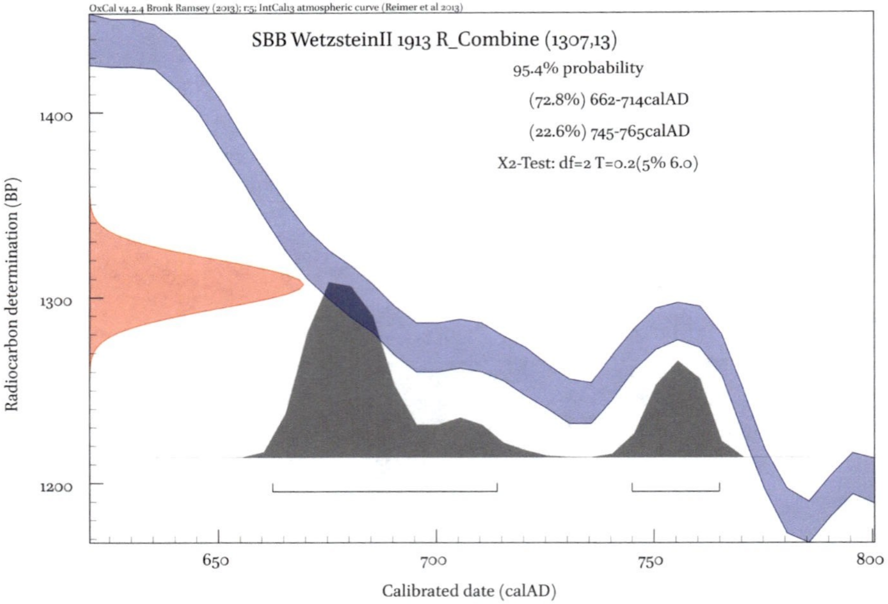

FIGURE 6.12 OxCal Combined plot and sample image of the manuscript (We II 1913, fol. 104r)

In order to narrow down the results, all measurements in Figs. 6.9–6.12 have not only been taken from the very same material (a singular folio of a manuscript) but also double as well as triple samples of different pages have been combined. This is due to the underlying assumption that in order to produce a codex, parchment of the same or of only slightly differing age was used. Therefore, from a statistic point of view, a merge of the individual results is permitted, which in light of the amount of time needed to produce the manuscript partially means a substantial improvement of precision.[44]

For the purpose of comparison alongside early Qur'ān fragments, *Coranica* also dated other texts of the first millennium,[45] i.e., Arabic papyri in cooperation with Eva-Mira Youssef-Grob (Zurich),[46] numerous wooden sticks with Ancient South Arabian texts in cooperation with Peter Stein (University of Jena),[47] Georgian manuscripts of the National Manuscript Center (Tbilisi), and Coptic texts together with Hugo Lundhaug (University of Oslo).[48] The method was confirmed by ^{14}C datings of papyri from Leiden and Heidelberg (see Youssef-Grob's contribution in this volume) as well as three Syriac parchment manuscripts from Berlin.[49] The ^{14}C study of three Kufic Qur'ān fragments—Berlin State Library We. II 1919,[50] University Library Leiden Or. 6814,[51] and a privately owned folio[52]—clearly demonstrated that Kufic text fragments

44 This statistical procedure was developed by Tobias J. Jocham in consultation with Irka Hajdas (Zurich) and Oliver Hahn (Berlin/Hamburg), although it reaches its limit at an accuracy of measurements of approximately ± 10 years BP: at this point the accuracy of the calibration curve—demonstrated by the "thickness" of the light-blue line in the displayed diagram—is reached.

45 For the dating of early Qur'ān fragments, see also Marx/Youssef-Grob/Jocham/Hajdas 2014.

46 On Youssef-Grob's ^{14}C-based dating of Arabic papyri, see her contribution to this volume.

47 See Stein/Jocham/Marx 2015.

48 See Hugo Lundhaug, "The Date of MS 193 in the Schøyen Collection: New Radiocarbon Evidence" (forthcoming).

49 The manuscripts are ms. or. quart. 528 (Syriac New Testament, *Pshitta*), Sachau 321 (Syriac church fathers), and Codex Philippi 1388 (Syriac New Testament, *Pshitta*), the data of which were measured through ^{14}C-analysis and matched paleographical datings by Eduard Sachau (Sachau 1899: 10–18; 94–100); on this also see Michael Marx, "The Dating of Three Syriac Manuscripts of the Berlin State Library by Means of ^{14}C-Analysis" (in preparation).

50 corpuscoranicum.de/handschriften/index/sure/12/vers/100/?handschrift=453 (last accessed 12 November 2018).

51 Witkam 2007, vol. VII: 311.

52 Special thanks to Professor Mark Mersiowsky (Stuttgart) for his kind permission to take samples of a Kufic Qur'ān fragment, Sig. Isl. 18 (1 fol.) in his possession.

are to be chronologically situated after the Ḥiğāzī fragments.[53] Merely due to the paleography of the four early Qur'ān parchments, a chronological order would result that cannot be confirmed by the ^{14}C results:

François Déroche classifies the writing of Arabe 331 as Kufic B 1 a, considering as type of script related to Ḥiğāzī.[54] Due to the fact that no colophons of early Qur'ān parchments have survived (or because early manuscripts may have had no colophons), the exact dating of Qur'ān manuscripts remains controversial. Because of ^{14}C dating the question remains whether the paleographical typology of Ḥiğāzī and Kufic writing types, as formulated by Déroche on the basis of the Parisian manuscripts, can be understood as being chronological. Here it looks as if the dating of the writing types within the Ḥiğāzī group and within Ḥiğāzī-similar writings will have to be constituted in a new way, in case further dating confirms the result.

Even though the conducted dating of papyri from Heidelberg and Leiden, as well as of three Syriac manuscripts (parchments) from Berlin, has demonstrated that the ^{14}C method offers reliable results, there are measurements such as the one of the Qur'ān parchment DAM 01-27.1 (Dār al-Maḫṭūṭāt, Sanaa) that offer odd results. It has to be kept in mind, however, that the scientific method can only date the material that was written upon—not the actual time of writing the text. It is highly possible that the parchments for the manuscripts Ma VI 165, ms. or. fol. 4313, We. II 1913, and Cod. or. 14.545b/c were bought by a writing workshop and that a certain amount of time passed before they were used as writing material. Nevertheless, it does not make sense to assume that the manufacturer would wait a long time with the production of a manuscript. For economic reasons, it seems unlikely that the time span between the production of the parchment and its acquisition by the producing atelier, on the one hand, and the moment the scribe began to produce the manuscript, on the other, would have encompassed decades. The studied manuscripts show no signs of having been inscribed twice, therefore these are no palimpsests.[55]

53 See Jocham/Marx: "Studie zum Vergleich von vier kufischen und vier *ḥiğāzī*-Handschriften: Orthographie, Paläographie und ^{14}C-Datierung" (Study on the Comparison of Four Kufic and Four *ḥiğāzī* Manuscripts: Orthography, Paleography and ^{14}C-Datings; in preparation).

54 "On palaeographic grounds, a *ḥiğāzī* style, B Ia, was included in Group B because a diachronic continuity could be recognized in this case between the early period and the third/ninth century. On the other hand, I made it clear from the beginning that the styles were overlapping and that there were possibly 'local schools' and 'regional peculiarities'" (Déroche 2013: 10).

55 After all, dating of the manuscript DAM 01-27.1 from Sanaa is problematic. In addition to the partly very early datings already conducted within the framework of the ANR-project

So far, the dating of ink that is not based on soot is not yet possible by scientific techniques, and a measurement of soot inks is very likely to fail due to the amount that needs to be extracted. The text of the four manuscripts Ma VI 165, ms. or. fol. 4313, We. II 1913, and Cod. or. 14.545b/c that is visible nowadays shows—to all appearances—the very first layer of text. Manuscripts Ma VI 165 and We. II 1913 underwent changes through a different ink, additions and corrections that still need to be studied in depth, as well as the vowel signs that have been added to the manuscripts later with red ink.

Because Qur'ān manuscripts can be dated precisely neither by paleography nor ^{14}C analysis, additional features such as their orthography must be taken into consideration;[56] codicological features and ornaments (e.g., forms of verse markers, ornaments marking the transition between two Surahs, etc.) may also offer additional evidence.[57] The scientific study of the ink's composition cannot contribute much to their dating, and then possibly only indirectly; yet in a large number of early Qur'ān manuscripts, it may be possible to draw conclusions from the applied ink about the age of the inks or the order of their application within a manuscript. The four manuscripts in concern use—as do most Ḥiǧāzī manuscripts—a dark-brown ink for the first layer, which was probably even darker, if not black, 1,400 years ago. The brown ink is clearly different from the deep-black ink of many of the Kufic manuscripts (e.g., We. II 1919, Or. 6814). Ma VI 165 also uses such a black ink for corrections and vowel signs, as does the almost complete (210 fol. that contain 85 % of the text of the Qur'ān) Berlin codex We. II 1913, where most of the dark-brown ink has been overwritten with black ink. Possibly, scientific ink analyses will one day be able to provide an informative basis on its point of origin—provided there are by then a larger number of analyses available, from which conclusions can be drawn about different ink compositions in different regions.

Even without an ink analysis, the orthography gives important indications about a manuscript's age: Archaic writing forms in the manuscripts Ma VI 165, ms. or. fol. 4313, and We. II 1913—such as *dw'd* for *Dāwūd*, *š'y* for *šay'* ("thing, issue"), or the variant readings (see Fedeli 2012, vol. III: 403–440) in Ma VI 165—

"De l'Antiquité tardive à l'Islam" (Christian J. Robin), the *Coranica* project conducted complementary research; see Robin 2015; coranica.de/computatio-radiocarbonica-de (last accessed 12 November 2018).

56 See, e.g., the orthographical comparison of the "Codex Parisino-petropolitanus" with five other manuscripts, Déroche 2013:47.

57 See the study on a monumental manuscript DAM 20-33.1 (Sanaa), von Bothmer 1989: 4–20, who proposed a convincing suggestion for its dating in the first decades of the 7th century, based on the similarity of ornaments in the Surah headings and in ornaments in Umayyad architecture.

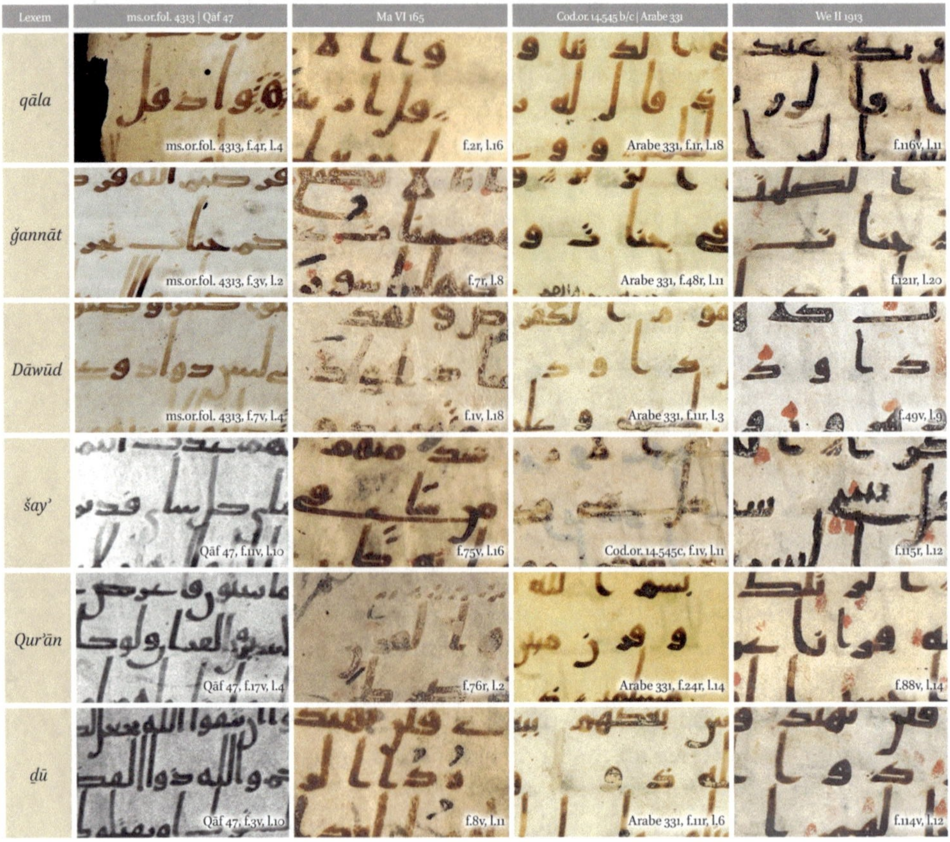

FIGURE 6.13 Comparison chart for key words in different Qurʾānic manuscripts
© TOBIAS J. JOCHAM

can be considered indications for being older. Also, the frequency of the spelling *qāf-alif-lām* for *qāla*, i.e., with *alif* for the long vowel /ā/, as compared to the spelling *qāf-lām*, can serve as an indicator for the dating together with other keywords; yet it is also conceivable, of course, that the scribe had copied an archaic spelling. Figure 6.13 contains six keywords, each with an image section of the four manuscripts: (1) *qāla* spelled *ql* (without the *alif*) or *qʾl*; (2) *ǧannāt* generally with *alif* for the long vowel /ā/; (3) *Dāwūd* in the archaic orthography *dwʾd*; (4) archaic spelling of *šayʾ* as *šʾy*; (5) *Qurʾān* often without *alif*; (6) *ḏū* spelled *ḏwʾ*, but interestingly in Tübingen sometimes with *ḏāl-alif*.

The long vowel /ā/ in old texts sometimes being written with an *alif* (as in *ǧannāt*) and sometimes not yet (as in *qāla* written with *qāf* and *lām*), is not a usual phenomenon in papyri documents. For the word *šayʾ* with the letters *šīn-alif-yāʾ* a number of papyrus documents are known, such as in PERF

600.10, in the letter P.SijpesteijnArmyEconomics.5, in P. Khalili I 14, and in P. Khalili II 34.7—all four being papyri that are datable before 800 CE—and in two letters dated to 710 CE (P.BeckerNPAF 1.13 = P.Cair.Arab. 146.13; P.Cair.Arab. 158.17). Also in documents after 800, this spelling occurs (P.David-WeillLouvre II.recto 23; P.RagibLettres 19 verso.4). It is mentionned in ad-Dānī's treatise on Qur'ānic orthography, entitled *al-Muqniʿ fī rasm al-maṣāḥif*, only for *li-šay'in* (Q 18:23). In the Cairene print of 1924, whose spellings follow ad-Dānī's work, the word *šay'* is spelled without an alif following the šīn more than 280 times; interestingly, in one verse, 18, 23, it is spelled in the Cairene print (1924) لِشَاْىْءٍ with the letter *alif*. This spelling appears today as an odd spelling; in the Cairene print, against the predominant spelling *šīn-yā'* (e.g., in Q 18:33; 18:45; and 18:54).

It is interesting to see that archaic spellings such as the one of *Dāwūd* were overwritten and changed in the manuscripts Tübingen and We. II 1913 from *dw'd* to *d'wd*. Since the long vowel /ā/ in early times was written by the letter *alif*—and apparently *yā'*—at the end of the word on a regular basis, for a long vowel in the middle of the word the letters *yā'* and *wāw* were used. Yet even the oldest manuscripts contain the letter *alif* as a sign for the long vowel in a center position, as seen in the spelling of *ǧannāt* ("gardens"), i.e., in the early manuscripts *alif* in the central position of a word is used as a long vowel. In Qur'ānic Arabic the spelling of the long vowel /ā/ in words such as *ṣalāt* and *zakāt* still shows the old spelling, which noted the long vowel through a *wāw* (see Spitaler 1960), as attested in Nabataean. The spelling *dw'd* could be understood as an archaic spelling of the name *Dāwūd*, in which the *wāw* notes the long vowel /ā/ and the *alif* the guttural sound (*hamza*), which the form *Dā'ūd* contains according to some grammarians. The spelling *dw'd* is well documented in the early manuscripts Dublin Is. 1615 I, Bibliothèque nationale Arabe 328a/b, British Library Or. 2165, and St. Petersburg E-20. The fact that in Ma VI 165 *Dāwūd* is constantly spelled *dw'd* could indicate a high age; Arabe 331, in contrast, contains the name once and in the common form: *d'wd*. It remains striking that in We. II 1913, as well as in Ma VI 165, the archaic form of the name *dw'd*, the common spelling of the name, almost constantly appears "corrected" into *d'wd*. All four dated manuscripts contain archaic spellings: Ma VI 165 contains, next to the archaic spellings of *Dāwūd*, the spellings *qāla* and *šay'*—also variant readings that are not to be found within the canonical readings—to a greater extent than does ms. or. fol. 4313.

The scribe of We. II 1913 often—but not always—writes *alif* in the central position for a long ā, more often than can be found in the other three manuscripts, e.g., in the case of *qāla* or *qālū*, yet shows other features of archaic

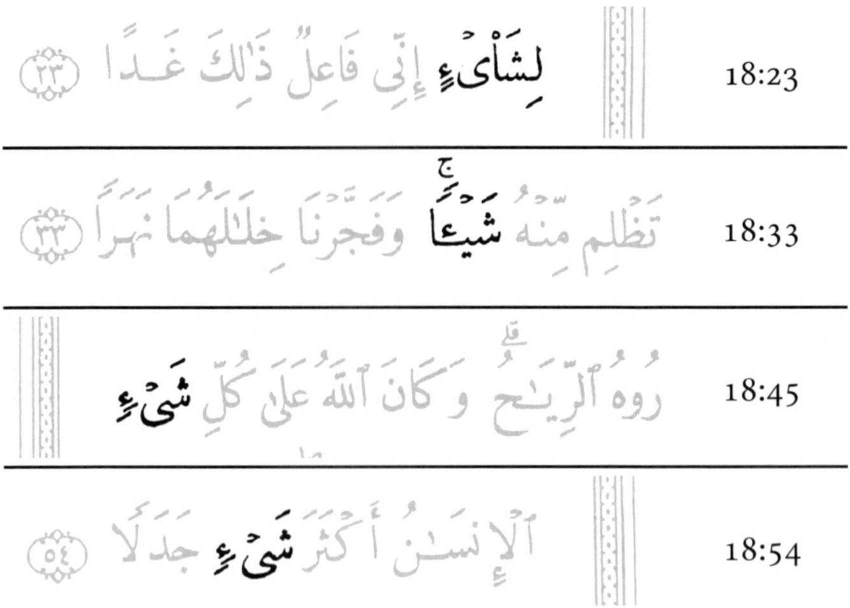

FIGURE 6.14 Two ways of spelling the word *šay'* in Surah 18 of the Egyptian print of the Qur'ān (Cairo 1924)

writing such as *dw'd* or *ḏw'*. Arabe 331, however, contains an orthography quite similar to the Egyptian print (Cairo 1924), but also includes archaic spellings such as *ḏw'*. The Egyptian print for its part refers, in its epilogue, to the two authorities ad-Dānī (d. 1053/1054) and Ibn Naǧāḥ (d. 1102/1103). The question whether the manuscripts consulted by ad-Dānī[58] were the oldest ones probably has to be answered in the negative. One cannot exclude the possibility that he had seen old manuscripts, but it is doubtful that he was in the position to understand the chronological order of scripts and spelling. The spelling of the Egyptian print of 1924, which lives on in the nowadays very widespread text output of the King Fahd Glorious Quran Printing Complex (Medina), apparently does not always include the oldest verifiable spelling, for it never writes *dw'd*, and only once *šay* with an *alif* after the *šīn*.

All in all, ^{14}C datings could confirm the high age of manuscripts, so far only dated by paleographic classification, especially those in Ḥiǧāzī script. The observations on the four manuscripts can be summarized as follows: (1) Tübingen Ma VI 165, in a Kufic script, although paleographically located in the

58 See ad-Dānī's *al-Muqniʿ fī rasm maṣāḥif al-amṣār maʿa Kitāb an-Naqṭ* (1932).

8th century CE, belongs according to the ^{14}C datings, and as confirmed by orthography, in the 7th century. The additions and modifications of the first ink layer through the use of a similar ink can be seen with the naked eye (in the word *Qur'ān*, originally just *qrn*, an *alif* was added) and this should be supported through scientific ink-analyses. Moreover, the manuscript includes archaic spellings and variant readings that are not mentioned in later exegetical literature. (2) Berlin ms. or. fol. 4313, difficult to classify paleographically, shows similarities to the Ḥiǧāzī style of writing, yet according to its orthography and ^{14}C dating it belongs to the oldest textual witnesses preserved. The simple handwriting of the manuscript, without any vowel dots and ornamentation, appears to be among the oldest. (3) The fragments of Leiden Cod. or. 14.545b/c—sheets from a codex to which originally the fragment Paris Arabe 331 (56 fol.) and Marcel 3 (26 fol.) had belonged—are paleographically to be classified as Kufic B 1a and, according to ^{14}C, to be dated in the 7th century, although the orthography shows only very few archaic spellings. In this case the ^{14}C dating questions the fragments' classification as Kufic, because such a high age would better match a parchment in the Ḥiǧāzī style, with its upright format and its slightly uncalligraphic appearance. (4) The ^{14}C measurement results of the Berlin codex We. II 1913 (210 folios that comprise about 85% of the Qur'ān text, perhaps the oldest next-to-complete codex of the Qur'ān existing today)—together with the six folios of Arabe 6087 (Paris)—range over a long period of time, due to the calibration curve. Its orthography shows archaic forms such as *dw'd* for *Dāwūd*, but also spellings of the letter *alif* to note the long /ā/ in a central position, which is generally a feature of later manuscripts. All in all, the further philological evaluation of Berlin We. II 1913 will hardly be possible without the analyses of the different layers of ink—*inter alia* through the usage of ultraviolet images and scientific ink analyses.

By means of ^{14}C measurements, four Qur'ān fragments of vast text size (see Table 6.1) have turned out to be manuscripts of the 7th and the early 8th centuries. Without the radiocarbon dating procedure, the Tübingen manuscript and the Leiden fragment (together with Bibliothèque nationale Arabe 331) would most probably have been classified as manuscripts of the 8th century. The Berlin fragment, namely, the seven pages of ms. or. fol. 4313—together with the fragment Cairo *Qāf* 47, a large fragment[59]—seems to contain old spellings,

59 Pictures of the manuscript with the shelf mark *Qāf 47* from the photo archive of Gotthelf Bergsträßer (Munich) can be accessed via the online-publication of the Corpus Coranicum by now, see corpuscoranicum.de/handschriften/index?sure=2&vers=269&handschrift=73&anzeigen=Anzeigen (last accessed 12 November 2018).

pointing to an old-layer orthography; the fact that this fragment nevertheless actually belongs in the 7th century could only be determined due to ^{14}C dating.

Qurʾānic manuscripts are, in the light of scientific dating, a rather large corpus of primary sources that, in their physical shape in the form of a codex, precede scholarly exegetical literature by two or three centuries. This rediscovery of written transmission could help us to get a more precise idea of the historical development of the text of the Qurʾān: In an article written in 1954, Rudi Paret referred to a "void in the transmission on Urislam,"[60] and certainly rightly so, since the first Islamic century remains to this day an unknown epoch in fields such as law and exegesis. Due to a quite impressive number of textual witnesses—a first list of fragments from European collections, without consideration of auction sales, and the still-unknown manuscript collection of Sanaa count more than 2,000 folios (= 4,000 pages)—the Qurʾān is presumed to be a historically rather well-documented text.[61] We know that the first generations of Islamic scholars used writing materials but did not publish their writings, simply handing them on as written texts to their pupils. Up to the mid-8th century the transmission of knowledge was apparently oral, from teacher to student.[62] The early Qurʾān manuscripts indicate that the written form of the Qurʾān text played an important role, and—assuming that merely a part of the Qurʾān codices of the first century has been conserved—that the written text existed in numerous codices. This will have to be taken into account regarding the early textual history of the Qurʾān, especially when determining the crucial relationship between oral and written transmission. Many variant readings that have been documented by Islamic tradition show that single letters, oftentimes ambiguous, were interpreted in different ways, and that this was how variant readings emerged: many verses have variant readings due to the different interpretation of one and the same undotted letter. Most variant readings apply to the vocalization, however; for more than half of all Qurʾān verses, despite ambiguities in the spellings, a homogeneous text stock has been transmitted. Therefore it would be exaggerated to claim that the written transmission was stronger than the oral one, although it must be said that the track of transmission was apparently persistently influenced by the particularities of the written transmission. The seven canonical readings, implemented by

60 Paret 1954: 147–153.

61 For a first overview of fragments that can be dated back to about 750 CE, see Marx 2015b: 430–435.

62 See the research by Gregor Schoeler on transfer of knowledge in early Islam, e.g. Schoeler 2002.

	1	2		3		4			
Shelf mark	Ma VI 165	We II 1913	Arabe 6087	Qāf 47	ms.or.fol. 4313	Arabe 331	14.545 b	14.545 c	Marcel 3
Collection	Universitäts-bibliothek Tübingen	Staatsbiblio-thek zu Berlin	Bibliothèque nationale de France	Egyptian National Library Cairo	Staatsbiblio-thek zu Berlin	Bibliothèque nationale de France	Leiden University Library		National Library of Russia
Provenance	Damascus					al-Fusṭāṭ (Old-Cairo)			
Purchased / discovered by	Johann G. Wetzstein (1815–1905)		Charles Schefer (1820–1898)	Bernhard Moritz (1895–1939)		Asselin de Cherville (1772–1822)	C. Jorissen 1979, Beirut, Dutch ambassador		Jean-Joseph Marcel (1776–1854)
^{14}C-dating C.E.	649–675	662–765		606–652		652–763			
Extent (fol.)	77	210	6	31	7	56	1	1	26
Script	*kūfī* B 1a	*kūfī* B 1a		*ḥiǧāzī* II		*kūfī* B 1a			
Range of the Qur'ānic text (Sura:Verse)	17:35–36:57	2:30–21:112; 22:18–24:33; 24:51–27:84; 34:47–74:1; 78:35–90:18	31:23–34:6	2:269–3:14; 3:56–78; 3:100–4:137; 6:45–51; 6:53–79; 8:1–53; 9:94–11:42; 11:92–120; 14:32–15:6; 21:37–45; 21:55–66; 63:8–64:14	4:138–155; 4:172–5:87	2:125–191; 2:201–258; 7:162–9:35; 14:9–16:64; 6:114–17:4; 17:78–18:6; 25:65–26:19; 43:81–44:28; 45:9–46:8; 46:21–47:16; 47:36–53:62; 54:41–60:1	16:96–114	63:1–64:4	4:92–5:5; 6:25–6:153; 70:44–85:10

TABLE 6.1 Four large fragments of Qur'ānic Codices on parchment before 770 CE.

the Baghdadi scholar Ibn Muǧāhid (d. 936), most probably cannot be detected within the early manuscripts at hand in their exact wording. At least to date, no manuscript before 800 CE has been found that would perfectly match one of the canonized seven readings.

The broad material evidence gives us the possibility to go farther back into textual history than had been deemed possible until now—at least fragmentarily. The euphoric media coverage of the ^{14}C dating is understandable, however, since the Islamic religion and the Qur'ān are still considered to be historically controversial. The fact that the examination of some of the oldest manuscripts raises so many new questions—some of which could challenge the historicity of the presently used way of spelling in modern print editions—could also raise further questions. Based on a corpus of ancient manuscripts, one could ask, for example, why many modern print editions—such as Cairo 1924, prints from the Medina based King Fahd Complex, or the modern Iranian edition—still rely on the descriptions of ancient manuscripts given by the Andalusian scholar ad-Dānī (d. 1053/1054). Since many features, described by ad-Dānī and his pupil Ibn Naǧāḥ seem to correspond only to some degree to evidence gained today from manuscripts and their spellings that are believed to originate from the time of ʿUṯmān, these might have to be counterchecked again.

After our look into four manuscripts, we may extend our approach to other early Qur'ānic manuscripts. Meanwhile, the results of carbon dating of fourteen Qur'ān manuscripts—thirteen fragments on parchment and one papyrus, displayed in the following Table 6.2—suggest a correlation between script style and carbon age. Arranged in numerical order of the obtained measurements, starting with the highest date on top, the Ḥiǧāzī script is attested to as being oldest, followed by Kūfī, with a period where manuscripts of both styles would mingle. The Ḥiǧāzī DAM 01-27.1 (palimpsest) shows in the lower layer considerable deviations from the Qur'ān text as we know it today, recalling to us variations types known from the reports about non-canonical variant reading in Muslim exegetical sources. The fragments of Leiden, two of them Kufi, the other one Ḥiǧāzī, show both less frequent "variant spellings and readings" compared to the mainstream text of today. Kufi We. II 1913 and Ma VI 165, and the Ḥiǧāzī-style manuscript ms. or. fol. 4313, show more odd spellings, indicators of their rather high age.

If we accept the dates obtained by the analysis of radiocarbon, we see that different spellings were developing at a different pace. Of course we know still very little about the places where these manuscripts were produced—two of them (the Leiden parchments and Berlin ms. or. fol. 4313) can be retraced to Cairo, whereas Tübingen Ma VI 165 and Berlin We. II 1913 were bought by the Prussian diplomat Johann Wetzstein (1815–1905) in Damascus—so the features we were discussing might have been caused by regional variations of pronunciation and regional spelling conventions. If the spellings according the Nabataean style (long /ā/ written by *wāw* or *yāʾ*) were still practiced in the middle of the 7th century, as becomes evident by words like *ṣalāt* ("prayer") or *zakāt* ("alms") spelled with a *wāw* for /ā/,[63] as the two words and some others appear in Qurʾānic manuscripts as well as in the orthography of the Cairene print, then one could imagine that the "odd" spelling for *Dāwūd* (or, according to some grammarians, the name has a glottal stop: *Dāʾūd*) could be explained by the usage of the letter *wāw* for /ā/.

All of our manuscripts show the usage of *alif* for the long vowel /ā/, e.g., *ǧannāt* ("gardens") or *qāla* ("he has said"), perhaps because there was some need to distinguish these words from *qul* ("say!") and *ǧanna*(*t*) ("garden" in its singular form, with the feminine ending *tāʾ* in context form). A spelling without *alif* could have caused misunderstandings at that early period, since *ǧanna*(*t*) could be easily confused with *ǧannāt*, and analogously *qul* with *qāla*, so the scribe could opt for an explicated spelling by writing the *alif*.

Even today, the complex function of the letter *alif* remains obscure in some respects. Spellings like *ḏū* with *ḏāl-wāw-alif* occur frequently in manuscripts of the 7th and 8th century, although we do not understand clearly the motivation behind it. If *wāw* in continuous script of the old codices was ambiguous, in the sense that it would in most cases belong to the following word, then the combination of *wāw* and *alif* could be seen as a way to avoid confusion when writing down a long vowel /ū/. Other words, such as the third-person plural *kānū*, spelled in modern orthography *kāf-alif-nūn-alif*, seem to be another case of a "more precise spelling" in a sign system that had not yet fully developed. The spelling for *šayʾ* with the *alif* in middle position remains a strange case, too. Generally speaking, it appears that the frequency of *alif* denoting /ā/ increased over time: manuscripts of the 7th century show fewer *alifs* denoting a long vowel in middle position than do manuscripts of the 8th century. The opposite seems to be true for the spelling of the word *šayʾ* (with more than 280 occurrences in the text), for manuscripts of the 8th century show this feature less frequently than those of the 7th.

Since we have reason to believe that we have an important corpus of early witnesses on parchment for what is believed to be the oldest Arabic book—at least some 2,000 fol., stretching over the first two centuries in accessible collections—historical research into the development of Arabic script and its paleo-

63 Spitaler 1960.

TABLE 6.2 Fourteen carbon-dated manuscripts, listed according to the calculated time span in increasing chronological order

No.	Collection	Manuscript	Radioactive carbon age in BP (= years before 1950)	Time span to which the carbon was dated in CE	Script (Déroche 1983)
1	Birmingham* (Oxford laboratory)	1572a	[1456, 21], fol. 1 or fol. 7	568–645	*ḥiǧāzī* I
2	Sanaa	DAM 01-27.1	1440, 16 (fol. 2), 1404, 16 (fol. 11), 1439, 16 (fol. 13)	606–649	*ḥiǧazī* I
3	Berlin	ms. or. fol. 4313	1422, 19 (fol. 2) 1424, 19 (fol. 5)	606–652	*ḥiǧāzī* II
4	Sanaa	DAM 01-29.1	1378, 16 (fol. 7/8) 1400, 16 (fol. 13)	633–665	*ḥiǧāzī* I
5	Tübingen	Ma VI 165	1357, 24 (fol. 23), 1388, 24 (fol. 28), 1319, 24 (fol. 37)	649–675	*kūfī* B Ia
6	Leiden	Cod. or. 14.545a	1335, 24 (fol. 4) 1322, 24 (fol. 2/3)	652–763	*kūfī* B Ib
7	Leiden	Cod. or. 14.545b Cod. or. 14.545c	1327, 24 (fol. 1) 1331, 24 (fol. 1)	652–763	*kūfī* B Ia
8	Leiden	Or. 8264 (papyrus)	1324, 24	653–766	close to *kūfī* B II
9	Berlin	We. II 1913	1300, 27 (fol. 21), 1313, 19 (fol. 104), 1305, 19 (fol. 151)	662–765	*kūfī* B Ia
10	Berlin	We. II 1919	1288, 19 (fol. 13)	670–769	*kūfī* C III
11	Leiden	Or. 6814	1247, 24 (fol. 6) 1256, 24 (fol. 28)	680–798	*kūfī* B II
12	Stuttgart	Sig. isl. 18	1233, 21 (fol. 1)	690–877	*kūfī* B Ib
13	Munich	Cod. arab. 2569	1227, 21 (fragment 1) 1211, 24 (fragment 2)	720–880	*kūfī* D IV
14	Munich	Cod. arab. 2817	1210, 21 (fol. 9)	725–886	*kūfī* D IV

graphy can be applied in a new way. It seems crucial to develop an approach and a perspective independently of the narratives of later sources. As we have tried to show, in the case of the history of Qur'ānic spellings and scripts, we seem to be in a position to look at the textual sources with the glasses of the historian. Comparison with the spellings observed in dated papyri could enhance an historical approach in that field. Also the study of so-called Middle Arabic and the question of the development of Arabic grammar could benefit from these inquiries.

Bibliography

Abbott, Nabia. 1939. *The Rise of the North Arabic Script and its Ḳur'ānic Development, With a Full Description of the Ḳur'ān Manuscripts in the Oriental Institute*. The University of Chicago Oriental Institute Publications, vol. 1. University of Chicago Press.

Adler, Jakob Georg Christian. 1780. *Faksimilia kufischer Koranhandschriften der Kgl. Bibliothek in Kopenhagen mit einer Untersuchung über die arabische Schriftentwicklung*. Kopenhagen: n.p.

ad-Dānī, Abū ʿAmr ʿUṯmān ibn Saʿīd b. ʿUmar al-Umawī. 1932. *al-Muqniʿ fī rasm maṣāḥif al-amṣār maʿa Kitāb al-Naqṭ*, ed. Otto Pretzl. Istanbul: Maṭbaʿat ad-Dawla.

Amari, Michele, and Hartwig Derenbourg. 1908. *Bibliographie primitive du Coran: par Michele Amari, extrait tiré de son mémoire inédit sur la chronologie et l'ancienne bibliographie du Coran, publié et annoté par Hartwig Derenbourg*. Palermo: Virzì.

Arnold, James Richard, and Williard Frank Libby. 1949. "Age Determinations by Radiocarbon Content: Checks with Samples of Known Age." In *Science* 110: 678–680.

Bergsträßer, Gotthelf. 1930. *Plan eines Apparatus Criticus zum Koran*. München: Bayerische Akademie der Wissenschaften.

Bothmer, Hans Caspar Graf von. 1989. "Architekturbilder im Koran: eine Prachthandschrift der Umayyadenzeit aus dem Yemen." In *Bruckmanns Pantheon* 45: 4–20.

Christie's. 1992. "Islamic Art, Indian Miniatures, Rugs And Carpets: London, Tuesday, 20 October 1992 at 10 a.m. and 2.30 p.m., Thursday, 22 October 1992 at 2.30 p.m." London: Christie's, 1992, 88 (= Lot 225).

Creasman, Pearce Paul. 2014. "Tree Rings and the Chronology of Ancient Egypt." In *Radiocarbon* 56, no. 4: 85–92.

Déroche, François. 1983. *Manuscrits musulmans, vol. 1: Les manuscrits du Coran*. Catalogue des manuscrits arabes, vol. 2. Paris: Bibliothèque nationale.

Déroche, François. 1992. *The Abbasid Tradition: Qur'ans of the 8th to 10th Centuries AD*. London: Nour Foundation in association with Azimuth Editions and Oxford University Press.

Déroche, François. 1999. "De Fourmond à Reinaud: les péripéties de l'identification des plus anciens manuscrits du Coran." In *Comptes rendus des séances de l'Académie des Inscriptions et Belles-Lettres* 143: 563–576.

Déroche, François. 2009. *La transmission écrite du Coran dans les débuts de l'Islam: le codex Parisino-petropolitanus*. Leiden: Brill.

Déroche, François. 2014. *Qur'ans of the Umayyads*. Leiden: Brill.

Dutton, Yasin. 2007. "An Umayyad Fragment of the Qur'an and Its Dating." In *Journal of Qur'anic Studies* 9, no. 2: 57–87.

Fedeli, Alba. 2014. "Variants and Substantiated *Qirā'āt*: A Few Notes Exploring their Fluidity in the Oldest Qur'anic Manuscripts." In *Die Anfänge einer Weltreligion, vol. 2: Von der koranischen Bewegung zum Frühislam*, ed. Markus Gross; Karl-Heinz Ohlig. Berlin: Hans Schiler, 403–440.

Graf von Bothmer, Hans-Caspar, Karl-Heinz Ohlig, and Gerd-Rüdiger Puin. 1999. "Neue Wege der Koranforschung." In *Magazin Forschung* (*Universität des Saarlandes*) 1: 45.

Grohmann, Adolf. 1958. "The Problem of Dating Early Qur'ans." In *Der Islam* 33: 213–231.

Grohmann, Adolf. 1959. "Zum Problem der Datierung der ältesten Koran-Handschriften." In *Akten des Vierundzwanzigsten Internationalen Orientalisten-Kongresses München 28. Aug.–4. Sept. 1957*, ed. Herbert Franke. Wiesbaden: Deutsche Morgenländische Gesellschaft, 272–273.

Ibn an-Nadīm. 1970. *The Fihrist of al-Nadīm, Vol. 1*, ed. and trans. Bayard Dodge. New York and London: Columbia University Press.

Ibn an-Nadīm. 1971. *Kitāb al-Fihrist*, ed. Riḍā Taǧaddud. Teheran: al-Bank al-Bāzargānī.

Jocham, Tobias J., and Michael J. Marx. In preparation. "Studie zum Vergleich von vier kufischen und vier *ḥiǧāzī*-Handschriften: Orthographie, Paläographie und ^{14}C-Datierung."

Lundhaug, Hugo. In preparation. "Dating the Nag Hammadi Codices: A Multidisciplinary Approach".

Lundhaug, Hugo. Forthcoming. "The Date of MS 193 in the Schøyen Collection: New Radiocarbon Evidence."

Marx, Michael J. 2015a. "Der Korantext als Herausforderung." In *Wege zur Weltliteratur: komparatistische Perspektiven der Editionswissenschaft*, ed. Gesa Dane, Jörg Jungmayr and Marcus Schotte. Berliner Beiträge zur Editionswissenschaft, vol. 15. Berlin: Weidler, 253–278.

Marx, Michael J. 2015b. "Manuscript British Library, Or. 2165 and the Transmission of the Qur'ān." In *Comparative Oriental Manuscript Studies: An Introduction*, ed. Alessandro Bausi et al. Hamburg: Tredition, 430–435.

Marx, Michael J. In preparation. "Datierung dreier syrischer Handschriften der Staatsbibliothek zu Berlin durch ^{14}C-Analyse."

Marx, Michael J., and Tobias J. Jocham. 2015. "Zu den Datierungen von Koranhandschriften durch die ^{14}C-Methode." In *Frankfurter Zeitschrift für islamische Theologie* 2: 9–43.

Marx, Michael J. and Tobias J. Jocham. 2018. "Über neue Möglichkeiten zur Datierung von Koranhandschriften durch die ^{14}C-Methode. In *Kodex* 8 (= *Book Studies and Islamic Studies in Conversation*, ed. Marta Dominguez): 149–163."

Marx, Michael, Eva Mira Youssef-Grob, Tobias Jocham, and Irka Hajdas. 2014. "The Chronology of Holy Scriptures." In *ETH Yearbook 2014*, https://www1.ethz.ch/ams/publications/annual_reports/2014/Annual_report_2014, 37. (last accessed 29 September 2016).

Nehmé, Laïla. 2010. "A Glimpse of the Development of the Nabataean Script into Arabic Based on Old and New Epigraphic Material." In *The Development of Arabic as a Written Language*, ed. M[ichael] C.A. Macdonald. Supplement to the Proceedings of the Seminar for Arabian Studies, vol. 40. Oxford: Archaeopress, 47–88.

Paret, Rudi. 1954. "Die Lücke in der Überlieferung über den Urislam." In *Westöstliche Abhandlungen: Rudolf Tschudi zum siebzigsten Geburtstag überreicht von Freunden und Schülern*, ed. Fritz Meier. Wiesbaden: Harrassowitz, 147–153.

Pretzl, Otto. 1934. *Die Fortführung des Apparatus Criticus zum Koran*. München: Verlag der Bayerischen Akademie der Wissenschaften.

Rezvan, Efim A. 2000. "On the Dating of an 'Uthmānic Qur'ān' from St. Petersburg." In *Manuscripta Orientalia* 6, no. 3: 19–22.

Robin, Christian J. 2006. "La réforme de l'écriture arabe à l'époque du califat médinois." In *Mélanges de l'Université Saint-Joseph* 59: 157–202.

Robin, Christian J. 2015. "L'Arabie dans le Coran: réexamen de quelques termes à la lumière des inscriptions préislamiques—Appendice." In *Les origines du Coran, le Coran des origines*, ed. François Déroche, Christian J. Robin, and Michel Zink. Paris: Académie des Inscriptions et Belles-Lettres, 27–74.

Sachau, Eduard. 1899. *Verzeichnis der syrischen Handschriften*. Die Handschriften-Verzeichnisse der Königlichen Bibliothek zu Berlin, vol. 23. Berlin: Asher.

Sadeghi, Behnam, and Uwe Bergmann. 2010. "The Codex of a Companion of the Prophet and the Qur'ān of the Prophet." In *Arabica* 57: 343–436.

Schoeler, Gregor. 2002. *Écrire et transmettre dans les débuts de l'Islam*. Paris: PUF, 2002.

Silvestre de Sacy, Antoine-Isaac. 1808. "Mémoire sur l'origine et les anciens monuments de la littérature parmi les arabes." In *Mémoires de littérature tirés des registres de l'Académie royale des inscriptions et belles-lettres* 50: 247–440.

Spitaler, Anton. 1960. "Die Schreibung des Typus صلوة im Koran: ein Beitrag zur Erklärung der koranischen Orthographie." In *Wiener Zeitschrift für die Kunde des Morgenlandes* 56: 212–226.

Starcky, Jean. 1964. *Pétra et la Nabatène. Supplément au Dictionnaire de la Bible*. Paris: Letouzey et Ané.

Stein, Peter, Tobias J. Jocham, and Michael Marx. 2016. "Ancient South Arabian Correspondence on Wooden Sticks: New Radiocarbon Data, Wooden Sticks." In *Proceedings of the Seminar for Arabian Studies* 46: 263–276.

Wansbrough, John. 1977. *Quranic Studies: Sources and Methods of Scriptural Interpretation*. Oxford: Oxford University Press.

Witkam, Jan Just. 2007. *Inventory of the Oriental Manuscripts of the Library of the University of Leiden*, vol. 7. Leiden: Ter Lugt.

Internet Media Reports Mentioned

Anon. "Almanya'da 14 Asırlık Kur'an-ı Kerim Sayfaları Korunuyor." In *Haberciniz*, 14 December 2014. http://haberciniz.biz/almanyada-14-asirlik-kuran-i-kerim-sayfalari-korunuyor-3382078h.htm. (last accessed 12 November 2018).

Anon. "Eine der ältesten Koranhandschriften in der Staatsbibliothek." In *Berliner Morgenpost*, 4 April 2015. http://www.morgenpost.de/printarchiv/kultur/article139114891/Eine-der-aeltesten-Koranhandschriften-in-der-Staatsbibliothek.html. (last accessed 12 November 2018).

Anon. "Oldest Quran Fragments in Leiden." n.d. library.leiden.edu/library-locations/university-library/university-library/ancient-quran-fragments.html. (last accessed 16 September 2016).

Anon. "Tawağğuh-i muḥaqqiqān-i ālmānī ba-nusḫa-ī az qur'ān bā čahār-dih qarn-i qidmat." In BBC *Fārsī*, 9 December 2014. bbc.co.uk/persian/world/2014/12/141209_sam_koran. (last accessed 12 November 2018).

Anon. "V nemezkom Tubingene obnaruzhena starinnaya rukopis' Korana." In TASS, 10 November 2014. http://tass.ru/obschestvo/1563280. (last accessed 12 November 2018).

Anon. https://www.uni-tuebingen.de/aktuelles/pressemitteilungen/newsfullview-pressemitteilungen/article/raritaet-entdeckt-koranhandschrift-stammt-aus-der-fruehzeit-des-islam.html. (last accessed 12 November 2018).

Anon. n.d. www.mashreghnews.ir/fa/mobile/365829. (last accessed 12 September 2016).

Harrer, Gudrun. "Was die Muslime schon immer sagten." In *Der Standard*, 13 December 2014. derstandard.at/2000009325749/Was-die-Muslime-schon-immer-sagten. (last accessed 12 November 2018).

Hennig, Kay-Uwe. "Uraltes Pergament an Uni Tübingen. Koranhandschrift aus der Frühzeit des Islam." In *Landesschau Aktuell Baden-Württemberg*, swr.de/landesschau-aktuell/bw/tuebingen/uraltes-pergament-an-uni-tuebingen-koranhandschrift-aus-der-fruehzeit-des-islam/-/id=1602/did=14521010/nid=1602/16710sm/index.html. (last accessed 30 April 2015).

Husain, Rahat. "World's Oldest Quran Discovered and May be Linked to Imam Ali."

In *Communities Digital News*, 19 November 2014. www.commdiginews.com/world-news/middle-east/worlds-oldest-quran-discovered-and-may-be-linked-to-imam-ali-30011/#bJcUe9hZKuZh3Dsh.99. (last accessed 12 November 2018).

Lotze, Jana. "Staatsbibliothek zu Berlin. Älteste bekannte Koran-Handschriften entdeckt." In *Der Tagesspiegel*, 2 April 2015. tagesspiegel.de/berlin/staatsbibliothek-zu-berlin-aelteste-bekannte-koran-handschriften-entdeckt/11593442.html. (last accessed November 12th, 2018).

Salam, Khaled. "Aus der Frühzeit des Korans." In *DW.de*, 18 April 2015. http://dw.de/p/1FAT9. (last accessed November 12th, 2018).

Salāma, Khālid. "Aqdam maḫṭūṭa li-aǧzā' min al-Qur'ān tastaqṭib al-aḍwā' fī Barlīn." In *DW*, 18 April 2015. www.dw.de/p/1F9zU. (last accessed November 12th, 2018).

Sevak, Sufa. "Eine der ältesten Handschriften des Koran entdeckt. Aus der Epoche des Propheten." In *WDR 5.de*, 13 November 2014. wdr5.de/sendungen/scala/handschriften_des_koran100.html. (last accessed April 30th, 2015)

Vlasblom, Dirk. "Vragen over oude Koranfragmenten." In *NRC*, 31 July 2014. nrc.nl/handelsblad/van/2014/juli/31/vragen-over-oude-koranfragmenten-1405130. (last accessed November 12th, 2018).

Tagesschau of 10 November 2014, 8:00 pm, accessed under tagesschau.de/multimedia/sendung/ts-5347.html (last accessed November 12th, 2018); the report runs from minutes 11:42 to 12:10.

Quoted Editions

BKU I–II *Ägyptische Urkunden aus den Königlichen Museen zu Berlin: koptische Urkunden, vol. 1; 2,1*, ed. Generalverwaltung der Königlichen Museen zu Berlin. Berlin: Weidemann, 1895–1905.

BKU III *Ägyptische Urkunden aus den Staatlichen Museen zu Berlin: koptische Urkunden, vol. 3*, ed. Helmut Satzinger. Berlin: Hessling, 1967–1968.

Chrest.Khoury I Grohmann, Adolf and Georges Raif Khoury. *Chrestomathie de papyrologie arabe: documents relatifs à la vie privée, sociale et administrative dans les premiers siècles islamiques*. Handbook of Oriental Studies, Ergänzungsband 2,2. Leiden: Brill, 1993.

Chrest.Khoury II Grohmann, Adolf and Raif Georges Khoury. 1995. *Papyrologische Studien: zum privaten und gesellschaftlichen Leben in den ersten islamischen Jahrhunderten*. Codices Arabici Antiqui, vol. 5. Wiesbaden: Harrassowitz, 1995.

CPR III 1 Grohmann, Adolf. *Allgemeine Einführung in die arabischen Papyri*. Corpus Papyrorum Rainer, III: Series Arabica, vol. 1,1. Vienna: Burgverlag, 1924.

CPR XVI Diem, Werner. *Arabische Briefe aus dem 7.–10. Jahrhundert*. Corpus Papyrorum Raineri, vol. 16. 2 vols. Vienna: Hollinek, 1993.

CPR XXVI Thung, Michael. *Arabische juristische Urkunden aus der Papyrussammlung der Österreichischen Nationalbibliothek*. Corpus Papyrorum Raineri, vol. 26. München; Leipzig: Saur, 2006.

O.Crum *Coptic Ostraca from the Collections of the Egyptian Exploration Fund, the Cairo Museum and Others*, ed. Walter E. Crum. London: Kegan Paul, 1902.

P.AbbottMarriageContracts Abbott, Nabia. "Arabic Marriage Contracts Among Copts." In *Zeitschrift der Deutschen Morgenländischen Gesellschaft* 95 (1941): 59–81.

P.AbbottMutawakkil Abbott, Nabia. "Arabic Papyri from the Reign of Ǧaʿfar al-Mutawakkil ʿala-llāh (A.H. 232–245/A.D. 847–861)." In *Zeitschrift der Deutschen Morgenländischen Gesellschaft* 92 (1938): 88–135.

P.AbbottUbaidAllah Abbott, Nabia. "A New Papyrus And a Review of the Administration of ʿUbaid Allāh b. al-Ḥabḥāb." In *Arabic and Islamic Studies in Honour of Hamilton A.R. Gibb*, ed. George Makdisi. Leiden: Brill, 1965, 21–35.

P.Alqab Muġāwirī Muḥammad, Saʿīd. *al-Alqāb wa-asmāʾ al-ḥiraf wa-l-waẓāʾif fī ḍawʾ al-bardīyāt al-ʿarabīya*. 3 vols. Cairo: National Library and Archive, 1421–1423/2000–2002.

P.AnawatiPapyrusChrétien Anawati, Georges C. and Jacques Jomier. "Un papyrus chrétien en arabe (Egypte, IXe siècle ap. J.-C.)" In *Mélanges Islamologiques* 2 (1954): 91–102.

P.Aragon Alarcón y Santón, Maximilian. *Los documentos árabes diplomáticos del Archivo de la Corona de Aragón*. Publicaciones de las Escuelas de Estudios Árabes de Madrid y Granada, Serie C, vol. 1. Madrid: Imprenta de Estanislao Maestre, 1940.

P.Bad. V Grohmann, Adolf. "Islamische Zaubertexte." In *Griechische, arabische und koptische Texte zur Religion und religiösen Literatur in Ägyptens Spätzeit*, ed. Friedrich Bilabel and Adolf Grohmann. Veröffentlichungen aus den badischen Papyrussammlungen, vol. 5. Heidelberg: Universitätsbibliothek, 1934, vol. 1, 415–447; vol. 2, pl. 1–12.

P.BeckerNPAF Becker, Carl Heinrich. "Neue arabische Papyri des Aphroditofundes." In *Der Islam* 2 (1911): 245–268.

P.BeckerPAF Becker, Carl Heinrich. "Arabische Papyri des Aphroditofundes." In *Zeitschrift für Assyriologie und verwandte Gebiete* 20 (1906): 68–104.

P.BeckerPapyrusstudien Becker, Carl Heinrich. "Papyrusstudien." In *Zeitschrift für Assyriologie und verwandte Gebiete* 22 (1909): 137–154.

P.Berl.Arab. II Diem, Werner. *Arabische Briefe des 7. bis 13. Jahrhunderts aus den Staatlichen Museen Berlin*. Documenta Arabica Antiqua, vol. 4. Ägyptische Urkunden aus den Staatlichen Museen Berlin, Arabische Urkunden, vol. 2. 2 vols. Wiesbaden: Harrassowitz, 1997.

P.BlauJudaeoArabicPapyri Blau, Joshua and Simon Hopkins. "Judaeo-Arabic Papyri—Collected, Edited, Translated and Analysed." In *Jerusalem Studies in Arabic and Islam* 9 (1987): 87–160. 2nd edition in Blau, Joshua. *Studies in Middle Arabic*. Jerusalem: Magnes, 1988, 401–474.

P.Cair Arab. Grohmann, Adolf. *Arabic Papyri in the Egyptian Library*. 6 vols. Cairo: Egyptian Library Press, 1934–1962.

P.Clackson *Monastic Estates in Late Antique and Early Islamic Egypt: Ostraca, Papyri, and Essays in Memory of Sarah Clackson (P. Clackson)*, ed. Anne Boud'hors et al. American Studies in Papyrology, vol. 46. Cincinnati: American Society of Papyrologists, 2009.

P.David-WeillEdfou David-Weill, Jean. "Papyrus arabes d'Edfou." In *Bulletin de l'Institut Français d'Archéologie Orientale* 30 (1931): 33–44.

P.David-WeillLouvre David-Weill, Jean et al. "Papyrus arabes du Louvre." In *Journal of the Economic and Social History of the Orient* 8 (1965): 277–311; 14 (1971): 1–24; 21 (1978): 146–164.

P.David-WeillMarchand David-Weill, Jean, Mireille Adda and Claude Cahen. "Lettres à un marchand égyptien du III/IXe siècle, 1." In *Journal of the Economic and Social History of the Orient* 16 (1973): 1–14; pl. I.

P.DelattreEcrire Delattre, Alain, Boris Liebrenz, Tonio Sebastian Richter, and Naïm Vanthieghem. "Ecrire en arabe et en copte: le cas de deux lettres bilingues." In *Chronique d'Egypte* 87 (2012): 170–188.

P.DiemAmtlicheSchreiben Diem, Werner. "Drei amtliche Schreiben aus frühislamischer Zeit (Papyrus Erzherzog Rainer, Wien)." In *Jerusalem Studies in Arabic and Islam* 12 (1989): 146–164; 13 (1990) Corrigenda.

P.DiemAphrodito Diem, Werner. "Philologisches zu den arabischen Aphrodito-Papyri." In *Der Islam* 61 (1984): 251–275.

P.DiemDienstschreiben Diem, Werner. "Vier Dienstschreiben an ʿAmmār: ein Beitrag zur arabischen Papyrologie." In *Zeitschrift der Deutschen Morgenländischen Gesellschaft* 133 (1983): 239–262.

P.DiemFruheUrkunden Diem, Werner. "Einige frühe amtliche Urkunden aus der Sammlung Papyrus Erzherzog Rainer (Wien)." In *Le Muséon* 97 (1984): 109–158.

P.DiemGouverneur Diem, Werner. "Der Gouverneur an den Pagarchen: ein verkannter arabischer Papyrus vom Jahre 65 der Hiğra." In *Der Islam* 60 (1983): 104–111.

P.DiemKontoauszug Diem, Werner. "Ein arabischer Kontoauszug in Briefform aus dem 9. Jahrhundert n. Chr. (Pap. Berlin P. 15128)." In *Forschung in der Papyrussammlung: eine Festgabe für das Neue Museum*, ed. Verena M. Lepper. Ägyptische und Orientalische Papyri und Handschriften des Ägyptischen Museums und Papyrussammlung Berlin, vol. 1. Berlin: Akademie-Verlag, 2012, 411–423.

P.DiemMauleselin Diem, Werner. "Schwieriger Verkauf einer Mauleselin (Pap. Berlin 24008)." In *Studien zur Semitistik und Arabistik: Festschrift für Hartmut Bobzin zum 60. Geburtstag*, ed. Otto Jastrow et al. Wiesbaden: Harrassowitz, 2008, 57–72.

P.DietrichTopkapi Dietrich, Albert. "Die arabischen Papyri des Topkapı Sarayı-Museums in Istanbul." In *Der Islam* 33 (1958): 37–50.

P.FahmiTaaqud Fahmī Muḥammad, ʿAbd ar-Raḥmān [Fahmy, Abdel Rahman]. "Waṯāʾiq li-t-taʿāqud min fağr al-Islām [Early Islamic Contracts from Egypt]." In *Mağallat al-Mağmaʿ al-ʿĀlī al-Miṣrī* [Bulletin de l'Institut d'Egypte] 54 (1972–1973): 1–58; pl. 1–10.

P.Fay.Monast. Abbott, Nabia. *The Monasteries of the Fayyūm*. Studies in Ancient Oriental Civilization, vol. 16. Chicago: University of Chicago Press, 1937.

P.Frantz-MurphyContracts Frantz-Murphy, Gladys. "Papyrus Agricultural Contracts in the Oriental Institute Museum from Third/Ninth Century Egypt." In *Itinéraires d'Orient: hommages à Claude Cahen, textes réunies*, ed. Raoul Curiel and Rika Gyselen. Res orientales, vol. 6. Bures-sur-Yvette: Groupe pour l'étude de la civilisation du Moyen-Orient, 1994, 119–131.

P.Giss.Arab. Grohmann, Adolf and Fritz Heichelheim. *Die arabischen Papyri aus der Giessener Universitätsbibliothek: Texte aus den Sammlungen Papyri Bibliothecae Universitatis Gissensis, Papyri Gissenses und Papyri Iandanae*. Abhandlungen der Giessener Hochschulgesellschaft, vol. 4,1. Nachrichten der Giessener Hochschulgesellschaft, vol. 28. Giessen: Schmitz, 1960.

P.GrohmannBerlin Grohmann, Adolf. "Arabische Papyri aus den Staatlichen Museen zu Berlin: Teil 1: Protokolle und Rechtsurkunden." In *Der Islam* 22 (1935): 1–68.

P.GrohmannDating Grohmann, Adolf. "The Problem of Dating Early Qur'āns." In *Der Islam* 33 (1958): 213–231.

P.GrohmannQorra-Brief Grohmann, Adolf. "Ein Qorra-Brief vom Jahre 90 H." In *Aus fünf Jahrtausenden morgenländischer Kultur: Festschrift Max Freiherr von Oppenheimer zum 70. Geburtstag gewidmet von Freunden und Mitarbeitern*, ed. Ernst F. Weidner. Archiv für Orientforschung, vol. 1. Berlin: Selbstverlag des Herausgebers, 1933, 37–40.

P.GrohmannUrkunden Grohmann, Adolf. "Einige bemerkenswerte Urkunden aus der Sammlung der Papyrus Erzherzog Rainer an der Nationalbibliothek zu Wien." In *Archiv Orientální* 18 (1950): 80–119.

P.GrohmannWirtsch. Grohmann, Adolf. "Texte zur Wirtschaftsgeschichte Ägyptens in arabischer Zeit." In *Archiv Orientální* 7 (1935): 437–472.

P.Hamb.Arab. I Dietrich, Albert. *Arabische Papyri aus der Hamburger Staats- und Universitätsbibliothek*. Abhandlungen für die Kunde des Morgendlandes, vol. 22,3. Leipzig: Brockhaus, 1937.

P.Hamb.Arab. II Dietrich, Albert. *Arabische Briefe aus der Papyrussammlung der Hamburger Staats- und Universitäts-Bibliothek*. Veröffentlichungen aus der Hamburger Staats- und Universitätsbibliothek, vol. 5. Hamburg: Augustin, 1955.

P.HanafiBusinessLetter Hanafi, Alia. "An Early Arabic Business letter." In *From al-Andalus to Khurasan: Documents From the Medieval Muslim World*, ed. Petra M. Sijpesteijn et al. Islamic History and Civilization, vol. 66. Leiden: Brill, 2007, 153–161.

P.HanafiContracts Hanafi, Alia. "Two Contracts of Marriage of Papyrus Collections in Cairo and Copenhagen." In *Atti del XXII Congresso Internazionale di Papirologia: Firenze, 23–29 agosto 1998*, ed. Isabella Andorlini et al. Florence: Istituto papirologico G. Vitelli, 2001, 571–584.

P.HanafiPrivateLetters Hanafi, Alia. "Two Private Letters." In *Akten des 21. Internationalen Papyrologenkongresses: Berlin, 13.–19.8.1995*, ed. Bärbel Kramer et al. Archiv für Papyrusforschung und verwandte Gebiete, Beihefte 3. Stuttgart: Teubner, 1997, vol. 1, 51–56.

P.HanafiTwoArabicDocuments Hanafi, Alia. "Two Unpublished Arabic Documents." In *Akten des 23. Internationalen Papyrologenkongresses, Wien, 22.–28. Juli 2001*, ed. Bernhard Palme. Papyrologica Vindobonensia, vol. 1. Vienna: Verlag der Österreichischen Akademie der Wissenschaften, 2007, 261–265.

P.Heid.Arab. I Becker, Carl Heinrich. *Papyri Schott-Reinhardt, vol. I*. Veröffentlichungen aus der Heidelberger Papyrussammlung [VHP], vol. 3. Heidelberg: Winter, 1906.

P.Heid.Arab. II Diem, Werner. *Arabische Briefe auf Papyrus und Papier der Heidelberger Papyrus-Sammlung*. [Publications of the] Heidelberger Akademie der Wissenschaften, Philosophisch-historische Klasse, Kommission für Papyrus-Editionen. Wiesbaden: Harrassowitz, 1991.

P.HindsNubia Hinds, Martin and Hamdi Sakkout. "A Letter From the Governor of Egypt to the King of Nubia and Muqurra Concerning Egyptian-Nubian Relations in 141/758." In *Studia Arabica et Islamica: Festschrift for Ihsan Abbas*, ed. Wadād al-Qāḍī. Beirut: American University of Beirut, 1981, 160–187.

P.Horak 85 Sijpesteijn, Petra M. "Request to Buy Coloured Silk." In *Gedenkschrift Ulrike Horak (P. Horak)*, ed. Hermann Harrauer and Rosario Pintaudi. Papyrologica Florentina, vol. 34. Florence: Gonnelli, 2004, 255–272.

P.Jahn Jahn, Karl. "Vom frühislamischen Briefwesen: Studien zur islamischen Epistolographie der ersten drei Jahrhunderte der Hiğra auf Grund der arabischen Papyri." In *Archiv Orientální* 9 (1937): 153–200.

P.KarabacekPapyrusfund Karabacek, Josef. *Der Papyrusfund von El-Faijûm*. Denkschrift der Philosophisch-historischen Classe der Kaiserlichen Akademie der Wissenschaften, vol. 33. Vienna: Kaiserliche Akademie der Wissenschaften, 1882.

P.Kell.Copt. I Gardner, Ian, A. Alcock and W.-P. Funk. The Coptic Documentary Texts from Kellis, vol. 1: P. Kell. V (P. Kell. Copt. 10–52; O. Kell. Copt. 1–2). Dakhleh Oasis Project Monographs, vol. 9. Oxford: Oxbow, 1999.

P.Khalili I Khan, Geoffrey. *Arabic Papyri: Selected Material from the Khalili Collection*. Studies in the Khalili Collection, vol. 1. Oxford: Azimuth, 1992.

P.Khalili II Khan, Geoffrey. *Bills, Letters and Deeds: Arabic Papyri of the 7th to 11th Centuries*. [Publications of] The Nasser D. Khalili Collection of Islamic Art, vol. 6. London; New York: Azimuth; Oxford University Press, 1993.

P.Khurasan Khan, Geoffrey. *Arabic Documents From Early Islamic Khurasan*. Studies in the Khalili Collection, vol. 5. London: Nour Foundation, 2007.

P.KisterQuran Kister, M.J. "On an Early Fragment of the Qur'an." In *Studies in Judaica, Karaitica and Islamica Presented to Leon Nemoy on His Eightieth Birthday*, ed. Sheldon R. Brunswick. Ramat-Gan: Bar-Ilan University Press, 1982, 163–166.

P.KölnKauf. Diem, Werner. *Eine arabische Kaufurkunde von 1024 n. Chr. aus Ägypten: Aus der Sammlung der Max-Freiherr-von-Oppenheim-Stiftung*. Schriften der Max-Freiherr-von-Oppenheim-Stiftung, vol. 16. Wiesbaden: Harrassowitz, 2004.

P.Kratchkovski Kračkovskaja, V.A. and Ignatij J. Kračkovskij. "Drevnejškij arabskij dokument iz Srednej Azii." In *Sogdijskij Sbornik* [*Recueil Sogdien*] (1934): 52–90. Reprint in Kračkovskij, Ignatij. *Izbrannye sočonenija, vol. 1*, Moscow: Izdat. Akad. Nauk SSSR, 1955, 182–212.

P.Lond.Copt. Crum, W.E. *Catalogue of the Coptic Manuscripts in the British Museum*. London: British Museum, 1905.

P.Loth Loth, Otto. "Zwei arabische Papyrus." In *Zeitschrift der Deutschen Morgenländischen Gesellschaft* 34 (1880): 685–691.

P.Louvre David-Weill, Jean et al. "Papyrus arabes du Louvre." In *Journal of the Economic and Social History of the Orient* 8 (1965): 277–311; 14 (1971): 1–24; 21 (1978): 146–164.

P.Marchands I–III; V/1 Rāġib, Yūsuf. *Marchands d'étoffes du Fayyoum au IIIe/IXe siècle d'après leurs archives (actes et lettres)*. Suppléments aux Annales Islamologiques, cahiers 2; 5; 14; 16. Publications de l'Institut Français d'Archéologie Orientale, vol. 586; 631; 727; 768. Cairo: Institut Français d'Archéologie Orientale, 1982–1996.

P.MargolIouthMonneret Margoliouth, David S. and Eric J. Holmyard. "Arabic Documents from the Monneret Collection." In *Islamica* 4 (1930): 249–271.

P.MargoliouthSelectPapyri Margoliouth, David S. "Select Arabic Papyri of the Rylands Collection, Manchester." In *Florilegium ou Recueil de travaux d'érudition dédiés à … Melchior de Vogüé à l'occasion du quatre-*

vingtième anniversaire de sa naissance. Paris: Imprimerie nationale, 1909, 407–417; 2 pl.

P.MariageSéparation Mouton, Jean-Michel, Dominique Sourdel and Janine Sourdel-Thomine. *Mariage et séparation à Damas au moyen âge: un corpus de 62 documents juridiques inédits entre 337/948 et 698/1299*. Documents relatifs à l'histoire des croisades, vol. 21. Paris: Académie des inscriptions et belles-lettres, 2013.

P.Mird Grohmann, Adolf. *Arabic Papyri from Ḫirbet el-Mird*. Bibliothèque du Muséon, vol. 52. Louvain/Leuven: Institut orientaliste, 1963.

P.Ness. III Kraemer, Casper J. *Excavations at Nessana, vol. 3: Non-Literary Papyri*. Princeton: Princeton University Press, 1958.

P.Philad.Arab. Levi Della Vida, Giorgio. *Arabic Papyri in the University Museum in Philadelphia, Pennsylvania*. Atti della Accademia Nazionale dei Lincei, vol. 8. Rome: Accademia Nazionale dei Lincei, 1981.

P.Prag.Arab. Grohmann, Adolf. "Arabische Papyri aus der Sammlung Carl Wessely im Orientalischen Institute zu Prag." In *Archiv Orientální* 10 (1938): 149–162.

P.Qurra Abbott, Nabia. *The Ḳurrah Papyri from Aphrodito in the Oriental Institute*. Studies in Ancient Oriental Civilization, vol. 15. Chicago: University of Chicago Press, 1938.

P.RagibLettreFamiliale Rāġib, Yūsuf. "Une lettre familiale rédigée en 102/721." In *Annales Islamologiques* 45 (2011): 273–284.

P.RagibLettres Rāġib, Yūsuf. "Lettres arabes." In *Annales Islamologiques* 14 (1978): 15–35; pl. VI–XI; 16 (1980): 1–29; pl. I–XII.

P.RagibPlusAncienneLettre Rāġib, Yūsuf. "La plus ancienne lettre arabe de marchand." In *Documents de l'Islam médiéval: nouvelles perspectives de recherche. Actes de la table ronde (Paris, 1988)*, ed. Yūsuf Rāġib. Textes arabes et études islamiques, vol. 29. Cairo: Institut Français d'Archéologie Orientale, 1991, 1–9.

P.RagibQalamun Rāġib, Yūsuf. "Les archives d'un gardien du monastère de Qalamūn." In *Annales Islamologiques* 29 (1995): 25–57.

P.RagibQurra Rāġib, Yūsuf. "Lettres nouvelles de Qurra b. Šarīk." In *Journal of Near Eastern Studies* 40 (1981): 173–187.

P.RagibSauf-Conduits Rāġib, Yūsuf. "Sauf-conduits d'Egypte omeyyade et abbaside." In *Annales Islamologiques* 31 (1997): 143–168.

P.ReinfandtLeinenhändler Reinfandt, Lucian. "Leinenhändler im Herakleopolites in arabischer Zeit: P.Vindob. A.P. 15021 (PERF 576)." In *Bulletin of the American Society of Papyrologists* 44 (2007): 97–123.

P.ReinfandtWeingutbesitzer Reinfandt, Lucian. "Die Sorgen des Weingutbesitzers: der Wiener Papyrus P.Vind. inv. A.P. 11378." In *Orientalistische Stu-*

dien zu Sprache und Literatur: Festgabe zum 65. Geburtstag von Werner Diem, ed. Ulrich Marzolph. Wiesbaden: Harrassowitz, 2011, 203–216.

P.RémondonEdfou Rémondon, Denise. "Cinq documents arabes d'Edfou." In *Mélanges islamologiques* 1 (1954): 103–112.

P.Ross.-Georg. IV Zeretelli, Gregor and Peter Jernstedt. *Die Kome-Aphrodito Papyri der Sammlung Lichačov*. Papyri russischer und georgischer Sammlungen [P.Ross.-Georg.], vol. 4. Tbilisi: Universitäts-Lithographie, 1927/Reprint Amsterdam: Hakkert, 1966.

P.Ryl.Arab. I Margoliouth, David S. *Catalogue of Arabic Papyri in the John Rylands Library Manchester*. Manchester: Manchester University Press, 1933.

P.Ryl.Copt. Crum, Walter E. *Catalogue of the Coptic Manuscripts in the Collection of the John Rylands Library*. Manchester: Manchester University Press, 1909.

P.Séoudi Seif, Theodor. "Zwei arabische Papyrusurkunden." In *Wiener Zeitschrift für die Kunde des Morgenlandes* 32 (1925): 275–285.

P.SijpesteijnArchivalMind Sijpesteijn, Petra M. "The Archival Mind in Early Islamic Egypt: Two Arabic Papyri." In *From al-Andalus to Khurasan: Documents from the Medieval Muslim World*, ed. Petra Sijpesteijn et al. Islamic History and Civilization, vol. 66. Leiden Brill, 2007, 163–186.

P.SijpesteijnArmyEconomics Sijpesteijn, Petra M. "Army Economics: An Early Papyrus Letter related to *ʿAṭāʾ* Payments." In *Histories of the Middle East: Studies in Middle Eastern Society, Economy and Law in Honor of A.L. Udovitch*, ed. Adam Sabra et al. Islamic History and Civilization, vol. 79. Leiden: Brill, 2011, 245–267.

P.SijpesteijnQurra Sijpesteijn, Petra M. "Une nouvelle lettre de Qurra b. Šarīk: P.Sorb. inv. 2345." In *Annales Islamologiques* 45 (2011): 257–268.

P.SijpesteijnTravel Sijpesteijn, Petra M. "Travel and Trade on the River." In *Papyrology and the History of Early Islamic Egypt*, ed. Petra M. Sijpesteijn and Lennart Sundelin. Islamic History and Civilization, vol. 55. Leiden: Brill, 2004, 115–152.

P.Steuerquittungen Diem, Werner. *Arabische Steuerquittungen des 8. bis 11. Jahrhunderts aus der Heidelberger Papyrussammlung und anderen Sammlungen*. Documenta Arabica Antiqua, vol. 5. Wiesbaden: Harrassowitz, 2008.

P.Terminkauf Diem, Werner. *Arabischer Terminkauf: ein Beitrag zur Rechts- und Wirtschaftsgeschichte Ägyptens im 8. bis 14. Jahrhundert*. Wiesbaden: Harrassowitz, 2006.

P.VanthieghemCoran Vanthieghem, Naïm. "Un fragment coranique sur papyrus (Coran 19, 43–49)." In *Chronique d'Égypte* 90 (2015): 420–422.

P.Vente Rāġib, Yūsuf. *Actes de vente d'esclaves et d'animaux d'Égypte médiévale*. Cahier des Annales islamologiques, vol. 23; 28. 2 vols. Cairo: Institut Français d'Archéologie Orientale, 2002–2006.

P.Vind.Arab. III Diem, Werner. *Arabische amtliche Briefe des 10. bis 16. Jahrhunderts aus der Österreichischen Nationalbibliothek in Wien*. Documenta Arabica Antiqua, vol. 3. 2 vols. Wiesbaden: Harrassowitz, 1996.

P.World Grohmann, Adolf. *From the World of Arabic Papyri*. [Publications of the] Royal Society of Historical Studies. Cairo: Al-Maaref, 1952.

PERF Karabacek, Josef. *Papyrus Erzherzog Rainer: Führer durch die Ausstellung*. Wien: Selbstverlag der Sammlung, 1894.

Index

Page references in **bold** type indicate a more in-depth treatment of the subject.

Abbott, Nabia 192
abǧad letters 119
Abū Bakr (1st caliph, r. 632–634) 8, 67
Académie des Inscriptions et Belles-Lettres (Paris) 3, 188n1
Accelerator Mass Spectrometry (AMS) *see* AMS dating
accounting, Qur'ānic formulae in 94
acid-base-acid (ABA)/acid-alkali-acid (AAA) pre-treatment 142n7, 164, 164n82
Adler, Jakob Georg Christian 6, 192–193
administrative documents 92
adversaries, amulets against 131, 132
afterlife (*dār al-āḫira*) 88n5, 95, 95n18
Agence nationale de la recherche (ANR, France) 1, 3n6, 206n55
'ahd allāh ("the promise/command of God"), in papyrus legal documents 96*tab.*, 98, 99
aḥmadu ilayka llāha allaḏī lā ilāha illā huwa (introductory formula for letters) 42, 71
'Alī ibn Abī Ṭālib (4th caliph, r. 656–661) 4, 190
alif 65
  plene v. non-*plene* 128
  position of 129, 209, 215
  rightward-leaning ascender 11, 192, 192n25
  spelling with or without 56, 58, 59, 64, 127, 188, 208, 209, 210, 211, 215
allaḏī ḫalaqa s-samawāti wa-l-arḍ, in Arabic papyrus letters 59
allaḏī huwa ḫayr, in Arabic papyrus letters 58
allaḏī lā yuḫlifu l-mī'ād, in Arabic papyrus letters 58
allāhu llaḏī lā ilāha illā huwa see Šahāda
allusions, Qur'ānic 43, 44, 102, 106
  biblical 75
Almbladh, Karin 69, 71, 71n32
Altıkulaç, Tayyar 4
Amari, Michele 6, 192, 193
Amari project 3, 4
'Amr ibn al-'Āṣ Mosque library (al-Fusṭāṭ) 3
AMS dating (Accelerator Mass Spectrometry) 140
  accuracy/precision 141, 141n5, 142, 143–144, 146, 150, 153, 158, 160, 160*tab.*, 166, 176, 178, 179
  castor oil contamination 141, 142n7, 143, 164
  checklist for scholars 179–183
  chronology of Egypt 144–145
  contacting AMS Labs 180
  Dead Sea Scrolls 140–144, 142n9, 164
  Early Islamic manuscripts 145–148
  evaluation of test results (checklist) 178–179
  interpretation of test results 149, 176–178, 181–182
  method/technique 150, 158–161
  modeling results 172–173
  papyrus v. parchment 161, 163–165
  presentation of test results 182–183
  sampling/sample measurement 140, 159, **166–172**, 176–177, 179, 180, 181, 198–199, 205
    pre-treatment of samples 142, 142n7, 143, 145, 159, 161, **164**, 179
    stages of measurement 159–160, 181
amulet writers *see* scribes
amulets 112–114
  Arabic isolated letters in 119
  disposal of 115–117
  Ḥadīṯ/Tafsīr manuals used for 130–133
  irregularities in text
    dialectical influences 123*tab.*, 124
    grammatical and other 123*tab.*, 124, 127, 129–130, 129*tab.*
    misheard/misunderstood verses 124, 124*tab.*, 125*ill.*, 126, 128
    variant readings of Qur'ānic quotations 123, 123*tab.*, 124, 126, 127, 129
    writing mistakes 122, 126–127*tab.*, 127–128

layout variants 118–121, 121*ill.*, 133–134
magical signs, drawings and script 118–119, 133–134, 188
preservation 118
Qur'ān verses/quotations on 122–133
against adversaries 131, 132
on enemies of God 132, 133
on healing 114–115, 120, 122, 130, 131
on Judgment Day 132
on omnipotence of God in 131, 132, 133
on protection 114–115, 122, 130
on redemption 132–133
real amulets v. templates 116
secrecy around 115, 116, 119
wooden tablets as 120
ANR (Agence nationale de la recherche, France) 1, 3n6, 206n55
De l'antiquité tardive à l'Islam (DATI project) 3n6
Antiquity, letter-writing culture in 74
APD (Arabic Papyrology Database) 43, 87, 88*tab.*, 94, 112
"Apparatus Criticus" project (Bavarian Academy of Sciences and Humanities) 190–191
Arabia 1–2
Arabic formulae, in papyrus legal documents 97
Arabic language 74, 119
affiliation to Islam 71, 72, 76
dialects 123
Arabic letters 74, 75
Arabic Palaeography (Bernhard Moritz) 6, 9, 10
see also Moritz fragment
Arabic papyri
number of documents 112
published papyri 112
Arabic Papyrology Database (APD) 43, 87, 88*tab.*, 94, 112
Arabic papyrus amulets *see* amulets
Arabic papyrus letters *see* letters, Arabic papyrus
Arabic script 119, 215, 217
affiliation to Islam 71, 72
history and formation 2–3, 192–193, 192n23
Arabization 71, 74
Aramaic formulae, in papyrus legal documents 97
archaeological discoveries 1–2
archaeology, radiocarbon dating in 139, 148
archaic spelling 207–210
Arendonk, C. van 11
Artemidorus papyrus 144n16
Atwill, Joseph 143
authentication of legal documents 90*tab.*, 92–93
Āyāt al-ḥifẓ ("Verses of Protection") 114–115, 122
Āyat al-kursī ("Throne Verse", Q 2:255), in amulets 122, 131, 133
Āyāt aš-šifā ("Verses of Healing") 115, 122
Ayyūbid Period (1171–1260), letters from 68

al-Balāḏurī 3
baraka (blessing) 46, 66, 67, 115, 119, 122, 130, 131, 132
Basmala ("in the name of God, the Most Gracious, the Most Merciful") 2, 193, 198*ill.*, 199*ill.*
in Arabic papyrus amulets 119
in Arabic papyrus letters 44–46, 68
in Christian-Arabic letters 72, 74–75
in Judaeo-Arabic letters 45, 69–70
precursors of 74–75
Bavarian Academy of Sciences and Humanities 190–191
Bayesian analysis, in radiocarbon (^{14}C) dating 145, 180, 180n106–107, 182
al-Bayhaqī, Abū Bakr Aḥmad b. al-Ḥusayn 130–131
bayt allāh (House of God) 95, 95n18
Bergmann, Uwe 147
Bergsträßer, Gotthelf 6, 191, 192, 211n59
Berlin manuscripts
Berlin State Library, Codex Philippi 1388 205n49
Berlin State Library, ms.or.fol. 4313 198*ill.*, 201*ill.*, 206
dating of 188, 189, 198, 201*ill.*, 206, 211–212, 213*tab.*, 216*tab.*
ink analysis 207
origins 214
orthography 207, 211
script style 193, 211

Berlin State Library, ms.or.quart. 528 205n49
Berlin State Library, Sachau 321 205n49
Berlin State Library, We. II 1913 199*ill.*, 204*ill.*, 206
dating of 188, 198, 204*ill.*, 206, 213*tab.*, 216*tab.*
ink analysis 207, 211
origins 214–215
orthography 207, 209, 211, 214
script style 193
Berlin State Library, We. II 1919 205, 207, 216*tab.*
Neues Museum, P.Berl.inv. 24017 9, 12, 35–36*ill.*
Berlin-Brandenburg Academy of Sciences (BBAW) 188n1, 190
see also Corpus Coranicum
Betz, Hans-Dieter 113
bi-ahli t-taqwà, in Arabic papyrus letters 59
bi-l-qisṭ, in Arabic papyrus letters 57
bi-smi llāhi r-raḥmāni r-raḥīm see Basmala
Bible
as legal source 86
quotations from/allusions to 75, 97
Bibliothèque nationale de France 3n7, 6, 7, 192, 193
Bibliothèque nationale et universitaire, Strasbourg, P.Stras.inv. Ar. 142 9, 12, 28*ill.*
Bi'r Ḥimā-inscriptions 2
Birmingham University Library, M 1572 190, 216*tab.*
Blair, Sheila S. 146
blessings (*baraka*) 46, 66, 67, 115, 119, 122, 130, 131, 132
Bonani, Georges 141, 141n4, 142, 142n7, 143
Braunheim, Steve 143, 143n15
British Library, Or. 2165 3n7, 5, 6, 209
Bronk Ramsey, Christopher 155n56, 160, 176, 178n105
Brussels Coptic Database 74
al-Buḫārī, Muḥammad ibn Ismāʿīl 105–106
Bulliet, Richard W. 72n36
al-Būnī, Aḥmad ibn ʿAlī 130
business, conducting 95
business letters 43
dating of 42
full Qur'ānic quotations in 61–63*ill.*, 65
Qur'ānic formulae in
Basmala 45–46
Greeting to Muslims 52, 53
Ḥamdala 47–49
Ḥasbala 56
in šāʾa llāh/Istiṯnāʾ 55, 56
lā šarīka lahu 54
Šahāda 49–50
"sufficiency" formula 94
Taṣliya 51
short Qur'ānic quotations in
allaḏī huwa ḫayr 58
fa-llāhu l-mustaʿān 58
fa-tawakkal ʿalà llāh 57
innahu samīʿu d-duʿāʾ in 57
subḥāna llāh 56
Byzantine formulae, in papyrus legal documents 97

^{12}C 149–150, 199
^{14}C *see* radiocarbon
^{14}C dating *see* radiocarbon dating
Cairo Geniza 68–69, 117
Cairo Qur'ān (1924) 191, 210, 210*ill.*, 214
orthography 5, 210, 210*ill.*, 214
overview of quotations found in letters 77–84*tab.*
Caldararo, Niccolo 141
calendar years, calibration of radiocarbon years to 150–155, 176, 200
CALIB (software) 155n56, 178n105
calibration 169*tab.*
accuracy/precision **155–156, 169–172**, 174, 176, 178
calibration curves 142n10, 143n12, 146–147, 152–153, 152*ill.*, 154*ill.*, 155, 156*ill.*, 157*ill.*, 170–172*ill.*, 175*ill.*, 176, **179**, 200, 201–204*ill.*
confidence ranges 155, 169, 170, 171, 172, 173, 176, 177, 178, 182
offsets in 141, 142, 143, 157–158, 171–172
peculiarities for Early Islamic documents 155–157, 157*ill.*
radiocarbon years to calendar years 150–155, 176, 200
software/online programs 155n56, 173, 178, 178n105, 179, 182n111, 183
tree-ring measurements 153, 153n51, 159, 160*tab.*, 161, 163, 200n42

Canonical Law 86
carbon, main stable molecular forms used in radiocarbon dating 162*tab.*
carbon dating *see* radiocarbon (^{14}C) dating
castor oil contamination 141, 142n7, 164
Cellard, Eléonore 5
Center for Isotope Research (University of Groningen) 189n7
Central Library of Islamic Manuscripts 4
Central Library of Islamic Manuscripts (Cairo) 5
Centre National de la Recherche Scientifique (CNRS) 188n1
Cherville, Asselin de 213*tab.*
Chester Beatty Library Dublin, CBL 1431 (Codex of Ibn al-Bawwāb) 5
Chester Beatty Library Dublin, Is. 1615 I, fol. 7r 198*ill.*, 209
Chester Beatty Library Dublin, Is. 1615 II 193n1
Christian formulae, in papyrus legal documents 97
Christian-Arabic letters 70–71, 73, 77
  Biblical quotations/allusions 51–52, 71, 75, 76
  dating of 71
  epistolary traditions 71, 72, 74
  identification of 70–71, 75–76
  Qur'ānic formulae/short quotations in 44, 45, 54, 56, 71, 72
  script 70, 71
Christianity 2, 74
Christie's (auction house) 145–146, 197
church marriages 106
civil marriages 106–107, 106n38
classification of manuscripts, by script style 7, 192, 193, 194–197*ill.*, 206
Codex Amrensis 1 (*Documenta Coranica*) 3, 5
Codex Amrensis 2 (*Documenta Coranica*) 5
Codex Damascensis 1 (*Documenta Coranica*) *see Tübingen University Library Ma VI 165*
Codex of Ibn al-Bawwāb (Chester Beatty Library Dublin) 5
"*codex of the nurse*" (*muṣḥaf al-ḥāḍina*) 197
Codex Sanaanensis 1 (*Documenta Coranica*) *see Sanaa, House of Manuscripts, DAM 01-27.1*
Codex Sanaanensis 2 (*Documenta Coranica*) 5, 216*tab.*
codices
  late antique codex culture 13
  publication of 3–5
coercion (*karh*) 100
collagen extraction 164
colophon, dating by 5
Commission of Semitic Philology (Bavarian Academy of Sciences and Humanities) 190–191
Common Law 86
conditio jacobaea ("if it is the Lord's will, we will live"), in Christian letters 54
condolences, short Qur'ānic quotations for 58, 69
consonants
  repetition of 128
  šadda rule 127
conversion, invitations to 67
Coptic language/script 73, 74, 76
Coptic legal documents 94
  divorce documents 106–107, 107*tab.*
  marriage contracts 106–107, 106n37
Coptic letters 205
  biblical quotations/allusions in 75
  epistolary tradition 71, 74–76
  expression of religious affiliation in 76
  Qur'ānic formulae in 74, 98
Coranica Project 1, 148, 188n1
  media response 148n42, 189–190
  objectives 3
  radiocarbon dating in 139, 140, **148–149**, 172–173, 188, 198, 205
Corpus Coranicum (project, Berlin-Brandenburg Academy of Sciences and Humanities) 5, 188n1, 190–191
Corpus Papyrorum Raineri (CPR), Vienna collection 9, 112, 119n7
Cuneiform inscriptions 100
Cyriacus (King of Nubia, r. 747–768) 59, 66

daily life, role of Qur'ān in matters of 65–66
Damascus
  early Qur'ānic manuscripts from 1n2
  letters from 46
ad-Dānī, Abū ʿAmr ʿUṯmān ibn Saʿīd b. ʿUmar al-Umawī 209, 210, 214

Danish National Library (Copenhagen) 193
dār al-āḫira ("the afterlife") 88n5, 95, 95n18
ad-Dārimī, Abū Muḥammad ʿAbd Allāh b. ʿAbd ar-Raḥmān 130, 131, 132
DATI (*De l'antiquité tardive à l'Islam*) project 3n6
dating of manuscripts
  by colophon 5
  see also AMS dating; orthography/orthographic analysis; paleographic dating; radiocarbon (^{14}C) dating
David-Weill, Jean 112
Dāwūd, spelling variants 188, 207, 208, 209, 211, 215
Dead Sea Scrolls
  origins of 141, 142–143
  radiocarbon/AMS dating of 140–144, 142n9, 164
  storage conditions and physical treatment 141
Dee, Michael W. 157–158, 163, 171–172
delivery orders 88*tab.*, 92
Della Vida, Levi 113, 121n25
demons, drawings on Arabic papyrus amulets 118–119
Demotic contracts 100
Déroche, François 3, 4, 7, 147–148, 188n1, 190n15, 197
  classification of Qur'ānic fragments 7, 192, 193, 206
Deutsche Forschungsgemeinschaft (DFG) 1, 188n1
dialectal influences, in Arabic papyrus amulets 123*tab.*, 124
dialects, Arabic 123
Diem, Werner 11, 51n9, 53, 58, 67, 112
Dietrich, Albert 113, 114
divorce 102
  divorced wives 96, 106–107
  initiated by wife (*ḫulʿ*) 106
divorce documents 87
  Qur'ānic quotations in 101, 105, 106–107, 107*tab.*, 108*ill.*
Documenta Coranica (series) 3, 4–5
donation, acts of 88*tab.*
  Qur'ān quotations in 94, 97, 98
Doudna, Gregory 141, 142n8, 143
dowries 100, 101
drawings, on Arabic papyrus amulets 118–119
ḏū, spelling variants 188, 208, 215
Dublin manuscripts
  Chester Beatty Library Dublin, CBL 1431 (Codex of Ibn al-Bawwāb) 5
  Chester Beatty Library Dublin, Is. 1615 I, fol. 7r 198*ill.*, 209
  Chester Beatty Library Dublin, Is. 1615 II 193n1
Duke University, Papyrus No. 274 9
Dutton, Yasin 146–147, 173, 174*tab.*, 193

Early Islamic manuscripts 67
  peculiarities of calibration for 155–157, 157*ill.*
  radiocarbon dating of 145–148
Egypt
  development of religious identity 74, 76–77
  epistolary traditions in 74, 76–77
  Islamic conquest 119, 120
  letters from 46, 48, 61*ill.*, 62*ill.*
  manuscript discoveries 42
  papyrus production 163, 165
  radiocarbon concentration in 157–158
  radiocarbon dating of objects from Ancient 144–145
Egyptian National Library, Cairo, Ms. Qāf 47 6–7, 9–10, 13, 15–16*ill.*, 211, 213*tab.*
emancipation, acts of, Qur'ānic citations in 88*ill.*, 97, 98
ETH Zurich 7, 148, 149, 150, 159n64–65, 166, 189n7, 198n38
Europe
  parchment production 163
  radiocarbon concentration in 158
Exorcist *Sūras* (*al-Muʿawwiḏatān*, Q 113–114), in amulets 133

fa-innahu raḥīmun samīʿun qarīb, in Arabic papyrus letters 57
fa-llāhu l-mustaʿān, in Arabic papyrus letters 58
fa-rabbuka ʿazīzun raḥīmun qarībun muǧīb lā ilāha illā huwa, in Arabic papyrus letters 57–58
fa-sayakfīyakahumu llāhu, in amulets 131

fa-tawakkal ʿalà llāh
in Arabic papyrus letters 56–57
in Jewish letters 56
al-Faraǧ baʿd aš-Šidda (at-Tanūḫī) 130, 133
Fātiḥat al-kitāb ("the Opening of the Book", Q1), in amulets 122, 123, 131, 133
Fāṭimid period 67n19, 93, 105
Fayyūm (Egypt), Arabic papyrus letters from 61*ill.*, 62*ill.*, 64
Fihrist (Ibn an-Nadīm) 3, 192
Frankfurt Institute for Islamic Theology 190
Frantz-Murphy, Gladys 100–101
free will (*ṭawʿ*) 100
Fuʾād I (King of Egypt, r. 1922–1936) 191
full/longer Qurʾānic quotations 44
in Arabic papyrus amulets 122–130
in Arabic papyrus letters 59, 60–63*ill.*, 64–66, 73
in marriage contracts 101–102, 102–104*tab.*, 105–106, 107
in papyrus legal documents 87, 88, 101–107, 102–104*tab.*, 107*tab.*
Futūḥ al-buldān (al-Balāḏurī) 3

Ǧaʿfar aṣ-Ṣādiq 123
ǧannāt an-naʿīm, in Arabic papyrus letters 58
ǧannāt (gardens), spelling variants 58, 208, 209, 215
Geniza, Cairo 68–69, 117
Georgian manuscripts 7, 188, 205
Glossarium Coranicum (*Coranica* project, part II) 1
glottal stop (*hamza*) 64, 65, 120, 188, 209
Graf von Bothmer, Hans Caspar 197, 197n36
grammar
grammar skills of scribes 65–66, 126–128, 129
grammatical irregularities 123*tab.*, 124, 127, 129–130, 129*tab.*
Great Mosque (Sanaa) 3, 117
Greek language/script 74, 76
Greek letters 74–76
biblical quotations/allusions in 75
expression of religious affiliation in 75–76
Qurʾānic formulae in 74
Greek magical papyri 112–113
Greeting to Muslims (*as-salāmu ʿalaykum wa-raḥmatu ilāhi wa-barākatuhu*)
in Arabic papyrus letters 51–53
first part 51–52
in prayer rituals 52
pre-Islamic use 52
second part 52
use in Christianity and Judaism 51–52
Greeting to Non-Muslims (*as-salāmu ʿalà man ittabaʿa l-hudà*)
in Arabic papyrus letters 53–54
in passports 53, 54
Grohmann, Adolf 6, 9, 10, 51n9, 57, 112, 113, 114, 120, 133n49, 191
Guo, Li 113n4

Ḥadīṯ manuals/literature, used for Arabic papyrus amulets 130–133
Ḥadīṯs 86, 89, 92
disposal of 117
Haeuptner, Eleonore 8
Hajdas, Irka 7, 205n44
Ḥamdala ("praise be to God")
in Arabic papyrus letters 46–49, 92
in Christian letters 46
in marriage contracts 92
in papyrus legal documents 92
use as or next to signatures 92
verbalized 46–47, 48–49, 71, 72
with/without *rabb al-ʿālamīn* 47
Ḥamdala-cum-Taṣliya 92
al-ḥamdu li-llāhi rabbi l-ʿālamīn see Ḥamdala
Hamidullah, Muhammad 67
hamza (glottal stop) 64, 65, 120, 188, 209
handwriting *see* paleography
Hārūn ar-Rašīd (5th ʿAbbāsid caliph, r. 786–809) 51, 72
ḥasb (sufficiency, calculating) 94
see also "sufficiency" formula
Ḥasbala ("God is enough for us and an excellent guardian")
in Arabic papyrus letters 56
in Judaeo-Arabic letters 70
ḥasbunā llāhu wa-niʿma l-wakīl see Ḥasbala
healing, amulets for 114–115, 120, 122, 130, 131
Hebrew formulae 45, 51, 69, 70, 97
Hebrew script 68, 69, 70, 72, 73
Heidelberg manuscripts 112, 148, 205

Heid.inv.Arab.2 166, 166n97, 167*ill.*, 169*tab.*, 171*ill.*, 171*tab.*, 176, 177*tab.*
Heid.inv.Arab.9 166, 168*ill.*, 169*tab.*, 171*ill.*, 171*tab.*
radiocarbon dating of **166–172**
Hellenistic formulae, in legal papyrus documents 97
Heraclius (Emperor of the Byzantine Empire, r. 610–641) 67
Ḥiǧāzī fragments/manuscripts 3n7, 10, 173, 194–197*ill.*, 206
dating of 148, 210, 214
ink analysis 207
Ḥiǧāzī script 7, 188, 192, 193, 194–197*ill.*, 214
Ḥiǧāzī (term) 192
Himyarites/Himyarite Kingdom (fl. 110 BCE–520s CE) 2
Ḫirbet al-Mird 9, 64
Hopkins, Simon 123, 127, 128
House of God (*bayt allāh*) 95, 95n18
house sales 86, 95
houses, in afterlife 95
ḫulʿ (divorce initiated by wife) 106

Ibn ʿAbbās 123, 123*tab.*
Ibn al-Bawwāb 5
Ibn an-Nadīm 3, 6, 192
Ibn Kannān, Muḥammad b. ʿĪsā 117–118
Ibn Muǧāhid 214
Ibn Naǧāḥ 210, 214
Ibn ʿUmar 123
in šāʾa llāh ("God willing", *Istiṯnāʾ*), in Arabic papyrus letters 54–56
ʿinda ʿuqdat niqāḥih ("at the conclusion of his marriage"), in papyrus legal documents 96*tab.*, 99
inheritance, of houses and land 95
inheritance documents 88*tab.*
ink analysis 207, 211
innā li-llāhi wa-ilayhi rāǧiʿūn ("We are from God and to him are we returning"), in Arabic papyrus letters 58
innahu ʿalà kulli šayʾin qadīr, in Arabic papyrus letters 57
innahu l-waliyyu l-ḥamīd, in Arabic papyrus letters 59
innahu samīʿu d-duʿāʾ, in Arabic papyrus letters 57
inšāʾ literature 67–68
inscriptions, pre-Islamic 2, 52, 119, 192n23
IntCal curves 143n12, 147, 152, 152*ill.*, 153n51–52, 154*ill.*, 154n56, 156*ill.*, 157*ill.*, 178, 178n105, 180
IntCal Working Group (IWG) 152n49
introductory formulae in letters 42–43
IRCICA (Research Center for Islamic History, Art and Culture, Turkey) 4
iṣdāq ("contract about the dower") 101
Islam, emergence of 190
Islamic Law 86, 97
Rabbinical Law v. 86–87
Islamic-Arabic letters 72, 73, 74, 77
isotopic fractionation 150
Istanbul, manuscript discoveries in 1, 1n2
Istanbul Museum of Turkish and Islamic Arts 4
Istiṯnāʾ, in Arabic papyrus letters 54–56
IWG (IntCal Working Group) 152n49

Jeffery, Arthur 8, 123, 191
Jerusalem, Rockefeller Museum, P. Rockefeller inv. Mird A 31 a 1 9, 10, 23*ill.*
Jewish formulae 45, 51, 69, 70, 97
Jewish letters 75, 76
Qurʾānic formulae/short citations in 44, 45, 56
Jocham, Tobias J. 148, 189n7, 190, 198*ill.*, 205n44
John Rylands University Library (Manchester) 9
Jorissen, C. 213*tab.*
Joseph 95n17
Judaeo-Arabic letters 68–70, 73, 76, 77
dating of 68
epistolary traditions 71, 72, 74
Hebrew script v. Arabic letters 69, 70
Qurʾānic formulae in 51–52, 69–70
Tanakh quotations in 68, 69, 70
tawakkul references in 70
Judaism 2
Jull, A.J. Timothy 141, 142, 142n7, n10, 143

kafā bi-llāhi šahīdan ("God suffices for a witness") 92
Kairouan, Qurʾān fragments from 197
Karabacek, Josef von 6, 10, 13, 113, 127, 129, 192

karh (coercion) 100
Khedival Library (Cairo) 6, 9
Khorasan
 letters from 46, 48, 53
 manuscript discoveries 42
King Fahd Glorious Quran Printing Complex (Medina) 210, 214
"King Fu'ād Edition" *see* Cairo Qur'ān
Kister, Meir J. 9, 10
Kitāb al-Muǧarrabāt (as-Sanūsī) 130
Kitāb an-nikāḥ (Aḥmad aṭ-Ṭahāwī) 105
kitāb (term) 8
knowledge transfer, oral v. written transmission 212
kōl 'ašer-ḥāpēṣ 'āśāh ("he does whatever he pleases", Ps. 95.3) 97
Kufic manuscripts/fragments 121*ill.*, 193, 205–206, 210, 211
 ink analysis 207
Kufic script styles 7, 121*ill.*, 216
 dating of 214
 Type B 10, 193, 206, 211
Kuweit LNS *19ab* (*Codex Amrensis 2*) 5

lā šarīka lahu ("He has no associate")
 in Arabic papyrus letters 54
 in papyrus legal documents 89–90
 in protocols 54
Laboratory of Ion Beam Physics (ETH, Zurich) 7, 148, 149, 150, 159n64–65, 166, 189n7, 198n38
land, inheritance, purchase, lease and sale 86, 95, 100
languages
 impact on Qur'ānic vocabulary 1, 97
 in Late Antique Arabia 1, 97
Late Antiquity
 formulae from 97
 letter-writing culture in 74
lease documents 88*tab.*
lease of land 86, 100
legal documents, papyrus 86–88, 88*tab.*, 108*ill.*
 authentication of 90*tab.*, 92–93
 full Qur'ānic quotations in 87, 88, 101–107, 102–104*tab.*, 107*tab.*
 marginal Qur'ānic notes/sentences in 87, 88–95
 Qur'ānic formulae in 92, 92n10, 97
 scarcity of Qur'ānic quotations in 87, 95, 107
 short Qur'ānic phrases in 87, 90*tab.*, 95–101, 96*tab.*
 "sufficiency" formula in 89–92, 93
Leiden manuscripts
 dating of 148, 174*tab.*, 205, 206
 origins of 214
 orthography 214
 University Library Leiden, Cod. or. 14.545a/b/c 203*ill.*
  dating of 174*tab.*, 188, 189, 198, 203*ill.*, 206, 211, 213*tab.*, 216*tab.*
  ink analysis 207
  orthography 211
  script style 211
 University Library Leiden, inv. Or. 8264 9, 10–12, 25–26*ill.*, 151*ill.*
dating of 148, 150, 154, 154*ill.*, 156*ill.*, 173, 174*tab.*, 175*ill.*, 216*tab.*
 University Library Leiden, Or. 12.885 11
 University Library Leiden, Or. 6814 205, 207, 216*tab.*
letter formulary, changes in 71–73
letters
 classification of 76
 transmitted in literary sources 66–68
 letters, Arabic papyrus 42
 closing formulae 56
 criteria for being Islamic 72
 dating of 42, 72
 full Qur'ān quotations in 59, 60–63*ill.*, 64–66, 73
 introductory formulae 42–43
 overview of all Qur'ānic quotations found 77–84*tab.*
 Qur'ānic formulae in 44–56, 73
 short Qur'ānic quotations in 56–59
 see also business letters; official letters; private letters
letters (characters)
 Arabic isolated letters in papyrus amulets 119
 numerical value of 119
li-waǧhi llāh ("for the Sake of God") 96*tab.*, 97–98
 in papyrus legal documents 98, 99
Libby, Williard Frank 140, 141, 150n46, 199

literary letters 66–68
long vowel /ā/ 188, 192n23, 208, 209, 215
Louvre papyri collection 112
Lundhaug, Hugo 205

magical papyri 115
  Arabic 113
  disposal of 115–117
  Greek 112–113
  lack of interest by scholars 113, 116
  see also amulets
magical script, in Arabic papyrus amulets 133–134
magical signs/symbols, on Arabic papyrus amulets 118, 133
magical texts
  disposal of 115–117
  preservation 118
  secrecy around 116, 119
  storage of 118
  see also amulets
magical/magic (term) 114
maġribī style, in Arabic papyrus amulets 120
Maḥmud II (Ottoman Sultan, r. 1808–1839) 4
Mamlūk Period (1250–1517) 101
  letters from 68
Manichean letters 75, 76
Manichean scriptures, quotations from/allusions to 75
Manuscripta et Testimonia Coranica (*Coranica* project, part I) 1, 190–191
manuscripts
  discoveries 1, 42
  editing and publication of 3–5
  see also amulets; legal documents, papyrus; letters, Arabic papyrus; radiocarbon (^{14}C) dating; *under* individual manuscripts
Marcel, Jean-Joseph 1n1, 213*tab.*
Margoliouth, David S. 113
markup system for Arabic text 4n8, 14*ill.*, 17–18*ill.*, 21–22*ill.*, 24*ill.*, 27*ill.*, 29–30*ill.*, 33–34*ill.*, 37*ill.*, **38*ill.***
marriage contracts 88*tab.*
  Coptic 106–107, 106n37
  full/long Qurʾānic quotations in 101–102, 102–104*tab*, 105–106, 107
  Ḥamdala in 92
  husband's behavior 101–102
  Jewish 100
  marital obligations 102–104*tab.*
  marriage to minors 105
  "pleasant company and association" 105
  short Qurʾānic quotations/phrases in 95, 96*tab.*, 98, 99, 100–101
  women's rights and obligations 102, 105
  see also divorce
Marx, Michael 3, 148, 188n1, 190
mašdūda consonants 128
material evidence
  dating of 5–7
  for early history of Qurʾān 1–3, 9, 13, 190
  see also amulets; legal documents, papyrus; letters, Arabic papyrus
Mecca 8, 122, 192
Medina 8, 122, 192
Melkites 71
memorization of Qurʾān 128
Michaélides Collection (*P.Michael. inv. 32*) 9, 10, 12, 19–20*ill.*
Michaélides Collection (*P.Michael. inv. 190*) 9, 12, 31–32*ill.*
Michaélides, Georges 9
Middle East, radiocarbon concentration in 163
misheard/misunderstood recitations/verses, in Arabic papyrus amulets 122, 124, 124*tab.*, 125*ill.*, 126, 128
monotheism 2, 73
monotheist formulae/statements
  in Arabic papyrus letters 44, 73
  in papyrus legal documents 89, 93
monotheistic letters 73, 76
Moritz, Bernhard 6, 9, 213*tab.*
Moritz fragment (*Egyptian National Library, Cairo*) 9–10, 13, 15–16*ill.*
Muʿallaqāt 8
Muʿāwiya (1st Umayyad caliph, r. 661–680) 68
al-Muʿawwiḏatān ("the Two Exorcist" *Sūras*, Q 113–114), in Arabic papyrus amulets 133
Muḥammad (the Prophet)
  letters ascribed to 67

in Qurʾānic quotations in legal documents 91
scribes employed by 8
muḥammadun rasūlu llāh (second part *Šahāda*) 50
mummy tablets 119–120
Munich, Cod. arab. 2569 216*tab.*
Munich, Cod. arab. 2817 216*tab.*
al-Muqniʿ fī rasm al-maṣāḥif (ad-Dānī) 209
al-Muqtafī (31st ʿAbbāsid caliph, r. 1136–1160), letters by 68
Mūsà b. Kaʿb (Governor of Egypt, 758–759), letter to Cyriacus 59, 66
Museum of Islamic Art (Doḥa, Qatar) 5
muṣḥaf al-ḥāḍina ("codex of the nurse") 197
muṣḥaf (codex of the Qurʾān) 8
Muslim-Arabic letters 72, 73, 74, 77
al-Muʿtaṣim (8th ʿAbbāsid caliph, r. 833–842) 68
mutual satisfaction 99

Nabataean inscriptions 2
Nabataean letters/style 192, 215
Nabataean scripture 192n23
Nağrān (Saudi Arabia) 2, 67
names, religious affiliation and 72n36, 75, 76
Naṣṭān (Palestine), letters from 42, 46
National Library of Russia 1n1
National Library of Russia, Marcel 3 211, 213*tab.*
National Manuscript Center (Tbilisi) 205
Neuwirth, Angelika 3, 188n1
Nöldeke, Theodor 6
non-*plene* writings, in Arabic papyrus amulets 128
Noja Noseda, Sergio 3–4, 9, 10
"*the Nurse's Qurʾān*" (Qayrawān) 5

official letters 43, 92
dating of 42
from Egypt 46, 59
full Qurʾānic quotations in 59, 64, 66
Qurʾānic formulae in
Basmala 46
Greeting to Muslims 52, 53
Greeting to non-Muslims 53–54
Ḥamdala 47, 48
in šāʾa llāh/*Istiṯnāʾ* 55
Šahāda 50
Taṣliya 51
short Qurʾānic quotations in
allaḏī ḫalaqa s-samawāti wa-l-arḍ 59
bi-ahli t-taqwà 59
fa-rabbuka ʿazīzun raḥīmun "qarībun muǧīb" "lā ilāha illā huwa" 58
ǧannāt an-naʿīm 58
style 66–67
old texts, recycling of 117
omnipotence of God, in amulets 131, 132, 133
"Opening of the Book" (*Fātiḥat al-kitāb*, Q1), in amulets 122, 123, 131, 133
oral transmission, written v. 212
organic material, dating of 199
orthography 207–210, 208*ill.*, 210*ill.*
Arabic orthography 188
combination with radiocarbon and paleographic dating 188, 207
Egyptian orthography 191, 210*ill.*
Ottoman orthography 191
ostraca 74
Ottoman orthography 191
OxCal (software) 155n56, 173, 178n105, 182n111, 183
Oxford Radiocarbon Accelerator Unit (ORAU) 155n56, 159n64, 160, 162n72, 178n105

pagan letters 76
paganism/pagans 2, 74, 76
paleographic dating 7, 42, 146n24, 147, 192, 193, 200
combination with orthography 207, 210–211
combination with radiocarbon dating 141n4, 142n9, 143, 147, 174, 179, 188, 193, 206, 210
paleography, Qurʾānic 7
classification of script styles 7, 192, 193, 194–197*ill.*, 206
Palestine, manuscript discoveries in 42
paper, replacing papyrus 43
Papyri Graecae Magicae (Karl Preisendanz) 112–113

papyrus
  production 162, 163, 164, 165
  replacement by paper 43
  reuse 165
papyrus manuscripts 8–9, 13
  number published 112
  origins 163
  preservation/conservation 42, 69, 118, 164
  (radiocarbon) dating 6–7, 139, 142n9–10, 145, 148, 161, **163–165**, 205, 206
  see also amulets; legal documents, papyrus; letters, Arabic papyrus; radiocarbon ^{14}C dating; *under* individual manuscripts
parchment
  production 162–163, 165, 206
  reuse 165
parchment manuscripts 8, 13
  origins 163
  preservation 163
  (radiocarbon) dating 5–6, 7, 139, 140, 142n9, 145–146, 148, 161, **163–165**, 205, 206, 213*tab.*
  see also radiocarbon ^{14}C dating; *under* individual manuscripts
Paret, Rudi 212
Paris, Bibliothèque nationale de France, Arabe 326a 5
Paris, Bibliotheque nationale de France, Arabe 328 192
Paris, Bibliothèque nationale de France, Arabe 328a 4, 194*ill.*
Paris, Bibliothèque nationale de France, Arabe 328a/b 209
Paris, Bibliothèque nationale de France, Arabe 328e 5, 195*ill.*
Paris, Bibliothèque nationale de France, Arabe 330a, fol. 1r 196*ill.*
Paris, Bibliothèque nationale de France, Arabe 330g 193
Paris, Bibliothèque nationale de France, Arabe 331 206, 211, 213*tab.*
Paris, Bibliothèque nationale de France, Arabe 334c, fol. 41r 197*ill.*
Paris, Bibliothèque nationale de France, Arabe 6087 211
passports, greeting to Non-Muslims in 53, 54
payment orders 92, 93, 94, 100
personal names, religious affiliation and 72n36, 75, 76
Peshitta inscriptions 52
photosynthesis 149, 153, 161
plant-based materials
  incorporation of radiocarbon 149–150
  radiocarbon dating of 145
plene writings, in Arabic papyrus amulets 128
Plicht, Hans van der 189n7
Polosin, Valery V. 1n1
polytheism 74
polytheistic letters 76
pre-Islamic documents and inscriptions 1, 2, 52, 119, 192n23
  Qur'ānic formulae in 45
pre-Islamic formulae 74–75, 97
pre-Islamic letters
  formulae in 74–75
  religious identity in 74–76
pre-treatment, for radiocarbon/AMS dating 142, 142n7, 143, 145, 159, 161, **164**, 179
Preisendanz, Karl 112–113
preservation
  of papyrus 42, 69, 118, 164
  of parchment 163
Pretzl, Otto 191
private letters 43
  dating of 42
  full Qur'ān quotations in 59, 60*ill.*, 63*ill.*, 64, 64–65
  Qur'ānic formulae in
    Basmala 45
    Greeting to Muslims 52, 53
    Ḥamdala 47–49
    Ḥasbala 56
    in šāʾa llāh/Istiṯnāʾ 54–55
    lā šarīka lahu 54
    Šahāda 50, 57–58
    Taṣliya 51
  short Qur'ānic quotations in
    allaḏī huwa ḫayr 58
    allaḏī lā yuḫlifu l-mīʿād 58
    bi-l-qisṭ 57
    fa-innahu raḥīmun samīʿun qarīb 57
    fa-llāhu l-mustaʿān 58
    fa-rabbuka ʿazīzun raḥīmun qarībun muǧīb lā ilāha illā huwa 58

ǧannāt an-naʿīm 58
innā li-llāhi wa-ilayhi rāǧiʿūn 58
innahu ʿalà kulli šayʾin qadīr 57
innahu l-waliyyu l-ḥamīd 59
innahu samīʿu d-duʿāʾ 57
subḥāna llāh 56
private property 95, 98
professional enchanter (*šayḫ*) 122
protection 114–115
amulets for 115, 122, 130
protocol sheets (cover sheets of papyrus rolls) 165n90
protocols, *lā šarīka lahu* in 54
purchase
of houses 95
of land 95

al-Qāʾim (26th ʿAbbāsid caliph, r. 1031–1075) 93
qāla ("he has said"), spelling variants 208, 209–210, 215
qāla taʿālà ("He says may He be elevated") 44
al-Qalqašandī, Abū l-ʿAbbās Aḥmad 67n19
qawl allāh ("the Word of God") 59
in marriage contracts 101, 105
qirṭās/qarāṭīs (term) 8
Quaternary Isotope Lab (University of Washington) 155n56, 178n105
Queens University (Belfast) 155n56, 178n105
Qumran 141
Qumran Documents *see* Dead Sea Scrolls
quotations *see* Qurʾānic quotations
Qurʾān
authenticity of 189
copies of 8–13, 191
disposal of worn-out copies 117
knowledge of 77
role in daily life 65–66
spelling variants of *Qurʾān* 208
standardization of 9
textual history 1–2, 6, 9, 13, 190, 212, 214
"*Qurʾān of Amāǧūr*" 5
Qurʾānic formulae 44
in Arabic papyrus letters 45–56, 73
dating of 97
in Jewish and Christian Arabic letters 44, 51–52
in legal papyrus documents 92, 92n10, 97
see also Basmala; Greeting to Muslims; Greeting to Non-Muslims; *Ḥamdala*; *Ḥasbala*; *Istiṯnāʾ*; *Šahāda*; *Taṣliya*
Qurʾānic marginal notes, in legal documents 87, 88–95
Qurʾānic quotations
categorization of 43–44, 87
dating of 97
disposal of 117
overview of quotations found in papyrus letters 77–84*tab.*
see also full/longer Qurʾānic quotations; Qurʾānic formulae; short Qurʾānic quotations
Qurʾānic vocabulary 1, 97
Qurra b. Šarīk (Governor of Egypt, 709–714)
letters of 42, 46, 48, 49, 50, 52, 53, 54, 55, 78*tab.*, 82*tab.*, 166, 168–169*ill.*
see also Heidelberg manuscripts
al-Quṣayr 113n4
quwwa (strength) 90, 93

Rabbinical Law, Islamic v. 86–87
radioactive carbon age 200, 216*tab.*
radiocarbon age
calibration of radiocarbon years to calendar years 150–155, 176, 200
correlation between script style and 214
radiocarbon (^{14}C) 199
half-life of 150, 150n46
incorporation into organisms 149–150
production 149–150
radiocarbon concentration
in Egypt 157–158
in Europe 158
in Middle East 163
radiocarbon (^{14}C) dating 7, 139–140
accuracy/precision 143–144, 173–174, 179
of animals' remains 161
in archaeology 139, 148
Bayesian analysis/statistics 145, 180, 180n106–107, 182
castor oil contamination 141, 142n7, 164
checklist for scholars 179–183

combination with paleographic dating and orthography 141n4, 142n9, 143, 147, 174, 179, 188, 193, 206, 210
duration of process 181
of Early Islamic textiles 148
history/evolution of 140
method/technique 149–150
of oriental manuscripts 139, 140–149, 193
of papyrus documents 139, 140, 142, 142n9–10, 145, 148, 161, **163–165**, 205, 206
of parchment documents 139, 140, 142n9, 145–146, 148, **163–165**, 205, 206, 213*tab.*
of plant-based materials 145
pre-treatment of samples 142, 142n7, 143, 145, 159, 161, **164**, 179
radiocarbon years v. calendar years 150–155, 176, 200
stable molecular forms of carbon used in 162*tab.*
standard deviations 150, 153, 154, 155, 158, 160
see also AMS dating; calibration
Radiocarbon and the Chronologies of Ancient Egypt (dating project) 144–145
ar-raḥmān ("the Merciful", monotheistic god) 2
Rapoport, Yossef 106, 106n37
raqq see parchment
Rasmussen, Kaare L. 141
receipt orders 88*tab.*, 93, 94, 100
recitations, misheard/misunderstood, in Arabic papyrus amulets 122, 124, 124*tab.*, 125*ill.*, 126, 128
redemption, in amulets 132–133
Reimer, P. & R. 155n56, 178n105
religious identity/affiliation
criteria for identifying 75–76
expression by formulae 69, 72, 73
expression in Greek and Coptic letters 75–76
of scribes 65, 66, 70, 73
representative script, transmitting script v. 133–134
Research Center for Islamic History, Art and Culture (IRCICA, Turkey) 4
revelation (*tanzīl*) 95n18
Rezvan, Efim A. 4, 197
rḥmn-n/raḥmān-ān ("the Merciful", monotheistic god) 2
Richter, Tonio Sebastian 71, 74, 75
Rightly-Guided Caliphs, letters by 67
Roads of Arabia (exhibition) 2
Robin, Christian 3, 188n1
Rockefeller Museum, Jerusalem, P.Rockefeller inv. Mird A 31 a I 9, 10, 23*ill.*
Rodley, G.A. 141, 141n5, 143, 143n12
Roman formulae, in legal papyrus documents 97
Roman Law 86
Rotulus (series of scholarly sales catalogues, C. van Arendonk) 11
Royal Library of Paris 3n7, 6, 7, 192, 193

aṣ-Ṣābi', Abū Isḥāq 68
sacred texts, disposal of 117
Sadan, Joseph 117
šadda-rule (consonants) 127–128
Sadeghi, Behnam 147, 197
Ṣafaitic inscriptions 52
Šahāda ("There is no god but God. Muhammad is the messenger of God.") 44, 46, 72
in Arabic papyrus letters 50–51, 57–58
first part (*allāhu llaḏī lā ilāha illā huwa*) 49–50, 71
in papyrus legal documents 89
second part (*muḥammadun rasūlu llāh*) 50
shortened form 49
St. Petersburg, manuscript discoveries 1
St. Petersburg, E-20 209
St. Petersburg Institute of Oriental Manuscripts 4
St. Petersburg, Marcel 9 5
as-salāmu ʿalà man ittabaʿa l-hudà see Greeting to Non-Muslims
as-salāmu ʿalaykum wa-raḥmatu llāhi wa-barakātuhu see Greeting to Muslims
sale 86
of houses 95
of land 95
sale contracts 88*tab.*, 92, 97, 99
ṣallā llāhu ʿalà muḥammadin wa-sallama see Taṣliya

sampling/sample measurement (AMS dating) 140, 159, **166–172**, 176–177, 179, 180, 181, 198–199, 205
pre-treatment of samples 142, 142n7, 143, 145, 159, 161, **164**, 179
stages of measurement 159–160, 181
Sanaa, manuscript discoveries 1
Sanaa, House of Manuscripts, DAM 01-25.1 (*Codex Sanaanensis* 2) 5
Sanaa, House of Manuscripts, DAM 01-27.1 (*Codex Sanaanensis 1*) 3, 5, 173, 173n101, 206, 206*ill.*, 214, 216*tab.*
radiocarbon dating of 146, 147, 148
Sanaa, House of Manuscripts, DAM 01-29.1 (*Codex Sanaanensis* 2) 5, 216*tab.*
Sanaa, House of Manuscripts, DAM 20-33.1 5, 207
Sanaa Qurʾān manuscripts 3, 197, 212
as-Sanūsī 130
Šarīʿa 86–87, 97
Sasanian formulae, in legal papyrus documents 97
šayʾ, spelling variants 188, 207, 208–209, 210, 210*ill.*, 215
šayḫ (professional enchanter) 122
Schefer, Charles 213*tab.*
Scherling, Erik von 11
scribes
grammar and writing skills 65–66, 126–128, 129
religious identity/affiliation 65–66, 70, 73
training and way of work 128, 129–130
writing style 67
script, magical 133–134
script styles, classification of 7, 192, 193, **194–197***ill.*, 206
secrecy, around magical texts/amulets 116, 119
"sectarian" works 141
short Qurʾānic quotations/phrases
in Arabic papyrus letters 44, 56–59, 73
dating of 97
in papyrus legal documents 87, 88, **95–101**, 96*tab.*
Sīdī ʿUqba Mosque (Kairouan) 117
signing documents, Qurʾānic quotations/formulae as means of 92, 93
Sijpesteijn, Petra 10
Silvestre de Sacy, Antoine-Isaac 192, 193
as-sirāṭ al-mustaqīm ("the straight path") 123
slavery 93, 95, 133
South Arabian inscriptions 2
spelling
archaic 207–210
mistakes 11, 122, 126–127*tab.*, 127–128
spelling variants 208–210, 208*ill.*, 210*ill.*
stable carbon (^{12}C) 149–150, 199
standard deviations, in radiocarbon/AMS dating 150, 153, 154, 155, 158, 160
Stein, Peter 149, 205
Strasbourg papyrus (*Bibliothèque nationale et universitaire, Strasbourg, P.Stras.inv. Ar. 142*) 9, 12, 28*ill.*
Stuiver, M. 155n56, 178n105
Stuttgart, Sig.isl. 18 216*tab.*
sūʾ al-ʾadāb, in Arabic papyrus letters 57
Šuʿab al-īmān (al-Bayhaqī) 130
Subḥ al-aʿšà (al-Qalqašandī) 67n19
subḥāna llāh ("Glorified is God")
in Arabic papyrus letters 56
in Christian letters 56
Süddeutsche Zeitung 86
Südwestfunk (German regional news channel, SWR) 189
"sufficiency" formula
in Arabic papyrus letters 94
in papyrus legal documents 89–92, 93
Sūrat al-Baqara (Q 2:285–286), in amulets 131
Sūrat al-Fātiḥa (Q 1), in amulets 122, 123, 131, 133
Sūrat al-Iḫlāṣ (*Sūra* of the Redemption, Q 112) 132–133
Sūrat at-Tawba (Q 9:129), in amulets 132
Sūrat Yā Sīn (Q 36), in amulets 132
SWR (Südwestfunk, German regional news channel) 189
Syria
letters from 46
manuscript discoveries 42
Syriac church marriages 106
Syriac manuscripts 205, 206
Syriac script 192n23

tabula ansata (tablet with handles) 119–120
Tafsīr (Aḥmad aṭ-Ṭahāwī) 105

Tafsīr manuals/literature, used for Arabic papyrus amulets 130–133
Tagesschau (German news program, ARD) 189
aṭ-Ṭahāwī, Aḥmad 99, 101, 102*tab.*, 104*tab.*, 105, 106
ṭāʾiʿan ġayra mukrahin ("voluntarily and not against His will"), in papyrus legal documents 96*tab.*, 100
talismanic clothing 115
Tanakh, quotations from/allusions to 68, 69, 69n26, 70, 75
at-Tanūḫī, Abū ʿAlī al-Muḥassin b. Abī l-Qāsim 130, 132, 133
tanzīl (revelation) 95n18
ʿan tarāḍin ("by mutual satisfaction"), in papyrus legal documents 96*tab.*, 99
Ṭarafa 8
Taṣliya ("peace be upon him") 77
in Arabic papyrus letters 50–51, 72, 73
ṭawʿ (free will) 100
tawakkul references
in Judaeo-Arabic letters 70
in papyrus legal documents 89, 93
tawfīq (success) 90
tawḥīd (statement on oneness) 98
tax administration/receipts 86, 93, 94
ṭayyibatan lahu nafsuhu ("His Soul being satisfied with it"), in papyrus legal documents 96*tab.*, 100–101
textiles, Early Islamic, radiocarbon dating of 148
Thiering, B.E. 143
"Throne Verse" (*Āyat al-kursī*, Q 2:255), in amulets 122, 131, 133
Thung, Michael 94n14, 112
Tillier, Mathieu 13
at-Tirmiḏī, Abū ʿĪsā Muḥammad b. ʿĪsā 130, 132–133
Topkapī Sarayī Museum (Istanbul) 4
Torah scrolls, disposal of 117
trading 99
transactions, witnessing of 94
transmitting script, representative script v. 133–134
tree-ring measurements 153, 153n51, 159, 160*tab.*, 161, 163, 200n42
Tübingen University Library, Ma VI 165 (*Codex Damascensis 1*) 4, 5, 199*ill.*, 202*ill.*, 206
dating of 148, 174*tab.*, 188, 189, 198, 200, 202*ill.*, 206, 210–211, 213*tab.*
ink analysis 207, 211
orthography 207, 208, 209, 211, 214
radiocarbon dating of, variant readings 211
script style 193, 210

Ubayy b. Kaʿb 123
ʿUmar b. al-Ḫaṭṭāb (2nd caliph, r. 634–644) 67
Umayyad dynasty (661–750) 9
Umayyad Mosque (Damascus) 117–118
University of Birmingham, M 1572 190, 216*tab.*
University of Groningen 189n7
University of Hamburg 13
University of Oslo 205
Uṣūl al-Ḥikma (al-Būnī) 130
Utah, Inv. 342 9
ʿUṯmān ibn ʿAffān (3rd caliph, r. 644–656) 4, 8, 191, 214
ʿUṯmānic Qurʾān, radiocarbon dating of 145–146

Vanthieghem, Naïm 12, 13
variants readings of Qurʾānic citations, in Arabic papyrus amulets 65–66, 123, 123*tab.*, 124, 126, 127, 129, 214
Vienna papyrus collection (*Corpus Papyrorum Raineri*) 9, 112, 119n17
vocabulary, Qurʾānic 1, 97
vowels
long 127, 188, 192n23, 208, 209, 215
vowel dots 211
vowel signs 192n23, 207
voyages, Qurʾānic quotations for 69

li-waǧhi llāh ("for the Sake of God"), in papyrus legal documents 96*tab.*, 97–98, 99
Wansbrough, John 190
wāw, use of letter 129, 188, 209, 215
Wetzstein, Johann G. 213*tab.*, 215
wiggle matching (technique for testing tree rings) 153n51–52, 163, 163n80
Wilamowitz-Moellendorff, Ulrich von 113

witnessing of transactions 94
wooden sticks (Yemen), dating of 7, 149, 205
wooden tablets 120
Wright, William 6
writing materials 8, 165, 212
writing mistakes, in Arabic papyrus amulets 122, 126–127*tab.*, 127–128
written transmission, oral v. 212

yā', use of letter 65, 120, 188, 192, 209
years BP (before present) 150, 200
Youssef-Grob, Eva Mira 148, 205
Yūsuf ʿAs'ar Yaṯ'ar (Ḏū Nuwās, Jewish king, r. 515–525/27 CE) 2

Zaid b. Ṯābit 8
Zarafšān, letters from 46, 48